Kiviuq

McGill-Queen's Native and Northern Series
(In memory of Bruce G. Trigger)
Sarah Carter and Arthur J. Ray, Editors

1 When the Whalers Were Up North
Inuit Memories from the Eastern Arctic
Dorothy Harley Eber
2 The Challenge of Arctic Shipping
Science, Environmental Assessment, and Human Values
Edited by David L. VanderZwaag and Cynthia Lamson
3 Lost Harvests
Prairie Indian Reserve Farmers and Government Policy
Sarah Carter
4 Native Liberty, Crown Sovereignty
The Existing Aboriginal Right of Self-Government in Canada
Bruce Clark
5 Unravelling the Franklin Mystery
Inuit Testimony
David C. Woodman
6 Otter Skins, Boston Ships, and China Goods
The Maritime Fur Trade of the Northwest Coast, 1785–1841
James R. Gibson
7 From Wooden Ploughs to Welfare
The Story of the Western Reserves
Helen Buckley
8 In Business for Ourselves
Northern Entrepreneurs
Wanda A. Wuttunee
9 For an Amerindian Autohistory
An Essay on the Foundations of a Social Ethic
Georges E. Sioui
10 Strangers Among Us
David Woodman
11 When the North Was Red
Aboriginal Education in Soviet Siberia
Dennis A. Bartels and Alice L. Bartels
12 From Talking Chiefs to a Native Corporate Elite
The Birth of Class and Nationalism among Canadian Inuit
Marybelle Mitchell
13 Cold Comfort
My Love Affair with the Arctic
Graham W. Rowley
14 The True Spirit and Original Intent of Treaty 7
Treaty 7 Elders and Tribal Council with Walter Hildebrandt, Dorothy First Rider, and Sarah Carter
15 This Distant and Unsurveyed Country
A Woman's Winter at Baffin Island, 1857–1858
W. Gillies Ross
16 Images of Justice
Dorothy Harley Eber
17 Capturing Women
The Manipulation of Cultural Imagery in Canada's Prairie West
Sarah A. Carter
18 Social and Environmental Impacts of the James Bay Hydroelectric Project
Edited by James F. Hornig
19 Saqiyuq
Stories from the Lives of Three Inuit Women
Nancy Wachowich in collaboration with Apphia Agalakti Awa, Rhoda Kaukjak Katsak, and Sandra Pikujak Katsak
20 Justice in Paradise
Bruce Clark
21 Aboriginal Rights and Self-Government
The Canadian and Mexican Experience in North American Perspective
Edited by Curtis Cook and Juan D. Lindau
22 Harvest of Souls
The Jesuit Missions and Colonialism in North America, 1632–1650
Carole Blackburn
23 Bounty and Benevolence
A History of Saskatchewan Treaties
Arthur J. Ray, Jim Miller, and Frank Tough
24 The People of Denendeh
Ethnohistory of the Indians of Canada's Northwest Territories
June Helm
25 The *Marshall* Decision and Native Rights
Ken Coates

26 The Flying Tiger
Women Shamans and Storytellers of the Amur
Kira Van Deusen

27 Alone in Silence
European Women in the Canadian North before 1940
Barbara E. Kelcey

28 The Arctic Voyages of Martin Frobisher
An Elizabethan Adventure
Robert McGhee

29 Northern Experience and the Myths of Canadian Culture
Renée Hulan

30 The White Man's Gonna Getcha
The Colonial Challenge to the Crees in Quebec
Toby Morantz

31 The Heavens Are Changing
Nineteenth-Century Protestant Missions and Tsimshian Christianity
Susan Neylan

32 Arctic Migrants/Arctic Villagers
The Transformation of Inuit Settlement in the Central Arctic
David Damas

33 Arctic Justice
On Trial for Murder – Pond Inlet, 1923
Shelagh D. Grant

34 Eighteenth-Century Naturalists of Hudson Bay
Stuart Houston, Tim Ball, and Mary Houston

35 The American Empire and the Fourth World
Anthony J. Hall

36 Uqalurait
An Oral History of Nunavut
Compiled and edited by John Bennett and Susan Rowley

37 Living Rhythms
Lessons in Aboriginal Economic Resilience and Vision
Wanda Wuttunee

38 The Making of an Explorer
George Hubert Wilkins and the Canadian Arctic Expedition, 1913–1916
Stuart E. Jenness

39 Chee Chee
A Study of Aboriginal Suicide
Alvin Evans

40 Strange Things Done
Murder in Yukon History
Ken S. Coates and William R. Morrison

41 Healing through Art
Ritualized Space and Cree Identity
Nadia Ferrara

42 Coyote and Raven Go Canoeing
Coming Home to the Village
Peter Cole

43 Something New in the Air
The Story of First Peoples Television Broadcasting in Canada
Lorna Roth

44 Listening to Old Woman Speak
Natives and Alternatives in Canadian Literature
Laura Smyth Groening

45 Robert and Francis Flaherty
A Documentary Life, 1883–1922
Robert J. Christopher

46 Talking in Context
Language and Identity in Kwakwaka'wakw Society
Anne Marie Goodfellow

47 Tecumseh's Bones
Guy St-Denis

48 Constructing Colonial Discourse
Captain Cook at Nootka Sound
Noel Elizabeth Currie

49 The Hollow Tree
Fighting Addiction with Traditional Healing
Herb Nabigon

50 The Return of Caribou to Ungava
A.T. Bergerud, Stuart Luttich, and Lodewijk Camps

51 Firekeepers of the Twenty-First Century
First Nations Women Chiefs
Cora J. Voyageur

52 Isuma
Inuit Video Art
Michael Robert Evans

53 Outside Looking In
Viewing First Nations Peoples in Canadian Dramatic Television Series
Mary Jane Miller

54 Kiviuq
An Inuit Hero and His Siberian Cousins
Kira Van Deusen

Kiviuq

An Inuit Hero and His Siberian Cousins

Kira Van Deusen

McGILL-QUEEN'S UNIVERSITY PRESS
Montreal & Kingston • London • Ithaca

ISBN 978-0-7735-3499-5 (cloth)
ISBN 978-0-7735-3500-8 (paper)

Legal deposit second quarter 2009
Bibliothèque nationale du Québec

Printed in Canada on acid-free paper that is 100% ancient forest free (100% post-consumer recycled), processed chlorine free.

This book has been published with the help of a grant from the Canadian Federation for the Humanities and Social Sciences, through the Aid to Scholarly Publications Programme, using funds provided by the Social Sciences and Humanities Research Council of Canada.

McGill-Queen's University Press acknowledges the support of the Canada Council for the Arts for our publishing program. We also acknowledge the financial support of the Government of Canada through the Book Publishing Industry Development Program (BPIDP) for our publishing activities.

Library and Archives Canada Cataloguing in Publication

Van Deusen, Kira, 1946–
Kiviuq : an Inuit hero and his Siberian cousins / Kira Van Deusen.

(McGill-Queen's native and northern series ; 54)
Includes bibliographical references and index.
ISBN 978-0-7735-3499-5 (bnd)
ISBN 978-0-7735-3500-8 (pbk)

1. Kiviuq (Legendary character). 2. Inuit–Nunavut–Folklore. 3. Legends–Nunavut. 4. Legends–Russia–Siberia. 5. Shamanism–Nunavut. 6. Storytelling–Nunavut. I. Title. II. Series.

E99.E7V2235 2009
398.2089'9712
C2008-906114-4

This book was designed and typeset by studio oneonone in Electra 10.5/14

Image on page iv:
Kiviuq, portrayed by Lamech Kadloo in the film *Kiviuq*, longs for his goose-wife and family. Photo by Megan Wennberg for drumsong communications inc.

The images on pages 115, 247, and 328 have been reproduced courtesy of drumsong communications inc.

Contents

Acknowledgments

I would like to express my appreciation to the many people who have helped me with this work. Among the elders who generously told Kiviuq's story to John Houston and me, some are no longer with us. My heartfelt appreciation goes to those who are, as well as to the memory of those who are gone. Thanks to Mariano Aupilaarjuk, Elisapee Karlik, Bernadette Okpik Patterk, Madeleine Makkigaq, Ollie Ittinuar, Felix Kopak, Peter Katorkra, Henry Isluanik, Leo Ahmak, Peter Suqaksiork, Phillip Kigusiutnak, Samson Quinangnaq, Elizabeth Tunniq, Simon Tookoome, Janet Uqajuittuq Kigusiuq, Leo Nimialik, Joe Issaluk, Theresa Kimaliadjuk, Eli Kimaliadjuk, Henry Evaluardjuk, Celestin Erkidjuk, Herve Paniaq, Madeleine Ivalu, Rachel Ujarasuk, Zippora Innuksuk, Annie Peterloosie, Jacob Peterloosie, Cornelius Nutaraq, Joanasie Macpa, Naujarlak Tassugat, Judas Aqilgiaq, Jimmie Qiqut, Ruby Eleeheetook, Gideon Qitsualik, Bernadette Uttaq, Niviuvak Marqniq, Mary Ittunga, Frank Analok, Moses Koihok, Margaret Nakashook, and Matthew Nakashook.

Thanks also to our excellent interpreters Percy Tutannuaq, Philip Paniaq, Simon Okpakok, Peter Mannilak, and Julia Ogina, and to our super videographers Albert Kimaliakyuk, Jolene Arreak, Pacome Qulaut, and Linda Tucktoo. We had marvellous unit managers in every community: Noah Tiktak in Rankin Inlet, Tiffany Muckpah in

Arviat, Sam Itkilik in Baker Lake, Phillipa Aggark in Chesterfield Inlet, Jolene Arreak in Iqaluit, Tam Akittirq in Igloolik, Jaco Anaviapik in Pond Inlet, Uriash Paqiqnak in Gjoa Haven, Eva Kootook in Taloyoak, and Kim Crockatt and Trisha Marie Ogina in Cambridge Bay. With pleasant memories I send heartfelt thanks to the schools, museums, and centres that hosted us and to many others in Nunavut who facilitated this work.

For making my trip possible, thanks go to Triad Films, drumsong communications (including Albert Kimaliakyuk, Alethea-Ann Arnaquq-Baril, Kirt Ejesiak, and Tracy Wallace), St Mary's University, John Houston, Peter d'Entremont, Marnie Bienias, Stephen Fielding, and their generous funders, including Nunavut Film, Kivalliq Inuit Association/Aboriginal Language Initiative, Aboriginal Peoples Television Network, Vision TV, Kakivak Association, Nova Scotia Film Development Corporation, and the Kitikmeot Heritage Society.

My gratitude goes out to many colleagues and friends who have given me their feedback and ideas, to Gizelle Ryon-Berry, Birgitte Sonne, Lorne Balshine, Leah Otak, and Michael Kusugak for sharing their expertise on the North, to Johanna Kuyvenhoven, Helen Mintz, Bruce Grant, and two anonymous readers for reading early drafts of the manuscript and giving useful feedback. I am grateful to Eva Aariak for providing the Inuktitut pronunciation guide and to Mary Nashook for further help with subtleties of Inuktitut involving both the meanings of words and their spelling. Big thanks also to Kerry Rodriguez for her excellent research on Kiviuq.

Thanks to the British Columbia Folklore Society and especially to Mike Ballantyne and Murray Shoolbraid for creating the list of folklore types and motifs and for publishing a mosaic version of the story and an article about it (Van Deusen 2005). Thanks to Robert MacNevin for his work on the maps. The map of Nunavut is reproduced with the permission of Natural Resources Canada 2008, courtesy of the Atlas of Canada.

Thanks to McGill-Queen's University Press, University of Washington Press, and the Canadian Museum of Civilization for permission to use previously published material; to Nunavut Arctic College for permission to quote from their publications; and to drumsong communications, John Houston, Megan Wennberg, and Alethea Arnaquq-Baril for the use of several photos.

As always, I am grateful to the wonderful people at McGill-Queen's University Press who have brought this book to life. It is a pleasure to work with Joan McGilvray, John Zucchi, Judith Turnbull, and many others who do such a fine job in editing and design.

My gratitude goes always to John Houston for including me in his exciting work, for answering endless questions, and above all for his friendship and guidance on this wonderful journey.

Providenia
Sireniki
CHUKOTKA
SAKHA REPUBLIC
Lena River
EASTERN RUSSIA
Yakutsk
Amur River
Khabarovsk
Gvasyugi
Yenisei River
Abakan
Lake Baikal
KHAKASSIA
Kyzyl
TUVA
MANCHURIA
MONGOLIA

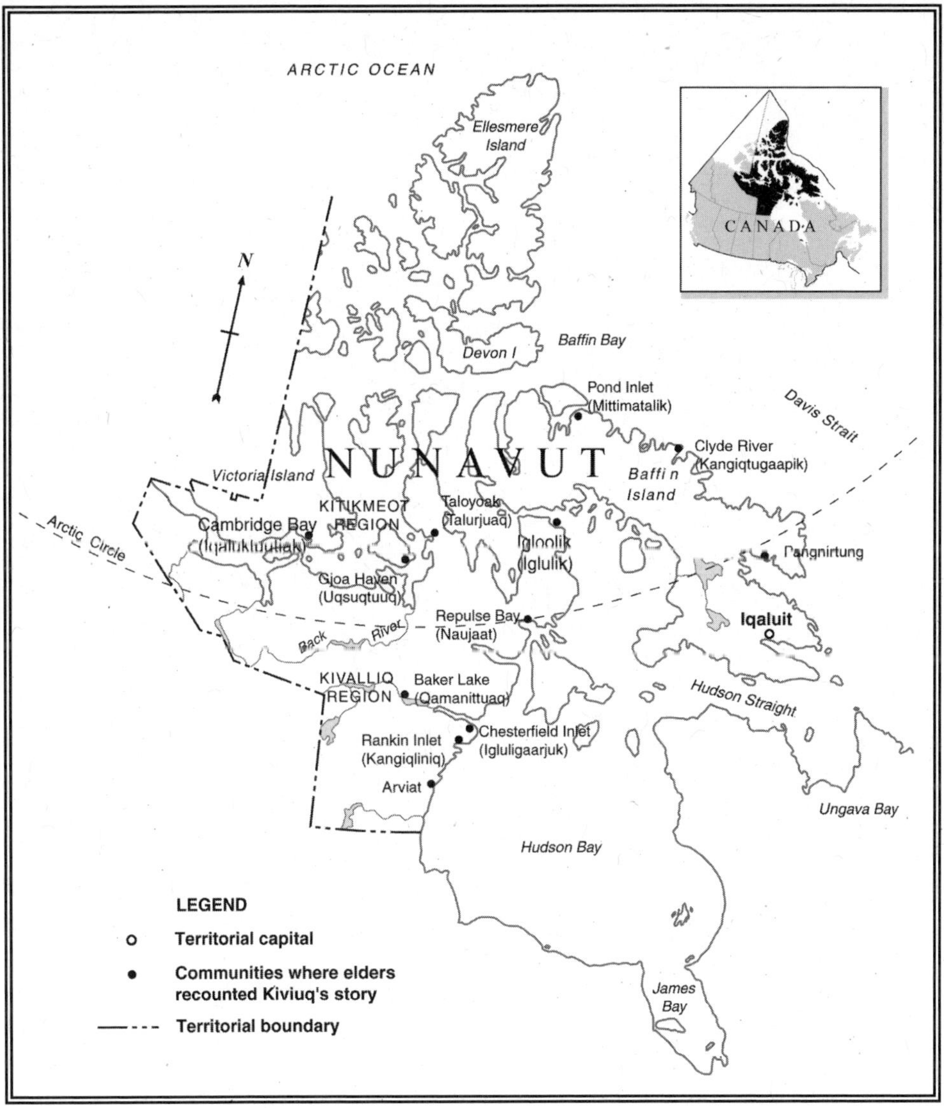
ARCTIC OCEAN
Ellesmere Island
CANADA
N
Devon I
Baffin Bay
Pond Inlet (Mittimatalik)
Davis Strait
Clyde River (Kangiqtugaapik)
NUNAVUT
Victoria Island
Baffin Island
KITIKMEOT REGION
Taloyoak (Talurjuaq)
Cambridge Bay (Iqaluktuuttiaq)
Igloolik (Iglulik)
Arctic Circle
Pangnirtung
Gjoa Haven (Uqsuqtuuq)
Repulse Bay (Naujaat)
Iqaluit
Back River
KIVALLIQ REGION
Baker Lake (Qamanittuaq)
Hudson Straight
Rankin Inlet (Kangiqliniq)
Chesterfield Inlet (Igluligaarjuk)
Arviat
Ungava Bay
Hudson Bay
LEGEND
Territorial capital
Communities where elders recounted Kiviuq's story
Territorial boundary
James Bay

Kiviuq

Introduction

"Have you seen the great Kiviuq? Have you met him on your travels?"

A century ago European travellers in the Canadian Arctic were met with these surprising questions. "Who is Kiviuq," they wondered, "and why are you asking me about him?" They were told that this legendary Inuit hero had gone south into exile among the white people after a life of continuous journeying. That was why the local people thought the white visitors might have seen him. Some travellers, including the Danish ethnographer Knud Rasmussen, recorded Kiviuq's whole life as told to him by storytellers across the Arctic – an epic tale that had been passed down from one generation to the next since time out of mind. The shaman-hero had inspired each new listener in a way that was fresh and meaningful. This multi-layered story is a cornerstone of traditional Inuit life.

In the fall of 2004 I followed in Rasmussen's footsteps,[1] and my journey encompassed one of the most remarkable listening experiences of my life. As part of a team doing research for a film on Kiviuq,[2] I visited ten Nunavut communities over the course of a month and listened to forty Inuit elders telling Kiviuq's story as they had heard it in childhood and remembered it down through the decades. The elders spoke eloquently of Kiviuq's triumphs and tragedies, fleshing out details early story collectors had not recorded. But times have changed. Although many elders are certain Kiviuq is still alive, none of them told me they had seen him in recent times. Nor did they ask, except in jest, if I had seen him myself.

One of the planes we travelled in

My focus is the art of oral storytelling, which I have practised professionally since 1991, and this was the perspective I brought to the film project. I wondered how the Inuit relationship to their hero and his shamanic tradition would have shifted over nearly a century of social, religious, and political change. What is Kiviuq's relevance today? As a performing artist I wondered how to approach telling this long story in a cross-cultural context. The difference between film, books, and oral storytelling is huge. While a film or book is done once and for all, storytelling shifts with each new set of listeners. We see our audience face to face, feel their pain, enjoy their laughter. Which of my own assumptions would I need first to identify and then to set aside? What background would I need to provide in my telling in order to set the stage for those unfamiliar with the Arctic? In carrying a story to a new world, we must help our listeners into the social and cultural context of this world, as well as into the story itself. Some of these questions are common to filmmaking and writing, some unique to live performance.

This was not the first trip I'd taken far from home, meeting new cultures. I had spent parts of a decade with indigenous Siberian peoples, travelling through the arctic tundra, the great taiga forests, and the steppes near the Mongolian border, developing friendships while learning stories and much more about ancient traditions and modern problems.[3] I had participated actively in the renewal of native culture that began in the early 1990s after the fall of communism. I had told stories, given talks, published several books, and contributed to the creation of educational materials in collaboration with aboriginal colleagues. My view of life had expanded tremendously through that learning and from the generosity I was shown.

As my Canadian journey began, I hoped to encourage a connection between our two northern countries. I was eager to find out how life in Nunavut would be similar to life in the Siberian north, and how different. Even with a strong background in indigenous cultures, I found this quest challenging, not least in terms of what I experienced about my own country and its sometimes reprehensible history. Any story comes more fully to life when told aloud and face to face. That includes stories of abuse of power by incomers as well as ancient legends. It was clear that I would need to delve deeply into the story and the culture, and perhaps more deeply into myself in order to acknowledge and honour this powerful ancient tradition.

I travelled with filmmaker John Houston. John grew up in the Arctic with Inuit children as playmates, but he left when his parents took him away to school. He returned as an adult, relearning Inuktitut, the language of the Inuit, and he renewed old acquaintances as he began documenting ancient stories on film. His creations have won many awards and are deeply appreciated in Inuit households. Together we listened.

Many Siberian people had welcomed me as a foreigner, a non-Russian, and I quickly came to be seen as a promoter of their indigenous culture and language in my own world. I was encouraged when Siberian colleagues read my books and heard my performances. They told me I had caught important qualities of their own beloved storytellers, the lively engagement, attention to detail, and sense of humour. I was pleased when they gently corrected my misconceptions. The fact that I tell stories in addition to studying them seems to have contributed to their accepting me so warmly.

I felt cautious as I approached aboriginal storytelling in my own country. I am fully aware of the debates about cultural appropriation and what happens when outsiders bend indigenous stories to their own mould. In general, Inuit stories are not owned by families and individuals the way some West Coast First Nations stories and songs are, but there is more to it than that.[4] John Houston assured me I'd soon feel part of the northern family, and this proved to be so. The elders were open and gracious. There was no reserve in the way they gave me their permission to use the story in performance and writing.[5] I felt most honoured by the then 104-year-old Niviuvak Marqniq. We sat with her after her storytelling, swirling in the shamanic reality she had brought forth, surrounded by her several large statues of the Virgin Mary. John introduced me to her, saying, "Kira is a writer and a storyteller." Feeling pleased that I had been able to understand this simple sentence in Inuktitut, I listened for her reply. She nodded. "*Unipkaqti. Iii* … A storyteller. Yes …" Her eyes were bright, her smile full of warmth and good humour. I felt blessed and came away with an even stronger sense of responsibility to be true to her traditions.

I had three projects in mind. Vitally important to most of the elders was the development of a bilingual project involving a website and book.[6] I am currently working on this in collaboration with Inuit colleagues in the fields of education, heritage, and literacy. Then there was oral performance, a project that has since developed, blending the story with original instrumental and vocal music. The third project is the book you hold in your hands.

In *Kiviuq's Journey: An Inuit Epic Hero and His Siberian Cousins*, I present the Kiviuq story in all the variations I have experienced through listening, reading, and telling, variations that include historical as well as present-day tellings. This book shares the knowledge I've gained about certain images within Inuit culture and about Inuit spiritual and social structures. I learned about these things from reading, from discussion with Inuit colleagues, and also from the elders' gestures and facial expressions, which convey so much of the emotional content.

Another level that is woven into the text is related to a question John Houston put to me when we first discussed the project. While pleased with having a practising storyteller beside him, he was also interested in what I could share from my deep involvement with Siberian culture. He asked me if there were parallels to Kiviuq's story in Siberia. I could find no direct parallel to Kiviuq as a living shaman in the works of ethnographers on either side of the Bering Strait or in my own notes; nor does Kiviuq's name resemble any I have heard on the Siberian side. But many story details are stunningly similar, going beyond the kinds of details found nearly universally in stories around the world.

Of course, any direct contact across the Bering Strait would have happened so long ago that it would be virtually impossible to draw any real conclusions about the transmission of the story. Even language connections are tenuous, except right at the point of continental contact.[7] Nonetheless, in the following sections of this book, I have juxtaposed certain stories and other key aspects of Siberian cultural tradition with their Inuit counterparts, calling them "cousins" in a loose sense, leaving readers to make up their own minds about whether and how Kiviuq may have crossed the Bering Strait. But even apart from the ancient story, there are many parallels in the contemporary lives of Inuit and Siberian aboriginal people.

The last and perhaps most important question I wish to address is how performers, writers, and readers can get to know a culture different from their own well enough to act usefully as its advocate. Surely stories can open many doors from the inside, as can music and long-term friendship. I believe that with great care and attention it is possible to find a way to pass our learning to others. I also believe that in the process we learn as much about ourselves as we do about others, forging the foundations of peace and mutual respect. Fuelled by our curiosity and willingness to give up preconceptions, we are constantly challenged to remain clear about what part of a story belongs to the original culture and what we consciously add to it from our own background. We cannot fully explain any story, be it our own or someone else's. We can only live and learn within it, and emerge to share our responses.

The act of live storytelling is a unique art form. Hearing storytellers is very different from seeing theatre or reading stories and books. Storytelling has been downgraded in the modern world, both in academia, where it joins other undifferentiated forms of "narrative," and in everyday life, where it has come to mean entertainment for children, any exaggerated reminiscence, or something written by a best-selling novelist. It can be all those things, but much more. Down through the ages and across the world, tellers of tales and epics have been highly respected by their communities for their artistry, their sense of humour, and their ability to convey history as well as social and spiritual values to all age groups at once. Their ability to create stories that spoke truly to both young and old is one of the storyteller's greatest talents, whereas written historical records were usually aimed at a particular readership. It was a rare privilege for me to spend so much time listening to today's fine Inuit storytellers, to enter the world of story with such experienced guides. It was a pleasure to explore the kinds of changes the Kiviuq story has undergone since it was recorded nearly a century ago, and to trace its similarities to and differences from Siberian tales.

In conveying their sense of history, ancient story-singers included both the physical and the spiritual events that shaped their people, combining them in story, poetry, and song. In many cultures, a split came about when events began to be recorded in writing. The spiritual aspect of history became the province of religious professionals, and the physical aspect had no place for magic. Oral stories lost their validity as historical records. Years ago a Skagit woman approached me after hearing me tell a Tuvan epic. "I love the way these old stories are so historical," she said. The story had been full of shape-shifting, clairvoyance, and horses that could talk and fly, and the heroine had miraculously returned her dead father to life. "How do you mean, historical?" I asked. She replied, "I think the people who told your story are like my own in that we see ourselves primarily as spiritual beings." To her, as to many indigenous people, the important part of history involves spiritual development. Imagine how differently we would order events with that point of view.

In some cases, probably more than we know, the same events have been preserved in both the written and the oral traditions. One of my favourite examples comes from Korean written history of the seventeenth century and the Nanai oral tradition.[8] The Korean version describes how the Korean army made its way up into what is now Russia, but was turned back by a freak snowstorm in late summer. The soldiers left a stone engraved with the information about who they were and why they had turned back. The Nanai story tells of a shaman who outwitted a foreign military commander, coming back to life every time the commander had him executed. Eventually the shaman told the commander that he could be killed if the commander cut off one of his fingers. The commander did so. The shaman's finger flew north and turned into a female shaman. She conjured up a terrifying summer snowstorm that forced the commander's men, who had set off after the shaman's people, to turn back. Some storytellers add that the foreigners left a stone commemorating the place they had reached, although local people were unable to read the inscription. Others omit this detail, which is one that tends to confirm that we are talking about the same event. In this way, through many oral retellings of historical events, a story becomes unrecognizable as history to outsiders, who cannot accept magical events as true.

There is another level of difference in historical renderings when representatives of two different cultures record the same event, as in the story above. Often the differences in the cultures' perspectives, laws, and moral codes make the event unrecognizable to the other side, even without magic or shamanic power entering the picture. This question is thoroughly examined in Sheila Grant's *Arctic Justice* (2005) and Julie Cruikshank's *The Social Life of Stories* (1998). Grant follows the story of Nuqallaq, one of the first Inuit to be tried for murder under Canadian law. In his own culture, he had performed an act that was not only permitted but required, since the man he killed was a serious threat to the community. Cruikshank recounts the events surrounding the Klondike gold rush as told from inside and outside the culture of one of the main figures, Skookum Jim. His motivations and actions as portrayed in the oral records of his own family are very different from the way they are portrayed in the writings of Pierre Berton.

As often as not, those who write their history and those who tell it orally come from very different cultures or even subgroups with the culture, so that both writing and orality may play a role in the resulting differences in the tale as we encounter it today. Even within an oral culture the passage of time plays a role. The people who told the stories to Grant and Cruikshank had heard about the events from those who had participated in the action. This sets them apart from the tellers of the story of Kiviuq, a tale so ancient that today there is no link to those who told it for the first time, even though certain details, such as the glass beads that

Kiviuq brought home from his first journey, were undoubtedly added at some point. The elders we spoke with did not comment on whether the glass beads were evidence of Inuit contact with Europeans. Their interest was more easily aroused by questions about the mapping of Kiviuq's journey.

Over the years my own storytelling has come to focus on long stories. I love the opportunities provided by a story experience that lasts days rather than minutes, and have organized and performed in several "epic weekends" in Vancouver in which about thirty storytellers gather once a year to tell a long story from a particular culture, each teller taking a section. I have also heard long stories performed by a single teller and have told some as well.

While writing this book, I circulated a questionnaire among the storytellers most strongly involved with long stories, asking them to describe what is special about telling and hearing long stories.[9]

Canadian storyteller and writer Celia Lottridge had this to say about the differences between listening to a skilled storyteller and reading the same epic: "When I read I have control. I can go back and reread, stop and take a break, look something up. As a listener I'm taken into the world of the epic. I'm just there. The epic happens a lot like life. It just washes over me."

Storyteller Naomi Steinberg says: "The transmission of images and emotions is so different when there is a live teller in front of you – moving, talking, and emoting. There are voice modulations, pauses or emphasis where you might not have put them or expected them. These force you to rethink or re-understand what before was simply your assumption of the way truth goes. It forces new perspectives and teachings to be accepted."

Some storytellers speak of the ways that hearing epics helps us get deeply acquainted with a culture. When meeting a new culture, we often bump up against things that seem impossible to grasp, but once we live those events with story characters, much understanding is possible. Later and throughout the book, we'll hear still more storytellers' responses to the questionnaire.

My own experience with both storytelling and research tells me that what we learn from telling and listening is very different from what we learn from comparing and analysing written texts. To engage in both methods is to involve both heart and head.

Kiviuq is known by many names as his story moves from Alaska through northern Canada to Greenland, among them Kiviu, Kivioq, Qivioq, Kiviung, Kiviuna, Giviok, Qaaweiluq, and Upaum.[10] In some stories he is not named at all and is just called "the bachelor." Like those who track him, Kiviuq was a great traveller, mapping the world as the Inuit knew it, from his home with the great rocks, where his parents had worn indentations, waiting for his return, across raging seas, to the place where the salt water did not freeze and to the place of extraordinarily long tides. He journeyed over mountain ranges and huge bodies of water to the place where the goose people wintered. He even had a hand in creating some of the mighty landforms of the Arctic. And no matter how difficult his voyage, he came home singing.

We see the dangers of life in the Arctic reflected in the dark side of these tales – cannibalism and murder. We see its beauty in Kiviuq's bright heroism as master of the kayak and as the only one who was kind to a poor orphan. As a great *angakkuq*, or shaman, Kiviuq seems to "just know" things that others don't. He has mastered the power of words and can call on his helping spirits, the small snow buntings or the great polar bear, to help him in times of trouble. As a man he is willing to go to any lengths to find his beloved goose-wife when she flies away on migration.

Some Inuit believe Kiviuq is still alive, perhaps sleeping in the rocks. They say he will die only when the world ends, when there is no more air to breathe. But others say his legend is just a bedtime story for children. This is one of the changes that have come about after decades of outside influence. I wonder what role Kiviuq's lessons will play as Inuit continue to move forward. Many cultural myths, from the Tibetan spiritual warrior Gesar to the Christian Messiah, tell of a hero who has gone away for centuries but will return. Will Kiviuq come back from exile to provide inspiration to his people in a new time?

Although Inuit told episodes of Kiviuq's story to the early travellers in all the Arctic regions, only the master storyteller Kuvdluitsoq of Ilivileq, relating the story to Rasmussen in the early 1920s, told it as a connected epic. His telling takes the form of a hero's journey, similar to that described by Joseph Campbell in *The Hero with a Thousand Faces*. At its most basic, the journey, which Campbell has traced in stories from around the world, involves a problem that propels the hero from his home, meetings with obstacles and helpers, a crisis, and a return.

I thought that today people would only be able to tell fragments of the story and that probably no one would know the whole thing. How wrong I turned out to be! The very first person we recorded, Elisapee Karlik, told a very complete version. And so did many others afterwards, although the story took on various forms of organization and there was some disagreement about which parts were from Kiviuq's life and which were about someone else. Many Inuit refer to the story as a legend, likely because it is the life story of a man who truly lived among them. I began to question the whole concept of what constitutes an epic, having formerly thought that an epic was a long story with a beginning, middle, and end. Kiviuq's story shows us an epic with a more cyclical form, beyond any sense of what is correct in terms of Western genres. It can be told in pieces or all at once, rearranged to suit different audiences and to convey various levels of information. I think of it as an epic because of its length, spiritual values, musical components, and rich complexity. Some non-Inuit refer to it as a fable, but I cannot agree. Fables are literary creations of single known authors, generally very short. Each fable carries one clear moral. Kiviuq's story has been passed orally and carries within it the genius of many storytellers. It contains history and practical life skills, but also works as a powerful tool for spiritual development. Kiviuq's story is very long, with many complex and multi-layered morals. It compares better with Homer than with Aesop.

Outside influences have hugely damaged the Inuit storytelling tradition. The move away from living on the land, Christian and secular Canadian schooling, the change of language, and finally television have all taken their toll. That elders could recall the story in complete detail and in all its variety after decades of neither hearing nor telling it is certainly a tribute to the power of memory and to the power of the story itself. Not only did they remember plots, characters, and details, but they often spoke in poetic rhythm and used elements of Inuktitut spoken many generations ago – elements that have been preserved to emphasize pivotal moments in the story.

Inuksuk at Rankin Inlet

With the elders' permission I came home and told the story in English to people of all ages. The preparation was arduous with so many threads to follow. I heard the elders' voices over and over again on our tapes, listened to Inuit music, studied art works, and read new works on Inuit culture. I have since learned much from listeners' responses. All of this has joined learning I gleaned from telling and hearing other world epics over many years. I have come to see that we can contact the culturally specific heart of a story by listening carefully to the voice and detail offered by storytellers who have known it since childhood. We can contact the cross-cultural heart of a story by preparing it for and telling it to new audiences, by making connections between the unknown and the familiar, and by reading audience responses.

Besides the imagery and plot of the story itself, there is something transformative about sitting for many hours in the space of a storytelling. In the words of American storyteller Antoinette Botsford,

> In the live telling and live listening, certain stories encourage the spontaneous creation of a "parareality." This world allows us to be comfortably in two places at once, at least one of them somewhat magical. It allows for events that in ordinary life might be pretty far out of reach. If we collectively engage and are embraced in such a metaworld for hours, or even days, it becomes increasingly possible to stay present within the two realities. The metaworld created by live story can invite us into a refined state of consciousness, modeling for us some highly empowering material, both symbols and actions. Thus partaking of the long story can be a gateway into a world of shamanic potency.

This book is organized around the "chapters" in Kiviuq's epic, each of which might have been told on a separate evening in earlier times. My arrangement of incidents is based on that of the majority of elders who told the story to John Houston and me. I will go on to explain how others told it differently.

Within this book's chapters we will consider questions such as shamanism, music, social change, and the parallel male and female stories that emerge. I will take you along on my own journey as I face storytelling challenges, knowing that my need for explanations is much stronger than that of many Inuit listeners and readers. This is natural, in part because like indigenous people the world over, Inuit were raised not to ask too many questions about the mysteries of story. As Elisapee Karlik said to us, "I asked my father about that and he said, 'If you knew, what would you do?' He didn't explain."[11] This doesn't mean that Inuit and other indigenous peoples don't ask questions about the world outside story, and sometimes within it. When indigenous Siberians visited me in Canada, they asked what seem to me to be endless questions about everything from the way we eat and dress to what makes us tick. Some of these questions were difficult to answer simply because, living in my home culture, I have never looked at it from an outsider's point of view. Some of their questions felt judgmental, although they were not intended to hurt. Others needed answers that were long and complex.

The same curiosity goes for this visitor to the Arctic. An ancient Inuit story tells of a woman who married a dog. Some of her children turned out to be dogs, and it is from them that white people are descended. Like a dog with a bone, it seems to the Inuit that white people never stop their obsessive chewing things over. A dog-child, I indulge that instinct in this book, both in terms of the story and in terms of everyday life. I do my best to identify what I've learned from elders and to separate that from my own thoughts, showing their evolution. This care is something I've learned from the elders themselves. They always distinguish what they learned from their own elders and what they think themselves. The wisdom passed down through generations holds much more weight with them. I too return again and again to the voices of the elders.

In this book I include other stories that enhanced my understanding of Kiviuq's, some from Inuit tradition and others from Siberian. I've placed the Siberian stories in short "Siberian cousins" chapters following each of the main chapters. These connections have deepened my understanding of Kiviuq. They also signal the seeming universality of certain images and the uniqueness of others as stories move in time and space.

Inuit and Siberian naming systems can be confusing to those unfamiliar with them. Both come out of older traditions in their own languages and have incorporated English or Russian names first for official and then for everyday purposes. Some Inuit use a name that goes back to the time when any given Inuk had just one name, given at birth (for more information on Inuit names, see the "Seal, Tuutalik, Storm at Sea" chapter). Two of the Siberian elders mentioned in this book also go by just one name, and this comes from a similar tradition.

Inuit have adopted certain European names, sometimes recalling early traders and whalers – people they actually knew. The names have changed slightly under the influence of Inuktitut pronunciation. Thus, John has become Joanasie, Philip is now Pilipuusi, and Elizabeth is Elisapee. In the words of interpreter Philip Paniaq, "My name is Pilipuusi the son of Paniaq of Clyde River. Even today, we still use a naming system where a newborn is named after a dear friend or relative and given a 'Christian' name for the birth certificate. We use the traditional name for everyday use and the 'Christian' or *qallunaaq* [non-Inuit] name for the records. Younger people in each successive generation are going more towards a first and last name that they use exclusively. Even though the relatives and friends still use the one 'they' named the person after."

Most Siberian people have adopted Russian names, at first under social and political pressure. Under communism a person couldn't get a decent job without a Russian name. Some have chosen the names of Russians who befriended and helped them at crucial moments. The names follow Russian form, which includes first name, patronymic, and last name – for example, Evdokia Batovna Kimonko. People also use Russian nicknames such as Sasha or Valya. Some of the last names, such as Kyalundzyuga, are taken from clan names. For simplicity's sake I have generally not used the patronymics or nicknames in this book. In most areas only a few elders still use traditional names, while younger people use exclusively Russian names. The native names tend to stand alone – for example Ulchi shaman Anga and Yupik elder Nununa. One regional exception is Tuva, where many Tuvan names are in everyday use – the name Mongush, for example, can appear as either a first name or a last name.

In writing Inuktitut words, I follow the Inuit Cultural Institute (ICI) orthography. Exceptions are elders' names, which I've tried to write as they themselves prefer, and words used within citations from other published works that differ from ICI orthography.

The complete story stands here at the book's opening. In the interest of a smooth read, I follow one storyline instead of forty, which inevitably means that many variations are left out. We will pick these up again in the book's chapters. Each chapter includes the details of all the Inuit elders' telling, set off in the text by small triangles. After much internal debate I decided to do it this way for two reasons. First, I want to share with you the delight I experienced forty times over – the pleasure of hearing the story in one voice, of sinking into its internal rhythm and flow. At the same time, I want to be true to the story, with all its wealth of detail, and to the voices of the individual elders, remembering their names and faces and what they said. When a story has been written down, there is a tendency to think that the written version is correct and others are variants. We are privileged with Kiviuq to meet a story that has been retained much more strongly in oral memory than in writing. It becomes crystal clear that there is no one correct version. Each is unique and valid, expressing a heady mix of strong tradition and individual expression.

I must offer this note to storytellers. Generally I grant others permission to retell stories I have published. But in this case the elders granted their permission specifically to me, so I must ask interested tellers to find their own sources, either from Inuit storytellers or from earlier published accounts. In particular I hold the rights to my retelling of the legend as put forth in this book as "Kiviuq's Life Story.

Kiviuq's Life Story

The story comes leaping into existence. It holds us captive. There is no escape.
– Canadian storyteller Jan Andrews, 2006

Our hero Kiviuq lived a long time ago.
He travelled far and wide, over water and land,
Through a hole in the water, through a hole in the earth, through a hole in the sky.
He travelled far and wide, over water and land,
A man of power, a man of kindness, a great hero, on his long journey home.

The Seal-Child

It all began one winter, a winter worse than many another. The winds howled, the storms seemed never to abate. Much of the time the hunters could not get out at all, and even when they did, they often returned empty-handed. The people were hungry, on the edge of starvation.

In the community where Kiviuq lived there was one Tuutalik, half man, half seal. Since time out of mind the *tuutaliit* have lived in the waters of the Arctic – in the water, under the water, never far from the water. They are good hunters and good neighbours. They live close to the Inuit, who are also masters of the arctic climate, also good hunters and good neighbours.

When Inuit meet *tuutaliit*, most often they perceive them as people, exactly like themselves. Sometimes they see the *tuutaliit* as seals. And

Mountains seen from Pond Inlet

there are some with double vision who experience the *tuutaliit* at one and the same time in both sides of their dual nature. They see a being who is half human and half seal. Such a man was the great *angakkuq*, the great shaman Kiviuq.

Tuutalik was fond of people and wanted to help them. During that terrible winter he spoke to the hunters and said, "Come with me. I will take you out on the ice to the places where the seals come up to breathe. I will help you find seals who are willing to give their lives so that you may survive."

The hunters went with him. They went far out over the ice. At last Tuutalik stopped and cleared the snow from around one of the small holes where the seals come up to take breath. "I will go down into this hole and call the seals," he said. "Just one thing. When I come back I will call out, telling you that I am a person. Do not harpoon me."

The hunters agreed. Down Tuutalik went into the icy water. As his body passed the boundary between the realm of air and the realm of water, it changed from the body of a man to that of a seal.

I wish I could tell you that what happened next was an accident. But it's hard to be sure. One man waited, standing over the hole, his harpoon at the ready. This was a man who had always been envious of Tuutalik and his abilities. And this was a man who was very hungry.

Tuutalik swam back and called out, "I am an Inuk. I am human. Do not harpoon me."

Whether the hunter didn't hear him or whether he acted deliberately is not certain, but we do know that he did not hesitate. He struck with his harpoon. The water filled with blood. The hunters set to work. With their sharp snow knives they cut blocks of ice from around the hole, enlarging it. They pulled from the water a large seal.

They carried the seal to the home of the successful hunter, rejoicing that there would be food. His wife came out and the other women joined her as she began to clean the seal. The women were the first to notice that something was different about this animal. It seemed cleaner on the inside than seals usually do.

Tuutalik's spirit was hovering around the place. He hoped that his own wife would stand over his former body as she worked. When she did, he communicated to her, "I want to be reborn through you." His spirit entered her body.

A shiver went down her spine. Time passed and she gave birth to a child. Everyone realized that this was Tuutalik returned, and they called the child Tuutalannuaq, or "little Tuutalik." The child grew strong and healthy.

But times were hard. Tuutalannuaq was raised mainly by his grandmother. She did her best but often there was not enough to eat. Because they had no hunter in the family, there was no one to bring fresh meat and hides. She could not make new clothes for the child. Instead she patched his old clothes and they became tighter and tighter on his growing body.

It should not have been this way. Inuit traditional law is very clear on this point. We must look after those who are less fortunate than we are. We must share what we have with them – food, stories, laughter. But that's not the way it was in this community. Not only did people refuse to help, they openly tormented the child. When he went out to play with the others, children teased him as children do, and even the adults joined in. There was one who loved to pick Tuutalannuaq up in his teeth by the tip of the parka hood and twirl him around until the dizzy child ran home in tears and in tatters.

Only one person did not take part in this torment, and that was the hero of our story, the great shaman Kiviuq. He even tried to convince the others that they were doing wrong. To no avail.

The grandmother worried. She tried to bring the people to their senses but they did not listen to her. They had killed her son and tormented her grandchild. Long she considered her options. At last she decided on revenge. She knew that in taking revenge on the hunters she could also teach the child important skills and lessons for his whole life.

She called Tuutalannuaq to her. "I have no more materials to repair your clothes. You are getting bigger and the clothes are getting smaller as I patch them together. Go over to that deserted camp where the gulls are circling and see if you can find any piece of sealskin." Off the child ran.

He didn't find much. But he did find one small piece of skin from a baby seal's face. He took it back to his grandmother and she said it would do very well indeed.

She chewed the sealskin as Inuit women do and stretched it, singing all the while. At last it was big enough to cover the child completely, and she sewed it together using sinew from seagull wings.

"Now you must learn to hold your breath under water," she said. She filled her biggest cooking pot and trained him. Gently she held his little head down under the water. At first he couldn't hold his breath very long and came up sputtering, but as the days went by, he learned to hold his breath longer. She kept track by watching the shadows on the tent wall. At last he held his breath so long that she saw the sun move.

"You are ready," she said. "Now, will you be afraid if I put you down through this wet spot in the floor?"

And perhaps because he had no idea what was about to happen, he replied, "No, grandmother, I will not be afraid."

She told him what would happen when he got into the water and how he should behave. Then she put him down through the wet spot in the floor, singing, "Go down, go down through the earth. Come up in the sea."

Down through the earth he went. He came up in the water right beside the place where the people were gathered, playing a ball game on the shore. Tuutalannuaq was now in the form of a baby seal.

The Storm at Sea

The young seal bobbed up in front of the hunters. "A seal!" they called to each other. "Let's go hunting!" They raced to their kayaks and pushed off. If they had been paying close attention, they would have noticed that this seal was completely white, the way the pups are in early spring. Now it was full summer and normal seals were no longer white. But they didn't notice. The grandmother had made it so.

Tuutalannuaq headed out to sea, the hunters hot in pursuit. He bobbed up here and there, always staying out of the way of the harpoons. Farther and farther from shore he led them. And when he was sure they were too far from shore to get back easily, he raised his right hand from the water. He called out as his grandmother had taught him, "*Silaga nauk, ungaa!* Where's my weather?" He was calling for the weather of the day he was born. And that child had been born on a stormy day!

The winds began to blow. Big waves rose up on the sea. Too late the hunters realized what had happened. "Look," one shouted. "That's a human hand. That's the orphan child." They recognized the hand because it was deformed. He had raised that hand so they would realize that this was revenge.

The winds howled and the waves rose as high as mountains. One by one the kayaks turned over. One by one the hunters drowned.

At last only Kiviuq was left alive in his kayak. The grandmother had spared him because he alone had been kind to the family and had tried to stop the others from tormenting the child. But even he was struggling to stay afloat. At first two other men survived as well. They had been thrown from their kayaks and he was holding them up in the water beside his own. These two were also shamans from the community. He held them as long as he could but at last one called out to him, "I can't hold on any longer. You go ahead. Let me go."

Kiviuq had to let him go.

And then the other one called, "I can't hold on any longer. You go ahead. Let me go." Kiviuq had to let him go as well.

Now he was truly alone in the raging sea. It was all he could do to keep his kayak upright. From time to time he thought he saw land. "*Nuna tauvva, iqqaq tauvva,*" he called.[1] "There's the land. There's the bottom under shallow water." But each time he was mistaken – what he saw was just a giant wave.

Time passed and at last the storm started to die down. Now Kiviuq heard a sound coming from inside his kayak. And shore birds appeared in the air.

When Kiviuq was born, his grandmother had chosen carefully the kind of skin she would use to clean the baby's skin. She chose the skin of a sandpiper. She spoke powerful words into his ear.

"You will always be able to come home, no matter what the obstacles."

The sandpiper became his helping spirit, his *ikajuqti*. When his first kayak was built, they put a sandpiper skin between the wood frame and the sealskin cover to prevent the wood from poking through. Any time he needed help, he could call on the sandpipers. And he needed them now. With unerring instinct the birds guided him to shore.

At last Kiviuq called, "Nuna tauvva, iqqaq tauvva," and it was true. He saw land, he saw the bottom under shallow water.

Gratefully he pulled his kayak up on shore. He got out, turned the kayak upside down, and cleaned it out. He had been out at sea for a long time, unable to get up and urinate over the side for fear of capsizing in the storm. He had been at sea for so long that his kayak had filled almost to capacity. He was much relieved to clean the kayak and his own clothes. And when that was done, he lay down on the shore and went to sleep.

Kiviuq slept long and then awoke to a voice. "Get up!" it said. "You have to move your kayak." He looked around and saw no one. But sure enough, although he had pulled the kayak well up on shore, the waves were now lapping around it. He pulled it further up and went back to sleep.

After a while the voice called again, "Get up! You have to move your kayak. You have to turn your boots over." He looked and saw that again the water had come up to the place where he had left the kayak. His boots were drying unevenly and needed to be turned. When he had taken care of his things, he went back to sleep.

At last he awoke of his own accord. The kayak was now well above the high water mark. He had slept through a whole cycle of tides.

Kiviuq looked around. Nothing looked familiar. He was certainly far from home in an unknown land. Further up on the shore he saw a sod house without a cover. He went to investigate.

Bee Woman

As he got closer to the house, he heard singing coming from inside. He climbed up the wall and looked down over the edge. Inside he saw an interesting being. She was working with a big crescent-shaped knife, cleaning a human skin. A pot filled with chunks of human meat was boiling in front of her. Kiviuq was taken aback but decided to get her attention. He spat down on her head.

At first she didn't notice him, and so he spat again. "That's funny," she said. "This house has never dripped before, and now it's dripping." She looked up, but her floppy eyelids covered her eyes and she couldn't see a thing. This didn't bother her though. She took her *ulu* and cut her eyelids off. She put one of them in the pot and popped the other in her mouth.

Kiviuq was so horrified, so terrified, that he passed out and fell off the sod house. He lay there on the ground all winter, dead.

In the spring, the one with the big *ulu* came out. She was Iguttaqjuaq, or Big Bee Woman. She looked like a big bumblebee. Spotting the body lying on the ground, she poked at Kiviuq. "Aha, it's a human person. *Inunguna*. Person, wake up!"

Kiviuq woke up, but he did not see Big Bee Woman. Instead he saw her in the form of Arnatiaq, Good Beautiful Woman.

"Come into my house," she said. "Your clothes are wet, you must be hungry. I'll dry your clothes and give you some food." He followed her inside and took off his outer clothing. She hung his things up on her drying rack. Pointing to a bed in the other room she said, "Lie down and sleep some more. I'll get firewood and cook you up a meal." With that she was gone.

Kiviuq looked around. The bed had a solid wood frame, but it was strung from side to side with human intestines.

And then he saw the skulls, on the floor in a ring around the base of the wall. What was worse was that he recognized them. These were the skulls of his former companions – the men who had died at sea.

One of the skulls spoke to him. This was the last shaman who had died at sea, the one Kiviuq had tried to save. "If you don't want to turn out like me, get out of here fast!"

Kiviuq didn't have to be told twice. He reached for his boots and clothes up on the drying rack. But every time he reached, the rack moved higher in the air. He stretched and jumped but couldn't get his clothes down.

"Come in here and help me!" he called to the woman. But she replied from outside, "I put them up, you get them down!"

Now Kiviuq called on his *tuurngaq*, his powerful shamanic helping spirit. This was the giant polar bear. "Nanurluk, come and get this woman!"

A loud growling and snuffling came from outside. The door flew open and in came Bee Woman. "H-here are your b-boots. H-here are your c-clothes," she said, fearfully pulling his things down from the rack. He threw on his clothes and headed out the door so fast that he had one boot on and the other only halfway on. She was waiting by the door and tried to slice him with her *ulu* but only succeeded in cutting off the flap of his parka. He ran down to his kayak and pushed off.

She was right behind him, but too late. She stood complaining with one foot in the water and one on the shore. "Tee hee. Tee hee."

He paddled parallel to shore, and she walked along beside him. "Come back, my husband. I won't hurt you. Come back."

She came out on a point of land, the last place where she had a chance of getting him. She took up her great *ulu* and sliced a boulder on the shore. "This is the way I would have sliced you." Her gesture was so powerful that it almost knocked him out of his kayak.

He took up his great spear and speared an ice floe. "This is the way I would have speared you." His gesture was so powerful that it knocked her over backwards.

She got up and threw her great *ulu* out over the water the way you would skip a rock. The *ulu* sank, and then it rose up again. As it came up, it turned into sea ice. This was the first time that ice ever appeared on the salt water.

It froze up all around Kiviuq's kayak. Pretty soon she would be able to get out to him over the ice. He remembered an incantation that his maternal aunt had taught him, and gesturing forward with one finger, he sang the incantation. The ice broke up with a sound like breaking glass.

Kiviuq paddled away, leaving Bee Woman alone on the shore.

A man of power, on his long journey home.

Giving and Receiving Help

He paddled along, watching out for familiar landmarks.

After a while he began to feel he was paddling hard and getting nowhere. The landmark he was orienting himself to had not moved for a long time. Then he heard a voice calling out to him, "Come up here and help me clean this dirt out of my eye." Kiviuq pulled his kayak up on shore and looked around. There was no one to be seen. At last he looked down on the ground and saw a small seal bone. This is the bone people call "the dog" in a game played with bones. The dog bone has a little hole called "the dog's eye." Kiviuq picked up the bone and sure enough, the "eye" was full of dirt. Taking a few blades of grass, he carefully cleaned the bone and placed it back where he had found it. He got back into his kayak and now he was able to paddle freely away.

After a while it happened again. Paddling and getting nowhere. Another voice called out, "Come up here and help me climb this cliff." Kiviuq went up on the shore and looked around. He couldn't see anyone, and the land was quite flat, no cliff in sight. Again he looked closely at the ground. A tiny lemming was trying to climb a sandbank and kept falling back. Kiviuq was amused to see that the lemming could have easily gone around but was determined to get up his cliff. The man picked the animal up gently in his palm, and set it down at the top of the sandbank. He then got back into his kayak and was able to paddle freely away.

As he moved along, he saw two *inuksuut* (or two *inuksuks*) up on the shore.[2] One of them called out to him, "Watch out. The giant mussels are trying to bite your kayak." Kiviuq looked back and saw huge mussels in the water, about to bite the stern of his kayak. One of them spoke up and said, "Kubleroq is lying." Kubleroq was the name of the *inuksuk* that had spoken. Having their plot exposed, the mussels sank into the water and Kiviuq paddled away, on his long journey home.

Mother and Daughter – Two Women and a Log of Wood

He met fighting grizzly bears, giant caterpillars, sprightly mer-people, and dangerous beings wielding tiny knives. He was nearly exhausted when he came to an island and saw smoke rising from a campfire. Hoping this indicated that real people were living there, and not other extraordinary beings, he left his kayak on the shore and walked in the direction of the smoke.

Not only were they people – they were women. It had been so long since Kiviuq had met any human women that he was completely tongue-tied by the time he got to their camp. The only thing he could think of to say was, "Could I have a drink of water?"

The two women, mother and daughter, were amused, since he had passed a freshwater pond on the way and now appeared not to have noticed it. The mother said, "You can have a drink of water if you stay here with us."

Kiviuq agreed to stay. He quickly learned that these two women were living with a log of wood. The knots on the log were stained with the juices of mating. When night came, the two women placed the log between them in the bed. Kiviuq lay down with the mother. During the night the log poked him and moaned in a jealous voice.

"Who is this log?" Kiviuq asked.

"It's my mother's husband," the daughter replied.

"Not just mine," said the mother. "It's our husband."

In the morning the women carried the log down to the water and it sailed away. All day long they could hear the log singing happily out in the water, and towards nightfall it came back with seals draped over its knots. This is the way the log provided for his wives.

That night Kiviuq lay down and slept with the daughter, and that night the log's moans were even louder than before. In the morning when they put the log in the water, Kiviuq spat on it. The log sailed away and never came back.

Now Kiviuq began to provide for the two women. He went hunting every day, both on the sea and over on the mainland. He began to spend more time with the daughter. This was a very happy period in his life, as their love blossomed.

It was pleasant for Kiviuq and the young woman, but not so happy for the mother. She grew lonely as the young couple left her alone more of the time. She was frightened they would move away, leaving her behind. She was frustrated by the nearness of their lovemaking, which excluded her. As time passed, a plan formed in her mind. It was something she would never have considered before, so terrible it was, but now it took on a life of its own.

One day while Kiviuq was away hunting she called her daughter. "Let me pick the lice from your hair," she said. The daughter sat down at her feet and the mother ran her hands through the younger woman's hair. It was so relaxing that the daughter fell asleep. When she was sure the daughter would not awaken, the mother took a skewer and thrust it into the girl's ear, killing her.

She lost no time. She skinned her daughter carefully and put the skin on herself. And how good it felt! Firm youthful skin, shiny black hair. The mother felt young again. She waited eagerly until Kiviuq returned.

Usually when he came back in his kayak, his young wife would come down to the shore and help him. No matter what he had brought, be it a caribou from the mainland or a big seal from the sea, she would pick it up easily and carry it up to camp on her powerful shoulders.

But today things were different. The woman who came to meet him looked the same, but she guided him in to shore at a different place. The seal he brought was not the largest, but nonetheless she had great difficulty getting it up on her shoulders. As she walked away he saw that her legs trembled.

Then he noticed something that froze his heart. At the place where her pants met the top of her boots a bit of skin was exposed. This was not firm youthful skin, but was slack and wrinkled – the skin of a much older woman.

At once he realized what had happened. His heart filled with grief for his young wife, and with rage for what her mother had done. He wanted to race after her and take revenge.

But before he could move, the voices of his elders came to him strong and clear. "Walk away from trouble. If someone does you a wrong, do not engage with them. Do not let your emotions get the better of you. If it is at all possible, just walk away."

It was difficult, but he walked back to his kayak and paddled away.

Tiny Spiders and Homecoming

In spite of his grief, or perhaps because of it, Kiviuq now had the sense that at last he was truly on the way home.

After a while he came to a place where tiny spiders were busy stringing glass beads and making beautiful embroidered clothing. Kiviuq thought of his wives, the ones he had left at home so long ago. It would be nice to bring them something. He took beads and clothing from the tiny spiders and left them crying on the shore.

Now he was exhausted. He called to his sandpiper spirits and said, "Please help me. I am so tired."

"We will help you. Just go to sleep and we will tow your kayak."

Kiviuq drifted off and the sandpipers towed the kayak. Every now and then they woke him up to ask if he recognized any landmarks. At first he did not, but after a while the scenery became more familiar. They came to a place where two young men were checking their meat cache. Kiviuq greeted them and they spent the evening telling each other stories. The young men told of how their father had been carried away at sea by a big storm long ago, and Kiviuq told them of his many adventures.

One of the young men took a good look at Kiviuq's teeth and said, "I recognize you. You are our father!"

And so it was. His sons, who had been just small children when he left, were now fully grown men. They travelled home together.

"*Aasiggai, aasiggai, aasi aasi aasiggai!*" Kiviuq sang his homecoming song.

Kiviuq's mother had been waiting, standing on a rock, gazing out to sea. She had stood there for so long that her feet had worn indentations in the rocks. People brought her food, but she refused to leave her post. Now she saw her son and heard him singing, and rushed home to prepare for his arrival.

His father had been sitting on a rock watching the sea for so long that he had worn indentations in the rock. He had been sitting for so long that he could no longer walk. But now he heard his son's voice and jumped up. He made the rounds of the tents, announcing joyfully, "My son is coming home at last."

Kiviuq's wives heard his singing. One of them had taken another husband, and she was well dressed and well fed. The other had not taken a new husband and she was very thin, dressed in tatters. She came down to shore and called out, "Kiviuq, my husband, I have waited for you all this time. My vagina has been closed, unused, but now it is wide open."

Kiviuq pulled up on shore and everyone came to meet him. He gave beads to all the women in the community except for his favourite wife, the one who had waited for him. He tore her rags from her body and dressed her in the beautiful beaded clothing from the tiny spiders.

There was only one sad thing about Kiviuq's homecoming. His parents had waited long, living only to see their son return home. Now that he was there, they used the last of their energy in their joy and died as he arrived on shore.

Kiviuq fulfilled the prophecy made at his birth. He arrived home in spite of all the obstacles.

A man of power, a man of kindness, a great hero, on his long journey home, *ajaajaa*.

The Penis in the Lake

Kiviuq challenged the young man his second wife was living with. They engaged in a contest of arm wrestling, and Kiviuq easily won her back. Fall came and he set off caribou hunting with his two wives. They found a good place and set up camp.

At first everything went well. Kiviuq hunted and his wives worked at dressing the hides and preparing food. They did their work well. But after a while something changed. He would come home in the evening and find the two women asleep, cold and shivering. He woke them and asked what was going on, but they gave him no sensible reply. He decided to find out for himself.

Next day he only pretended to go hunting. He hid and watched as his two wives left the tent, ostensibly going to collect firewood. He followed them as they walked to a nearby lake. When they got there, they picked up pebbles and threw them into the water. "Penis, come up," they called.

A large penis rose above the surface of the lake. One of Kiviuq's wives took off her pants, waded out into the water, and had sex with the penis. When she was finished, she came back, and the second wife did the same. When both were satisfied, they went home, gathering a token amount of firewood on the way. When Kiviuq came home, he found them both asleep, as usual.

Next day he sent his wives on an errand far away from camp. When they were gone, he went out to the lake. He tossed pebbles into the water and called out, "Penis, come up!" The penis came up out of the water. Kiviuq waded out and cut the penis off at water level. He took it home and boiled it up. When his wives came home he served it to them.

They seemed to enjoy it. One said, "What is this, so hard but so delicious?"

"It's your second husband's penis, you two," Kiviuq replied.

One wife was quite distressed by this but the other continued to eat.

From then on, when Kiviuq was out hunting he collected maggots in a caribou skin. When he had enough, he came to his first wife.

"Which are you more afraid of, maggots or the knife?" he asked her.

"We can squash maggots," she replied. "I'm not afraid of them."

Now he forced her to take off her pants and sit on the maggots. She tried to pull the flap of her parka under her but he cut it off. The maggots entered her body through every opening.

She spoke about what was happening. "Now they are eating my intestines. Now they are done. Now they are eating my liver. Now they are done. Now they are eating my lungs. Now they are done."

When she said, "Now they are eating my heart," she died.

The maggots came back out of her body through every opening, but now they were in the form of small animals, mainly lemmings. Kiviuq was still so angry that he took a coal from the fire and burnt one lemming, who went away with a bent nose.

Now he faced his second wife. "What are you more afraid of, maggots or the knife?"

She knew what was coming and replied, "Give me the knife. At least it will be quick."

He killed her using his knife, and buried both of his wives under rocks, as was the custom.

Now he moved his camp to a new location.

The Fox-Wife

For some time Kiviuq lived alone. Not just alone, but lonely.

Then one day he came home and found cooked food waiting for him inside his tent. No one was there. The first time this happened the food was cold when he arrived. Next day he came home and the food was lukewarm, and after a few more days the food was piping hot. His mysterious helper must have just left.

Next day he hid where he had a good view of the tent. He saw an arctic fox with silvery white fur emerge from the grave of his favourite wife and go into the tent. After a few moments a beautiful woman came out. She had long silvery white hair and was carrying a fox skin, which she hung out over the tent ropes. Then she went in and began cooking.

Every day he watched, moving closer to the tent. He made sure to stay out of the wind. At last he was close enough, and while she was inside he ran forward and grabbed the fox skin. The woman came out and demanded, "Give me back my skin!"

"I will give you back your skin only if you become my wife," he replied.

At first she objected but at last she agreed. He gave her back the fox skin and the two began to live together happily as man and wife. They made excellent hunting partners.

Winter was coming and they decided to move camp. They moved quite a long distance and then stopped at a place where a wolverine was living alone. They built their igloo next to his, and the wolverine helped. Time passed and the wolverine began to envy Kiviuq his lovely wife. "I wish I had a wife like that," he thought. "I can just picture her – rosy cheeks, chewing coyly on the tip of her mitt."

Then he got an idea. "I'll shit myself a wife." And he succeeded.

It wasn't long afterwards that the wolverine came and proposed to Kiviuq that they swap wives for the night. Kiviuq didn't much like the idea, and he was sure his wife would like it even less. But the wolverine was persistent – and after all he had helped build the igloo. At last Kiviuq gave in, but not without conditions.

"Don't offend my wife. She is terribly shy. Whatever you do, don't mention her smell! And make sure you close the igloo up tightly."

"Yeah, yeah," said the wolverine eagerly.

The two retired to each other's igloos.

When the time came to go to bed the fox-wife wanted to pee, so she went to the spot at the end of the bed.

"Ugh, what a foul smell," said the wolverine. "Where's it coming from?"

"Maybe from me?" said the fox, terribly embarrassed.

She quickly pulled on her fox skin and slipped out through a crack around the door, where the wolverine had not closed it tightly enough.

The wolverine went over to his own igloo and said to Kiviuq, "I was not able to lie with your wife."

"I told you not to offend her," said Kiviuq. And he set off following the fox tracks. But before he left, he noticed an unpleasant smell in the wolverine's igloo. The dream wife had reverted to her original state.

Kiviuq walked quickly. After a while he noticed that he was following one fox track and one human track.

At last he came to what appeared to be the opening to a fox den.

A lemming came out, looked at him flirtatiously, and said, "Take me!"

He looked the little animal over and replied, "I won't have you – your nose is bleeding." The lemming went back into the den and said to the fox, "He won't have me because I'm prone to nosebleeds."

Now a weasel came out and said, "Take me!" But Kiviuq replied, "I won't have you – you are too skinny." The weasel went back in and said, "He won't have me because I'm too skinny."

Now a ground squirrel came out and said, "Take me!" Kiviuq replied, "I don't want you – you are too fat." The ground squirrel went back in and said to the fox, "He won't have me because I'm too fat."

Now an arctic hare came out, but Kiviuq told her her eyes were too close together. The hare went back in and said, "He won't have me because my eyes are too close."

Now a pretty wolverine came out and offered herself, but he said her nose was too short. The wolverine went back in and said, "He won't have me because my nose is too short."

A wolf came out and she was the most attractive of all. Kiviuq was very tempted by her but he thought of his fox-wife and replied, "I won't have you – your nose is too long." The wolf went back to the fox and said, "He won't have me because my nose is too long."

Now the lemming came back out and said, "You can come in but you must come backwards, and keep your eyes closed."

Kiviuq backed into the den, but he couldn't resist opening his eyes a little. As he did so, he felt the earth closing tightly around him. He closed his eyes and got the rest of the way in.

He looked around. The place was full of animals. The lemming was living on a shelf over the door. A pair of ground squirrels were making up their bed. Kiviuq thought to himself, "They look exactly alike."

One of the squirrels said to the other, "He thinks we look exactly alike."

In a side room Kiviuq saw his fox-wife, combing her beautiful long white hair. She had wept so long that a pillar of frozen tears reached from her face to the floor. He went to sit next to her, but she jumped up and ran to the other side of the den. He followed her but she was always too quick for him – he couldn't catch up with her. At last he spat on the floor in front of her. She stopped and the two were reunited.

Feast and Lampoons

The animals were happy that Kiviuq had become one of the family, and they called for a feast. Each animal brought something to eat. Wolf brought caribou meat. Wolverine also brought caribou but his was stolen. The seagull brought a beautiful arctic char. The only one who brought something no one else wanted was the raven, and he brought frozen dog shit.

"That's disgusting," said the other animals. "Take it out into the porch and eat it yourself." Raven went out, and they heard his happy sounds as he ate by himself.

After supper the animals got ready for a session of lampooning. They paired up and sang songs making fun of each other. First up were wolf and wolverine.

The wolverine sang, "*The wolf is smart, the wolf is fast. The wolf tells stories that seem to be true. But I have seen him chasing an arctic hare up a hill, and the hare was faster – the wolf could not get him.*"

Wolf replied, "*Wolverine, you are a nuisance. You create anger. You make trouble for people all the time around their meat caches. You should be chased with howling, you should be stabbed or strangled.*"

Seagull sang to raven, "*Once the creeks are open I'll use my spear to catch fish, and you'll just be making sounds in the distance.*"

Raven replied, "*During the cold time you won't be here at all while I'm feasting on dog droppings and getting fat on garbage.*"

Fox sang to hare, "*I am a predator looking for seal breathing holes. I smell them but can't find them. This is the hard part for me – and the same goes for the nest with eggs.*"

Hare also sang to fox, "*You say you can catch swimming caribou from a kayak, but everybody knows that's ridiculous. Your snout is growing longer from your lies!*"

When the singing was over, Kiviuq let out a huge fart, and the animals scattered, racing for the door. The fox was first to go out, and Kiviuq tried to follow her. But he was hindered by a scratching being who fell down in front of him from over the door. As the fox was the reincarnation of his first wife, this being was the reincarnation of the second wife. She was so determined to stop him that he had to turn back and go out through a window. By the time he looked for his fox-wife she had disappeared. Since it was now spring, there were no tracks to follow. He was left alone again.

The Grizzly Bear

Meat was being stolen from the cache in the community where Kiviuq had come to live. No one had been able to catch the thief, although they suspected it was a bear.

Kiviuq offered to help. "Bury me in the cache," he said, "and I will find out who is stealing the meat."

They took him out and buried him under rocks. He lay there for many months like a dead man. From time to time people came and took meat from the cache, but still Kiviuq stayed there.

At last one day he heard someone approaching on powerful paws. Then rocks were being tossed away from the cache, and Kiviuq found himself face to face with a huge grizzly bear. He pretended to be dead.

The bear pulled him out and looked him over, a little disappointed that it was only a human. Nonetheless he decided to bring Kiviuq home for his children to eat. But how would he carry him?

This was no problem for the bear. He took off his bearskin and laid it out on the ground, placed Kiviuq's body on top, and pulled it like a travois. Under his bearskin, the grizzly looked like a man.

After a while the bear began to have doubts. Was the man really dead? He came back to check, sniffing around Kiviuq's nose and mouth. Kiviuq started to breathe through his rear end. But the bear was still suspicious. He sniffed around Kiviuq's rear and at that time Kiviuq breathed through his nose.

At last, convinced that the man was dead, the bear continued on his way. They passed through a place where willows grew close to the trail. Kiviuq reached out and held onto the willows, making himself harder to pull. Of course he stopped holding the willows when the bear turned around to look.

The grizzly bear–man arrived at his own home. His children came running out to greet him. "*Ataata*, Papa! What have you brought us?"

"I've brought you a man to eat. And when we've finished, you can have his bones to play games with."

The bear's wife came out of the igloo. She too was in human form. She took Kiviuq's body inside and tried to cut him up. But he held his muscles so tight that she couldn't cut him. Thinking he was frozen, she set his body up to thaw out, and sat down to sharpen her *ulu*. Her husband lay down for a nap.

The children came over to investigate the thawing body. Snot was dripping from his nose and they licked it from his face. Meanwhile Kiviuq wanted to find out if there was some kind of weapon in the igloo, so he surreptitiously opened his eyes.

"*Ataata*," the children cried, "the dinner is opening its eyes!" The bear-man dragged himself awake. "Let him open his eyes," he said. "I thought he was alive all the time. I thought he was holding on to the willow branches to make my work harder."

Kiviuq noticed an axe over on the other side of the igloo. He leapt over there, grabbed the axe, and struck the bear-man a terrific blow on one leg, putting him out of action. He headed out the door and began running.

The bear-woman came after him, stopping in the porch just long enough to get into her bearskin, which would help her run faster.

Kiviuq looked back over his shoulder. The bear was gaining on him. He came to a small mound of earth, took saliva on his finger, and ran it around the mound.

"Grow a big mountain!" he called. And the mound grew into a big mountain. This slowed the bear-woman down for a while but pretty soon she was gaining on him again.

Kiviuq came to a small creek. He jumped to the other side and then took saliva on his finger and ran it along the edge of the creek. "Grow a big river," he called. The creek grew quickly into a river that was swift and wide. Now Kiviuq waited.

The bear came up to the creek bank. She sniffed in both directions.

"How did you get over there?" she asked Kiviuq.

"Me?" said Kiviuq, "I just drank the river. I ate and kissed and licked the river. I fought the river, and then I crossed." The bear did just that.

She drank and ate and kissed and licked and fought the river, and came across. But when she got near Kiviuq's side, she shook herself to get the water off her fur. Her big stomach burst, and because the water inside was so warm, it turned into mist and fog. And that was the very first fog that ever appeared on earth.

The bear's body was carried downstream, Kiviuq following along onshore. At last it got snagged and he pulled it out of the water. He skinned the bear on a big boulder that you can still see today if you go to the place. It is called Paniqsiivik, the drying place.

After that Kiviuq walked away through the new fog.

The Goose-Wife

He walked through the fog and after a while he heard the sound of girlish laughter. He approached carefully. He came to a big lake and saw several girls in the water, enjoying a swim. They had left their feather coats on the shore, for these were water birds – a sandhill crane, a loon, and a Canada goose.

Kiviuq watched the girls and then picked up all the feathers.

The girls came up to him. First was the sandhill crane. "Give me back my feathers," she said. He noticed that she was quite flat-chested and unattractive, so he gave the feathers back.

Next the loon approached. "Give me back my feathers." She was eyeing the area around his kidneys and her long beak made him feel profoundly uncomfortable. And so he gave her feathers back.

Then came the Canada goose. "Give me back my feathers," she said. What a beauty she was. Kiviuq had already fallen in love. He replied, "I will give you back your feathers only if you become my wife."

At first she refused but she liked the look of him as much as he liked her. She agreed at last, and he gave the feather coat back.

They began to live together and in time she gave birth to several children. She taught them to eat as she did. This displeased Kiviuq's mother.

"Why do you have to eat sand?" she said. "We have good meat here, seal and caribou. Why don't you eat as we do? Besides, I don't like you tracking sand in the tent like this. It's damaging the caribou skins I'm working on."

Kiviuq supported his wife. "Let her be, Mother," he said. "Sand is her natural food." He even went out and collected grasses for her and the children. And with this uneasy truce, time passed.

Fall came, the time of migration. The goose-wife heard her relatives getting ready for their long flight south and she felt the pull in her blood and bones. She was torn, loving her husband and yet yearning to join the formation in the sky. She worried about the children. How could she find food for them when everything froze up in the winter?

She decided to go. She took the children down along the shore and collected feathers. She placed the feathers between their fingers and taught them to fly. When they were ready, they all rose up into the air and flew around Kiviuq's mother. Then they flew out on the land to where Kiviuq was hunting and flew around him too. "Wait for me," the goose-wife called out. "I'll be back in the spring." And then they were gone.

Kiviuq returned home and confronted his mother. "Did you offend my wife? Why has she left?"

"I don't know," she replied. "She just took the children and flew away."

"I think you offended her. I'm going to find her and I won't give up until I do."

Now his mother was frightened. "If you truly go and leave me alone, may your way be difficult," she said.

He set off, following the flight of the geese. And his way was difficult indeed. He met obstacles so strong that he could only surpass them by singing his way through.

I am going to the land of the birds, to the place where winter never comes.
Over mountains I go. Through a hole in the water, through a hole in the earth, through a hole in the sky.
To the land of the birds.

Before me I see a qulliq, *a seal-oil lamp.*
Wherever I move, it is there blocking my way.
I jump from one chunk of fat to another and at last come to the other side.

When I look back the lamp is gone.

I am going to the land of the birds, to the place where winter never comes.
Over mountains I go. Through a hole in the water, through a hole in the earth, through a hole in the sky.
To the land of the birds.

Before me I see a cooking pot full of chunks of meat.
Wherever I turn it is there before me, blocking my way.
I walk carefully around the rim of the pot and jump down on the other side.

When I look back the pot is gone.

I am going to the land of the birds, to the place where winter never comes.
Over mountains I go. Through a hole in the water, through a hole in the earth, through a hole in the sky.
To the land of the birds.

Before me I see huge rocks, clashing together and apart.
I must time my passage carefully.
I run between the rocks and they clash shut, cutting off the tail of my parka.

When I look back the rocks are gone.

I am going to the land of the birds, to the place where winter never comes.
Over mountains I go. Through a hole in the water, through a hole in the earth, through a hole in the sky.
To the land of the birds.

Before me I see the lower half of a woman's body.
Wherever I turn it is there, blocking my way.
At last I have sex with that body.

When I look back the female body is gone.

Kiviuq arrived in a warm country, far from home.

The Fishmaker

He saw a huge shining lake in the distance. Realizing it would be very difficult to cross, he camped for the night so as to approach in the morning when his energy would be stronger.

Next morning he came to the shore of the lake. There a giant of a man was working with an axe. Kiviuq came up behind him and noticed something strange. He could see daylight through the man's body. The man had an opening that ran from his anus to his mouth.

Guessing that the man might be sensitive about this, Kiviuq approached from the side. He was right to be cautious. The big man raised his axe threateningly. "Which way did you come from?" he demanded.

"I came from your side," said Kiviuq.

At first the man didn't believe him, but after a few more reassurances he calmed down.

This was the Fishmaker, Iqaliraq. He was working with a big piece of wood, whittling chips which he rubbed on his penis and put into the water. The wood chips turned into fish and swam away. From the hardwood the Fishmaker made arctic char and from the softwood he made lake trout.

Now Kiviuq asked if the Fishmaker had seen his family of geese. "They crossed this lake," the Fishmaker replied, "and now they are somewhere on the other side."

"I truly wish I could get over there and find them," said Kiviuq.

"I will help you," said Iqaliraq.

He called out into the lake. The thing Kiviuq had taken for an island turned out to be a huge fish. "Get on his back," said the Fishmaker. "Sit behind the second to the last fin and he will take you across. The journey will be long. You can do whatever you want on the way. Sleep if you need to sleep. When you reach the other side, the fish will shake with excitement – get off then. Put your ear to the ground, and you will hear your family and know which way to go."

Kiviuq got on and rode the giant fish across the lake. He got off on the far shore and put his ear to the ground. He heard the sounds of a large encampment of geese and headed in that direction.

Reunion

His children saw him coming and rushed in to tell their mother. "*Anaana*, Mama! *Ataata* is here."

"That cannot be," she replied. "We left him too far away, beyond the second step. We left him beyond two great bodies of water."

Now Kiviuq arrived. She looked out and saw that it truly was her husband. But in the meantime she had taken another husband, one of the geese. He said, "Kiviuq is not one to be afraid of." Nonetheless he rushed out of the tent. Then he came back – he had forgotten to take his bag, which was really his stomach. Now he jumped into the water and swam away.

Kiviuq's goose-wife came out of the house but she was in too much of a hurry. She forgot to bring the amulet that would allow her to turn back into a human. At that moment she forgot the words to her transformation song. She remained in the form of a goose, and when the time of migration came, she flew away north with her children.

Kiviuq stayed in the south. He is still alive today, although no one has seen him in a long time. As he gets older, it becomes more difficult for him to move. In the cold days of winter he hardly moves at all, while in the warm days of summer he moves around a bit. Lichens have grown on his face, which makes it embarrassing for him to be among people.

No one knows for sure whether Kiviuq will ever return to the north. When he dies, they say there will be no more air to breathe and life on earth will end. But for now he and his wives are still alive in the minds and hearts of those who live their stories with them, gaining strength every time their story helps one of us to live a better life here on earth. Their intelligence and wit, observant nature, deep humanity, and ability to overcome obstacles, including those of their own making, as well as their forgiveness and compassion are an inspiration for the time to come.

Journey to Nunavut, 2004

If it weren't for head lice I wouldn't know stories! When I was young there was no medicine and no shampoo – mother or grandmother would pick our lice. The child says yes to the story and thus gets their lice picked at the same time.

– Mary Ittunga, 2004

For the last month I'd made the rounds of the sporting goods stores in a sunny September 30°C Vancouver, dressed in sandals and shorts, buying clothes for sub zero Nunavut. The Arctic in October – what would that mean? It would be hot, with jacked-up central heating indoors and variable temperatures outdoors as we moved from south to north, from early to late in the month.

"Make sure you have wind pants," said one friend.

"Nothing but snowpack boots will do," said another.

"Fleece, fleece, and more fleece," they all agreed. Practically nothing that I already owned seemed right except my trusty down jacket, although on such a hot day it was hard to imagine wearing that. The boots were the last piece to arrive in our stores. Who would want them in Vancouver in September? I felt I was going to the end of the world.

Mountains from molehills. True, the Arctic requires different clothes than Vancouver, but what was really boggling my imagination was the fact that the place I was going is part of Canada. The snowy tundra was so far off my beaten track that I couldn't fathom it being in the same country as my British Columbia home with its old-growth forests and multicultural restaurants. Under all the questions about snowpacks and fleece lurked this excitement and anxiety about the unknown.

Nunavut is Canada's newest territory, formed in 1999 from the eastern part of the Northwest Territories.[1] Geographically it is enormous – one-fifth of Canada at 1.9 million square kilometres. If Nunavut were a country, it would be the thirteenth largest in the world, almost the same size as Mexico. It spite of that, the whole territory has only twenty kilometres of highway! It reaches so far north that the Nunavut community of Baker Lake (west of Hudson Bay) is near the geographic centre of Canada. But Nunavut's population is only 29,000, which makes for a density of one person per seventy square kilometres. Communities range in size from Bathurst Inlet, population 25, to the capital, Iqaluit, with about 6,000. Inuit represent 85 per cent of the population, and their ancestors lived on what is now Canadian soil far longer than most of our ancestors inhabited land in the south.

Clothing was the least of my worries, but it seemed to be the only one I could act on. I was concerned about many things. Would I get along with the people I was going to live and work with intimately for the next month? In Siberia I work alone. Would there be adequate translation to allow me to do my work? In Russia I speak the language fluently, while I know practically no Inuktitut. Would the Inuit accept or resent my presence, my studying their ancient story? I was used to a warm welcome. Would I enjoy the northern "country food" or not? Often in my Siberian travels my own stomach has been my worst enemy, and now I was concerned about such things as whale blubber and even seal meat – how would I balance my tastes with not offending my hosts?

At last the day came. Sweltering on the way to the airport under bundles of clothes, stopping in Edmonton with friends. Then Yellowknife, and at last I was stepping off the plane in Rankin Inlet, on the western shore of Hudson Bay. I nearly fell flat on my face descending the plane's narrow ladder, tripping on the duck feet of my new boots. Lots to learn in getting a new footing. The wind was howling. Already on October 4 it was colder than it ever gets in Vancouver.

The plan was that I'd wait at the airport for John Houston, my partner on this voyage, who would be arriving from Halifax via Iqaluit. Imagining a drafty airport building with inadequate seating, conjured from my memories of the Russian north, I hoped he would be on time! Instead I entered a well-equipped modern building and was met by a smiling young man who introduced himself as Noah Tiktak, our unit manager for Rankin Inlet. He was dressed in running shoes, jeans, and a light jacket. He told me that there had been a bad storm, the power was still out in many places, and John's plane might be delayed until the next day. Further, it turned out that the hotel we were booked into did not exist. Well, it was under construction. Somehow the hotel chain that had cheerfully booked us in almost every community had neglected to mention this small detail.

Noah whisked me off to Rankin's other hotel on his all-terrain vehicle (ATV), which everyone calls a Honda here in the north no matter what the brand. The power was still off in the hotel but they managed to check me in after a few calls back and forth with Halifax. Then John arrived safely. Things were getting back to normal, and before long we were sitting at the Wild Wolf Cafe with Noah and our videographer, Albert Kimaliakyuk, eating delicious caribou burgers with Caesar salad and discussing the days to come. Albert told us he knew an elder in Chesterfield Inlet who claimed to have gone hunting with Kiviuq.

And so it began – a whirlwind month through ten of Nunavut's twenty-six communities. The territory has three administrative regions, and we were to have a new camera person and interpreter in each one, as well as as a local unit manager in each community to handle logistics. The reason for the frequent changes of interpreter lies in the wealth of dialects spoken in Nunavut – it would have been difficult for any one person to do justice to them all. We recorded forty elders, all telling the story of Kiviuq, each in his or her own way, as they had learned it from parents, grandparents, aunts and uncles, friends, and hunting partners.

A month listening to one story? Houston had decided on this focus, since he knew that Kiviuq's is one of the most important Inuit stories, and he wanted to collect as many versions as possible while today's elders are still alive. But people at home ask if we weren't bored listening to one story repeated so many times. Why didn't we record many stories in so much time? I wouldn't have traded this experience for anything. There were moments when I drifted, true, hearing for the thirty-third time about a grandmother encasing a child in sealskin and sending him

The research crew at Pond Inlet: Jaco Anaviapik, Kira Van Deusen, John Houston, Jolene Arreak, and Philip Paniaq

out to sea to take revenge on the hunters who had tormented him. But the elders always brought me back quickly, each with a new detail or interpretation.

Proof of the importance of devoting much time to one story is the fact that we had as many questions at the end of the trip as at the beginning, but these were deeper questions. I had learned a lot about the seal-child, about Kiviuq's journeys and animal wives, about the lessons today's elders had learned in childhood from the story. Now I wanted to know whether Kiviuq was the only who had lived many lives. Perhaps his wife did the same, reincarnating through the animals he married. Or were they in some strange time warp where he lived one long life while she reincarnated several times? Who set the obstacles he encountered in his initiation – the grandmother, the giant bee, or the wolf mother? How did glass beads, which came to the Arctic only after European contact, get into this ancient story? What is the system of justice that underlies the action?

How does the extensive evidence of deep shamanic philosophy relate to today's world, and what practical use do the elders see for reviving this philosophy or keeping it hidden?

Some of the questions I had come with became irrelevant. I had wondered whether storytellers in the past had selected the stories they told publicly in order to address difficult issues in their communities at the time, such as disputes between neighbours or marital discord. My question came from my experiences in Siberia, where middle-aged people today recall storytelling in their childhood as a large community event where such issues might be indirectly addressed and thus resolved. Of course, there may have been times when Inuit used storytelling in this way, but it would have been an adult matter. Our elders were calling on memories from early childhood, when they would not have been party to such discussions. For the most part they recall storytelling in small family groups, rather than larger gatherings. Today's young people, for the most part, have not been brought up on traditional storytelling.

The kinds of questions my storytelling friends and I love to debate, such as what stealing a person's skin says about identity, now seemed too far from concrete reality and from what the elders would have heard from their own parents. Their strong conviction that Kiviuq was a real person who lived in a barely remembered past may explain why they interpret his story the way they do.

Although I had been invited on the trip because of my knowledge of storytelling and of Siberia, my job now was simply to listen. It was a lesson in the value of listening not only for myself but for the storytellers. When there was technical confusion over tapes and lights, I was sometimes the only one holding the energy of attentiveness with an eager elder. Often there was a trio – the teller, the interpreter, and me – keeping the level of humour up through the rather serious energy set by the video recording process. The story rolled over me in Inuktitut – and I began to understand a few words in this complex and beautiful language. Some tellers spoke with a strong poetic rhythm, others with an infectious good humour that made me laugh.

We had done extensive reading before setting out, digging out many versions of Kiviuq's story and stories related to it in ethnographic works. As the trip began, I was uncertain whether I actually liked our hero, having seen him in the works of Rasmussen bouncing characterless from one strange meeting to another and even engaging in rape and murder. I wondered what a woman could possibly find to inspire her in this tale of unfaithful wives, cannibalistic female monsters, and a mother who killed her own daughter to keep the hero for herself. The nicest females were Kiviuq's animal wives, but even the fox-wife submitted to his wife-swapping with the wolverine and the goose-wife to his mother's critique of her eating habits. Where was the strength and intelligence so obvious in northern women?

But of course this was the story as recorded by European men nearly a century ago, taken down painstakingly by hand, sometimes with indifferent translation. Was this the real Kiviuq, the man who had won the admiration and love of Inuit down through the centuries?

A different side of Kiviuq emerged through the elders' voices. By the time a week had gone by, I had seen him helping a tiny animal climb a sandbank. He returned the skin he had taken to convince the animals and birds to marry him, showing a respect for their nature that heroes in similar European and Asian tales did not. I saw him persist where others would give up, and even bring gifts when returning home. He was kind to the orphan and tried hard to save his companions at sea. Perhaps most importantly, I saw him turn away from troubling characters rather than kill them. All except his wife, that is. He still murdered her – and some elders point out that succumbing to his own anger in this way was very wrong. It seemed to me that his act came back to haunt him throughout the rest of the tale, contributing to his learning and growth.[2]

But that may be only my interpretation. Actually, I'm not sure that Inuit see him growing in the way heroes of modern novels and movies do. His own people see him as the embodiment of goodness. This contrast between the hero's obvious mistakes and his positive image creates a dynamic tension in the telling that contributes to its excitement. To me the telling becomes more like life than the folk tale.

And the women? Somewhere on the second day I came to understand an incredible act of forgiveness and what lay behind it. The wife he so brutally murdered reincarnated immediately as a fox and began preparing his food, concealing her identity until she was sure of him. And once having tested his devotion, she could let her love for him come back. Would I have had this strength? The orphan's grandmother and the goose-mother assert their nature and strength against the odds, making difficult decisions in order to protect their young – even transforming the children's small bodies and removing them from dangerous situations.

Children are much in evidence in Nunavut, where the median age is 22.1.[3] I saw them carried on their mother's back in the *amauti*, a large carrier attached to the fabric overcoat worn by virtually all women with babies. Children were playing in the streets, riding bicycles in blizzards, and watching television. Children listened eagerly to the elders when we recorded in school classrooms. In Pond Inlet two of the young teens listening to Annie Peterloosie stood poised, one foot ahead of the other, as if to take off racing as Kiviuq paddled his kayak away from Bee Woman. Others slept through the stories, stretched out on the floor, making me wonder if this was teenage lassitude, a language problem, or something more sinister. Amidst all the cheerful faces, laughter, and friendly hospitality I had to remind myself of the incredible level of teen suicide in these communities. None of the children we met could have been untouched by this terrifying and tragic phenomenon or by the levels of depression that surround it.

Change over Time

We found many differences between the stories we heard and the early twentieth-century stories we had read. Stories seem to change over time. Even when the words stay the same, the perceived meaning can change, since listeners are hearing in a new way. Even basic ideas about good and bad behaviour can change, and this shifts the overall meaning of a story. To bring a story back to life, to allow it to have the same benefit it once did, the cultural context sometimes requires a storyteller to add, delete, rearrange, or explain. I believe that most of the differences we experienced in Kiviuq's story are evidence of a shift in cultural context, the purpose of the telling, and/or the methods and purpose of collecting.

Today's Inuit have been successful materially and politically, having gained control over their own territory and set up a viable economy. Their brilliant artwork is known and valued throughout the world, and it contributes to the livelihood of most Inuit families. The promotion and distribution of art is as much a success story as the creative output itself.

Inuit have consistently marketed their work as high art – not as souvenirs. They ably took over management of the co-ops that first formed for art promotion and later expanded to include a large store and a hotel in nearly every community.[4] Inuit hold positions of responsibility and authority in all branches of territorial and local government, as well as in educational, health, and social services.

Nonetheless, success by the standards of others has not made for an entirely happy life. Inuit confront severe social problems, such as teen suicide, drug and alcohol abuse, and domestic violence. Elders look back longingly to the days when life was simpler, more focused, and they lived self-sufficiently on the land. Those were the days when a person's self-esteem came from being able to provide the family with the means of survival and from maintaining good relationships with neighbours. Today there are large and sometimes unexpected language gaps among generations. While most elders speak only Inuktitut, many small children speak only English. And then we find some older children who speak Inuktitut better than their parents. This could have come about because their parents were raised apart from their families in residential schools, where Inuktitut was forbidden. The children may have had more training in Inuktitut in local schools or they may have lived, not with their parents, but with relatives who spoke Inuktitut in the home. Storytellers lack an audience partly because of these language gaps and partly because of television. They recognize the need for old stories and the importance of recording and revitalizing them while the last generation of elders who know them thoroughly are still alive. We came to Nunavut to facilitate this process.

Our recordings and their purpose were very different from the those of the earlier ethnographers, who were working in igloos and tents, writing painstakingly by hand. Knud Johan Victor Rasmussen (1879–1933) is the best known of these story collectors.[5] Son of a Danish missionary and an Inuit woman, he grew up among Greenland Inuit, learning language and arctic survival skills. He carried out a number of expeditions across the north, meticulously recording both stories and details of material and spiritual culture. His works are still the best record of Inuit life in the nineteenth and early twentieth centuries.

Rasmussen used two hand-written methods. Sometimes he wrote quickly in Danish translation, almost keeping up with the teller, getting the storyline but missing some detail. Other times he slowed the teller down in order to record the precise words in Inuktitut, getting the rich language but missing the flow. Each method had advantages for his time, but disadvantages as seen through hindsight. When recording is done by hand, some of the more dramatic tellers simply lose patience with the process – even the patient ones may shorten the story. Poetic rhythm is lost, causing the teller to get mixed up or forget details. After a second round of translation a story feels dry and often confusing. We don't know whether to laugh or cry. I'm not sure if the tellers in earlier times were told how the recordings would be used. This must have affected their telling.

We owe Rasmussen a debt of gratitude and are lucky not to have had to make his choice of method. We recorded not only in well-equipped schools, where I could check my e-mail on their banks of computers, but also in teen centres and small museums. (These centres were twice plagued by broken heating systems that fazed the elders not at all, but we younger folks rushed back to hot baths in our hotels to warm up.) We used audio and video equipment that allowed us to preserve the full nuance of voice and gesture as well as normal speaking tempo. Some of the physical gestures are absolutely consistent across all regions: elders use their hands in the same way to show Kiviuq paddling his kayak, Bee Woman cutting off her eyelids, the goose mother putting feathers between her children's fingers, and Fishmaker working with his axe. All this reminds us that storytelling is much more than words. Oral stories live and breathe. Their meaning cannot be divorced from their tellers and listeners. How to convey it all in writing remains a difficult challenge.

In Rasmussen's time a storyteller's family may have been listening, since the home storytelling tradition was still fully alive. Today the ancient legends are rarely told at home, although some people still tell them on hunting trips. Our settings are more contrived – elders noticed the distraction of school bells, street noise, or a broken furnace being repaired. But I was pleased to see that nothing was left out for the children who were sometimes present. Elders insist that children need to learn about both good and bad times.

Consecutive interpretation can create some of the same difficulties as writing by hand; it slows down and breaks up the telling, but most of our tellers seemed unfazed by it.[6] In many cases they were engaged in studying my response. In spite of not understanding Inuktitut, I followed the emotional content attentively while waiting for details in translation. Suspense was often created by the gap between the response shown by John Houston, the interpreter, and the videographer and my response, which mirrored theirs, when I fully "got it" a few minutes later. I was struck by the elders' excitement and pleasure in telling the story, their certainty that it would be of interest. This was in contrast to what I had encountered in Russia, where elders often began by asserting that their story was not of any real interest to the outside world. They tended to take a while to thaw into enthusiasm in their recollection. The most articulate Siberian storytellers have been recorded so many times by people whose work has disappeared into archives in faraway capitals that they feel they are treated like a commodity rather than like human beings. With me, however, they enjoyed the curious possibility that their stories would be told live in my country and language.

In any time period the collector's viewpoints come consciously and unconsciously into play. We like to think ourselves more open and sympathetic than outsiders of earlier times, but the truth is that Inuit have come at least as far to meet us as we have to meet them. The early ethnographers met Inuit living their traditional lifestyle; they had the typical preconceptions of white European men of their time (never women) about what was "primitive," but they also had a healthy respect for the obvious strength and intelligence of the Inuit and others who could survive in the north. A number of them also had political agendas that served the interests of their governments. My sense is that the earlier ethnographers wanted to grasp the whole mythology of what they perceived as a dying culture and that they also used the stories as a way to learn the local languages. They saw change rapidly approaching. It's interesting that we have a similar sense of urgency around recording the story while it is still possible. Today's elders represent the last generation to have grown up living entirely on the land, speaking a language largely unchanged by English vocabulary and syntax.

I appreciate the elders' caution about bringing spiritual matters from the past back into play in the present, having seen the commercialization of spirituality and the competition among shamans and others attempting to revive their traditional culture in the context of Russia's economic chaos in the 1990s. At the same time, many Inuit elders sense a powerful need in their communities to bring back certain parts of pre-Christian tradition, including legend telling and the traditional justice system. It has become apparent that addressing the political issues involved in the formation and development of the new territory has not solved all the problems. Some say, "Let's take what is good and useful from our old ways and leave the damaging parts behind." The curses, for example. As we experience the power of words, we have to remember that they can be used for good or for evil. We believe that the elders' concern over social issues such as teen suicide led them to share greater detail with us than they might have ten years ago, understanding that our work will have concrete public results – films, books, and educational materials. They may also be feeling their own mortality. In the words of the venerable Samson Quinangnaq, "If I died and young people knew nothing about this story, it would hurt me in my heart."[7]

Landscapes

The landscapes of our physical journey varied as much as those in the story. The flat shorelines of Kivalliq Region reveal a world of water, with rivers snaking from the many lakes to the sea. One can readily imagine the confusion Kiviuq must have felt far from home, uncertain at times whether he was on an island or the mainland. I gloried in the soaring beauty of the mountains and fiords of Pond Inlet. I got used to seeing dogsleds being pulled by skidoos. As days grew shorter, I watched the red arctic sun moving in a low arc across the horizon – and this was still two months before the winter solstice. I knew that by January northern Baffin Island would have been without sun for six weeks and it would be another six before it showed itself again.

We met with warm hospitality – not only from Inuit but from hotel personnel, who rushed us to airports when we were late. One manager even came to my room to make sure I wasn't going to miss breakfast. We flew on three northern airlines in planes with anywhere from ten to fifty seats. The smallest of these airlines makes do without boarding passes, relying on the crew's ability to recognize the passengers. After all, as often as not there is no ground staff and it is the pilot who checks you in. I remember the cheerful co-pilot getting on at Resolute Bay, looking the passengers over and saying, "All familiar faces. Okay. The emergency exits are still in the same places. Anyone for ear plugs? Have a good flight!" We celebrated Thanksgiving Day on one of these planes, snacking on caribou jerky and tiny pumpkin pies made by cameraman Albert's wife, Tracey, and their children.

My load of bundles lightened as I welcomed more clothing layers, and even the boots began to feel comfortable as I got used to their wide bottoms and my feet stopped sweating. I'd had fears of unfamiliar food, but we ate mainly in hotels geared to construction worker tastes – what one fellow visitor called "food from the 1950s." Fried pork chops, french fries, mushy vegetables (if any,) Kool-aid, Tang. I felt great most of the time. Made me wonder about my carefully constructed organic low-fat diet at home!

Hotel at Igloolik

Often we would learn that the people serving our hotel dinners and making the beds were related to the people we were recording. I began to see the extensive family relationships in these communities. It became a joke with Albert and our interpreter, Percy. Whenever either of them introduced me to an acquaintance, I learned to say, "Don't tell me. This is one of your relatives." And of course I was right. Relatives by blood, by adoption, and even by carrying the same name. This gives Inuit a deep spiritual affinity, because for them a part of the soul is carried in the name. Meanwhile my notebook filled up and a new one was provided from a supply cabinet by the school principal in Chesterfield Inlet. As we added layers of clothing, we peeled layers of story.

In every community, from the smallest to the sophisticated capital city of Iqaluit, there are elders who remember Kiviuq. Most had learned his story while living out on the land year-round, and their memories of him are infused with the smells and sounds from times spent in igloos, wrapped in warm caribou skins, lying in bed with brothers and sisters, drifting off to sleep by the light of seal-oil lamps. Now they told the story in buildings created by a foreign government. One elder said that the ideal way to recall the story for us would be to tell it out on the land, perhaps in an igloo or tent, with no distractions or time restrictions.

Our unit managers had usually spoken with the elders beforehand to let them know what we were looking for. Now they went out on ATVs, snowmobiles, or foot to bring them to us one at a time. On three occasions we went to elders' homes. We met with the elders any time except Sunday morning and evening, when almost everyone can be found in either the Anglican or the Catholic church. John Houston had planned for this and tried to economize our recording time by travelling on Sundays. In reality our schedule was often changed by the weather. We might be stormed-in in a community on Sunday, unable to speak with elders, and then have to fly away leaving stories unheard. This was frustrating, but not only would it have been practically impossible to find an elder who didn't go to church, it would have felt wrong to set up an activity that conflicted with the services or the day of rest. This was yet another piece of learning for a person like me who lives in a multicultural community with many religious practices. I have never lived in a place where nearly everyone shared the same faith. Although I haven't heard of any religious intolerance on the part of the Inuit, it does seem that a person who turns away from the Christian churches in these communities is bucking a very powerful tide.

Missionaries first came to the Canadian Arctic in the late nineteenth century. They worked most actively from the 1920s to the 1950s, setting up hospitals and schools, teaching English, and distributing Bibles written in Inuktitut that used the syllabic alphabet devised by the well-known Anglican Reverend Peck. Working hand in hand with the Canadian government, they also contributed hugely to the deterioration of an ancient way of life.

Our interpreter Philip Paniaq laughs about the fact that early missionaries got the impression that Inuit were lawless. He says that Inuit accepted Christianity because they perceived it as having no rules compared with the elaborate system of taboos that had ruled their lives. Traditional rules had a solid basis in survival skills. Some of the reasons behind them were remembered, while other rules had lost their meaning over the course of time. The rules were particularly hard on women. Their every move was fraught with the possibility of a breach of taboo that could bring blame on their heads for misfortune in hunting and other aspects of life. Of course, men too had to be very careful to follow the elaborate rules, as we see in Kiviuq's tale.

Philip points out that some Inuit welcomed the possibility of redemption, as it softened the harsher Inuit rules that, like the arctic climate, allowed no second chances. Many missionaries are remembered fondly, and most of today's Inuit are sincere Christians, more dedicated and thoughtful about their chosen religion than many churchgoers in the south. A few Iglumiut, (people from the Igloolik area) became missionaries themselves, bringing Christianity to their home community before any foreign missionaries arrived there, and forming a system of beliefs that combined Christianity and shamanism.

But the missionaries also worked with the Canadian government to found the residential school system, which has been the subject of much notoriety throughout Canada in recent years. The schools were part of a plan to get Inuit to settle in the communities that formed around the trading posts. This move facilitated Canada's taking full sovereignty over the Arctic, including shipping lanes – a major international concern at the time. Inuit children were taken from the nomadic settlements to live throughout the school year in the schools. But many of the parents refused to be separated from their children and came to live nearly full-time in the communities where the schools were located, and so they too had to adapt to a new lifestyle.

I had been shocked to learn how children were abused sexually, physically, and emotionally in residential schools. Their ancestors' culture was beaten down. Often irreparable gaps formed between children and their families. In their zeal, certain missionaries told Inuit that they would burn in hell if they continued to tell the old stories, especially shamanistic ones like Kiviuq's. Celestin Erkidjuk tells us he knows certain followers of Reverend Peck who to this day will not tell the parts of stories with non-human elements, such as the goose-wife, because of these threats.

Although I had heard of these and other abuses for many years and had found parallels with the colonial policies in Russia and other parts of the world, I was shocked to learn of another level of damage in this Canadian schooling approach. Perhaps it struck me powerfully because I had been unaware of it. The schools had not eased the loss of the rich Inuit heritage with an introduction to European literature and world myth. Inuit children, only 25 per cent of whom complete high school even today, had to make do with a steady diet of simplified Bible stories and Aesop's fables. Their counterparts in Russia, also deprived of their own culture, studied everything from the poetry of Pushkin to the adventures of Sherlock Holmes, as well as being trained in contemporary professions. While this might look like forced assimilation, it did not seem that way to the Siberian peoples for several decades, and they still feel that this approach had a positive side.[8]

In contrast, not only have two generations of Inuit not heard their own ancient stories or had the benefit of other aspects of their ancient spiritual culture, they have been damaged in their ability to approach and enjoy world culture and thus to connect with people different from themselves. The schools were a cruel form of isolation in a time of increasing global connections. For Inuit children, an important avenue to life in the modern world remained closed. This is comparable to a phenomenon unfortunately common to many immigrants today – they are stuck between languages, fully fluent neither in their parents' language nor in that of the surrounding culture. Samson Quinangnaq shed light on another aspect of this isolation when he told us that white people have prophets and Inuit have shamans. In his understanding, the biblical prophets were white.

More recently there have been major improvements in Nunavut schools both in terms of technical facilities and curriculum content, connecting children with their own traditions and with mainstream life. Top-of-the-line computers and well-stocked libraries sit side by side with programs inviting elders in to teach children about everything from igloo building to traditional foods and from clothing to games and stories.

Many of today's elders can remember Kiviuq's story in rich detail, and their accounts are much fuller than the story recorded a century ago. The remarkable fact is that this memory leaps many decades. People now in their eighties and nineties are telling a story they heard when they were under ten years of age and have rarely told or heard since. This is a stunning testimony to human memory and the power of the story's ancient language. The elders convey a wealth of imagery that speaks strongly of shamanic meaning. Some point out the places that show shamanic power, while others may blushingly refer to magic and others say nothing about this aspect at all. When asked about the meaning, value, or lessons of the story, some elders wax eloquent and others say it has no meaning beyond being a good way to quiet children down in the evening.[9]

All the while there is a sense of something bubbling beneath the surface. Our interpreters, hardened by routine and often discouraging court work, found themselves in tears at inexplicable points in the story. They came away feeling new life possibilities opening up. People are now discussing the ways their ancient knowledge is similar to Christian beliefs. Kiviuq's walking away from trouble rather than resorting to violence, for example, reminds listeners strongly of Christ's exhortation to "turn the other cheek." Elders are gathering to discuss how traditional methods of justice can be integrated into the Nunavut criminal justice system. People were eager to chat with me about what their Siberian counterparts have undertaken in terms of culture and spirituality. While all these kinds of discussions and sentiments are still rather muted in the communities, I've heard they stronger than they were ten years ago.

Samson Quinangnaq discussed the ways an oral tradition is different from the Christian Bible. He felt that Kiviuq is like a prophet without a scribe, and that his message would be more widely known if he had had someone sitting beside him writing things down. Eli Kimaliadjuk disagreed politely, saying that if Kiviuq was a prophet he would be mentioned in the Bible. This did not at all detract from Kiviuq's value in Kimaliadjuk's eyes – to him they are two different things. At first I was curious that Quinangnaq would use the word prophet, but then I learned that the Inuit word *nalauttaiji* has a somewhat different meaning from the English word in its strict definition. The Inuit concept of a prophet puts a greater emphasis on understanding the consequences of things than on predicting the future or speaking out of unusual insight, vision, or as directed by a deity. Of course, both interpretations include the sense of an unusually wise person, common to many world religions. The interesting thing to me is that while prophets in most cultures are known largely through their speaking, Kiviuq is known through the example he set in his actions. It takes the storyteller to speak of them. Cornelius Nutarak confirmed this idea, saying that to his way of thinking not only was Kiviuq a prophet, but Samson Quinangnaq was also a prophet when he spoke of the meaning of the hero's life.

That people with such rich traditions could have been convinced that a written tradition from elsewhere is in any way superior to theirs evokes in me a profound sadness. And that they have not been taught that the Christian Bible springs from an oral tradition is equally misguided. Simon Tookoome told us that at a certain time writing had dropped from heaven. White people picked it up and prospered, while Inuit ignored it.

Bernadette Uttaq emphasizes that the story has life-giving meaning. "Kiviuq was a good person," she says, "and like him we can be great. The acts of legendary characters set a value, a way of living, of seeing consequences. Life has already been set out by Kiviuq for people and animals. I'm using analogy to simplify what will always be. It is set out but not written. It is very powerful."

Jacob Peterloosie says that his memory of legends goes back to about the age of six – which he calls an important formative period. "Later on there are many impressions and we may forget these things, but they resurface still later," he says. "Today it's as if even little kids are treated as adults – they are not given stories. Children don't know what to be afraid of, the dangers of water, blizzards, things like that."

Many elders speak of the story in terms of the hard times their ancestors survived. And they did more than survive. In the words of Aupilaarjuk, they created a life of tremendous quality and with frequent periods of joy out of circumstances many would consider impossible. Kiviuq went through hard times just as people do now, they say, and the methods he used for coping have much to teach us today. I was moved to learn yet another thing about life in the Arctic – elders are respected because they have survived to old age. Anyone whose behaviour was less intelligent, observant, and correct would simply not have made it.

Our journey through Kiviuq's world was facilitated by our interpreters, unit managers, and many other people in Nunavut. I gained a huge appreciation for John Houston's ability to shift gears and change plans when the weather made it necessary. It was also fascinating to experience the way a filmmaker's lens differs from mine, which is geared to books and oral storytelling. He was in a sense casting the film – looking for storytellers who convey their tale in a lively and authentic manner on screen – whereas I was more interested in a very detailed telling with rich language. Of course, he too is enriched by the detail and I learn much from a storyteller with good delivery, but in terms of our work the focus is different. On another level, he needed to know what everything looked like in the eyes of the tellers. To portray Kiviuq's entry into the fox den he needed to know if the man got smaller to fit through the narrow opening or if the opening got bigger. To me this makes little difference – each listener will see it in a unique way on the screen of inner vision. Thinking in media terms, John imagined that two hours with a storyteller would be a lot, but he quickly had to rethink this when some of our sessions stretched to seven hours. From the viewpoint of ethnographic research, which ideally stretches over many months or years of immersion in a culture, our time was short, although very rich.

I have lovely memories of being stormed in at communities, unable to fly out as scheduled. At first there was a small sense of panic and then gradual relaxation. If the plane's not going, well, there's no other way to travel so we're staying here. Nothing to be done. Philip Paniaq tells me he travelled for a period of six years and was stormed in only twice. It happened to us on five different occasions. I wondered if this was because the storm had been called several times a day within the story! Despite what seemed at best an inconvenience, wonderful things happened in the unplanned time. There were deep conversations in the Igloolik hotel's dining room, drinking coffee, looking out the steamy windows. We chatted with local people, including several actors from the popular film *Atanarjuat, the Fast Runner*, the first feature film made by Canadian Inuit. Stunningly beautiful, *Atanarjuat* tells another of the great stories and has won prestigious awards and popular acclaim. It was in Igloolik that Philip came up with his theory about Kiviuq's real geographic whereabouts in the goose-wife story, and where he told me about his own experiences with breathing-hole hunting for seals. It was in Igloolik that I came to understand more fully the nature of the fox-wife's forgiveness and saw the deep connections between the storytelling of the Inuit and that of my Udeghe friends in the Russian Far East.

Stormed-in at Pond Inlet we saw our hotel fill up with customers on the night the steamy dining room served Chinese food. At Cambridge Bay, we got a long way in our plans for a bilingual book containing Kiviuq's story. Snowed in at Gjoa Haven, we heard the wonderful Judas Aqilgiaq express the power of the grizzly like no other – we'd never have seen him had we left on time. It reached the point where when a plane was delayed John would look up expectantly and say, "I wonder what's waiting for us here!"

In Taloyoak it was the foxes. I've always felt an affinity with the fox, although I'd never met one before, and of course a lovely fox plays a big role in Kiviuq's life. On a morning when we should have already been gone, our translator Peter came into the hotel dining room and said casually, "Lots of foxes out there today." I rushed out so quickly that I forgot my camera. Sure enough, there sniffing around the Anglican church was an arctic fox – pure white – showing up against the snow only by her movement. I thought for an ironic moment that perhaps this master of transformation was considering converting to Christianity. She slipped away and I walked on. Look! There across the frozen bay another pure white animal was running full bore towards me. Could that be another one? Or was it a dog? Two women walked past me on the road. They looked at the animal and smiled. "Lots of foxes around today." Suddenly they were everywhere, raiding garbage cans and striking profiles against the sky. As the women continued down the road, a tiny fox pup appeared from under the steps of the town hall. It frolicked around them until they reached their destination, and then it joined me. Sniffing my big boots, running ahead, circling around, even chasing her tail on the road, showing me exactly the way Kiviuq's fox-wife moved.

ΔΔΔ

Our travel story was ending. But let's go back now to the beginning of Kiviuq's story and consider its implications in more detail. We'll trace many versions of the story, see how they differ from each other and from the historical versions, and look at parallels between shamanic and ordinary reality. We'll also consider the similarities and differences between Kiviuq's story and Siberian storytelling and shamanic traditions. This book is partly ethnographic, but it adds something more – an understanding that comes from telling as well as listening. My approach includes not only writing about what I've learned, but also speaking it aloud in the original genre. This speaking creates an understanding so rich that I've promised myself never again to write about a story without having first told it and experienced an audience's and my own responses to it.

Seal, Tuutalik, Storm at Sea

Have you seen Kivioq? You must have met him on your travels? For, like you, he has been in all countries, and the most wonderful things are told about him.

Kivioq is an Inuk, a man like ourselves, of our own tribe, but a man with many lives. He is from the times when the ice never laid itself on the sea up here by our coasts. He is so old that he was alive that time when the salt sea was open in winter too and people knew nothing of breathing-hole hunting from the sea ice; indeed, he is from the times when people hunted seals with kayaks [while in Rasmussen's time the Netsilik only used kayaks for hunting in freshwater lakes]. From the times when there was no fog, when the lands were never made invisible by haze, yes, from the times when the animals often turned themselves into human beings and human beings into animals, and when the wolves had not yet learned to overtake the caribou.

– Kuvdluitsoq, 1920s[1]

The Seal-Child: Storytelling and Picture Making

Taima! Listen now as the story begins. The word *taima* means simply "now." It calls attention to the storytelling. Over our month-long quest, almost every storyteller told us the story of the seal-child and the storm at sea. It is central to the life of Kiviuq.

Δ Some say it started in summer. There was plenty to eat and a group of people who had lived together since spring were relaxing and celebrating – playing a ball game on the shore. Naujarlak Tassugat locates the story's opening on a small island called Upirngivik, south of Clyde River on Baffin Island.[2] In that community there was an orphan boy who lived with his grandmother, although Henry Isluanik told us the orphan was a girl. Wisdom passed down through the generations says that people should be kind to those less fortunate, but it often happened that orphans were not treated well – and that was the case here. When the child went out to play with the others, adults would pick her up with their teeth by the tip of her hood and twirl her around, tearing the tip off. The children tore at her clothes and she returned home in tatters.

Others say it began in the hard times of winter. Men went out to the seal breathing holes to hunt but their luck was not good. Many were without food, and although ancient law said that a successful hunter should share with his family and neighbours, there was one who did not. Out of envy and anger, the other men killed this hunter, leaving an orphan child. The murdered hunter may even have stolen food or overhunted. Alternatively, others may have been jealous of his success. Simon Tookoome starts with caribou hunting. Most people tell us the child was left with his grandmother, although a few tell of the child's mother bringing him up. **Δ**

After returning home I set out to tell the story myself, both to share it with curious listeners and to understand it more deeply. I've often found that only in telling a story do certain mysteries get resolved. I like to work from the most detailed version I can find, and this was certainly the most variety of detail I'd ever had available. First I made a mosaic of the forty tellings to help me keep track. I then found my own logic about the order of events and what my particular telling would emphasize. It was a matter of combining my language with theirs, singing certain parts, recalling the elders' gestures, creating musical interludes with instruments and vocal sounds that give listeners time to digest. But the narrowing and selection could only come after a long period of listening, hearing new detail, and opening up new meaning. Listening to a story is not like reading a book, where you can always page back and check something you're not sure about. With oral stories we must hear them again and again, and each time something new pops out, either because a teller emphasizes it or because we are at last ready to absorb it. Images form spontaneously in our minds.

For me many of the details that are less frequently told point to the story's great spiritual depth and help me to make sense of the whole.

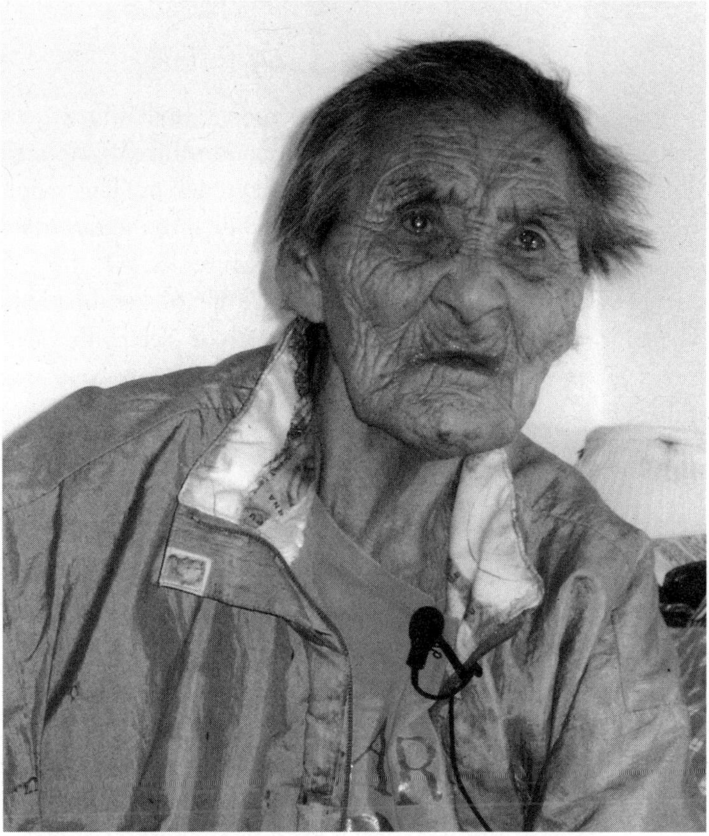

Niviuvak Marqniq, 104 years old at the time of the photograph. Her facial tattoos were done when she was a child.

I include these in my oral telling – Kiviuq's death and rebirth as opposed to a simple sleep, Bee Woman as a spirit of place, Tuutalik going down the breathing hole. Of the many arrangements possible, certain ones suit my sensibilities better than others.

Some of the solutions come from details that were told to us during question and answer periods, such as the connection of the sandpiper skins to Kiviuq's birth and to the gift bestowed on him of being able to return home. The nature of the *tuutaliit* and the logic behind what I call "survival morality" – which includes walking away from trouble – these and other aspects of the culture need to be filled in not only for non-Inuit audiences but also for some Inuit themselves, raised outside the traditional family.

As I listened to Inuit elders, I became aware that their telling came from a great sea of pictures and information. Like all storytellers who truly live inside the story, they select what to tell us. This is not because they are editing or censoring. They have their own messages they wish to emphasize, but primarily they are telling in response to the interest and energy that comes back to them. This is what makes the pictures flow. The next person to tell the tale may include details they saw on the screen of inner vision, without even realizing that they have added something. I believe this is one way a story can change over time, even among people who are determined to tell it exactly as they heard it. The changes come from an inner source that is just as true as what they have heard.

Annie Peterloosie agrees. "I say this thing and another person hears what I say. Since that other person understands it a little bit differently, if they tell it again then it'll be a little bit different. And so on – others would hear things in a little different way. That is the way stories change from one region to another. That's according to my grandmother."

An Inuit teller may simply say that people were on the shore playing the ball game, because that's where the story begins for them, the way their parents told it. But they see the hard winter that came before, the people who may have starved, the places where they held their winter camps, and how they arrived at the river where they were now. The teller takes for granted the bravery of the hunters who had provided food for a feast. The characters are based in the teller's complete knowledge of the intricate social and family relationships among them. Their families and neighbours see the background with them, while outside listeners dive in midstream.

The same process occurs for outside storytellers, which is why we owe it to ourselves and our listeners to be as well educated as we can be about the story's context, and then simply to acknowledge who we are and what we bring to the telling. There is nothing new about telling stories from cultures other than our own – this is the way they have traversed continents and time periods. But there are things we need to learn. I was not sure what a breathing hole was like or how the Inuit hunted at them. Now I wish we could just take the trip over, spending more hours with each of the elders, asking the questions that only arose afterwards. And yet the time for speaking of certain things is in the context of storytelling, while memory is fresh.

Some things were easy to understand. What kind of ball game were the people playing on the shore that happy summer? It turns out they still play it in the outpost camps. All those born in summer team up against the winter children. A ball is sewn of caribou skin, hair to the inside, stuffed with scraps of caribou skin till it's quite full, and then it's thrown and kicked up and down the hills, each team trying to keep possession of it. As John Houston recalls from summers in outpost camps, "There didn't seem to be a lot of pesky rules when we played it, just great exercise and summer fun."

Breathing-Hole Hunting

At first we didn't know why the grandmother and child were tormented by the hunters and other children. As we listened, we heard how resentment can carry over from one generation to another. Many take us back to the seal hunt so that we will understand the child's torment and the grandmother's eventual revenge. Deep in the preceding winter, hungry hunters had set out to try once more to find food for their families. Although seals spend the winter under the ice, they must come up regularly to breathe, keeping holes open in the ice from early winter to late spring. Ringed seals have razor-sharp claws for this purpose. They can go up to twenty minutes between breaths when relaxed and fully aerated, but they need to breathe more frequently when they have been exercising – every two minutes or so.[3] Hunters await their chance to spear one, standing motionless over the hole. Breathing-hole hunting certainly proves a hunter's strength and endurance, and provides the staples of the Inuit diet.

Houston's film *Diet of Souls* (2004), which includes footage from an earlier film made by Asen Balikci,[4] shows a hunter taking his young son out for his first seal hunt. The hunters must go far away from home. Today they ride snowmobiles but in former times they used dog teams. The dogs could sniff out the places where seals come up to breathe, which are covered with snow in winter. Once the hole is located, the dogs are tied far enough away that they will not betray the hunter's presence. The hunter scrapes down through the snow and feels around with his probe for the depth and angle of the hole. He also wants to find out how hard the ice within the hole has frozen since the hole was last used.

That will tell him now recently a seal has come to that hole to breathe. He can tell whether the seal will approach vertically or horizontally, knowledge essential to getting a good shot (Bennett and Rowley 2004, 52). He then re-covers the hole with snow, having installed the feather or piece of rabbit fur that will reveal the seal's presence when it comes up for air. The feather is visible to the hunter and is attached to a piece of sinew that goes down into the hole. The vibration caused by the head bumping the ice and the seal's breathing makes the feather move.

Hunters would stand immobile for as long as nine hours in temperatures of -40°C, waiting for seals to come to their hole to breathe. As the father in John's film left the boy to stand watch, he said, "You will get your first seal today. If you miss the seal when it appears, I will be unhappy with you and scold you." As soon as he saw the feather's movement, the boy was to shoot and call out. Once the seal was harpooned, the hunters cut out chunks of ice from the hole, using them to form a windbreak until there was room enough to pull the seal out. The seal was hauled home for the women to clean.

Our interpreter Philip Paniaq describes his own first seal hunt in the same way as it is portrayed in the film – his long watch and then, since it was his first time, losing his nerve when he finally saw the feather move. And his father's understanding and encouragement to try again. Naturally, when a boy made his first successful hunt, there was a celebration for the initiation passed – a separate celebration for his first of each kind of animal, land and sea. And every time hunters returned successful, there was rejoicing. The people knew that the food would be shared and that everyone would eat. There would be oil for heat, light, and cooking fuel, skins for clothing and kayaks. Bones would be used for tools and weapons, oil for cooking, caribou sinew for sewing. Nothing was wasted.

Killing the seal can be more complex with a high-power rifle than with a harpoon. The hunter has to wait for the seal to rise to breathe, holding the rifle to the ice, preferably using a slow bullet like a .303. If he has calculated the angle properly, he gets the seal, and if not, the seal swims away. If it has been injured, it may die under the ice but out of reach.

Hunters in pre-Christian times would bring gifts to spirits before going out on the ice.[5] Shamans would sometimes help with this. John Houston describes an island outside Arviat where people hung their gifts on wooden uprights. Today, under the influence of Christianity, such rituals are carried out very quietly and privately, if at all.

In the Inuit world, people are cautious in speaking about connections with spirits. They always have been. But now their silence goes beyond that caution. Christianity and community peer pressure contribute to an internal conflict that makes the hunter even quieter. And the younger hunters' exposure to Western scientific rationalism may also contribute to the silence.

Tuutalik, the Seal-Man[6]

Δ Many Inuit elders mention a hunter named Tuutalik, saying he either didn't share the seals or caribou he caught or was so successful that he garnered jealousy from others. Bernadette Uttaq says that Tuutalik was the orphan-child's mother. Felix Kopak says one man had lots of meat, while the others were hungry and they killed the one who had plenty. Simon Tookoome says Tuutalik was killed at a caribou crossing and that Kiviuq was the one to inform his wife. Mariano Aupilaarjuk describes the seal-person as human with claws like a seal. Δ

Kuvdluitsoq and other Netsilik and Utkuhikjalikmiut tellers of the past century imply that this story tells of the time when people first began to practise breathing-hole hunting, which seems to have happened at the transition from the Dorset to the Thule culture, possibly a thousand years ago. The breathing-hole aspect of the story is the first of many instances in Kiviuq's story where something is created or happens for the first time. Perhaps those early hunters learned their skills from a being similar to the one in Kiviuq's story – one that was half human, half seal. Balikci's film shows a hunter in sealskin clothing creeping up on a seal, pretending to be one. He made very realistic seal sounds. I would suppose Tuutalik was especially expert at this kind of hunting.

I'm impressed by the precision of Inuit hunters' understanding of weather and animal behaviour. This understanding developed over millennia. Generations of Inuit and their Thule ancestors survived in houses dug into the ground and topped with a bone structure and hides. The

Thule lived around AD 700–1800 and are called Tuniit in Inuktitut. Before that, the Tuniit of the Dorset culture (550 BC to AD 1100) survived many generations without breathing-hole hunting, dogsleds, snow igloos, or boats. Both groups had migrated across the Arctic from Asia. Their survival seems as magical to me as shape-shifting and journeying through the earth. Their practical skills arose from keen observation and persistence on the physical plane, and perhaps their magical skills come from a similar level of observation and discipline on the spiritual plane. The line is a fine one.

Inuit elders tell us that the practical information they extrapolate from Kiviuq's life is one of the most valuable aspects of hearing the story. Stories embed the practical so firmly in an individual that it will come back in life-saving ways later in that person's life.

Here is a story told in the 1920s about the *tuutaliit*.

Totalet[7]

The *totalet*, people say, are spirits that resemble both humans and seals. In fact, people call them the seal-men. Where they come from nobody knows, but some people believe that their first father was the *totalik* who avenged his father's death. In the story of Kivioq it is related how the mother drew the skin of a newly born seal cub over her own newly born child and taught it to swim. Afterwards, when the boy grew up, he became just as clever at living in the sea as a seal, and in that manner he enticed all the murderers in their kayaks out to sea so that they were lost in a storm. It is thought that this totalik was the first seal-man. Nothing is known of the totalet other than that they are splendid breathing-hole hunters who are not afraid of going down through the breathing hole when game is scarce. About this the story is told: Once upon a time some *totalet* were out hunting at the breathing holes. There a seal escaped, and one of them thought the best thing to do was to go down into the sea through the breathing hole to look for it. And he did so. He let himself slide down into the sea, and when he had caught the seal, he shouted up through the breathing hole that he had made his catch. The others peeped down and, true enough, found him stuck fast in the opening of the hole together with the seal he had caught.

No hunting is impossible to people who can catch seals in that way.

Today's elders tell it somewhat differently:

Δ Aupilaarjuk and others say that Tuutalik led the men out to a breathing hole and said, "I will go down into the hole, and then come back leading seals to you. I will always inform you that I am an Inuk, so that you will not spear me." He went down into the icy water. Leo Nimialik says Tuutalik went down under the ice attached to a rope, but that the rope broke and the man was lost.

Time passed and at last the feather placed at the breathing hole moved, showing that a seal was down there. Tuutalik called out, informing the hunters who he was. Why did the hunter spear him nonetheless? Did he not hear, through deadly inattention, or was he so hungry that he was willing to kill his neighbour? Perhaps he was so jealous of Tuutalik's success that he took the opportunity to kill him. However it happened, the men soon hauled the dead body up out of the icy water, still in seal form.

Annie Peterloosie says that the hunters had good luck in the winter when Tuutalik was with them, and that things turned bad for them after he died, so that in summer there were shortages. Δ

At first I wondered why Tuutalik would help in having his seal relatives killed. But my question failed to go deep enough into the intimate relationship between people and animals. The fact that a creature could partake in equal parts of both human and seal emphasizes the closeness and explains the desire to help. Basic to Inuit hunting practice is the idea that animals offer themselves to people and will reincarnate if treated properly. Hunters in many indigenous cultures worldwide share this understanding, which is reflected in story and ritual.[8] Inuit return parts of the animal, such as a bladder, to the water so that it can reincarnate and return to provide people with nourishment again, just as Northwest Coast peoples return salmon bones to the sea.

The kind of breathing holes where seals willingly offer themselves look different from the outside, and an experienced hunter can identify them. But animals are fussy about whom they will give their lives to. One elder, Peter Aningat, describes it like this:

> "I'm going to pop my head through a breathing hole that man is waiting from. You pop your head through that other breathing hole," said the first seal. But the other seal refused because it was known that the man had always been lazy to do chores as a child. The seal was terrified of the hunter. In the end they decided to go one by one to the one that wasn't lazy because they were pleased about him. He hunted with the thought of sharing his kill with other people. All animals are like that. They don't like going to lazy selfish people whose only concern is to survive alone. An animal will refuse to go to a person who is only concerned about his own survival. (Bennett and Rowley 2004, 45)

Generally I don't question how "real-life" events could have given rise to the seemingly impossible events in stories. When I listen to a good storyteller, I have no trouble picturing such things as talking animals and flying shamans. I often see them in my own dreams, so they seem almost normal. But sometimes my rational mind takes over. While sitting in hotel rooms in Nunavut, my thoughts turned that way.

Perhaps in "real life" a man went down into the breathing hole, I wrote in my journal. A seal appeared to the hunters above and the swimmer died down there. And so people sensed that an exchange had happened – a man for a seal. John tells a similar story from his own experience. An Inuit hunter was killed by a polar bear while hunting. John was mourning the tragedy but an elder said to him, "That's the way it goes. We hunt the polar bears. Sometimes we get one, sometimes they get one of us." The family of the drowned *tuutalik* suffered afterwards, I thought, as people did not show gratitude for the sacrifice by helping the widow and orphan.

Later in the month, I realized how small a breathing hole is in midwinter and began to wonder how Tuutalik could have gotten down there. In high winter the breathing hole is no more than a few centimetres across, and I imagine Tuutalik as being the size of an adult man. How did he get down through the tiny hole? If he did, it would be the first of many instances in this epic where a shaman adapts to impossibly sized openings. It offers a parallel to Kiviuq's impossible act of going down through a fox hole later in the story.[9]

Still later I realized that the holes get bigger in spring as the ice melts. It becomes theoretically possible for an adult human to go down through them. Indeed, looking back at my notes, I saw that Aupilaarjuk had said that the ice was getting soft. I had to step back and see that while listening I had formed a clear image in my mind that was different from what the storyteller had intended. I had seen a shaman squeeze through a pinhole, while Aupilaarjuk had seen a man diving among chunks of melting ice. Still, the breathing hole is a clear image of an opening between the worlds. Those with special gifts can traverse from our world to the one under water through such an opening, just as a Siberian shaman flies to the upper world through the smokehole of a dwelling or descends to the lower world through the hearth.

Evening speculations done, I returned to the world of the elders

Δ The men carried the seal home. Tuutalik's body was brought to the hunter's wife, according to custom. Other women helped her to clean it, and they were the ones to notice that something was different about this seal. The insides seemed "cleaner" than normal. Meanwhile Tuutalik's spirit hovered around the place. He waited until his own wife was standing astride the seal and then he communicated to her: "I want to be reborn through you." His spirit entered her body. And so when she gave birth it was understood that the child was Tuutalik returned. He was now called Tuutalannuaq, or little Tuutalik. He inherited his father's seal nature.[10] It's easy to imagine he would have special powers at sea, and so it was. Most elders say the child was a boy. On the other hand, interpreter Percy and cameraman Albert express their admiration for Henry Isluanik, the one elder who says the child was a girl. "Many Inuit men don't like to admit that a man could be defeated by a girl. But Henry doesn't knuckle under to that kind of pressure." **Δ**

At this point it makes little difference if the child was a boy or girl, although it will have different implications later.

Reincarnation, Naming, and the Soul

Reincarnation plays a big role in Inuit family relationships. This is not quite the same reincarnation we may know from other cultures. According to their beliefs, a human being has three parts: the physical body, the soul (called *tarniq*, or soul double), and the name-soul (*atiq*). *Tarniq* is "an immaterial copy of the living person. It resides within the body, somewhere in the groin, in the form of a miniature duplicate and enclosed within a bubble of air. When the person dies, the bubble bursts and the air returns to the atmosphere. The miniature double grows until it reaches the person's size at the time of death and goes to live eternally in a celestial or underwater hereafter." *Atiq* has been defined as "an entity passed down with a person's name from generation to generation. It carries all of the qualities that all who bear this name have acquired during their lifetimes" (Angilirq 2002, 53). The name-soul protects a child throughout his life (Bennett and Rowley 2004, 3). As soon as a child is born, or even before, relatives determine what the child's name will be, depending on who is returning. The information usually comes in a dream. Generally it is someone who has died recently, as it is not a good thing to stay long between incarnations. The child receives the name of the deceased relative, with no distinction between male and female names.

The upbringing of a child who takes a name from a relative of the opposite sex has more leeway than that of one whose name comes from a relative of the same sex. Such a child partakes of both male and female. But there could be restrictions as well. "A child named after someone of the opposite sex might be treated as such for a time or had to live with certain restrictions. George Agiaq Kappianaq, named after a girl, was dressed in girls' clothing until he was eight or nine years old. Martha Nasook, named after a man, was not allowed to own an *ulu* (woman's knife) when she was a child, and she could only use those belonging to others. Because Rachel Kalliraq was named after a man, she received no sewing instruction. She had to teach herself. Names could be changed if necessary, to protect a child or to remove sickness" (Bennett and Rowley 2004, 8). Besides being given a name, the child is also called by the kinship term of his or her namesake, and so family members may call a tiny baby "grandmother" or "uncle."

Philip Paniaq says, "It is only within the last couple of generations that children have begun to use the names of adults out loud. We never used to be allowed to utter the names of adults out loud and were scolded quite harshly sometimes for doing so. We were only allowed as children to use the terms for relatives – for example, uncle from my mother's side 'angak,' uncle from my father's side 'akkak,' or that person's mother or that person's uncle. That tradition seems to be used less and less these days but there are certain extended families that still use it exclusively."

Rasmussen recorded an interesting story about reincarnation through animals. It comes at the end of a fox-wife story similar to Kiviuq's and is told about a man named Maqo. After the man is reunited with his wife in the den, the fox puts the hero to sleep.

Maqo[11]

And then he fell asleep, and slept and slept, and when he awoke, there was a humming of flies about the window, and it was full summer. He had fallen asleep in the autumn, and had slept through the whole winter, to wake again in the summer time. And he went down to his kayak and found it all covered with grass and flowers, and when he saw this, he said: "Now what form shall I choose for my soul to wander in? If I change to grass, then I must die when the grass withers, and if I turn to angelica then I must die when their flowers fall. Ah, let me take the shape of a fjord seal!"

And so he became a fjord seal, and when he tired of that, he took the form of a spotted seal, and after having lived some time among them, and grown tired and weary of scratching about as the spotted seal do, he left them and took the form of a saddle-back seal. And now, after having taken the form of a saddleback seal, he saw one day the houses of men on the shore. In one of the houses nearest the shore lived a woman who was barren. She was a woman very greatly to be desired, for she owned two pearls, one blue and one white. Yet the other saddleback seals said: "Do not go to her. When she was a young girl, she brought neither salt water nor fresh to the house."

But one day Maqo lay in wait for that woman's husband, and came up to breathe just in front of where he was. The man harpooned him, and when he felt himself struck, he almost laughed aloud, but then the death struggle came upon him and he died. And now he was hauled ashore and the hunter's wife brought him up into the house to cut him up. And he thought: "If only she would stand astride over my head!"

And as soon as she stood astride of him to better get at her work, his soul crept into her body by way of her genitals. And now he found himself in a little house full of ice and turfs and therefore he began to clean it out. But while he was thus cleaning out that place, he heard a voice say: "She will bleed to death."

And then the soul thought: "Can it be that I am making her bleed?"

And when he stopped cleaning her out, she grew well again. And now while the soul was in there, one day a man with close-cropped hair came in, and kept on coming in and out, and spat upon him, and when this had happened, he felt himself growing fatter.

And at last the soul found himself more and more cramped for space in that house, and sometimes he would wonder if ever he would be able to get out again, because the opening was so small. But then he heard them talking outside "He is getting fatter every day," they said: "let us get him out."

And then he thought: "Can it be me they mean?" And as he came nearer to the opening he heard them say: "Now it is time: let us fetch a midwife."

"If only they will choose a young midwife" thought the soul.

> But when she did come it was a very old one. And when she tried to take away the bench from him, he was afraid, and strove as hard as he could to hinder her. She tried in vain to entice him out, but he, being afraid, only crept farther and farther up on the bench. And now when a young midwife came and tried to take the bench from him, he hurried towards the entrance, making himself as small as he could, and came out with a rush.
>
> "He might almost be a grown man, from the way he looks round at the things in the house," said they. And then they had to find a name for him, calling him after some dead one, but they did not call him Maqo, and therefore he began to weep.
>
> And the father, who was very fond of him, and looked after him, heard him one day saying: "I am Maqo!" The father was so astonished that he nearly let him fall. "Aha! He wants to be named after that Maqo who was lost," said he at last.
>
> And then he wept no more, and entered upon his human life again. And thus, when he grew old, he was able to tell us how once by means of his soul he became a man again. And here ends this story.

Stories like this one, as well as those that tell of marriages with animals, confirm that in the minds of indigenous people the line between humans and other animals is much finer than it is for non-indigenous peoples. In the Inuit legend of Nuliajuk, a girl refused to marry and was sent by her father to live with a dog. She gave birth to children whom she sent away for their protection. Those most like the Inuit followed the shore and became today's First Nations people, while those most like their father drifted southward and turned into white people – the dog children.[12]

Care for Those in Need: Story Morals

Tuutalannuaq was brought up by his grandmother, although Bernadette Uttaq says it was his mother. This would make a big difference in some cultures, but I am assured that it doesn't make too much difference today in Inuit society, at least in relation to the child. We'll see that there is a difference in the balance of their roles as teacher and protector, but for now the important thing is that the woman who cared for the child had a nurturing nature and took charge of the him. Adoption is frequent within families and some people, like our interpreter Percy Tutannuaq, know and love both their biological and their adoptive parents as part of their extended family. Members of the community have a responsibility to take care of orphans and anyone less fortunate – especially women and children who do not have a hunter to take care of them. As elder Rachel Ujarasuk says, "We should share what we have – our food, our laughter." Again and again the elders point to this as the main moral of the whole story.

Caring for those less fortunate is part of what I call "survival morality." In my own upbringing we were taught to be good simply for the sake of being good. But in Inuit culture there were clear practical reasons for obeying the rules, and these were shown in stories. Communities were small. Each individual was needed to help stave off starvation and accidental death, which were always possible. And so each individual needed to be cared for to ensure the survival of the whole. There were no "throw-away" people. Annie Peterloosie points out that those who had been abused always found the power they needed to survive and prosper, showing that violations of the rule were balanced in some way.

And yet it cannot have been easy. Instead of getting a really good meal and the certainty of enough food to last a long time, the family of a good hunter had to share with all, even those who did not work as hard. A poor family depended not only on their own less able or lazier hunters but also on all the hunters in the community. Problems did arise, such as those mentioned by the elders who said that Tuutalik was one who refused to share or who even stole from others. The story proves the rule by showing the exception.

Clothing

Δ And so it was that Tuutalannuaq and his mother or grandmother were not cared for. They did not have enough food, and there were no skins to make new clothes as the child grew. But not only was he neglected, he was also openly tormented. Children teased him with the cruelty of children anywhere. What was worse is that adults also tormented him. One man loved to pick the child up in his teeth by the tip of his parka hood and twirl him around before throwing him to the ground. More and more often the child came home crying and in tatters. Δ

In the Arctic, clothing is of vital importance and means the difference between life and death. Some of the female elder storytellers paid loving attention to the grandmother's sewing in their gestures as they portrayed how she tried to piece and patch the child's clothing back together after it was torn. Henry Evaluardjuk and Joanasie Macpa say she used eider duck skins, a sure sign of poverty. The pieces of skin got smaller as the child grew bigger, and eventually it became impossible to piece things together any more.

The grandmother and child resonate with Siberian cultures. Shamans and their families were often outcasts because the irregular nature of their working lives often left them in poverty and because people feared their enormous powers. Could it be that Tuutalik was also a shaman, as elder Peter Katorkra said? That same fear and guilt might have motivated the tormentors, since in a sense all the hunters had to take some responsibility for the death of the child's father.

Story Form – Who Is the Hero?

Only one person refrained from taking part in the torment, and he is the hero of our epic – Kiviuq. He helped the grandmother and tried to prevent the others from being so unkind to the child. Various explanations are given for his ability to swim against the social tide. He had a strong moral upbringing. He had powerful shamanic spirits who helped him. Even his brother was less implicated than the others.

After so much story, at last we meet the hero! It came as a shock to me to learn that the seal-child was not to be the main character of the rest of the story. While many world epics begin with the generation that precedes that of the main hero, it is the same family. Here the younger seal-child and Kiviuq seem to be unrelated. But might they be? There is some question as to whether the seal-child who tempted the hunters out to sea in the storm might have been Kiviuq himself. Most say he was not, but a few highly respected elders say he was.[13] If he was, it would certainly feel "right" to those of us raised on epics from other cultures. Otherwise our hero simply appears as a grown man, already highly competent. Here, as he's introduced into the story, we learn nothing of his parentage, childhood, and growth, those aspects of the hero that are almost invariably part of an epic. This was a signal to me that something was very different about this story.

"Kiviuq" does not follow a shape familiar to those of European background, and we should not try to impose one. Sometimes elders infer information about Kiviuq's childhood – such as the fact that he must have had a strong grandmother and a good upbringing to grow up as strong as he did. His family history can be read in his behaviour. This is an impressive form of storytelling, one that can only be appreciated by listeners who really understand the culture and the implications of the information they receive.

After digesting the story, telling it, and writing a first draft of this book, I heard new testimony from several of the elders who were participating in John's film as actors. Annie Peterloosie spoke of the way her grandmother had told the story: "She did not tell the whole story in one sitting. She would wait many days before telling the rest of the story. I'm starting to understand only now that the Kiviuq story is one big story as it develops." This reminded me of elders who had said they were unsure of the story's order or had even stated categorically that there was no such thing as a beginning or an end. I began to see that the order could have been imposed from the outside and later agreed to by Inuit, since there is in fact an innate logic to it. Regional and family preferences have developed for one order or another. In the Inuit tradition, the pieces could have been told in many different orders, with good spaces in between to allow the listeners to fully take in both what they had heard and the variety of ways a story could be understood, depending on what preceded or followed it. Just as life has no beginning or end (for those who believe in reincarnation), neither does the story.

This non-linear approach to storytelling reminds me of a tale told throughout the Siberian Amur River region in which, to take an example, the ice boasts that it is the strongest thing on earth. But the sun can melt the ice, a cloud can block the sun, the wind can disperse the cloud, and so on. After her conversion to Christianity, my friend Nadia's grandmother found an end with God in heaven, and in Soviet versions of such tales man is always the strongest. But I've heard that before the days of Christianity or communism the same story was somehow told with no beginning or end – and it had a completely different message. This sense that an epic or even a shorter story like the Amur one follows a cyclical pattern is based firmly in a tradition where people hear stories again and again over the years until they become part of the fabric of life.[14] Stories are very different in today's world. Now we usually look for a quick resolution and hear a story only once.

There are strong parallels between Kiviuq and the seal-child. The hunters tear the child's clothes, while giant mussel bites Kiviuq's kayak and both Bee Woman and the female grizzly bear later cut his clothing. Both child and man have extraordinary ability in the water. Both pass through the earth, journey to sea, and come home. Both have very powerful grandmothers. Both learned rules of conduct, hunting skills, and shamanic skills. These parallels are so strong that we can understand much about Kiviuq's early life through that of the child, even if they are not the same person. This use of parallelism, as well as of opposites, struck me repeatedly throughout the story. Parallels between characters who are similar but not the same show us the results of certain life choices. In seeing the seal-child and the hunter together, we can understand both the child and the man.

In an interview, Aupilaarjuk once referred to Kiviuq as being the one to invoke the storm, calling, "*Silaga nauk?*" (Saladin d'Anglure 2001, 91). This would indicate that he was the seal-child, although that is not the way Aupilaarjuk told the story to us. Still, the two interpretations are so close that it is possible to slip from one to the other. And as careful as I have been to emphasize the difference in my telling, invariably at least one listener thinks Kiviuq is the seal-child, as I did when I first read the story. Niviuvak Marqniq lends support to the idea through Kiviuq's name.

"Young seals have beautifully shiny skin and were often prized by hunters of that day. This particular type of sealskin is called *qiviuq* in our dialect. The grandmother made clothing out of *qiviuq* skin for Kiviuq, whose name is derived from *qiviuq*."

If Kiviuq is the seal-boy, we are left wondering how he grew from a seal in water to a man in a kayak. This provides a major challenge to Western-style logic but not to shamanic logic, the grammar of transformation. And it challenges logic only when we step outside the story and think about it. The image raises the tantalizing idea that a man in a sealskin kayak is encased just as the child is encased in the sealskin that his grandmother has lovingly stretched around him, transforming him. He grows from child to man during that long journey. A good kayak man imitates a seal while negotiating the water, just as a good hunter imitates the seal while creeping up to a seal basking on the ice. The fact that Inuit elders freely use the word analogy would indicate that this parallel may well be intentional. Having things bump up against each other this way can be more evocative than a strictly logical chain of events, and Inuit elders love to create space for listeners to play with possibilities and draw their own conclusions.

A real-life explanation for the dilemma about whether or not Kiviuq is the seal-child is that the grandmother builds a learner's kayak of sealskin. In a sense the kayak does encase the child in sealskin, and this resonates strongly with the image of the grandmother's sewing him into sealskin to effect his transformation into a seal. This would explain how the seal-child could *be* Kiviuq – it almost closes what feels like a logical gap between a seal in the water and a man in a kayak. Niviuvak has a simpler explanation: "Kiviuq, who was now in the water, took hold of a couple of kayaks, possibly his younger sibling's one and another relative's kayak. The three were the only survivors. They held the two kayaks together in the choppy waters until their strength gave out. Kiviuq got into one kayak and during that time the other kayak capsized drowning both of Kiviuq's companions."

In Siberia many indigenous people feel that teaching is a function of storytelling that has gained importance in relatively recent times, taking the place once held by historical, ritual, and healing functions. Of course, learning takes place but it is not in the form of something being deliberately taught. Canadian storyteller/writer Celia Lottridge spoke to me of her experiences listening to a long story: "I become totally immersed in the world and language of the story. It's a deep and complex experience having nothing to do with messages or lessons. The storyteller takes me somewhere, into a world I have not known from studying or thinking. I get that double reality of being somewhere in body and somewhere else in mind. If the telling goes on for many hours or days this is quite a mind-bending experience."

Those of us who frequently listen to First Nations storytellers hear repeatedly about the ways their elders taught them through story, but it's good to remember that in other times and places there were also several other purposes to storytelling and that these are still operational, though rarely acknowledged. The shift could have taken place as societies changed and as storytelling began to be seen as being primarily for children. At the same time, the younger generation required more overt "teaching," since in the course of daily living there was less learning going on about the skills and basic assumptions of traditional life. Even the very form of teaching has changed. Inuit elders were taught through story to think for themselves, a lifesaving skill to develop, whereas today's teaching takes a form more similar to the commandments handed down by the church.

Stories change as their purposes change, and this is the case when a teaching function has gained the upper hand. For this reason and others, one character may split into two. A simple story tells of an old woman, while a more complex version has two – a witch and a fairy godmother. One boy may become two, one smart and the other stupid. These opposites (or parallels) help listeners learn the difference between right and wrong. In Kiviuq's case, if this hypothesis holds true, the lesson about kindness to orphans doesn't work very well if the hero *is* the seal-boy. We then have no good person who stands aside from the torment, no one showing us how to live the right way. For a really clear lesson about kindness, characters who might have been united within one person when either the lesson or the story's function was different need to be separate now. Each variant shows a different strength of Kiviuq's. When he appears as an adult, he exemplifies the law about being good to orphans. On the other hand, if he is seen as the seal-child, he embodies the power of initiation at sea and the ability to control the weather.

Elders tell us that certain shamans had the power to control the weather, although not all of them, as this is a very difficult skill to master.[15] Both the grandmother and the seal-child have shown other shamanic skills, including the use of incantations and body transformation, which adds to our knowledge of their power. In linear epic terms it makes more sense to begin with the hero's birth and initiation, but in teaching terms it makes more sense to begin with a strong message about kindness. Both approaches are vitally important – the lessons because they help people live well, and the epic form because it contributes to healing and growth.

Shamans and Incantations

Δ The grandmother thought long and hard before deciding on revenge. After all, revenge is not to be undertaken lightly. Again and again we heard that a person should turn away from trouble whenever possible instead of giving vent to emotion. But in certain cases, for example when one's family has been harmed, revenge is justified according to ancient concepts of justice. Justified but not tolerated – the grandmother could expect reprisals. Nonetheless, after all attempts to deal with the situation peacefully had failed, she took action. Her revenge worked two ways, since besides punishing the hunters it acted as an initiation for the child. He now learned to pass through the earth, to change shape, and to call a storm.

First the grandmother sent the child out to a deserted camp to find a piece of sealskin. Annie Peterloosie says she saw seagulls and sent the child to look where they were circling. Bernadette Patterk says she told the child to ask someone he was not afraid of for some scraps. His training began by being made to go and look. The grandmother did much for him, but he had to do whatever he was able. Δ

As I began to tell the story, I felt it important to point out that the grandmother was teaching the child, that she was a woman of power and compassion. I didn't want her to appear as simply ruthless and cruel. That is my view. Aupilaarjuk acknowledges the grandmother's strength but says that she included Kiviuq in her revenge, though he was strong enough to survive it. Annie Peterloosie, on the other hand, says that the grandmother deliberately spared Kiviuq. The story gives leeway for all these ideas.

Long ago in Siberia I became interested in "shamanic story," which in my view goes beyond telling about the lives of historical shamans. A shamanic story is similar to the heroic journey popularized by Joseph Campbell, who showed how frequently this form appears in widely separated cultures around the world. It includes a disaster that forces the hero to leave home, meetings with dangers and with helpful friends, a crisis, and the return. The shamanic version often has two parts – the initiatory journey, where the crisis involves the shaman's own soul development, and a later journey, where that power is put to use to serve others. A shaman may undergo further initiatory adventures in addition to bringing back lost souls. A hero may journey a second time to bring back a wife or parents abducted by enemies. Although Kiviuq's story does not follow the form entirely, several parts reflect it strongly. The parallel lives of seal-child and hero give it strength.

This journey form rarely follows the life of only one shaman or person of power. Usually there are several of them, interacting, competing, complementing each other's actions. This epic purports to be about the *angakkuq* Kiviuq, but already we've seen the possibility that several other characters are also shamans – first Tuutalik, now the grandmother, and then the seal-child. And there will be others. Kiviuq works primarily in the element of water, although he later spends much time on land. He is not one of those shamans who fly. With few exceptions he has little to do with fire. Tuutalik, as expected, is also a water creature, as is his child Tuutalannuaq. The powerful grandmother, on the other hand, seems to work mainly in the air. Many of the elders say she is the one to call the storm with its high winds. She may also have power with the earth, for she is able to send her child down through the ground to the sea. Her power is very precise – she can pick the hunters off in the order of their sins. Kiviuq's legend is mainly about his life, but it includes these other strong characters to help point up the greatness of his powers. And such was the nature of life – a shaman never worked in isolation.

Many elders tell us the grandmother is a shaman. She introduces us to the power of singing incantations, *irinaliutit*. Again the use of breath puts her in the realm of the air and relates to the *tarniq* (soul). Aupilaarjuk says that an incantation is a very powerful use of words, like chanting. *Irinaliutit* can be good or bad, although they are definitely different from hexing, *ilisiiqsiniq*. He compares them to prayer, saying that *Silaup Inua* (the spirit of the air) is the one who would grant the request. Silaup Inua gives the breath of life – the same breath we use to sing – and takes it back at death. *Irinaliutit* can be used for healing (Saladin d'Anglure 2001, 48; Aupilaarjuk et al. 2002, 14).

Δ The grandmother sang the whole time she worked the sealskin that would aid in the child's transformation. As the grandmother sang and chewed, the child learned that a small piece of skin can contain the pattern for the whole. Annie Peterloosie says that the skin turned back into a live young sealskin as soon as it was stretched big enough to fit over the child. Jacob Peterloosie says her shamanic power made the sealskin fit the child. Rachel Ujarasuk says she sewed the clothing with sinew from seagull wings. Simon Tookoome pointed out that she was breaching the rules when she worked on clothing during the summer.[16] This could be another of the things that tells us something is "off."

The grandmother then trained the child to hold his breath under water, again singing. She used a big pot of water or the wet spot in the floor of the house. We see the passage of time in the way she watched the shadows on the tent to see if he could hold his breath long enough for her to observe the sun's movement. Then she asked him if he would be afraid when she put him down through the floor and he replied, "No, grandmother, I will not be afraid." Cornelius Nutaraq adds that perhaps the child had no idea what was about to happen. Many say she explained to him what he must do next. She continued singing as she put the child down through the earth. But not everyone tells it this way. Bernadette

Igloolik sky

Patterk says that Kiviuq, who was the seal-child in her view, started right out in a kayak and didn't swim. Zippora Innuksuk said the child sneaked into the water from the house. She speaks about the sealskin being used as a helping spirit. Δ

Calling the Storm

Journeying through the earth is basic to shamanic cultures nearly worldwide. In many cases it relates to the lower world, variously understood as a dangerous spirit world or as the land of the dead. "The entrance to the lower abodes started at the entrance hole in the floor, and proceeded through a subterranean tunnel, from where a lower tunnel, visible only in dreams or visions, branched off leading through the earth to the submarine abodes of other dead humans and the sea mammals" (Sonne 1992, 162). The underwater world is the realm of Nuliajuk, mother of the sea beasts.

In Siberian cultures there is a world under the water that is different from the one under the land. In some ways it is similar to our world but is inhabited by different beings. This is clearly represented in the Udeghe tale of the man who married a seal (see the "Seal Cousins" chapter). Tales of human marriage with seals or other sea mammals, and of creatures who are part human, part seal, exist wherever humans and these animals live near each other. From northwestern Canada through Iceland and the Celtic world to Siberia, such unions are a common intimacy.

Δ The child behaved as instructed and arrived in the river ready to lure the hunters out to sea. Jacob Peterloosie wondered why hunters were at home on such a good day with no wind. Eli Kimaliadjuk drew attention to the fact that the seal was completely white, as the babies are earlier in the spring. Since this was already summer and young seals had turned darker, the hunters should have been alerted to the fact that something was not quite right. This could not be an ordinary seal. But the grandmother made them forget this piece of very common knowledge. Off they went, in hot pursuit. Δ

Some things appear as they should be, and others are strikingly not as they should be. It is of vital importance to notice those things that are "off," since they can indicate that the hero is in the presence of non-human beings or is perhaps being influenced by a shaman's power. Even though hunters must respond very swiftly when they see an animal, warning signs should rise from deep in their consciousness.

In Kivalliq Region most people said that the child raised his left hand while calling the storm. When I asked why, Theresa Kimaliadjuk replied that the left hand was used for bad actions and the right for good. Bernard Saladin d'Anglure points out that shamans used the left hand for their powerful actions (2006, 96). But before I could learn more about this, we were in Baffin Island, where most elders said the child raised his right hand. Why? Expecting something parallel to Theresa's reply, I was stunned by Annie Peterloosie:

Δ "The seal-child used the right hand to call the storm because it was deformed. He wanted the hunters to know who he was, so he showed it." Zippora Innuksuk added another detail: "One of the hunters noticed that when the seal dove he had a human foot and not a flipper. 'That's not a real seal,' he called to his companions."

The child called, "*Silaga nauk, ungaa?* Where's my weather?" Some say he also called "Where's the sun?" He called upon the deity Sila to bring back the weather from the day he was born. The sound "ungaa" imitates the cry of a child, so Sila would understand that he was young. Zippora Innuksuk says *ungaa* is a word from shamanic language. A terrible storm came up, with high winds. Kayaks began to overturn. Too late the hunters tried to turn back. The only one who did not drown in the storm was Kiviuq. **Δ**

Annie has provided new information from the great storytelling well. The child had a deformed hand? This was the first we had heard of it but she saw it clearly.

In fact, any person can call the weather of the day they were born. "Iqallijuk from Igloolik called the good weather from her own birthday in order to help her father who was lost in bad weather. Her mother told her to stand naked and call '*Silaga nauk?*' just as the seal-child did" (Saladin d'Anglure 2001, 91). Of course the story does not state that the child was born on a stormy day, but again the elders work their way back from the results of his calling. They know this in the same way they knew that Kiviuq had a grandmother who gave him a very good upbringing, since he grew up to become a good man who obeyed the rules.

Then there is the detail about whether the child was cared for by a grandmother or a mother. The one real difference I can see is that in the ethnographic versions of the story the grandmother puts more into the hands of the child, whereas the mother does more for him. In versions from the past century, the grandmother taught the child to call the storm, while the mother called it herself from the shore. In the accounts of our time, almost everyone tells the story about the grandmother, with the exception of Bernadette Uttaq. She says the child was raised by the mother and that it was she who taught the child to call the storm.

Sila is a word of many meanings. "The term *sila* means many things at once: the intelligence, the order implicit in the universe, the atmosphere, the world, the air, the outside" (Saladin d'Anglure 2001, 179). It also represents an individual's intelligence or reason. Philip Paniaq says that *sila* means the whole air environment but in the expression *silaga nauk, silaga* tells us for sure what is meant is weather. *Sila* is the source of the earth eggs sometimes found in the tundra. These eggs can hatch into caribou and other animals but if broken bring bad weather (Saladin d'Anglure 2001, 180).

What happened to the seal-child after the storm? I sometimes wonder if the child died in the human sense while going down into the water. Or did the grandmother put his soul in a place of safety outside his body during the time he was in danger from the hunters? Protection of children's souls is one of the shaman's great skills among Siberian peoples. One Ulchi woman told me that a shaman held her children's souls in a place whose location not even she, the mother, knew until they were strong enough to survive.[17]

Non-Inuit listeners unfailingly ask what happened to the seal-child after the storm, but few of the elders even mentioned the child again after telling how he lured the hunters to their death. One or two of the elders say that the child came home alive and well, transformed now into a fine seal hunter well able to care for his grandmother. Rachel Ujarasuk and Joanisee Macpa tell us the other women came around and inquired but the grandmother told them he had been sick in bed.[18] But most likely both woman and child would have died if the venture had failed. I wonder if in real-life terms the child was sick to begin with, perhaps as a result of maltreatment by the neighbours.

What was the community like after most of the men died at sea? As several groups were living together at this time, it would have been a tremendous loss. Over time, as the people moved nomadically and met with other families, some of the women would have remarried and the children would have grown up. But there must have been some very difficult times the first year or two in a community composed mainly of women, and those hard times would have left a permanent scar on those who had lived through them. I can't help noticing that most of the beings Kiviuq meets up with on his journey after the storm at sea turn out to be females living without men – could this reflect the situation in his own community?

Geographic Locations

Many epics and legends speak of geographic locations. Where did this one take place? In most regions the elders had no precise answer, and Samson Quinangnaq told us that storytellers often don't like to name exact locations. Herve Paniaq agrees that the real names of places and people were never used in stories. Henry Evaluardjuk agrees but adds that much can be learned about location from the style of houses and other aspects of material culture portrayed in the story. Cornelius Nutaraq adds that dialect can also be a key. Nutaraq is a man with an intense interest in language. Besides studying dialects and writing systems, he is a writer, having kept a daily diary since the 1960s.

In spite of this reticence, certain places are known. In Arviat we pulled out the map. Elders there told us that Kiviuq had been born near modern-day Arviat, and they identified other places as well: Airaktuuq, where the parents waited and died of joy; Tikiraarjuk, where the mother waited; and Qikiqtaarjuk, where her footprints can be seen. They say Kiviuq travelled around the Kazan River and Yathkyed Lake after the death of his parents. Brothers Peter Suqaksiork and Phillip Kigusiutnak say he started off south of Igloolik and wintered in Nunavik and Baffin Island. We think this would mean that he returned by a route that took him frequently to land, possibly around the north, via Southampton Island, with stops on southern Baffin Island.

Henry Isluanik took us to see the rock where Kiviuq's mother had stood, hour after hour, year after year, searching the horizon for her son. When we got to Taloyoak, Niviuvak Marqniq and Bernadette Uttaq told us about a stone seat north of there where the parents had waited. In Iqaluit, Henry Evaluardjuk described the land Kiviuq had reached after being lost at sea as a red line, the way the thin line of the earth looks from far away as you approach Igloolik. The bear story also has identifiable locations, in the Back River Chantry Inlet area.

Weeks later, at the 2004 Vancouver Storytelling Festival, I met Inuit storyteller Michael Kusugak, who has studied the Kiviuq legend intensively. "Some Greenlanders told me that Kiviuq started off deliberately – he was not lost at sea in the storm," Kusugak said. "His wife had made a three-layered cover for his kayak that served him well, as the first two layers were eaten by krill. According to the Greenlanders, Kiviuq came across from Greenland to Baffin Island."[19]

Kiviuq's story is told all over the North, from Greenland to Alaska, and like many stories that reach far into the past there is often the sense that it happened "right here." Henry Evaluardjuk cites this as one reason it's difficult to determine the story's real location. Most elders are certain that Kiviuq really did live, and some say he's still alive today, so it is natural that the places in his story would be identifiable.

Helping Spirits – Arriving on Land

We have a long way to go before Kiviuq returns home to be welcomed by friends and relatives, but it will happen. I can readily empathize with those at home who waited, wondering if the man was still alive and how long they should hold him in memory before giving him up for lost. A person who survived would have good stories to tell. But that is yet to come.

Δ Kiviuq battled the storm for a long time. At first one or two other men survived, thrown from their kayaks into the water. Kiviuq tried to hold them up. Annie Peterloosie and others say that one man was his brother, whose amulet was the black-billed murre, and Samson Quinangnaq says there were two other shamans from his community. Kiviuq tried his best to save his companions but eventually they told him to give it up. "We can't go on any longer. You go ahead," they said. The Inuit sense of justice is very precise. In the eyes of many elders the hunters died in exactly the order of the severity of their injustice to the child. Those who had been the cruellest and most unrelenting died first. Those who partook less willingly and less often survived longer.

And so Kiviuq persisted. The waves rose like mountains around him – it was all he could do to stay afloat in his kayak. All the while he yearned to see land, any land, just to be able to go ashore for a rest and to orient himself. "*Nuna tauvva, iqqaq tauvva*," he called hopefully. "There's the land, there's the bottom under shallow water." Δ

How long did he stay at sea? Time in this story is not measured in days, weeks, and months. The North is not conducive to those divisions, with such huge differences in hours of daylight over the course of a year. One of the first Inuktitut phrases John taught me was "*Takulaarivuguk*," which means, "See you later, after at least one sleep" – not necessarily tomorrow, since sleeps could happen at various times, depending on the season.

Kiviuq could not stand up in his kayak, since to do so would certainly capsize the boat. And so he had to urinate inside the kayak. So much time went by that the kayak was almost completely filled. Think how long that would take, especially considering that most likely he had little or nothing to eat or drink in the meantime! This is the second of the many moments in the story that show us the passage of time in Inuit terms, and this instance provides a laugh as well.

We investigated the meaning of the word *iqqaq* with our interpreters, with the elders, and with oral historian Leah Otak, all of whom defined it as the place where you can see the rocks on the bottom under water. From Philip Paniaq I learned that the alternative – the bottom under deep water – is simply expressed as "bottomless," using the same root word. But it seems that in shamanic language, *iqqaq tauvva* could simply be another way of saying, "There's the land." Some shamanic words differ from normal language in subtle ways like this. Certain shamanic phrases use familiar words but with completely different meanings, while others use words unknown in normal speech.

Storyteller/educator Johanna Kuyvenhoven distinguishes two uses of words in the stories of her experience. One is the ordinary use, where words simply convey information that can be rearranged as the storyteller desires. Philip Paniaq is saddened that this is the only way words seem to be used today – for pure information. He says, "Today we regard words just as tools for information. But story words are very strong, coming from mind to mouth. Story reminds us about how strong words are." Johanna goes on to say, "The other kind of words are incantational sorts of words, including names. These are thoroughly inflexible. It matters that it is Baba Yaga,[20] for example. If you call her anything else you lose all the power invoked by her presence, history, and connectedness. These are the 'high words' in a story. They are pillars on which the story stands and is grounded, a kind of proof of the story's veracity and nature." "*Nuna tauvva, iqqaq tauvva*" is this kind of phrase. The story does not stand without it. As we go on, we will see many instances of these incantational words and phrases, delivered in an older form of Inuktitut than that used today. They make up a kind of skeleton of the whole story's structure, marking pivotal moments in story time.[21] Kiviuq called because he kept hoping to see land. Each time he thought he'd seen it, he was proven to be mistaken – what he saw was only the enormous waves. I think it is also possible that his calling acted as an incantation, which helped him reach shore at last.

We started hearing about sea birds. At first we were unsure what kind of bird they were, but in Chesterfield Inlet Joe Issaluk pointed with complete certainty to a picture of a Dunlin sandpiper (*sauraq* in Inuktitut), and others later confirmed his choice. In regions such as northern Baffin Island, where the Dunlin does not live, we simply heard of shore birds. According to some elders, sandpipers appeared in the air, giving our hero the encouraging thought that he must be nearing land. Leo Nimialik mentioned sandpiper skins that were inside the kayak. These turned out to be helping spirits (*ikajuqti*). Some said the sandpiper skins began making sounds that helped the kayak orient itself towards shore.

Certainly, sandpipers migrate over enormous distances – from their breeding grounds in Arctic Canada to their winter homes as far away as Mexico. Science has not completely explained the remarkable navigation system that allows them to find land and return home year after year. It may be a combination of sensitivities – to landmarks, the sun and stars, and magnetic forces. Their migration may also be driven in part by predators. While Inuit may not have known exactly how far the sandpipers fly in winter, they were observant and aware of the habits and abilities of all living creatures that lived in their territory, whether year-round or seasonally. Many hunters must have had the experience of being guided to shore by sandpipers. Later we will see that Kiviuq gained the ability to call the sandpiper spirits, whereas at this point in the story they appeared of their own accord.

When arrived in Philip Paniaq's home town of Pond Inlet, Philip decided to phone his father down in Clyde River. The next morning he described their conversation with some excitement: "Usually my father and I call each other once or twice a year, exchange a few words, and hang up. Literally, it's, How are you doing? Fine. Okay, bye. This time I mentioned this work I'm involved in on Kiviuq and he said, 'Oh yes.' Then he told me about sandpiper skins. He says people used to put them in the front tip of the kayak when they were building it, so that the frame wouldn't break through the sealskin cover. The same kind of skin was used in every subsequent kayak built for that person." Besides keeping Kiviuq awake, it seems the sandpiper skins helped keep the kayak afloat. As we started recording later that day, Annie Peterloosie told us that Kiviuq was spared in the storm because he had the bird skin as helper, given to him at birth. He was the last to survive in the water because he was able to float on top of the waves with the help of his bird helper. But she also believes that the sandpiper is the grandmother's helping spirit, sent by her to help Kiviuq.

This was just the beginning. Joanasie Macpa adds that Kiviuq wore a sandpiper amulet. From Cornelius Nutaraq and others we learn that sandpiper skins were part of a ritual. The women assisting at a child's birth would choose a particular kind of animal or bird skin to wipe the baby with. This would then become the child's personal helping spirit, or *ikajuqti*. An *ikajuqti* is distinct from a *tuurngaq*, or shaman's helping spirit. Anyone can have an *ikajuqti*, while only a shaman can have a *tuurngaq*. (Views about the meaning of these two words vary from one cultural region to another.) At the same time, the midwives can give children gifts that carry them through life. For Kiviuq the gift was that of always being able to get home safely, although as told today he did not return home after following his goose-wife, which seems to have broken the cycle.

The gifts are bestowed in words and are sometimes used to offset problems brought in from another lifetime. In Taloyoak Bernadette Uttaq explained this in more detail: "A child can be brought up with a certain discipline because of past life experiences that were too hard for the family. Parents don't want their children to suffer in the same way. They give the child certain words so that the past life will not affect the child in the future. For example, if the one coming back had been unable to have children, then voicing something out in words will make the thing take place. They might say, 'You'll have a lot of children.' There were no medicines in those days but there were people who lived from birth to death without sickness because of these words. They may be encouraged to hunt, to be good to others, or to be fast runners. The elders could make it happen through words and actions. They could set the life to be lived in a certain way. Choice words set a seed in the child."

Our interpreter Peter Mannilak told a story from recent experience. The child was the reincarnation of a woman from Taloyoak who had much trouble with her legs and at the end of her life could not walk. The women spoke into the baby's ear, saying, "You will be a fast runner!" And now at age three this has proven to be so. I am much impressed by the way Inuit used this truth about words in such a positive way. It connects to what we know about the ways storytelling creates worlds. It's clear that this power of words can also work negatively – people will be restricted by limitations created in the same way, often unconsciously. Inuit have made the positive use of the power of words one of the pillars of a child's upbringing.

Δ The sandpipers guided Kiviuq to shore and at last "*Nuna tauvva, iqqaq tauvva*" proved to be true. He managed to pull his kayak up onto shore, clean it out, and prop it up to dry, and then he fell into a long and much-needed sleep. Now we see another of those ways the elders have of showing the passage of time. A voice awakened Kiviuq several times, telling him to move his kayak further up the shore and turn his boots as they dried. But when he finally awoke to the voice of Bee Woman inviting him into her hut, the kayak was well above the high water mark.[22] Joanasie Macpa explains that Kiviuq slept through a whole month-long cycle of tides. Δ

And since his kayak nearly floated away, it could be that he had come to a place where the tides covered a greater distance than what he was accustomed to.

Another aspect of Kiviuq's power can be seen in the fact that his kayak lasted through such a long trip. Normally, sealskin kayaks need to be dried and oiled after about a week in the water, and his was obviously in the water much longer than that (Rousselot 1994, 254). It seems clear that thanks to his expertise and the help he received, he was being saved only to have to embark on even more difficult ventures. What happens next is the jumping-off point for a whole series of adventures as Kiviuq tries to find his way home. He has been compared to Odysseus on his way home from the Trojan War. In the words of elder Mariano Aupilardjuk, "It was a journey of maturation and development."

But before we continue, let's take a look at some of Kiviuq's Siberian cousins and how their stories show up new facets of the Inuit legend.

Seal Cousins

Orcas can help people. When they see a sinking boat they can take it up, two of them, and bring it to shore. I've seen it happen. People give them a bit of tobacco in thanks. The whales are very close to people.

– Gleb Nakazik, village of New Chaplino, 1994

Sireniki

On a chilly fall morning in 1994 I walked down to the beach in Sireniki, a village inhabited mainly by Siberian Yupik. The Yupik live along the shores of the Bering Sea and their language is related to Inuktitut. The village was deathly poor – people out of work, tuberculosis widespread, life expectancies in the forties. The food shelves in the store boasted a few canned goods and a single banana – the last a curiosity since no one could afford to buy it. It had taken us seven hours to get here from the regional centre, riding in the back of a military truck, bouncing across the tundra. I went for an early-morning walk to ease my bruises and lift my spirits. The wind was cold but Sireniki's setting is spectacular – a long pebbly beach with large jutting cliffs on either end. The cliffs look as though they had once formed the same rock but had split apart. As I walked along the beach taking photographs, I noticed a group of men sitting in front of a dilapidated building at the top of a sandbank on the trail leading back to the village. They were gazing through binoculars at the sea – hoping most of all to see a whale. They would have been satisfied with a seal or walrus, but that day they would catch nothing at all. Hunting is no longer a viable lifestyle owing to ecological damage and social change.

Whale bones

Later that day I heard Yupik elder Nununa, one of the last three speakers of her dialect, tell a story set on that beach. Young people had gathered there and paired up, but there was one girl who didn't get a partner. She put her foot into the hole in a whale vertebra and suddenly found herself being pulled out to sea. New flesh formed over the whale bone and the huge animal was reborn. The girl's brothers leapt into their boats and headed out between the two rocks, which were clashing together and moving apart. The young men followed small sea birds, dodging the cliffs in order to rescue their sister. Both of these images are reminiscent of Kiviuq – the clashing rocks he passed between while following his goose-wife and the sea birds who helped him to shore after the storm.

By the time they found the girl, she was pregnant. She came back with them and bore a whale-child, which she raised first in a basin, then in a protected body of water. Eventually she let him out to sea, but she put a talisman on him so that the hunters would recognize him and not kill him. The father came and accompanied his child out to sea. Nonetheless the baby whale was later killed by members of a neighbouring community, who did not follow the same rules. The woman watched the whale feast from afar, grieving for her child. Some say she slept with the bones, which came back to life, but Nununa did not tell it that way. The people's intimacy with sea mammals lives on in Nununa's story and in the hunters' strong attention to the sea. They watch now as they have watched down through the ages, although their prospects are meagre.

Ten years later I was carried back to that windy beach as I listened to Kiviuq's story. I was reminded not only of stories like the one about the woman who married a whale, but also of ideas expressed through the native languages, customs, and rituals. Today Inuit have better resources for survival than their Yupik relatives, but their relationships with the animals that feed them have been damaged just as much.

Inuit and many Siberian native peoples depended on hunting for their living, and this brought them into a complex intimacy with animals. Their knowledge is comprehensive and full of affection. We see this in stories of animals that not only talk and behave like humans, but also marry humans, recalling the times when communication was easier and the line between human and animal finer. Whether the stories are humorous or profound, they have similar hearts.

The opening of Kiviuq's tale focuses on seals, one of the staples of the Inuit diet and lifestyle. The *tuutaliit* – half human, half seal – express the closeness between people and animals in a way that few other images can. Although Siberian shamans take the form of animals in order to help people, I have not heard of beings anything like the *tuutaliit*, who live in close community with humans west of the Bering Strait. But I was reminded of the Ulchi boy who was helped by a Siberian tiger whose life he had spared (Van Deusen 2001, 176). The tigers were living parallel to humans, but not in the same community. Although I've never heard of anything like the *tuutaliit* in Siberian lore, I believe it's possible such stories exist somewhere under the surface. The basic concept certainly exists throughout the world in images of shapeshifting and marriages with animals.

Chukotka shoreline

A Man Who Married a Seal

One of my favourite places in Siberia is the village of Gvasyugi, thousands of kilometres south of Sireniki near the border with Manchuria. Located about four hours' drive from the city of Khabarovsk down a bumpy dirt road, it sits at the confluence of three rivers and is inhabited by about three hundred people, most of whom belong to the Udeghe tribe, which is part of the Tungus linguistic and cultural family. Also very poor, they have a more diverse livelihood, which includes hunting, fishing, gardening, and beekeeping. I have visited there many times, developing friendships and a deep fascination with their ancient culture.

When the Mongols invaded this part of the world, some of the local people assimilated, while others went off to live in isolation in the mountainous taiga forests. The forest dwellers are still there and include Udeghe, who have retained richly detailed traditions down through the centuries. At certain times they lived on the shore of the Sea of Okhotsk, where they hunted seals. I heard this story from storyteller Valentina Kyalundzyuga, whose people have now lived far from the sea for several generations. The images are so compelling that this story is still one of her favourites.

Kakta Ni[1]

Long ago Yegdyghe lived by the shore of the sea. His wife was Kakta Ni, a half-person with golden hair.

One day Yegdyghe went down to the shore hunting. There he saw a beautiful seal that had come out of the water and was sunning herself on the rocks. He approached her. They became friends. Truth to tell, the seal became Yegdyghe's second wife.

That evening when he went home, his human wife Kakta Ni noticed that something was different. Everything had been fine with them before but now he seemed to find fault with everything she did. She decided to find out what was going on.

The next day she followed as Yegdyghe went down to the shore. She heard how he sang to the seal and saw how she came up out of the water. She understood that the seal had become his second wife.

That night she prepared her husband an especially good meal. As he ate, she poured him cup after cup of strong drink. When he was soundly asleep, she took his hunting knife and cut his body in half, right down the middle. She attached one half of his body to her own. She took his great harpoon and went down to the shore of the sea.

She sang for the seal, imitating her husband's voice. The seal heard her and called back, "Why does your voice sound different?"

"I caught a cold," the woman replied. "That's why my voice sounds different."

"Ah well," thought the seal, "who else would be calling me?" She came up to the surface.

Kakta Ni threw the harpoon, holding tight to the cord. The seal struggled, severely wounded. When the seal was stronger, she almost pulled Kakta Ni into the water. And when the woman was stronger she almost pulled the seal onto the land. At last the seal broke free and swam away.

Kakta Ni went home. She put the two halves of her husband back together and went to sleep.

The next day Yegdyghe got up and went down to the shore of the sea. He called out for his seal wife but there was no answer. He called again and again – still no answer. At last he got worried and dove into the water. He lost consciousness at first but then he came to. The underwater world was much the same as ours. Yegdyghe saw a path leading into the forest and he followed it.

He walked for a long time and at last came to a place where an old woman lived.

"Have you seen my seal friend?" he asked her.

"I have seen her. She stopped here, and I tended her wound. Continue on the same path and you will come to the place where Sagdi Mama lives – the oldest woman of all. Perhaps she can help you find your friend."

Yegdyghe spent the night there and the next day he continued on his way. He came at last to Sagdi Mama and asked her, "Have you seen my seal friend?"

"You are too late," the old woman replied. "She is dying. But perhaps there is still a chance that you can save her. Take this birchbark container and run to the lake of red water. Fill the container with that water and use it to heal her wounds."

Yegdyghe took the container and ran as fast as he could go to the lake which was full of red water. He filled the container and then listened. He heard sounds – preparations for a funeral. He ran in that direction, shouting as he went.

Those who were carrying the seal were frightened and they dropped her. Yegdyghe poured red healing water into her wound and it began to heal before his eyes. Then he took saliva on his finger and rubbed it around the wound. It healed completely and the seal opened her eyes.

"Ah, it's you."

"Yes, I have come."

"Who was it who did this to me?"

"It was my human wife, Kakta Ni."

After a while, they started back. They stopped to visit Sagdi Mama. Yegdyghe went hunting and left her with a good supply of meat for the winter. They stopped to visit the other old woman and helped her too, leaving her with a good supply of firewood.

At last they came out to the place where Yegdyghe had entered the water. They came up onto the land, but Yegdyghe did not return to his human wife. Instead he and his seal wife found a new place of live, on another river, where there was much game and much fish. But people say he could no longer live on land, and before long he and his seal wife went back to live in the water. They say the sea takes people to itself.

This seal is similar and different from the *tuutaliit*. Her husband crosses down into the underwater world as Tuutalik did, and some say he did not survive it. But the seal never seems to have appeared in human form or to have lived in human community with anyone other than her husband. The sense of intimacy is just as strong because of the intensity of love and devotion.

The Udeghe often sing important conversations that cross between worlds of body and spirit, humans and animals. Both Yegdyghe and Kakta Ni sing to the seal in this story. Sung sound broadens communication into levels impossible with the spoken word. Like the Inuit grandmother's incantations, this use of singing is connected with the complexity of indigenous languages and the way they include both spiritual and practical meanings, as the sacred permeates everyday life.

When the seal-child called on the Inuit deity Sila for help in bringing up the storm at sea, I was reminded of the Udeghe word *bua*, which has a range of meanings similar to that of *sila*. *Bua*'s extensive meanings include the world, surrounding nature, the outdoors, here and there, around, a country or location, the taiga forest, a specific place or direction, a time period, God (male or female, in the sense of the forces of nature), a deity, and a person endowed with divine characteristics (Kyalundzyuga and Simonov 1998, 178–85). *Bua* appears in the story of Kakta Ni to indicate the place where Yegdyghe woke up under the sea and the way those who carried the seal ran off in different directions. A related Tungus word includes the sky and a certain kind of cumulous cloud layer. I'm amazed and fascinated by words that can range so easily from the sacred to the mundane.

Hunting and the Spirit World

Like that of the Inuit, the Siberian world is peopled with humans, animals, and other living beings, as well as spirits. The spirits can be good, evil, or changeable, depending on circumstances and how they are treated.

To ensure their success, indigenous hunters have long made offerings to spirits as they set out from home. Those Inuit hunters who perform such rituals today are even more quiet about them than their ancestors were in the past, when the rituals would have been included as a modest but vital part of any hunting trip. Siberian hunters have always made offerings to spirits and have done so openly since the collapse of Soviet power. Like the Inuit, however, they are cautious in speaking of spirits. The rituals are not taken lightly, nor should they be "demonstrated" for outsiders. Spirits do not like to be called when they are not needed. For most of the twentieth century, communism played a similar role in Siberia to that played by the church in Canada, almost taking the place of a religion. But since 1990, the old practices, such as the hunting rituals, have resurfaced in ways that are not yet evident in Nunavut.

Stopping at a place where the road forks, at a sacred spring or a mountain pass, travellers in Siberia may offer a bit of food or vodka to the spirits of the place. Even Russians have picked up this custom from the indigenous people, and they perform the rituals with more bravado. The hunters have often told me that spirits call the animals to the hunt if they are treated well. This reminds me of the Inuit tale of how the personal qualities of the hunter influence a seal's decision about which hole to pop up through.

For centuries Udeghe people have built special huts in the woods for the purpose of rendering respect to the spirits in a worshipful fashion.[2] The Udeghe word for the process is *khengki*, sometimes translated as prayer. Valentina Kyalundzyuga prefers to use a translation that indicates a bow or a worshipful rendering of respect. Of all the Amur peoples, only the Udeghe use these houses. Although they are called *miao* in Krasny Yar (derived from the Chinese name), the huts are known by the Udeghe name *khengginku bua* in the village of Gvasyugi, which is geographically further from Chinese influence. (The word *bua* appears again in this term, indicating a place for paying respects.) Other Amur peoples make offerings without building the little houses.

In 2005 I visited a new *miao* in the village of Krasny Yar. Together with a young shaman and several friends I walked to a little house newly built at the edge of the taiga forest. It is a place to be proud of, built of clean new lumber and decorated simply. The local people use it not only as a place to prepare for the hunt, but also as a place where they can spend time with children, teaching them the proper respect for the forest.

In the Turkic areas of southern Siberia, elders reminisce about how hunters would take storytellers and musicians along to their camps. Sometimes these men would hunt and sometimes their only function was to strike up and maintain connections with the spirits of forest and mountain, who love singing and stories. More than one man has told me about returning to camp and finding an elder uncle singing a story beside the fire, with no human listener present. Ethnomusicologist Liesbet Nyssen points out that a shared love of play – both in the sense of music and of laughter – was the common element between people and spirits, and the common ground for their communication (Nyssen 2005). When the hunt was successful, the storysinger would receive a share of the take. I learned more about this from Tuvan ethnomusicologist Valentina Süzükei, who told me stories about musical instruments.

The Shoor-*Flute*

There were two hunters. Every morning they went out separately and every evening they came back – one had empty bags, while the other had always caught something. One evening the one who had nothing sat playing his flute – the *shoor*. Now the one who was followed by success happened to be the kind of person who sometimes sees what we do not and hears things we do not hear. Tuvans call this kind of person *karang-körnür*.

When he looked at his companion playing the *shoor*, he noticed that the mistress of the taiga was sitting on his nose! She was listening so intently that she dozed off and slid down his cheek as if rolling down a hill. He started to laugh. His friend asked why he was laughing. He explained about seeing the mistress of the taiga and then laughed even harder. The mistress of the taiga was offended – first because he had told about seeing her and second because he had laughed.

And from that time on success deserted him, and the musician became a successful hunter.

Orphans

Although folk tale heroes are often ordinary people, the heroes of more magical stories are often set apart in some way. Many of them are orphans like the seal-child. Correct treatment of orphans is as vitally important to the dwellers of the Bering shore on the Asian side as it is to the Inuit. It is the main moral that most elders point out in Kiviuq's tale. In Chukotka the despised orphan often receives supernatural help and makes use of his own cleverness and persistence. The renowned Yupik storyteller Lubov Kutylina told me of one orphan boy who lived with relatives who hardly fed him at all. One night, out in the chilly corridor, he met a mysterious man who taught him to blow on his hand. The side of his palm became sharp enough to cut meat. When the stingy uncle saw this brilliant skill, it became a point of pride for him – he now trotted the boy out to show off to visitors. But he also saw the boy's power and a new fear led him to respect his nephew. The boy now got plenty to eat and lived well.[3]

In epic traditions of Turkic and Mongolian peoples, the hero or heroine is also often an orphan, although in the more complex epics the parents have not died but have been abducted by evildoers from whom the hero/ine must later win them back. This idea of the return of a lost loved one brings to mind the story of the man who married a seal. In the epics such a tale would take a two-part form – the first would be about the

Yupik storyteller with facial tattoos

hero's soul development and the second reminiscent of the shamanic ceremonies of soul retrieval.[4] Behind it all is often the image of the powerful orphan – so strong in Tuva that shamans adopt representations of orphans as amulets, called Öskus-eeren. Of course, from the child's point of view it makes little difference whether the parents are dead or abducted – they are not present to help the children, who must grow and learn on their own.

Orphans aren't the only ones to receive help – those who are despised or ill-treated do as well. In an Oroch tale a woman who has been unjustly beaten by her husband is helped by a goat who heals her wounds and eventually reunites her with her lost child. The child in turn is brought up by large river fish after being thrown in the water by the wife's rival. In Chukotka a wife with an overly demanding husband finds herself in trouble when her fire goes out. She receives help from a woman whose home appears only long enough for her to give the wife fire and some good advice.

Did Kiviuq Migrate from Asia?

When John Houston first asked me about Siberian parallels with Kiviuq, I thought about the many folk tales, life stories, and literary stories I had heard in Chukotka about a hunter being separated from land while out on the sea ice and returning home much later with supernatural help. More recently I've heard of hunters being stranded on an iceberg, calmly awaiting help from the government rather than from supernatural forces!

Being lost at sea is a common trauma. While the separation in the stories from Chukotka is similar to Kiviuq's ordeal at sea, the return is different. As we go along, we will see many Siberian parallels in Kiviuq's story, but my sense is that the whole epic, and especially the opening, was based on the life of a man who lived after the ancestors of today's Inuit had crossed the Bering Strait. My reasoning is simply that if he did originate in Chukotka, his story would also appear there in recognizable form. Of course, it's always possible that the story disappeared on the Asian side and was more fully elaborated on the North American side. Inuit elders say that Kiviuq has lived as long as their people have existed, which could imply that he was with them before the migration.

The section about the seal and the storm at sea is resonant with Siberian shamanic power, shape-changing, initiation and journeying through the earth, the place of the orphan, and the laws governing hunting and living within a community, but Kiviuq still seems to me to be a real North American Inuk.

Here is a Yupik story of the man who inadvertently went out to sea on an iceberg.

The Man and the Giant[5]

Long long ago, as they say in the stories, one man went out to the seashore. He walked along the ice, hunting for seals. Suddenly the weather worsened, the ice separated from the shore, and the hunter was carried far out to sea.

At home they waited long for him to return. He did not come back and they believed he was lost.

But the man had not died. He was an experienced and skilled hunter. The man built himself a dwelling of snow and ice out there on his strong iceberg. In it he sheltered successfully from the cold wind. He sat in his shelter while the blizzards blew, and only when good weather returned did he come out to hunt. And although the man met polar bears and other animals, he killed only seals. He had plenty of food, and the sealskins served him as comfortable bedding – after all, they never soak through even in the wettest weather. And in this way he spent the whole winter in his warm shelter on the iceberg.

Then spring came. The snow and ice began to melt. The higher the sun rose, the faster the hunter's snow house shrank. On the sunny side icicles even appeared. Inside things were still fine for the time being. But then trouble came – the iceberg began to melt quickly and break up. Then the man did some hard thinking.

One time, as he looked around, he noticed something dark in the clear water. The man rejoiced and ran to the edge. He saw that it was the interwoven roots of several big trees. Quickly the man prepared a rope with hooks on it and waited for the right moment. When the current brought the trees close, he threw out his rope and caught the tree roots. He pulled the trees to the iceberg and gracefully jumped across onto them.

The trees were big and held him well. Many seal pups were living there. Now they began jumping in the water but the hunter managed to kill many of them. He took off their little skins and dried them on the tree roots. They made him a good new bed. The man was glad that he had left his ice dwelling and come to live on the trees, which would not melt.

Thus he sailed around the sea on his trees. He had no idea where he was going. Then suddenly he caught sight of a giant walking through the sea – the water only came up to his knees. The giant approached the man and asked, "Little man, have you been through many troubles?"

The man was glad to see the giant and happily answered his greeting.

"Yes, many," he said.

The giant picked the man up and set him on his head. The giant walked through the sea and the man sat on his head, holding on by the hair. When the man looked down, he saw whales swimming at the giant's feet. And the giant began catching them. He would catch a whale and put it in his mouth and suck on it as if it were a tiny fish, spitting out only the bones. He gave pieces of meat to the man sitting on his head. That's the way the man ate.

At last the giant brought the man to shore. The man rejoiced in the solid ground when he stepped on it.

And now the giant politely asked the man, "Won't you help me to go to sleep? I want to rest."

The man was surprised, even lost his head a bit.

"What are you asking? I am so small. How will I put you to sleep?"

"Listen and I will explain," answered the giant happily. "I don't sleep well because animals bother me. Like mosquitoes and flies they buzz around me, they get in my nose and ears and don't let me sleep. I beg you, scare away the animals. I want to get a good sleep and get rested up. I will make you an earth hut and a meat cache."

The giant stuck two fingers in the ground and made two deep holes, one for an earth hut and the other for meat storage. And then he lay down on the ground.

The giant lay there and his body rose up like a huge mountain. And truly, as soon as he fell asleep, animals began to appear – foxes red and white, polar bears, and many more. The hunter killed various fur-bearing animals with his bow and his spear, warmed his earth hut with hides, and put up meat. He gathered many good hides. The man got a good fire going and scared the animals away with the smoke. And soon the animals stopped coming around.

The giant slept peacefully. Only as autumn approached did he stir and awaken. He talked a little with the man but then again began to doze. He stretched and then turned on the other side and fell back to sleep.

After a year had passed, the giant woke up. He got to his feet satisfied and joyous. The man had helped him well.

The giant thanked the man and asked him, "Wouldn't you like to go home?"

"I do so want to go home! But I just don't know where my home is."

"All right," said the giant. "I know where such little people like you live, and I will take you home."

And so the man got ready for the road. He tied up all the furs and put together the dried meat. The giant placed the man on his head and went along the water. After a while he spoke to the man.

"I'm going to stop here and put you down. It's not far from here to your home. You'll get there on your own. It's embarrassing for me to show myself there."

The man agreed. The giant thanked him again for helping him to sleep and get well rested.

"I don't want to go to your home," he said again. "The little people will laugh at me – I'm so huge."

He set the man on his palm, stretched out his arm, and placed him on the ground not far from a settlement.

The man continued on his way on foot. When he got there, everyone was overjoyed and came out to greet him. The man had returned home after more than a year away.

Those who cross the water embark on great adventures – life-changing, courage-building adventures. Each end is a beginning. The Yupik man rejoined his community, undoubtedly better able to face new challenges. Kiviuq pulled up on land after the storm at sea, and the first being he met proved to give him a real challenge indeed!

Bee Woman and Other Adventures

From my grandmother's storytelling I received the strength to live and survive. If there were no stories to go by, to survive or to learn to hunt and live, there would be nothing to learn from. My grandmother also passed the gift of storytelling to me.

As I understand it Kiviuq could have lived four thousand or even four million years ago, it doesn't matter. The story was passed on and eventually reached me. From me it goes to my son Albert and to my grandchildren. That's how I see it passing. All the generations found something in it to live by.

– Eli Kimaliadjuk, 2004

Taima!

Δ Kiviuq slept long and finally awoke. He spent a bit of time scavenging along the shore and then looked up away from the water. He saw a sod house and heard singing coming from inside. Now a woman came out and invited him in. "You're still tired and wet. You must be hungry. Let me dry your clothes while you sleep some more. I'll go get some firewood and cook you a meal," she said, directing him to a bed in the next room. She hung his clothes on her drying rack and then she was gone. He was distressed to see that the bed, although built on a solid wooden frame, had human intestines stretched across it.

Most elders say the woman looked frightening, exactly like a giant bumblebee, while at least one says she was beautiful. Many elders call her Big Bee Woman, Iguttaqjuaq, although Gideon Qitsualik calls her Arnatiaq, Good Beautiful Woman. Annie Peter-

Elder/performer Annie Peterloosie in costume, from the film *Kiviuq*. Photo by John Houston for drumsong communications inc.

loosie says she was a spirit of place called Ikpik, who lived in the low sandy area. Elisapee Karlik thinks Kiviuq may have turned small at this point instead of having met a large bee. **Δ**

I think Bee Woman may have changed into her beautiful shape in order to tempt Kiviuq into the house so she could kill him and eat him for supper. The house, the drying rack, and the bed are the first hints that something was not right about this woman. Madeleine Ivalu points out that if it was really still summer then it was odd to see a sod house, which is generally used only in fall or winter. Celestin Erkidjuk adds that people don't use drying racks at this time of year, and of course the bed of human intestines set off warning bells in Kiviuq's mind, even if the woman's appearance didn't. As in the past, today's storytelling audiences find this part of the story fun – Bee Woman provides delightful terror to children and laughter to adults. Nonetheless her story has much depth. Magical beings like Bee Woman do great service in an oral story by conveying deep meaning to listeners of all ages and degrees of understanding. For kids she is exciting, stimulating questions about everything from the dream world to the science of ice forming on the sea. For adults and elders, her story involves lessons on cannibalism and shamanic initiation, as we will see.

I was curious to find out what Kiviuq's meeting specifically with a bee might mean. I've heard that many Inuit are very afraid of bees, so naturally a giant bee would be particularly fearsome to them. I grew up cautious about bees but fond of the fuzzy bumblebees, which generally did not sting us – at least not as often or as painfully as other bees. As a child I loved to have them crawl on my hands, which may be why I've developed a certain affection for Bee Woman. Arctic bees survive the cold northern winter by means of an excellent system of temperature regulation, and they grow much thicker hairs than their southern cousins. They are key pollinators of tundra plants.

Even something that resembles the bee contains her power. In an excellent publication from Nunavut Arctic College, Aupilaarjuk shares some interesting information about the connection between bees and shamanism. He and Lucassie Naturaaluk had been discussing a man who had been brought back to life from the dead. Their conversation turned to Aupilaarjuk's nephew: "My father shaped my nephew's destiny so that he would be able to return, but I don't know whether it's going to happen or not … It's not through shamanism that he will come back to life, it's his destiny. We don't know all the marine life forms that are in the ocean. But we do see what is in the stomachs of bearded seals and ring seals. We can find what we call *igutsaup siggungit*, because they resemble bumblebee stingers. That is what my father put on the back of my nephew's parka so that, if he was going to die before his time, he would come back to life. This was taken out of a bearded seal's stomach, and placed on the back of my nephew's parka. They have a beak exactly like a bird. I don't know what they are but we call them bumblebees" (Saladin d'Anglure 2001, 29).

What works to revive a person also helps at birth. Elder Simon Inuksaq spoke about using bees to help a woman in labour: "I had mittens when I was a child and I had a pouch in each mitten. There were two adult bees in each, and baby bees were put there as well. These were there so that when a woman in labour had complications I could help ease the delivery. For example, when a woman was having a hard delivery I would touch her and the baby would come out easily. I used this method twice. When my first wife was having complications I touched her and the baby came out smoothly … I would just touch her on her belly. My second wife as well, when she told me the baby was having a hard time coming out and she asked for my help at that time, I did not even touch her body, I just made a movement towards her and the baby came out straight away" (Bennett and Rowley 2004, 202).

Rasmussen also recorded information about bees and childbirth "Two live bees must be rolled over the back of a pregnant woman and afterwards kept. When the child was born this bee would be an effective amulet: fastened to the top of the head in a hair-band it gives a long life" (1929, 170).

Naujarlak Tassugat and Cornelius Nutaraq say Kiviuq died on shore and was dead over the winter before meeting Bee Woman – a shock to us, as most of the elders said he merely slept. When she appeared and brought him back to life, or even when she awakened him from what could be a shamanic sleep, her bee form was a help, just like the amulets. Annie Peterloosie says Bee Woman carried him into the house. There is always a connection between death and birth in the Inuit understanding, since dying opens the door to a new incarnation. Bee Woman helps us to see that rebirth is more important than death, which goes a long way to explaining how she can be both good and evil at the same time, bringing him to life and then trying to kill him again.

Can we get a hint where this happened? Bee Woman went off to collect dry heather for the fire, which could happen nearly anywhere in the Arctic. Some say she collected firewood, which storyteller Michael Kusugak thinks places her most likely in the southern part of Nunavik, where there are trees. If that's the location, it ties in with the theory that Kiviuq crossed Hudson Bay in the storm. But it's also true that people gather firewood from small bushes instead of trees, and in that case this part of the story could have happened anywhere.

Bee Woman also had a wooden bed frame, possibly made from driftwood. But it seems unlikely that driftwood would have been used for firewood – it would be too valuable to burn. Driftwood is used in building both tent frames and kayaks, as well as harpoon handles, paddles, bow drill stands, sled runners, and other useful items. I was surprised to learn that Inuit didn't obtain wood through trade with their southern neighbours. Wood was a common trade item in the Russian arctic, where it would be transported long distances to meet the needs of Chukchi and Yupik on the treeless shores. The explanation for the lack of trade to the south in Canada probably lies in the hostility and fear that prevailed between Inuit and First Nations people.[1]

Michael Kusugak heard that Kiviuq kayaked up to an igloo – not a sod house – and he wonders how kayaking and igloos can go together, since they're usually associated with different seasons. Most elders tell us that Bee Woman was living in a sod house, although Peter Katorkra and Jimmie Qiqut say she lived in an igloo. Inuit artist Janet Kigusiuq (who also told us the story) portrays her in an igloo, which indicates that Kiviuq was at a place where the water remained unfrozen right up to the shore in winter. Or it could be one of those "off" things, a hint that the woman was not fully human. Kiviuq's long sleep on shore may explain these differences in season from version to version. On the other hand, the story does refer to a time when there was no sea ice, so kayaking up to an igloo would have been normal. Places and natural phenomena keep pulling us back from myth to history.

Ancient Language and Bones

Δ Kiviuq was uneasy in the strange woman's house but managed to fall asleep, only to be awakened by something poking at his body from below – meat skewers made of caribou leg bone were coming up through the floor, jabbing at him. And now it got worse! He noticed skulls lining the walls of the room. They spoke to him saying, "If you don't want to turn out like us, get out of here fast!"

Some people say the skulls were those of Kiviuq's former companions. Quinangnaq says that the one who spoke was the shaman who died last, while most others say it was one of Kiviuq's brothers. These were the men Kiviuq had tried to help, and now they helped him with this timely warning. Δ

As in many other places, when telling the story directly, the elders all use the same words, delivered in the older form of Inuktitut, preserved down through the centuries in story. This consistency could point to a ritual use of storytelling in the past and certainly helps pin down the structure of the Kiviuq story, ensuring that important ideas are never left out. The words affect both story characters and audience as well.

John Houston tried hard to determine whether or not the heads in Bee Woman's house had skin. For a filmmaker the distinction would be essential. Some tellers say "heads," while others say "skulls." The heads – with skin – appear in Janet Kigusiuq's 1979 work *Qiviuq Spits on the Evil Woman*, and indeed Houston thought that otherwise Kiviuq would not have been able to recognize his companions. Yet skulls would underline a different point. I believe that a person of Kiviuq's shamanic powers and hunting skill would have had no trouble in recognizing his companions from their skulls alone. The emphasis on bones points up how soul is retained in the bones. Bones carry incarnational information much as DNA carries characteristics on the physical plane. Inuit shamans of the past said that the lasting part of an *angakkuq* resides in the bones. The rest passes away. Animals are encouraged to return when people pay respect to their bones. Igloolik people told Rasmussen that breaking caribou bones was an offence to the animal that would be punished by death or disaster (1929, 57).

Gizelle Rhyon Berry, who has researched shamanic cultures worldwide, spent considerable time living in Nunavut. She says that the bones are the part of the body that contains the breath soul. Inuit have two kinds of soul: *atiq*, which is connected with the name, and *tarniq* (breath soul), which shamans describe as a tiny bubble that contains a scaled-down model of the individual. According to Aupilaarjuk, "The *tarniq* does not have blood. It does not have bones. It keeps us alive. We are told that God gave us *anirniq*, breath, to give us life. That is our *tarniq*" (Saladin d'Anglure 2001, 10–11, 19).

Western logic and a strong tendency to gather information visually at the expense of other senses can get in the way of our understanding how Kiviuq recognized his companions from their skulls. In my Siberian work I learned that people in indigenous cultures spread their information-gathering more equally among the senses and credit intuition more than Westerners do. It is important for us as story listeners to keep all senses open, as good hunters do. It seems to me that Kiviuq was able to recognize the skulls of his companions through the kind of simple knowingness possessed by both story characters and ordinary people. On the other hand, a representation with flesh clarifies the picture for the literal-minded. Ever practical, some elders point out that the skin shows us that these were the heads of people who had died relatively recently, since the skin had not yet decomposed.

How could the bodies have arrived at Bee Woman's house? You have only to glance at the map or take a look out the plane window to see how much water there is in Nunavut. The land is laced with hundreds of lakes and rivers connecting to the sea. They are less evident on Baffin Island but hugely present elsewhere. It should be no surprise in terms of geography that the men who died at sea wound up in Bee Woman's house, having taken a water route. But it's hard to believe that all those bodies just happened to come ashore at her place. Joe Issaluk says that Bee Woman was strong enough to call them there. Did they come up from the sea through the earth as the seal went down, or did she fish them up? We don't know, but their coming up out of the water provides a nice parallel to the seal-child's and Tuutalik's downward movement.

Cannibalism

Bee Woman, eater of human flesh, is surely an image of death, shown as female here as in many cultures. Some say that death has a more powerful reality for humans than for other animals, since we anticipate it. If you believe in reincarnation, then death in this life leads directly to birth in the next, and thus one goddess or spirit being may have power over what seem contradictory phases of human life (Walker 1996, 488). Bee Woman's ring of skulls within the house reminds me of the Russian witch Baba Yaga, whose house with its chicken feet was ringed with skull lanterns. Goddesses associated with death include the Hindu Kali Ma, who is associated with creation, preservation, and destruction, although she is best known for the last part of that cycle.

Bee Woman brings up the disturbing issue of cannibalism, of the eating of human flesh. I wondered at first if the story spoke of the possibility that cannibalism could turn a person into a non-human like Bee Woman. Although this sometimes happens in First Nations stories, I now believe I was way off base in this regard with the Inuit. For one thing, there are many kinds of mixed beings in the Inuit world. Bee Woman seems to be a type of animal-like mixed being (*uumajuit*), who are dangerous, rather than a human-like mixed being (*inurajait*), who are benign (Saladin d'Anglure 2001, 51). For her, eating a human would not be eating one's own species. My impression is that such beings do not change type.

For another thing, Inuit attitudes around eating human flesh do not support my thinking that it might have turned a human into a non-human. Cannibalism is morally ambiguous. Although considered very wrong, it was an unpleasant reality in times of starvation, and the trauma of it could pass from one generation to the next if not dealt with. There were times when people were forced to eat human flesh in order to survive. Usually this involved eating the bodies of those who had died of starvation, but occasionally people killed their companions for the purpose. In either case, the act had a profound effect on those who survived in this way. Whether or not a person had actually eaten human flesh could be determined by confession or by a shaman's spiritual journey to the sky. The inside of the mouth of those who had done so would turn completely dark, and they would suffer deep psychological trauma. They might also experience reprisals from the victim's family if they had killed someone in order to survive themselves, rather than having eaten the body of someone who had died naturally.

Those who ate the bodies of people who had starved to death could be held in awe, admired for their powerful courage and will to live. In one case a woman shaman named Ataguttaaluk was forced to eat the bodies of dead companions who had starved. She survived the ordeal and later remarried and had several children. As a means of compensation, she adopted these children out into the families of those whose bodies she had eaten. She kept her youngest son, who grew up to be the father of Paul Apak Angilirq, the writer of the screenplay for *Atanarjuat, the Fast Runner* (Angilirq 2002, 223). She was the grandmother of Herve Paniaq, one of the elders to tell us the Kiviuq story.

In an interview published in 1999, elder Elisapee Ottoova spoke of a woman she does not name but who may have been the shaman Ataguttaaluk. I am touched by her sympathy for the woman in her story, who appears to also have been one of her own ancestors.

> The way we see it, we don't think it's right for a human to eat another human. A certain woman ate her husband and she ate her children when they were going through starvation. There was another child that she was looking after at that time which wasn't her own, which she ate as well. We can state that we will never eat a fellow human being, but we do not know what our future holds. If it were our only chance for survival, we just might end up doing that too. She went through an experience which she had to go through. Amazingly, she was discovered and she pulled through it and had a chance to bear children again. If she didn't do what she had to do, there's no way we would be around today. We can see life meant a lot to this person. A lot of us today want to kill ourselves, hang ourselves because we can't deal with life's problems anymore. Imagine what she went through. It must have been hard. Alone all winter in the dark, and her husband dead. Imagine our own husbands; she had to eat her own husband and her own children to survive. It must have been hard. Yes, she must have had some rope to hang herself with, but her life meant something to her. She eventually died from sickness. If she had just given up on life, we wouldn't be around today. They had gone inland and they had nothing left to eat. (Oosten and Laugrand 1999, 15)

It was essential to confess the act, although there was no punishment attached to it and no *pittailinik*, or forbidden behaviour, if it was not confessed. Those who did confess usually then avoided eating light-coloured meat that might resemble human meat (Saladin d'Anglure 2001, 159–62). For example, people who have eaten human flesh never eat bear meat. It is said that bear meat is like human flesh (Rasmussen 1929, 169–203). If people don't confess, the trauma will stay with them. Aupilaarjuk and others frequently emphasize that we must talk things out to be free of them.

Storytelling is an excellent way to release the tension around painful realities such as these, which were hard on the whole community. Without naming individuals known to the community, storytellers would speak of painful issues and even find laughter in the pain. Certainly Bee Woman provokes laughter in audiences. My own listeners respond to her hugely – I can see them liven up with her antics. Inuit elders recall that in childhood they enjoyed this part of Kiviuq's story more than any other. Theresa Kimaliadjuk told us that children were often sent away while adults discussed very serious bad matters. But they did hear about Bee Woman. The story helped them understand harsh reality in a safe way. Siberian stories help people deal with spousal abuse in the same way that this one helps them deal with issues like cannibalism – by bringing the subject up in the safe world of story and pointing out ways of handling it.

The healing power of story in desperate situations is well attested to. The most moving personal story I have heard is that of a young man who survived the crash of a small plane in the mountains. Injured, blinded by blood in his eyes, he spent three days alone with his dead flying partner, waiting for rescue. He says he spent that time recounting to himself every story he had ever heard, and he attributes his survival to that link with life. It's hard to think of life in the Arctic without this very dark side. It must be part of what people think of when they say that times were tough in the old days. I've also noticed that stories tend to attribute the very worst actions to non-human beings – perhaps to distance those things that are most difficult to acknowledge in one's own kind. Some stories may be told one way or the other, depending on the situation – sometimes about a human and other times about a demon.

A woman living alone would have a particularly hard life and might be forced to desperate measures. Bee Woman, of course, was only masquerading as human and she seemed to kill for pleasure, living as she did outside the limits of normal human behaviour. The actions of humans have a resonance with, but are not directly parallel to, those of nonhumans. Kiviuq will meet more than one such being on his journey.

Shamanic Helping Spirits and Contests of Power

Δ Hearing the skull's warning, Kiviuq reached for his clothes on the drying rack, but the rack rose in the air, always out of reach. Although Bee Woman had gone outside, she was still aware of what was going on in her home. And she was still within earshot. Dodging the meat skewers, Kiviuq called out to her, "Come and get my clothes down!" She immediately taunted him in reply, "I put them up, you get them down!"

Human skill was not enough – the clothes were always out of reach – and he called his shamanic spirit helper. In Kivalliq Region people say this was a tiny bird, the snow bunting, who flew into the house and tossed his clothing down to him. Most important were his boots. Eli Kimaliadjuk and Samson Quinangnaq tell us that Kiviuq wore the bird as an amulet under his hood or on his hat. In Baffin people say Kiviuq called for his polar bear spirit, while in Kitikmeot we heard both one and the other. The contrast between the two helpers is dramatic – a tiny bird and the mightiest of animals – but it only proves that both have tremendous power.

Those who speak of the bear as Kiviuq's helping spirit say that the door was sealed shut, trapping him inside. Only when the bear appeared outside, growling fearsomely, did Bee Woman come back, open the door, and get the clothes down.

He rushed to shore with one boot only halfway on, parallel to the way Bee Woman stood with one foot in the water and one on land as she watched him leap into his kayak and push off. Δ

Bee Woman's words were a challenge to Kiviuq's shamanic power. Shamans worldwide are highly competitive with each other, and Bee

Woman, although non-human, engages Kiviuq on that level. Although such competition is a very serious matter in the spiritual world, it makes for good fun in storytelling.

There were only two exceptions to the regional division about whether the helping spirit was a snow bunting or a polar bear. Leo Nimialik of Chesterfield Inlet and Bernadette Patterk of Rankin Inlet both said the spirit was a polar bear, unlike others in Kivalliq Region. Leo is the grandson of a powerful shaman, the kind who could fly. He identifies the helping spirit specifically as Nanurluk, the spirit bear. Nanurluk is "a giant polar bear that lives in the ocean and is said to be bigger than large ships. An appreciated spirit helper of the *angakkuit*" (Aupilaarjuk et al. 2002, 67, 217).

I had my own experience with the power of the bear. Walking on the road at Chesterfield Inlet in the snow and moonlight, breathing deeply after a long day's recording, I felt strongly that someone was with me, a kind presence. I attributed this to the friendliness of the community, but local people told me that there is a polar bear who protects their village and that most likely that was the presence I felt.

Shamanic helping spirits, *tuurngait*, are quite different from the *ikajuqti* we have already encountered in the sandpiper. Although the elders who discussed this with us indicated that the *ikajuqti* was a personal spirit distinct from a shamanic helping spirit, other sources use the word for shamanic spirits as well (Saladin d'Anglure 2001, 247). But *tuurngait* and *ikajuqtit* (plural) are acquired differently. An *ikajuqti* can be bestowed on a person at birth or in childhood. *Tuurngait* come later. Anthropologist Bernard Saladin d'Anglure writes:

> The last phase of the apprenticeship was that of acquisition of *tuurngait*, i.e. helping spirits. Many such spirits would solicit an apprentice shaman if he had a brilliant *qaumaniq* [shaman's aura]. Caution, however, was needed before agreeing to enter into a relationship with them. It was better for an apprentice to wait for his mentor to offer to share one of his *tuurngait*. There were all kinds of *tuurngait*: *tarniit* [souls, described as bubbles] of deceased parents; great mythical figures; spirit masters of different animal species or of any entity belonging to space (such as heavenly bodies), the land world, or the sea world; spirits of lakes, mountains or rivers; and invisible spirits belonging to human-like groups. Some were composite in appearance, with chimerical forms. There

were also male and female spirits, giants and dwarves. (Saladin d'Anglure 2001, 33–4)[2]

Kiviuq had already acquired his helping spirits before we meet him, but we'll see one way the process works in his mutual courtship with the fox-wife, who may be a further helping spirit. One sign of evidence that Kiviuq has not died to this day is the fact that he has never appeared as anyone else's *tuurngaq*.[3]

Kiviuq managed to get out of Bee Woman's house, although the door shut abruptly behind him, cutting off the tails of his *atigi* (parka). Some say Bee Woman was standing outside the door with her *ulu* at the ready and that she cut the parka. This cutting of clothes reminds me of the seal-child, whose clothes were torn by the neighbours. Kiviuq himself later cut his wife's parka in anger after her visit to the penis in the lake. Kiviuq's clothing was cut again during his journey to find his goose-wife. Given the importance of arctic clothing, this may be a symbolic threat to life. I also wondered if it might explain a clothing style, and in fact that turned out to be the case. "The mountains crashed together, Kivioq narrowly escaped, losing only his parka's long back tail. That's how this style began," said Helen Poungat. This change took place only in the 1920s among the Paallirmiut, although they still use Kiviuq's story to explain it (Oakes 1987, 11). The incident Poungat alludes to happened while Kiviuq was pursuing his goose-wife. Similar images are the mussels that tried to bite the kayak (later in this chapter) and the door to the fox den that changed size as Kiviuq made his way in. I think that Bee Woman's standing with one foot on land and one in the water must have something to do with the clear separation between land and water in Inuit thought. It is forbidden, for example, to eat foods from land and sea together.

Δ Bee Woman wanted to keep Kiviuq. She even offered herself to him in marriage. "Come back, my husband, I won't harm you!" she called, in what Simon Tookoome calls an incantation.

She came out onto a point of land and threatened him with her *ulu*, slicing a boulder on shore. He responded in kind. "This is the way I would have sliced you," she called. "This is the way I would have speared you," he replied, spearing a nearby ice floe. Δ

This would be a marriage of power, but not one he was willing to accept. Both male and female shamans worldwide are known to marry in the spirit world – it's a good way of gaining helpers. But one must be very careful about which spirit beings to marry. Kiviuq sensed Bee Woman's dangerous deceit – she didn't want to marry him, she only wanted to have him for dinner. Another reminder to us that a shaman must be careful about helping spirits who are solicitous.

And so she became what Carlos Casteneda calls the worthy opponent – someone of sufficient power to give him a real challenge. Defeating her confirms his own power. The struggle contributed to his development and also served as a continuation of his shamanic initiation. Like Siberian shamans, he continually meets dangerous non-human beings, learns their tricks, and ultimately deals with them.

The contest on the water took the image of shamanic competition one further than the drying rack encounter – even their gestures were nearly enough to knock someone over. They threatened each other using an interesting verb tense. "This is the way I would have sliced you" shows her awareness that the moment of possibility was clearly past, as does his reply. Once Kiviuq was in his water element, Bee Woman had no power over him, whereas while on land he was in grave danger from her. Inuit storyteller Annie Peterloosie extends the contest for the greater pleasure of the listener by repeating her elaborate gestures. Udeghe storyteller Valentina Kyalundzyuga extends contests in exactly the same way when she has a receptive audience, adding rhythm and suspense to the telling. Gideon Qitsualik calls the contest a show of power.

Samson Quinangnaq says that Kiviuq speared the very ice that she had created. I kept my eye out for rocks on the shore that looked sliced but didn't see any that reminded me of this scene as I pictured it, with vertical slices. Perhaps the rocks she sliced were horizontally flat, like the shore where Kiviuq's mother waited – there are many of them on the eskers.

Acquisition of Shamanic Power

Going back to the way an Inuit shaman develops, I'd like to quote Bernard Saladin d'Anglure again: "Most shamanistic vocations began in adolescence and involved a training period under the supervision of one or more recognized shamans. The length of this apprenticeship varied from one Inuit group to the next, but it usually stretched over several winters. The first objective was initiation into the language of the spirits and into the conduct of rituals – both private and public. Then came the acquisition of clairvoyance, *qaumaniq*, which showed itself in a clear, brilliant aura visible to animals, spirits, and shamans. To acquire a strong *qaumaniq*, long periods of isolation and abstinence were needed. Some candidates never managed to acquire it. According to Aupilaarjuk, the shamans and *tuurngait* who committed bad actions had a very dark aura, *taarniq*" (Saladin d'Anglure 2001, 33).[4] Some shamans might acquire their gift spontaneously (Bennett and Rowley 2004, 177-8).

The third stage, the acquisition of helping spirits, is described above. Anthropologist Asen Balikci adds that novices joined an elder shaman's family and observed special rules. After a time, sleeping intermittently, they were sent to live in a special igloo, where they learned a secret vocabulary and necessary techniques. Novices received a ritual headdress and belt from their parents and spirits from the elder shaman (1970, 225). A person could also acquire shamanic power while wandering in the open air, as represented in the film *Atanarjuat*.

Shamans, as well as Celtic and other bards, commonly have a secret vocabulary. They devote much time to learning it and then engage in contests that make use of it (Matthews 2002, 211–36). Jeremy Narby calls attention to the similarity between coded shamanic languages and the "language" of our own DNA structure (Narby 1999, passim).

Siberian shamanic initiation is in many ways similar, as we'll see in the next chapter. Once initiated, shamans on both sides of the Bering Strait could journey through spiritual and physical realms to find information and effect healing. We frequently hear of Inuit journeys under the water to the realm of Nuliajuk, mother of the sea beasts, but *angakkuit* could also journey to the sky. A shaman's spiritual journey through the air is called *ilimmaqturniq*. Very powerful shamans can make such journeys to get information. People tie the shaman up very tightly with a rope and then he or she goes behind a screen. People can hear the shaman rising up. Once the shaman is in the upper world, the people up there play with the rope and it falls back to earth in a shape that can be read intuitively, just as certain clairvoyants read tea leaves. It is very hard for anyone to find the ends of the rope (Saladin d'Anglure 2001, 157–9).

An important lesson emphasized by the elders in this part of the story is that Kiviuq did not kill his enemies, but simply paddled away. This is how we must deal with trouble in life, they say. Killing an enemy involves too much dangerous emotion and can call up retribution from human relatives or from non-humans that are called up by animals or spirit beings. Whenever possible it is best to walk away from trouble rather than engaging with it. Once his power was established, Kiviuq paddled away. This "turning the other cheek" is strongly reminiscent of Christianity, but I believe it goes deep into ancient Inuit survival morality. High emotion can distract a person from life-threatening danger. Survival dictates correct action as well as concentration and self-control.

Creation

> Δ Bee Woman threw her *ulu* out over the water the way you would skip a rock. It sank and rose again, creating ice on the sea where it had never been before. Δ

This is one of several creation images in Kiviuq's legend. In real-life terms we can debate whether the Inuit moved from a place where the water did not freeze to one where it did, or whether Inuit oral memory goes to a time when the climate was warmer. In mythic terms the image is just one example of how story often seems to explain geographical and cultural phenomena, becoming an etiological story. Although such stories suggest something going back to the roots of creation, it is debatable whether such explanations always attest to a story's ancient roots. An explanation can easily be applied to an already existing feature, or it can be transferred to a similar one. One of the major features of the sacred landscape in Turkic cultures is a milk lake located high on a mountain. And in fact there are milky lakes located on mountains in Kirgizstan and Tuva, to name only two of a number of places that are considered to be the centre of the world. The milky whiteness of the water is caused by geological features. Still, taken with the testimony of elders and the fact that the Kiviuq story is told over the entire area of Inuit migration in the new world, the creation images heighten the sense that the story is ancient. And that may well be, for it seems probable that the story existed before the Inuit became geographically dispersed after leaving their former common home. More importantly, creation images like Bee Woman's underscore the fact that the story itself is one of the essential underpinnings of the Inuit world view. In the world of story, creation always happens "here and now."

Δ But now Kiviuq's kayak was stuck in the newly frozen ice. Celestin Erkidjuk told us that soon the ice would be strong enough to hold Bee Woman and she'd be able to get to him on foot. Kiviuq had been taught by his maternal aunt that if this ever happened he was to sing an incantation and strike the ice with his ring finger, pointing from his body outwards in the direction he wanted to go. He did as he had been instructed and the ice broke with a ringing sound. **Δ**

It's as if Bee Woman is creating an extension of her earth domain over his water domain. One Vancouver listener told me that Kiviuq's gesture reminded him of Moses parting the Red Sea. It worked and our hero paddled on.

Aupilaarjuk says Kiviuq used a tool to break the ice. The practicality of using a tool instead of an incantation reminds me of the way Udeghe storyteller Valentina Kyalundzyuga frequently emphasized the practical solutions found by her story's heroine. She did this not to downplay spiritual realities but to show that we must try to help ourselves before calling upon otherworldly support.

Hearing all these accounts daily, I began to wonder if Bee Woman could be another incarnation of the grandmother. At one point I thought she might have transformed herself in order to have another go at Kiviuq. As time passed, I began to think it more likely that Bee Woman was the grandmother's helping spirit. That could explain how the skulls got specifically to her house. But even those elders who say that much of the story has to do with the grandmother's revenge do not say that the bee was her helping spirit, so I had to abandon the idea. Bee Woman sets up the possibility of a connection between Kiviuq's adventures while away from home and the events that caused his journey. But it is just a possibility, and as so often happens with Inuit storytellers, we are left to reach our own conclusions.

In any case, the idea of that connection only works if you believe that the grandmother wanted to include Kiviuq in her revenge on the hunters. But Annie Peterloosie argues persuasively that the grandmother was helping Kiviuq all along – she spared him and him alone from dying in the storm. That made good sense to me. It went a long way to balancing the power between the grandmother and Kiviuq, as her power was now undiminished by his. She accomplished what she wanted, taking risks in order to protect her family and incidentally contributing to Kiviuq's ongoing initiation and growth by creating the storm and launching him on a great string of challenges. Looked at it that way, she appears as his teacher. Those who say she wanted revenge on Kiviuq may be taking a more patriarchal view, since in that interpretation she did not succeed in killing Kiviuq and his power proved to be greater than hers.

Theresa Kimaliadjuk is another who doesn't think the grandmother was taking revenge against Kiviuq. She says he overcame obstacles because he was so talented. Skilled people all encounter obstacles, she says, and so did he. It's as simple as that.

The logic most of us have been taught works in plain physical reality, while traditional story logic works in spiritual and story reality as well. Things can happen in the realm of spirit that simply don't happen in waking physical reality, and they make perfect sense, just as dreams do. I was amazed and pleased to learn that not only stories but also the ancient Inuit approach to law recognized that no system of problem resolution could be complete that did not include spirits and animals just as much as people. Kiviuq could not have moved on without dealing with Bee Woman and other dangers from the animal and spirit worlds. He must not only defend himself, but must also perform acts of kindness in order to complete his journey home.

Giving Help

Story heroes help those in need and receive aid themselves at key moments – an essential exchange. Kiviuq tried to help the grandmother and child and then the men drowning at sea. Now he came upon two smaller beings asking for help, which he offered readily. Annie Peterloosie says these incidents were like puzzles sent by Bee Woman, who wanted to see him fail. For story listeners, these tests reveal the hero's character.

> ∆ He paddled along and suddenly felt he was getting nowhere. A voice called out from the shore, "Help me! Help me to clean this dirt out of my eye!" Kiviuq went up onshore and saw no one. Finally, looking at ground level, he saw a small seal bone – the one that is called the "dog" in a game played by children. ∆

Who hasn't felt that frustration of working and getting nowhere? It must be a feeling well known to the Inuit. They describe a certain being that creates in a person the sense of making effort but without being able to move, just as Kiviuq is unable to move until he helps the lemming and seal bone. "*Ijirait* and other spirits of the land, *nunamiutait*, were often considered the cause of *taulittuq*. *Taulittuq* is the experience of moving but without the sense of getting any closer to one's destination" (Bennett and Rowley 2004, 155).

Philip Paniaq explained the bone game to me. Players reach into a bag with a loop to get small bones out and then build their own little camps – dogs, houses, sleds, etc. The dog bone can also be used for divination, to answer "yes/no" questions, so it might be connected to shamanic practices. In Siberia I had learned that children's games and toys often have their source in shamanic equipment or activities. No matter what the connection is, there are parallels in everyday modern life. Stuffed animals and dolls are really alive for children and give them comfort, just as the spirit figures are helpful to shamans. Objects that have received much loving attention seem to be able to give energy back.

One of Kiviuq's great qualities as a hunter is being observant – nothing escapes him. Many of us would have looked around at eye level and above and thus missed the thing we needed to see, on the ground at our feet. Not Kiviuq. John and I were much impressed by this, but when we asked the elders about what set Kiviuq apart, citing observance as a possible quality, most of them answered politely that it could be, but that what really impressed them was his kindness to the orphan. It seems to me now that being observant is such an essential part of being a good hunter that nobody would think of naming it. A hunter who is not observant will not survive.

Δ Using grasses, Kiviuq cleared a small hole called the "dog's eye," and was then able to paddle on. Perhaps clearing that eye made it possible for him to see the way forward, or perhaps he was simply obeying a request for help, so simple to give in this case and so useful to the one in need. Once again we see Kiviuq being kind to those weaker than himself.

Pretty soon it happened again – he paddled but couldn't move forward. A voice called out, "Come up here onshore and help me climb this cliff!" He went up onshore and saw no one, and no cliff – just a small sandbank. A tiny lemming was trying to climb up the sandbank, working hard to no avail. Annie Peterloosie and others say it was running from the tide. One elder pointed out that it could have gone around, and we laughed that it just had to do things the hard way! Kiviuq held the lemming affectionately in his palm and helped it up the bank. Now he was able to paddle on. Δ

Lemmings

Affection for animals seems to come naturally to the Inuit, whose very existence is so dependent on them. Evaluardjuk and others are more horrified by the mistreatment of animals they see today than by almost anything else. In fact it's one of the main reasons they believe this story is still so important.

A lemming returns to play an important role later in the story. Kiviuq will burn the lemming that comes from his wife's body after she dies, and some say that it is the same lemming who reproaches him when he arrives at the fox-wife's den. Why does such a small animal play such an

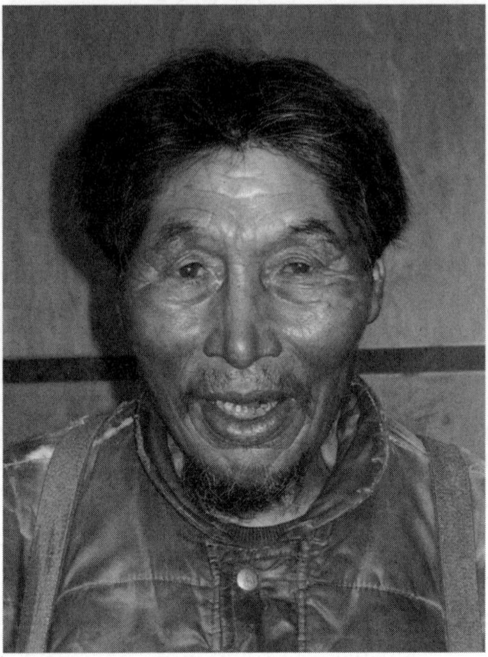

Storyteller Herve Paniaq

important role? It's like that in nature too. Lemmings lead a cycle of explosions and decline in population all the way up the food chain.

Lemmings are small mouse-like rodents. They control the rhythm of animal life on the tundra because they are an important food for ermines, arctic foxes, snowy owls, gyrfalcons, and jaegers. They remain active throughout the arctic winter without hibernating or freezing to death, living in the ridges produced by seasonal freezing and thawing and travelling in the depressions. They survive the cold by foraging in the relatively warmer space that forms between soil and snow, known as subnivean space, almost never appearing on the surface. In the High Arctic this "warmth" can be around -25°C.

Lemmings can reproduce within weeks of birth and have roughly four-year cycles of drastically fluctuating population. They peak with huge numbers and then crash, coming closer to extinction than any other animal. Those that survive are particularly strong, ensuring that the species continues and can adapt to change. Several animals that depend on lemmings for food have related cycles. Foxes produce few, if any, surviving young except during "lemming years" – when the numbers of lemmings peak. Inuit don't eat lemmings, but some animals they depend on do. There is much debate about what causes the lemming cycle. Is it ruled by change in vegetation, predators, or the length of the winter? It is difficult to distinguish cause and effect.

There are two main types of lemming in Nunavut, the brown lemming and the collared lemming. In summer the gentle collared lemmings, which live further north, use higher and drier sites. The more aggressive brown lemmings, which live down in the treed areas, use lower and wetter ones. By helping the lemming up the bank, Kiviuq may have played an important role in getting the animal home to its preferred habitat.

One of the Inuit names for the collared lemming is *kilangmiutak*, "one who comes from the sky." They give this impression, scientists believe, because after a winter when they have reproduced in great numbers, they suddenly all appear when the snow melts. These are the lemmings sometimes used by shamans as a source of supernatural powers. Rasmussen was told that "[b]ecause they fall from the sky they possess an altogether peculiar knowledge of the diseases of mankind and the causes of death" (Rasmussen 1929, 112). Philip Paniaq thinks the idea that lemmings fall from the sky is based on a certain atmospheric condition that creates an illusion of falling lemmings in the sky itself.

Danish ethnologist Birgitte Sonne tells me that lemmings were strong helping spirits of Inuit shamans. In some stories shamans use them as strong amulets that, like the maggots we will encounter in the episode with the penis in the lake, can bore their way through the inside of the body from anus to mouth, causing the enemy's death. Sonne thinks the association came about because of the way lemmings dig tunnels through earth and snow. This opening through the middle of the body will appear in Kiviuq's meeting with the Fishmaker, who is also open from anus to mouth. He uses that tunnel to bring fish to life from his wood carvings.

There is a well-known legend about lemmings committing mass suicide by throwing themselves into the sea. The legend, however, turns out to have no relation to reality. Where did it come from? Mainly from a

Disney movie of 1958, *True-Life Adventures – White Wilderness*. The lemming debacle in the film was not filmed where lemmings live, and the whole suicide idea has little basis in fact, virtually none in Canada. In Norway, lemmings do tend to move downhill and are funnelled into valleys. A large number eventually reach the sea or a large lake. They may go out onto the ice and jump into the water, but that doesn't amount to a mass suicide for the purpose of population control.[5]

The Irontail Spider Woman – More Death and Rebirth

Δ We now come to a place that is told in more than one way. Some say Kiviuq came to a second sod house – this one open on top with just the walls standing. He climbed up and looked down into the house. Inside he saw a woman cleaning a human skin, a boiling pot with chunks of human meat in front of her. Zippora Innuksuk told us that there were people hanging upside down in the house and that the woman was eating what came from their noses.

Kiviuq spat on her head, or some say onto the skin, to get her attention. The first time he spat she didn't notice him so he spat again. She said to herself, "This place has never dripped before and now it's dripping. It wasn't raining and now it's raining." She tried to look up but her big eyelids flopped down over her eyes, preventing her from seeing. With no hesitation she took her *ulu* and cut her eyelids off! Some say she tossed them into the cooking pot and others that she popped them into her mouth. Everyone who told this part made creepy gestures showing how she cut the eyelids, and Bernadette Uttaq even showed us that by making a slit in the eyelid the woman now appeared to have double eyes as she gazed at Kiviuq. This woman was a spider temporarily living in human form. Δ

A number of elders tell the story of the woman who cooks human meat and cuts off her own eyelids about Bee Woman, repeating those images when telling of the spider. Others truncate the story of Bee Woman and the story of the irontailed spider into one, as I do myself. Herve Paniaq says the difference between them is regional, although I haven't been able to trace that. We heard one person tell the two together, seven told them separately, and eleven told one or the other, with no particular regional pattern.

It is well known both in Siberia and among the Inuit that a smokehole is one of the main entranceways that a shaman uses to pass from our world to the upper world, just as the wet spot in the house, or the hearth in Siberia, is the entranceway to the lower world. Kiviuq's looking down on the fire is a reminder of this entry point, hinting that once again he is entering a strange world or state of consciousness.

Like Bee Woman, the spider woman is surrounded by the evidence of cannibalism – and she disgusts us even further by eating her own eyelids. In one fragmentary story associated with Kiviuq, a woman cut off pieces of her own cheeks and put them in the pot to replace meat she had eaten while cooking (Rasmussen 1930b, 111). Certainly the line between life and death is a fine one if a person considers eating her own flesh or offering it to her family to cover the fact that she has been taking more than her share.

Δ Kiviuq was so terrified by her appearance that he fainted and fell to the ground. Elder Felix Kopak, who told us it was Bee Woman who cut off her eyelids, said that Kiviuq died at that point and slept all the way through the winter until she brought him back to life in the spring. Celestin Erkidjuk says she used an incantation, "*Inunguna*. It's a person." Kopak adds, "Here is a person who died of terror. Wake up!" Δ

It's very possible that naming Kiviuq as a human was a significant step in Bee Woman's or the spider woman's gaining control over him. Some elders say he died when he first arrived on shore and lay dead through the winter, whereas others say he died when he fell off the house wall and, again, lay dead through the winter. In either case his death was obviously the work of the non-human woman.

This is the first of several places that Kiviuq dies and is reborn in this journey. It brings into focus the image of initiatory death and rebirth, which plays a major role in most shamanic traditions. Siberian shamans of the past often described being taken apart, bone by bone. The spirits would boil the bones, eat the flesh, and then count the bones. In some cultures they defecated the initiate out. An extra bone indicated shamanic destiny. If the person had that fate, he or she would be put back together and reanimated – if not, they would die. That would be the view from the inside. To an observer, it might appear that the person did nothing but sleep. Kiviuq's long sleep on the shore, as well as his fainting, is strongly reminiscent of shamanic death.

Rasmussen wrote: "In sleep the soul turns upside down, soul head downwards. It clings to the body by the big toe. Sleep and death are connected because of this frail bond" (1929, 93). He also learned that new Inuit shamans had to be able to see themselves as skeletons, divest themselves of blood and flesh, and name all the parts in shamanic language. They then consecrated themselves through the most lasting part of the body – the bones (1929, 114).

Felix Kopak, who some say was a shaman himself, told us he would like to see the story told, but not the shamanistic parts. He didn't specify which parts those were, but said that if young people learn shamanistic rites and become strong they might die young. In spite of that, he had no hesitation about telling all of Kiviuq's story to people of all ages.

As we read the ethnographic versions of Kiviuq's life, we often heard that Kiviuq lived many lives. What made this different from the usual reincarnation was that he always picked up at the age he had left off, rather than starting over as a baby. In the words of Kuvdluitsoq, "It is said that Kivioq has had many lives and that he is now at last living his last one. Formerly when he came to the end of a life he fell into a deathlike sleep, and when he awoke out of it he began a new life. But this did not mean that he began every time as a young man; he continued his age and become older and older" (Rasmussen 1931, 376). Ollie Ittinuar has heard elders say that some animals grow older and then go back to youth, some adding that Kiviuq does too. He himself has thought that Kiviuq might be alive, getting older and younger. In other stories a shaman who dies becomes a helping spirit of a younger one. The fact that we haven't heard of Kiviuq doing so might indicate he's alive. There are also stories of shamans who change to animals between human lives, as did Maqo. If Kiviuq was still in this world in human form, Ollie feels that someone would have recognized him, although if he was in animal form it would be more difficult.

We ask other elders about this. Henry Evaluardjuk says, "It was so long ago. We don't know what constituted a life in those days." Gideon Qitsualik says, "I think there were many Kiviuqs. After all, there are many stories. Some of the stories probably just got attached to his name. He would have had many sets of parents." Most elders are inclined to think of Kiviuq as having one very long life, one perhaps even continuing to the present day. If we were to think of Kiviuq as having several lives, the sleep on the shore and the fainting on the roof would be the kind of places where one life ended and another began.

Δ When the story of the spider woman is told separately from that of Bee Woman, the spider woman offered Kiviuq a place to sleep, but he, cautious by now and hearing a warning voice, only pretended to sleep and soon heard the sound of a tool being sharpened. Discreetly opening his eyes, he saw the woman sharpening a long tail of iron. Henry Isluanik says that the tails only turn to metal when the spiders want to kill someone. This is interesting in light of the fact that while spiders don't have actual tails, some have poisonous fangs. Gideon Qitsualik says that the woman had a tailbone like ours except it grew outside her body. In some versions there were two women in the house who welcomed Kiviuq in. In versions recorded long ago, he heard them discuss which parts of him they wished to eat – the younger one wanted the genitals.[6]

Kiviuq pretended to awaken and went outside for a moment. Resourceful as ever, he picked up a flat rock, the kind used as flooring, and put it under his shirt before lying back down. Now the woman – sometimes named Irontail – got up over him and tried to skewer him with her tail, but it bent painfully as it hit the flat rock and injured her knee. Some say the iron tail went right up into her body and killed her. Kiviuq got back in his kayak and paddled away, leaving her howling in pain. Δ

I see many images in Kiviuq's journey that reverse the normal, and surely a female spearing a male with her phallic-shaped tail is one of them. Perhaps the reversal is another indication that he was dealing with non-humans, that things were not as they should be. Many Siberians believe that in the land of the dead everything is the opposite of the way it is here – winter becomes summer, things that are broken become whole. Inuit also say the seasons are reversed in the land of the dead. Since Kiviuq met so many seasonal reversals and changes, it is possible that he was travelling in that realm.

Annie Peterloosie gives us a different view, explaining that "irontails" are a kind of parasite that lives in standing water. They have stiff tails and no legs. If the tail lodges in your body, it will kill you. Some of the people at her telling recall straining water through snow to get rid of parasites before drinking the water. Thus Kiviuq encountered the dangers of insects – again showing his understanding of microcosm as well as macrocosm.

Helpers and Obstacles

Δ As he paddled further he came to two *inuksuut*. One *inuksuk* called to him, saying, "Watch out! There are mussels behind you. They will bite your kayak."

He looked and, sure enough, two mussels were trying to bite at the back of his kayak. They now sank into the water, realizing they couldn't get him after all. One of them said, "Kubluroq is lying," as a kind of incantation. It seems that Kubluroq was the *inuksuk* who had spoken, but his words had turned into a lie, since the mussels would not be able to get Kiviuq. Margaret Nakashook says the *inuksuk* was one of Kiviuq's helping spirits. It counteracted the mussels, which had been sent by Bee Woman because she couldn't come after him on the water herself. Many years ago Kuvdluitsoq said the mussels were her helping spirits (Rasmussen 1931, 368).

Kiviuq came up onshore again and climbed a hill to explore, and when he looked back, he saw two grizzly bears fighting beside his kayak. They were rushing towards each other and he realized they would destroy his kayak when they met, so he ran back down the hill. As he approached them, they disappeared. Gideon Qitsualik says they were the grandmother's *tuurngait*.

Giant caterpillars worked a similar way: they came running on their hairy legs to steal his kayak. Kuvdluitsoq said they too were

Bee Woman's helping spirits (Rasmussen 1931, 367–8). But Kiviuq outran them, reached his kayak, and escaped out to sea. There were other obstacles as well. Samson Quinangnaq tells of snakes and Bernadette Uttaq tells of a long thin flame that appeared between Kiviuq and his kayak. Joanasie Macpa says the sandpipers towed the kayak between Kiviuq's adventures. ∆

Most of these adventures are told by many people, some more often in one region than another. Nearly all told of Bee Woman and Irontail. The *inuksuit*, the bone, and the lemming become more prominent in Baffin Island. Other things are told by only a few, including the parts about the grizzly bears and the caterpillars. Still, we heard of the fighting grizzlies even in areas like Baffin Island where the bears do not live, which suggests that this part of the story travelled there when people moved from a more southerly region. And some parts of the story are only told by one person.

Dangerous Tiny Knives

∆ Henry Evaluardjuk says that after the storm at sea Kiviuq came ashore on an island where many people were living. His brother, who was still alive in Henry's telling, wanted to trade his knife for some new *kamiks*. The brother was attacked, cut up, and eaten. The attackers used tiny knives.

Kiviuq was now in the gathering house where the men came for games and celebrations. One man approached him from the shore and he killed that man. He took out the man's eyes, left them dangling, and put the man's testicles around his own neck and the penis on his hood. This cruelty was justifiable revenge in Inuit terms because these men had killed Kiviuq's brother. But he could expect retaliation.

Kiviuq killed two men, and a third rushed back to the community to raise the troops. Kiviuq took off with all the men after him. Someone called after him, saying, "Non-humans can be vindictive." Later on, after Kiviuq's arrival home, these small beings came and attacked. Kiviuq warned his people to make arrows and they defeated the enemy. Little waves formed on the water as they disappeared. ∆

Their weapons are a hint that the attackers may be *tuurngait*, who often use tiny knives made either of antler or of bones taken from graves. In conversation with other elders in 2000, Felix Pisuk described the tiny knives and said that shamans sometimes wear them on their clothing as gifts for their helping spirits (Aupilaarjuk et al. 2002, 27–9). This story may tie in with the small spider beings called *nigjuarjuit* who took revenge on Kiviuq for taking the beads from the tiny spiders, a story we'll come to in the "Wolf Women, Tiny Spiders, and Homecoming" chapter. Since any animal or even insect can become a *tuurngaq*, this is entirely possible.

Tuutaliit

∆ Now Evaluardjuk says that Kiviuq came to the *tuutaliit*, who were human on top and fish on the lower half of their bodies, instead of half seal, as described at the beginning of the story by Aupilaarjuk. They had what Evaluardjuk describes as a bowl haircut. The women wore big necklaces, although he doesn't know why. Goaded by their father, some young *tuutaliit* came into the water and teased Kiviuq, who speared one of them with a trident. The ocean turned red. The others told Kiviuq to stay for three days, because after that time a dead *tuutalik* comes back to life, smiling. Kiviuq waited and, sure enough, the *tuutalik* came back and returned his trident to him.

Other elders tell of *tuutaliit* sporting around Kiviuq's kayak, daring him to spear one of them, but only Henry tells of the one who came back to life. ∆

The fact that such beings can readily return is part and parcel of ancient Inuit thought, but the term of three days suggests to me a Christian influence, especially as the number three does not figure as importantly in Inuit culture as it does in many others. Such a detail could have been adopted unconsciously.[7] It seems sad to me that Henry recalls the images of haircuts and necklaces without any sense of their meaning, although this does show that pictures stay with us more easily than explanations.

I wonder if these *tuutaliit* had any relationship to Tuutalik, the father of the seal-child, who was half human and half seal. Did they have some spiritual connection to Kiviuq? Why did they wish to be speared – was it only to prove that they could come back to life so easily? This could be a lesson for Kiviuq, about the way life always returns. Death and rebirth are central to this section and the *tuutaliit* provide a microcosm of Kiviuq's own experience.

Poisoned Food

Δ Another episode told by only one person was the one about poisoned food we heard from Madeleine Ivalu. Kiviuq came to a place where unknown people were living. Someone came to him and said, "My grandmother has made some delicious *allu*," identified by Madeleine as mixed brain of human and wolf. He went to eat. But knowing the food was poisoned, he swallowed and recycled it through his body into a bowl which he had turned upside down on his outstretched legs. He told the old woman stories to distract her. "After all, he is a shaman and that is why the food didn't kill him and why the food stayed in the bowl even upside down," said Madeleine. Then he turned the bowl right side up and it was full again. He gave it back to the old woman and her own food killed her just as evil thoughts and actions always turn back on the one who thinks and does them. Δ

Philip told me that a good shaman can kill a bad one by turning back his or her *tuurngaq*. It is safer for good shamans to do this rather than use their own spirits. Clearly *tuurngait* sometimes act independently, not under the instructions of a shaman. As Asen Balikci learned among the Netsilik in the mid-twentieth century, "When a shaman dispatched one of his spirits on an aggressive mission and the *tunraq* [alternate spelling] failed to achieve its task, it became a 'reversed spirit' or *tunraqkigdloretto*, a bloodthirsty being, blinded by frustration, totally out of control, who generally turned against his master and relatives and brought sickness and death into their camp. Under these circumstances, other shamans had to intervene and with their more powerful *tunraqs* harness the *kigdloretto*" (1970, 226).

Siberian storytellers often tell of similar clever ways a person manages to avoid taking poison – we'll see more about this in the "Bee Cousins" chapter.

Ordering the Anecdotes

I've placed the stories in this book in a particular order, following the practice of the majority of elders but certainly not all of them. Within the journey that starts with the storm at sea there is a lot of variation. Although most start with Bee Woman or Irontail, a few begin with the *inuksuit*. As I've noted above, some combine features of Bee Woman and Irontail into one episode, while others repeat the business of looking down into the sod house, with the Irontail episode coming right after Bee Woman's. Henry Isluanik and Elizabeth Tunniq tell the story of the two women and the log of wood (which we'll meet soon in the "Wolf Women, Tiny Spiders, and Homecoming" chapter) before the Bee Woman story. For Henry Evaluardjuk, the episode with the tiny knife people comes first after the storm, and Madeleine Ivalu's poisoned food episode comes after the Irontail story. Shorter episodes, such as the ones about the fighting grizzly bears and the caterpillars, can appear in various places.

The order seems to be a more individual than regional matter. I have a feeling that the rationale of any given order has to do with the lessons a certain family wishes to impart, and the elders are as precise as they can be in remembering it. Although most tellers are certain about their order, some got mixed up, and even wound up with a couple of episodes left over, uncertain about where they fit. Precision in every aspect of storytelling is very important to the elders. They would get upset with themselves for making a mistake in the order in which animals offered themselves to Kiviuq in the fox story, or for forgetting exactly what household implement was in use at a given point. It seems to me that the uncertainty about the order of episodes means that they could be told in various orders after all.[8]

Kiviuq entered another realm when he got lost in the storm, and he had many adventures. Some think he may even have been in the land of the dead. He passed through water and met many non-humans. He seems to have died and been reborn at least once on this journey. And there are more adventures to come. As we finish this chapter, Kiviuq is still paddling away from dangers, trying to find his way home. His Siberian cousins had many similar experiences.

Bee Cousins

Aaai – Basini bagdiani yegdyghe! Long ago a hero lived …

– Udeghe story opening

As I listened to Inuit elders telling Kiviuq's tale, I often thought of Udeghe storytellers I'd met in the Russian Far East. They seemed to have the same gentle humour, the same practicality, and even a similar way of using language – elongating vowel sounds, preserving ancient forms no longer in everyday use. Today, fewer Siberian people than Inuit speak their native language, but those who do speak it still use the ancient language in storytelling.

One of my favourite Udeghe storytellers was fondly called "Auntie Dusia," although her real name was Evdokia Batovna Kimonko. She was a relative by marriage of Valentina Kyalundzyuga, who told several stories in this book. Over two years she told me several of the most ancient Udeghe stories – including tales of her people's origins in the marriage of a girl with a bear and her brother with a tiger – all delivered with a sly sense of humour. She made divinations for me and my companion and sang traditional songs while working at her kitchen table. She stuck a knife in the threshold of her home at night to prevent evil from crossing her door. The last time we saw each other was in 1995. As we sat by the communal firewood pile waiting for my ride back to the city, Auntie Dusia looked me straight in the eye and said, "This is the last time we will see each other in this life." Never had anyone spoken to me so directly of life and death – I was momentarily speechless. Riding away I wondered if she would prove to be right. The following year

Udeghe storyteller Evdokia Batovna Kimonko, fondly known as "Auntie Dusia"

I came back to her village and asked about her. "She's still alive," my friend replied. "Perhaps she was wrong," I thought hopefully. But then my friend went on to explain that Dusia was so unwell that only her closest relatives could visit her. By my next visit she was gone. She had seen truly.

I think of Auntie Dusia as I work on books and storytelling here at home, wondering when I'll see those Inuit elders again. At this point, a number of the forty elders we met with are no longer with us – at least in the bodies they inhabited in 2004. Inuit souls are said to reincarnate quickly into new bodies.

As in the story of the man who married a seal,[1] Udeghe and other Tungus-language peoples often sing conversations, particularly those that cross worlds – between spirits or animals and humans. Musical sound is the language that spirit beings understand best. Storytellers also use what today seem to be nonsense syllables at the ends of lines – words with no known meaning that are personal to each teller. The word, which repeats throughout a given story, adds rhythmic unity to the telling. Some native scholars have linked these syllables to shamanic poetry. As in story, the poems contain words that belong to particular shamans, who may be the only ones to know their meaning. In both cultures, shamanic language has far more words that elaborate worlds of spirit than ordinary language does. To my knowledge, Inuit storytellers do not use such words, although some of them reminded me of the Udeghe women in their intonation.

Some Siberian peoples have a variety of concepts about both the soul and reincarnation, much as the Inuit do. Others speak of a variety of souls but not of any form of reincarnation. There may be up to seven parts of the soul, which generally include the life force, which operates on a spiritual level, and the breath, which animates the body. Some people say that reason is a part of the soul. Certain parts of the soul always stay with the body, whereas other parts can leave temporarily during sleep and permanently at death – the latter is the soul that may reincarnate. Parts of the soul can reside in bones and also in hair, which explains how people can take control of an unsuspecting adversary by running their hands through the victim's hair. Lice picking is a common excuse to get one's hands in someone's hair, as it is for the mother we'll meet later in Kiviuq's journey.

Shamans have a particular kind of soul, different from those of non-shamans, and they can relate to each other on that level. Whole peoples can have a collective soul. Sometimes the clan soul resides in a certain kind of tree, which members of that clan are forbidden to cut. This rule has a powerful ecological effect. If every clan is forbidden to cut one kind of tree, overcutting of the whole forest will be less likely to happen. There was probably a similar rule for the Yupik whale hunters, one that would be explained by the talisman the mother put on her whale child in the story of the woman and the whale in the "Seal Cousins" chapter.

Death and Rebirth

Bee Woman is a powerful image of death and rebirth. Many world cultures link the two in one female character. The Udeghe tell of the nameless wife of old man Kanda Mafa. She is simultaneously goddess of the earth and a cannibal like her husband, who is identified with the powerful bear. Storyteller Valentina Kyalundzyuga tells of an eldest sister who had been providing for her younger sisters. When she could no longer find animals for food, she became a cannibal and attacked strangers. She developed a taste for human meat. The sisters, not knowing what was disturbing her, tried their best to cheer her up, but at last they noticed that the inside of her mouth was dark from human hair. I was amazed to learn that Inuit also identify those who have eaten human flesh by the darkness inside their mouths. The sisters realized what had happened, and one day when the eldest sister was away, they took off on skis to get away from her. But soon she began to catch up to them, calling out to her sisters' ski straps to break. One by one she killed them all until only the youngest was left. But the youngest sister received help from the able hunter Yegdyghe, who carried her across the lake to his home. The cannibal sister arrived, messy hair streaming out behind her, but she was slowed down by her huge belly, which had formed because she ate humans. Yegdyghe pretended to help her across the lake, but rocked the boat until she fell in.[2] That cannibal sister turned into swamp plants and hummocks, which continue to claim the lives of unwary hunters to this day, while the youngest sister married the fine hunter (Van Deusen 2001, 138–40).

There are times when stories defuse tensions around difficult issues such as cannibalism. Although I know very few Siberian stories about eating human flesh, quite a few show up issues of spousal abuse and its solutions. From a Yupik tale showing how a wife can calm an angry husband to numerous Amur tales about the supernatural help that a severely beaten wife receives, a whole array of healing appears in story.

Games, Toys, and Bones – Life Skills and Shamanic Skills

As Kiviuq moved away from Bee Woman and helped the seal bone, I was reminded of Siberian games and the way they help children learn to function in adult society. Games also give support in difficult times, even connecting a child with spirit helpers. In the Amur region, a girl's dolls teach her practical lessons on caring for babies and making clothes. And the dolls are made in the same way as the shamans' spirit figures except that the toys have no eyes. Adding eyes would bring the figures fully to life and thus make them inappropriate for children's play.

Bones are used for games and shamanic divination in the Turkic Siberian world as they are in the Inuit. Children use sheep knucklebones in a game similar to jacks, and shamans use them together with stones to divine causes of illness. I have heard that the bone carries information about the animal's owner and can pass that information on to the shaman. The cracks in a shoulderblade bone charred in a fire pass information in the same way. This passing of genetic information is reflected in the words of a Tuvan heroine as she faces down her opponent, "The blood of a khan is in me and the bones" (Van Deusen 2000, 21).

Divination is one of a shaman's many skills. Healing and calling animals to the hunt are two among others. Bee Woman has engaged in a typical shamanic competition with Kiviuq, one that resonates strongly with Siberian shamanism in imagery of death and rebirth as well as in the introduction of the importance of bones. We have looked at the way Inuit become shamans. For Siberian shamans the process is similar.

It usually begins with an illness that cannot be diagnosed or cured by anyone other than a shaman. Sometimes novices spend time alone in the wilderness, where they are impervious to cold. During the course of their healing, they struggle with dangerous spirits who, once calmed, become their helping spirits. Sometimes this involves marriage in the spirit world. As the novice regains health, he or she gains the ability and strength to practise shamanism and is consecrated by an elder shaman, thus gaining recognition in the community. This phase often involves tests of clairvoyance and other abilities. In some areas the phase between the initiation by spirits and the consecration by humans includes a period during which an elder shaman teaches initiates the language involved in shamanic practice, acquaints them with various spirits and pathways in the spiritual world, and shows them how to conduct rituals. This phase can last as little as seven days. The degree of teaching involved in becoming a shaman varies significantly from one area to another, but the important stages in becoming a shaman are similar on both sides of the Bering Strait.

One of my favourite Siberian stories combines themes that are also apparent in Kiviuq's life, including shamanic competition and attempted cannibalism. It even contains an episode involving poisoned food, much like the story Madeleine Ivalu told us in Igloolik. The first time I visited an Udeghe village it was the end of summer – gardens were full of vegetables and hives full of fresh honey. I listened to storyteller Valentina Kyalundzyuga tell this tale, which involves cannibals attempting to poison the hero. As he foiled their plot by putting the poisoned food down a hollow reed held under his shirt, I filled up on pan bread with delicious fresh honey, little guessing that years later this story would connect in my mind with one about a giant Inuit bee.

Yegdyghe's use of the reed is reminiscent of a number of Turkic stories in which the heroine knows she is going to be either poisoned or forced to drink too much alcohol. She is rescued by her horse, who tells her to attach a thread between them. The poison follows the thread and the horse becomes ill. Since the animal is physically stronger than the human, both survive.

Elements of the story of "Yegdyghe and the Bones" arise again and again as I reflect on Kiviuq's life The hero's sister bestowed gifts, just as Kiviuq's grandmother bestowed gifts on him. The Udeghe hero was advised to listen carefully, much as Kiviuq is later advised by the Fishmaker. Like Kiviuq, Yegdyghe foiled attempts to stab him, created landforms by throwing objects out behind him, met cannibal beings, and engaged in shamanic competition. He even searched for a wife in ways that mirrored Kiviuq's pursuit of his animal wives.

In other Udeghe stories we meet helpfulness along the way that is reminiscent of Kiviuq's helping the bone and lemming. The singing style is similar. In the Udeghe shamanic rite of accompanying the dead, a tunnel appears through the earth, reminding me very much of Kiviuq's journey to find his goose-wife. Many of these motifs appear in the stories and rituals of other cultures as well, but I feel the connection most strongly with the Udeghe and the south Siberian Turks. This could simply be because of my personal affinity for these particular peoples.

Yegdyghe and the Bones[3]

A sister lived alone with her brother. He hunted, bringing back fish and meat, while she prepared skins and made clothing, boots, and food.

One morning the sister woke up, took up her drum, and began to sing. She must have had a dream. She said to her brother, "You will go out. On the way you'll find a dead owl. Take it with you. Farther along you'll find a dead rabbit. Take that too. And go on. You'll hear some people. Hide and listen to find out who is going by. Then you'll see how to act."

And so she played her drum and told her brother Yegdyghe what she had seen. He got ready and set out. Before he left, she gave him half of her comb and half of her sharpening stone, and he put them in his hunting bag. True, on the way he found a dead owl. He took it in his bag and went on. And then he found the dead rabbit, put it in his bag, and went on.

It was quiet in the taiga. Suddenly he heard someone driving, making a sound. Chok chok chok chok! He got up into a tree that was helpfully bending down and looked to see who would appear. He saw old man Kanda Mafa and his wife sitting on a sleigh pulled by wild boars. They were driving along, chok chok chok chok. They passed by without noticing Yegdyghe.

He waited and heard someone else coming. It was Emenda, the elder daughter of Kanda Mafa and his wife. Female wild boars were pulling her. She passed by without noticing him.

He thought he could come down now, but then … He could barely see her, all bent over. She could just barely pull the sleigh, she had no dogs or anything. He sat and watched. It was Belye, the younger daughter. She went by without looking at him, just pulling the sleigh, tired and bent over.

He saw that the sleigh was full of bones. Why bones, he wondered?

He jumped down from the tree, took his stick and hooked it on to the end of the sleigh so that it stopped. The girl pulled and pulled and couldn't move it. She turned around and said, "What's going on here? Why can't I move this sleigh?"

Now she saw Yegdyghe holding on with his stick. He threw the bones out of the sleigh.

"What are these bones for?" he asked.

"My parents eat human meat," she said. "If they don't find anyone, they make soup from the bones."

"I want to come with you."

"You can't do that," she said. "They'll kill you."

"We'll see about that!"

So they went on, and he helped her pull the sleigh.

When they stopped for the night, Belye make camp further from her parents than usual. They made a hut of fir branches and got a fire going.

Then Emenda came running, all ragged and uncombed. She saw Yegdyghe and her face changed; she turned red, she turned white.

She ran home and called to her parents. "Mother, father, Belye has a man there with her, and he's so good-looking! He's big and healthy. We'll have a feast!"

They were all happy there would be something to eat.

"I'll wait 'til he goes to sleep," said Kanda Mafa. And so they boiled up some bones to make broth.

When it was time to go to sleep, Belye put the dead owl beside her, and Yegdyghe lay at her feet. In the night Kanda Mafa came with his spear and whispered, "Belye, Belye, where is Yegdyghe?"

"He's next to me, next to me," she replied.

The old man struck with his spear, and heard the satisfying crunch of bones. Yegdyghe moaned in a dying voice. The old man didn't realize it was the owl he had struck, and he went away well satisfied.

Next morning Emenda came running, looking for meat, eager for breakfast. She saw Yegdyghe sitting beside the fire, smoking his pipe. She turned red, she turned white! She ran back to her parents.

"Father father, he's still alive, sitting by the fire smoking his pipe!"

"That's odd," said the father. "But never mind, tonight I will get him for sure."

Night came and Yegdyghe asked, "How else will he try to kill me?"

"Tonight he will come with a heated spear."

That night he lay beside her and they placed the dead rabbit at her feet. In the night the old man came and whispered, "Where is Yegdyghe?"

"He's at my feet."

He struck with his spear and there was a sound of crunching bones and the smell of cooking meat. Yegdyghe moaned in a dying voice. The old man went away well satisfied and the next morning Emenda came running again. And there was Yegdyghe, sitting by the fire, smoking his pipe.

She ran back to her parents. "Father, he is still alive."

"How can that be?" said Kanda Mafa. "I heard the bones break, I smelled the meat cooking. He must be a powerful shaman. But tonight I will kill him before my own eyes. I too am a great shaman."

"What will they do today?" Yegdyghe asked Belye.

"Today they will invite you to eat and they will serve you poisoned food."

Her parents made *salome*, a dish made from berries mixed with dried fish – and they added poison. Emenda came and invited him. He prepared by putting a hollow reed down his shirt.

Meanwhile Emenda was hungry and sneaked some of his food. She fell down unconscious.

"What's the matter with her?" asked Yegdyghe.

"She's just embarrassed," replied her parents, and they took her away.

Yegdyghe just pretended to eat and put the poisoned food down the hollow reed. When no one was looking he emptied it out into the fire. They waited for him to die, but he didn't die.

"All right," said Kanda Mafa. "Yegdyghe, tonight you and I will compete as shamans. Show me what you can do. We'll meet by the fire."

Yegdyghe agreed. That day he made seven wooden spirit figures and when night came he set them up around the fire. Kanda Mafa was first to take up the drum. He danced and drummed and sang until he was tired and then he sat down.

Spirit figures

Now Yegdyghe took up the drum. He danced and sang and drummed. He had made those spirit figures in a special way so that they would be funny. Each one had strange features and when the shadows fell on them they seemed to be laughing. Yegdyghe himself was dancing in a funny way. The old people began to laugh uncontrollably. They fell on the ground and rolled around laughing.

At this point Yegdyghe and Belye ran away. By the time Kanda Mafa and his wife came to, they were far away.

Now they came running after the young people. They were getting closer and closer. Yegdyghe remembered the things his sister had given him. He took out the half comb. "Grow up into dense bushes," he called and threw the comb out behind him. Dense bushes grew up.

This slowed the old people down, but after a while they were getting closer again. The young people were getting tired and could feel the hot breath on the backs of their necks.

Yegdyghe took out the half sharpening stone. "Grow into big rocky mountains!" he called.

The stone turned into rocky mountains. The old people tried to climb but they couldn't get to the top. Yegdyghe and Belye could hear them scrambling up and falling back.

And so Yegdyghe and Belye got back to his home and there they were married.

Kanda Mafa and his wife stayed beyond the mountains.

Yegdyghe and Belye arrive home safely, and so does Kiviuq, eventually. But he still has more adventures to go through before his homecoming.

Wolf Women, Tiny Spiders, and Homecoming

The story was and is alive for me. It helps Inuit to survive and live. All Inuit feel the story is real and that it has usefulness in life. If we were raised in only happy times we wouldn't learn. We have both good and bad in life. To survive is to do our best even in hard times, and grow mature, strong, and respected. As children we were taught to live well and to follow things through even if we didn't like it.

– Mariano Aupilaarjuk, 2004

Taima!

Δ Kiviuq paddled on. He came to an island where two women were living alone. Some say these were wolves temporarily living in human form, and others that they were human women living on an island.

Kiviuq forgot that he had seen a freshwater pond on the island and he asked them for a drink of water. The mother said, "You can have a drink if you stay with us." He agreed and stayed on with them. In spite of the fact that he was eager to get home, he needed more clothing, and these women would sew for him.

The human women most Nunavut tellers describe in 2004 were living with a big log of driftwood. The first thing Kiviuq noticed was that the log had stains around its knots, which had been smoothed by much use. The stains were the source of much laughter, as Annie Peterloosie explained that the log was serving the women sexually. The first night Kiviuq lay down to sleep with the mother. The log, which lay between the two women, poked him and moaned in jealousy. Madeleine Ivalu tells us that the second night, when he lay with the daughter, the log moaned even more loudly. Kiviuq asked the daughter about it and she said, "The log is my mother's husband." The mother quickly retorted, "It's OUR husband!" not wanting to be seen as the only one to resort to desperate measures.[1]

During the day the women sent the log to sea. He could be heard out in the water singing happily, and he came back in the evening laden with seals. That is the way they lived and ate. After the second night Kiviuq spat on the log as they placed it in the water. The log never came back. Δ

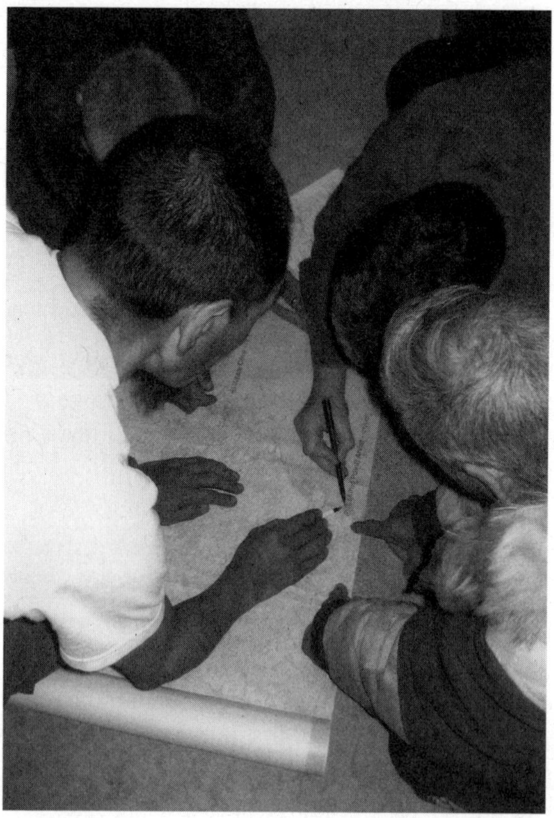

Mapping Kiviuq's voyage

The wolves were shape-shifters, and the humans were not. The wolves could take care of themselves hunting, and the human women seemed to need help. Both were highly attractive to Kiviuq, as they were strong, friendly, and at times ruthless. After all, it had been a long time since he had been with women. Henry Isluanik feels that this story had its basis in real life.

For the most part the Kivalliq, Netsilik, and Back River elders tell the story about wolves, while people from Baffin Island and Igloolik tell about human women. The wolf women as presented in Rasmussen's time taught Kiviuq how to hunt where the tides were dangerously long and fast-moving (Ostermann 1939, 52–5). They ran faster than he could when the water rushed in, and they hauled him out of the water in the nick of time. Storytellers in the early twentieth century said that in return Kiviuq taught the wolves who had saved him how to hunt wild caribou, and that these wolves then taught the skill to all other wolves (Rasmussen 1931, 369). Real-life wolves are noted for their strong family and social instincts – they even babysit! They have a hierarchy of respect and affection. They are fast and have wonderful endurance – tracking wild caribou for up to five hundred miles. It is possible, though not certain, that wolves mate for life. A wolf is certainly a worthy mate for an expert hunter like Kiviuq.

Saliva exercises personal power, as we'll see again when Kiviuq spits to control his fox-wife and when saliva helps him to create landforms that slow a pursuing grizzly bear. After he spat on it, the log never returned and Kiviuq began to provide for the two women with his hunting.

I'm fascinated by the fact that people who might never have seen trees could personify their living nature so graphically. Of course, they would have heard reports about forests and some might have actually travelled into treed areas themselves. Sometimes driftwood arrived on their shores in the form of a whole tree, but the wood still enters the story with a feel of something distant and exotic. The Netsilik used to say that driftwood came from great underwater forests (Balikci 1970, 210). I was surprised to find that this image had come from a book without illustrations, with no accompanying story. I had formed a clear mental picture of thick-trunked trees seen through deep sea water, their branches moving subtly with the ocean currents.

From here on, the two tracks of the mother-daughter story – the one with the wolves and the other with the log of wood – converge. But there are different implications. If the mother and daughter are wolves, they have more in common with the other beings he has met so far, being part animal, part human. The warm relationship he has with the daughter is the first positive relationship he has with any of the shape-changing animals, beginning a shift that continues later with the fox and the goose.

But if the women are human, they have more in common with his human wives, whom we will meet in "The Penis in the Lake" chapter. The daughter episode begins the long cycle of stories about Kiviuq's wives. Besides that, she and her mother need help in providing themselves with food, either from the spirit world or from a man. Make no mistake – many Inuit women were able hunters who worked as partners with their husbands. Later on the fox-wife shows this side of female life. In an emergency they could survive goodly periods of time without men, just as men were able to sew good clothing and boots and did so when out hunting on their own. But it would have been difficult for either a woman or a man to carry on for very long doing the whole load of work – the food preparation and clothes making and mending as well as the hunting. Besides, the women could not go out to hunt during late pregnancy or while taking care of small babies.

It's a challenge for some Western women to see such a division of labour as egalitarian, but it seems to have worked very efficiently. The very climate constrains people to live in community, to keep the birth rate up, to develop specialized forms of work while remaining conversant with all survival skills. Survival favours specialization. Social mores have always favoured maintaining the community, and thus the division of labour has been emphasized in story. Among peoples of Siberia a similar situation has applied. The difference between these northern societies and our own is that in northern communities both kinds of labour were equally valued, while we have put greater value on "men's work." In the North the women's creation of clothing was every bit as essential to survival as the men's hunting. This is not to say that women did not have problems in those societies – they did – but we should not associate the division of labour with their problems or see it as demeaning.

Needles in the Ear

Δ Time passed. Henry Evaluardjuk says it was a whole winter. He is certain the mother and daughter were human women, since they spoke Inuktitut. They had somehow been left behind by their group on an island.

Kiviuq and the daughter enjoyed a romantic idyll. But the situation was not so pleasant for the mother. She was jealous of her daughter, frustrated now that even the log was gone, lonely and afraid of being completely abandoned. She wanted Kiviuq all to herself. One day while he was away hunting, she called her daughter and offered to pick the lice from her hair. The daughter dozed and her mother put a skewer in her ear and killed her.[2]

"This is where tragedy began in Kiviuq's life," says Henry. Δ

Having lice picked from one's hair can be very soothing. Elder Mary Ittunga greeted us at the beginning of our session, saying, "If it weren't for lice, I would never have heard any stories! My mother used to tell me stories while she picked my head, and I sat still to listen!" But with the kind of characters Kiviuq was meeting, the offer to pick lice was a warning sign. According to one teller, the irontails had picked Kiviuq's lice to put him to sleep – and their intent was to kill him.

In many Siberian stories a woman will soothingly pick lice from someone's head to cast a spell – and the intent is also to get rid of bothersome sexual competition. And so it was here. What happened next was a matter of identity theft.

Δ The mother skinned her daughter carefully the way the Inuit skin a fox, through the mouth so as to keep the skin whole. The mother put the skin on herself, hoping to deceive Kiviuq. Leo Nimialik says she took her own skin off and exchanged the two skins, which makes it seem more like borrowing a dress for the evening than like murder. Samson Quinangnaq says she took only the face and hair. However it was, her objective was to transform herself into a younger woman and to have Kiviuq.

That evening she was the one to come down to shore to meet him. Usually his young wife came down, helped him secure his kayak, and lifted the heavy seal or caribou onto her powerful shoulders and carried it up to camp. Annie Peterloosie says she flipped the seals into her *amauti*. This time the woman might have looked the same but she directed him to a different landing place, and when she lifted the seal, she had a hard time getting it to her shoulders. Her legs trembled as she walked away. Looking more carefully, Kiviuq noticed that the exposed skin between her pants and her boots was wrinkled, not youthful at all. Henry Evaluardjuk says that because the daughter was the larger woman, her skin was floppy on the mother. With instant shamanic knowingness Kiviuq realized what had happened. He was horrified and grieved for his young wife, whom he had come to love.

Some say he simply paddled away, but others say he stayed on a while to practise a deception of his own. A man needs many pairs of mittens over the course of the winter, as they get worn out. He needed a good supply to get him home, so every time the mother made a new pair, he would hide them inside his kayak, pretending to have lost them. She then made more.

The woman was suspicious and said, "I think you are going to leave me."

He replied, "I will not leave you because I am fond of you." But this was not true. When he had enough mitts he paddled away. **Δ**

This exchange is one of the places where the language reverts to the old style and most elders use exactly the same words – a signpost to the story's architecture. The mitt trick appears as a motif at several places in this story as well as in others. In Kiviuq's story it appears to have a role in his preparation to leave a woman, sometimes his mother or wife, who he knows will object to his going. Herve Paniaq and Zippora Innuksuk say that in the wolf story he did it before the mother killed the daughter, rather than after. Zippora says it was beaded clothing he took, whereas Annie Peterloosie says it was beaded mitts.

When I tell the story myself, I leave out the mitt trick (as do some of the elders), since it seems to derail the story's emotional energy. I was feeling Kiviuq's grief and rage and wanted to stay with that rather than turn to the tensions that would arise from his knowing he was living with a murderer. To a non-Inuit audience I felt I had to explain why he just left, without taking any action against the woman. My words are the ones the elders use to explain this action and others. "He heard the voices of his own elders running through his head. 'Don't let your emotions get the better of you. If you let yourself get distracted by emotion, you can die in a second out on the land or water. If someone does you a wrong, do not engage with them. If possible, just walk away from trouble.' And so he paddled away." This is one of the most vital pieces of survival morality. On the other hand, those elders who instead tell of the mitt trick are tacitly acknowledging another aspect of what it takes to survive – you must have the right clothing and a man generally relies on a woman to get it.

Only one elder, Joanasie Macpa, thought that the mother tried to bring her daughter back to life after Kiviuq left and that she may have succeeded. We made jokes among ourselves about how unpleasant the family dynamic would have been after that, but the suggestion seriously grabbed my imagination. Siberian story heroines who died with needles in their ears all came back to life – in fact they were not really dead at all. I'm not sure where "killing through the ear" came into human story-making, but we even find it in Shakespeare's *Hamlet*. One friend suggests that the needles could symbolize words, which can certainly kill when they enter the ear.

The death seems not to be permanent in most stories. If this one did cross from Asia, the return to life would have been an important part of it. This aspect of the story now seems to have fallen away, perhaps because the story is not primarily about the girl. But the daughter resonates strongly with Kiviuq's human wife in the same way that Kiviuq resonates with the seal-child – they are separate characters with strong similarities. The daughter's experience recalls an initiation. With her mother training her, she undergoes a classic dismemberment. As terrible as killing someone may be in ordinary reality, in shamanic reality a person who appears to do a wrong by killing someone is often actually catalyzing the "victim's" initiation. The killer presents the challenge and kickstarts the process of transformation. Seen from this point of view, the story has quite a different flavour – one that suggests the shamanic life path, with its death and rebirth. Inuit easily understand that this action in the story world does not give licence to kill in our world.

The mother is led astray by jealousy and fear, but she is still human. This is one of several things in the story that, for me, jump out as very contemporary. The gut desire to change one's appearance in order to get a man is reflected in ads that bombard us daily – about everything from eliminating wrinkles by peeling facial skin to changing our hair colour and style. Facelifts and tummy tucks – are those the modern-day pre-occupations of wolf mother? Not quite, since we don't kill our daughters to achieve them, but the parallels show us that the desire to improve the body at any cost is still with us and that perhaps the glorification of youth is not as new a phenomenon as it seems.

Does this desire to change the female body begin in a female response to what seems to be a very deep-seated male tendency to judge women by their appearance? An interesting point here is that only the North American story husbands – Kiviuq and his First Nations counterparts – recognize the deception, while the north Asian and European story husbands are completely fooled. We'll hear more about them in the "Wolf Cousins" chapter. Perhaps part of Kiviuq's strength is his ability to resist the spell cast by the deceiver, an ability that may be part of his shamanic power. The husbands in similar Siberian and European stories are not shamans, although they are able hunters and highly observant men. Some of them go through initiations of their own, falling under the spell that a woman undoubtedly casts on them. Kiviuq, with well-developed shamanic powers, is impervious to such spells. The fact that the Inuit hero is a shaman may be a development that took place as the story crossed the Bering Strait and shifted from a focus on initiation for both male and female to a different message – one of shamanic power, its use and abuse.

I'm beginning to think that this story is partly about the growth of the human family. Unlike certain animals and birds, humans do not instinctively mate for life – it's a social construct. On the road from random mating to more or less stable family and group relationships, such things as stealing mates and children may have been commonplace. And at a certain point stories began to show that these and other behaviours had become unacceptable.

In Asian stories that involve face stealing, the male and female are sometimes reconciled. In Kiviuq's story they are not reconciled, while mother and daughter may be, at least in the eyes of Joanasie Macpa. Inuit stories tend to keep the shadow out in plain sight.

Skin and Clothing

In certain tales similar to the one of the wolf mother, the imposter steals a woman's clothing. In places where the clothing that people depend on for survival is made from animal hides, human skin and clothing can be seen as nearly identical. In places where style and decoration are sure markers of region, family, and gender, to change clothes is to change identity.

Clothing made from animal hides emphasizes a close identity with the animal involved. This is one reason seamstresses try to keep the skin whole and, when possible, to cover specific parts of the human body with the corresponding parts of the animal skin. Arctic researcher Valerie Chaussonnet writes: "Animal skin, transformed into a second skin for humans by the work of the seamstresses, still maintained its animal identity. From the killing of an animal through the tanning, cutting, and sewing of its skin into a piece of clothing, the qualities and characteristics attributed to it in life were maintained and passed on to the wearer of the finished garment. This important spiritual principle linked animals, hunters, and seamstresses together in an intricate and circular set of relationships" (1988, 212). This is one of the ways an animal continued to live after death. A person takes on part of the animal nature by wearing its skin. Likewise an animal's voice lives on in a drum head. In some places this identification with the animal extended as far as retaining unsuitable styles in new climates. The Chukchi women's one-piece *kerker* has heavy sleeves that so impede motion that the women have to take one sleeve off while working, but the garment fulfils the important spiritual function of keeping the hide whole.

Shape-Shifting

The ways identity is held and expressed through skin and clothing brings us to the idea of shape-shifting. The mother and daughter appear to Kiviuq in human form, as do bee, spiders, fox, bear, and goose. In the Inuit story world, the difference is not so rigid as in the Western perception. People and animals change their form regularly. Animals are not considered to be a lower life form – in many ways they are more intelligent than humans. In Siberia, where clan structure comes into the picture, people may wish to gain some of their wisdom and strength for their genetic line by marrying one. Inuit, on the other hand, consider that marrying an animal is very dangerous and can shorten your life considerably. Theresa Kimaliadjuk says that Kiviuq's ability to marry in the animal world is evidence of his tremendous strength. I'm not sure where the danger lies in the Inuit understanding, but it's clear that one should stay in human society whenever possible. It could be that living too much in another world is a drain on a person's vital energies. But are these normal animals that people marry, or are they somehow set apart?[3]

A different take on the relationship between humans and animal forms comes from the Nivkh people of Sakhalin Island. A boy challenged a Siberian tiger, and after showing mercy to the injured animal instead of going in for the kill, he was taken to the tiger's home on the mountaintop. The tiger now took off his skin, revealing that he was a man underneath. He introduced the boy to his parents, who explained, "We are really people. We only put on these tiger skins when we are around you." What they were getting at, I think, is that they had the same kind of soul as people do, that animals and people are relatives under the skin. Tuutalik seems more equally gifted than either humans or animals, his nature truly half human, half seal. It's not as if he resides mainly in one form or the other. Sometimes a *tuutalik* appears as a kind of mermaid, with both sides of its nature showing at once.

My own interest in shape-shifting goes back to my college days. In a course on Russian folk literature I met the epic hero Volkh Vseslavevich, who turned himself and his army into ants in order to get into an impregnable fortress. Once inside they took their own human form and defeated their enemies. Then they all changed into hawks and flew away. The thing that struck me most was that Volkh could change himself and his men into any form that suited him. Before that, the only shape-shifters I had heard about were werewolves.

The mother attempts an interesting form of shape-changing, if you can call it that. She takes the physical process into her own hands by killing her daughter and stealing the whole skin. She breaks an unspoken taboo by taking someone else's form rather than changing her own. Clearly it works only superficially and temporarily. Her willingness to sacrifice her own child breaks one of the strongest taboos, one that is embedded in nature – animals do not kill their young; rather they will fight to the death to protect them. Just a few years ago our news was full of the case of a woman who killed her own children because her new lover didn't want them. Again humans are set apart from animals in an unfavourable light.

Shape-changing does involve appearing in a different skin, but usually the second form is an integral part of the shape-shifter's nature. The case of a human shape-shifter is qualitatively different from that of an animal that can take human form. The animal can only change into a human, whereas certain shamans and story heroes like Volkh, whose very name means wolf, can change into many different forms. A Siberian shaman might change into the form of any of the spirits under his or her control in order to journey. Inuit shamans did sometimes change into the form of their spirit helpers, but Kiviuq never changed shape in the stories that we heard.

Animals appearing temporarily in human form are a normal occurrence in the Inuit story world. But when a person sets out to appear in another person's form, something profoundly wrong is happening. Taking a step beyond simple disguise, the mother actually displaced the soul that owned the body; it was as if she had forgotten that her daughter had a separate existence from her own.

This step – moving from changing aspects of one's own nature to stealing the external part of someone else's nature – is a misuse of power and as such it came back on the mother. She was ultimately left alone on her island – the very thing she feared in the first place. Think how different her story is from that of the grandmother who transformed the child into a seal. First of all, that child had a seal nature, being descended from Tuutalik, and so she was teaching him to use aspects of his own nature. Secondly, she did it for his own good, to save his life and initiate his growth. The wolf mother acted to benefit only herself, and thus she failed. As we saw with the poisoned food, magic undertaken with selfish aims bounces back. As Philip Paniaq is fond of saying, there are no second chances when one makes a serious mistake.

Rachel Qitsualik Tinsley (daughter of elder Gideon Qitsualik) pointed out to John Houston that the monstrous beings are those who don't quite succeed in their transformation. This could apply to Bee Woman and the giant spiders, and now resonates with the mother's failure to transform.

Soul displacement as practised by the mother is not the same as soul theft. Instead of leaving the body soulless, the mother tries to inhabit body herself. Yet another way of looking at the mother's act is that she overidentified with her daughter. She failed to let go, thinking the daughter was still a part of herself. This feels like a very modern view, but there must have been people who would have seen things that way in the past as well. The mother also tested Kiviuq's powers of observation. If he had not noticed the piece of exposed skin, she would have succeeded in deceiving him.

Still, I wonder if we really understand what motivated the Inuit wolf mother. I wonder how old she actually was and whether the idea of having more children was what appealed to her. Maybe she simply wanted to have sex with a man instead of with a log.

Soul Retrieval

In cases of soul displacement or soul theft, the logical cure is shamanic soul retrieval. This is the most important form of healing in Siberian shamanism, one that is echoed in many world shamanic traditions. The soul might have been stolen or shocked from the body, and its absence caused illness. Modern Western shamanic practitioners practise soul retrieval today and have been successful in many settings, including work with criminals, as well as with drug and alcohol addicts.[4] Although rarely mentioned by Inuit today, their ancestors also practised soul retrieval.

Rasmussen tells us that illness was caused by soul loss (1929, 93) and that a shaman must be able to go to the land of the dead to bring back the souls of those who are alive but have been called to the land of the dead by relatives who love them (109). This reminds me of what Udeghe elder Valentina Kyalundzyuga told me about attending a funeral as a child. She became very ill, and the presiding shaman discovered that the dead man, who was very fond of the small Valentina, had tucked her soul under his arm, wanting to take her along. He had no intention of harming her and gave her back when the shaman pointed out his error.

The Inuit locate the world of the dead in at least two places – there is an upper world of the dead as well as one under the water. Some of the dead go to live on the moon (Saladin d'Anglure 2001, 149, 169). Here is what Aupilaarjuk said about how a shaman gets to the underwater realm: "In the Nattilik area we say *atqaqtuq* [for going down into the sea to Sedna and to fetch animals]. My father saw the *angakkuit* do this but I haven't seen this particular *saka* ritual myself. [*Saka* is a ritual where a shaman's helping spirit enters him.] The *angakkuit* are said to be very *nangiaqtut*, fearful of falling, because there is only one passage they can go through and it is very dangerous. We call this ritual, when the *angakkuit* go down through the earth, *atqaqtuq*. This one passage that they have to pass through has a very smooth, slippery rock. That part is very dangerous and when they reach it they make the sound, 'uh, uh, uh.' It is like the sound one makes when one falls into the water because of the cold … Once they pass this, then the *angakkuit* are no longer in danger. The people who live down there are said to be very friendly" (Saladin d'Anglure 2001, 88).

Of Inuit soul theft, we read: "A shaman might use his powers to steal the *tarniq* [soul] of someone he disliked or was jealous of, by secretly performing *ilisiirniq* [hexing] with the assistance of his *tuurngaq*. Some *tuurngait* thus became vicious through improper use. The victim might also succeed in blocking the evil *ilisiiqquti*, or hex, which would then boomerang back against the sender and kill him. When a shaman was accused and convicted of this, the group could execute him" (Saladin d'Anglure 2001, 181).

On the subject of returning a soul to a sick person, Luke Nuliajuk described a situation where the *tarniq* no longer wanted to be with a person and that person became ill. The *angakkuq* took the sick person's parka outside, and the people inside pulled very hard on a rope to bring it back in. Pulling was very difficult as long as the parka was outside, but it became light once it was back inside. After that the sick person got better (Aupilaarjuk et al. 2002, 23–4). Tuvan shamans do a similar form of healing using clothing. The use of the rope reminds me again of Siberian ceremonies of accompanying the dead to the next world. Assistants would tie a rope around the shaman's waist so that they could pull her back from the next world once her job was finished. This protected the shaman from being held there against her will.

Women Living Alone

When circumstances forced women to live alone, they sometimes resorted to magic to eke out a living – or at least it probably seemed like magic. A society built on the essential interaction of male and female would inevitably recall any individual's nearly miraculous survival in terms of magic, something beyond the realm of the natural. This applies to men as well as women, as we've seen in the story of the man who survived on an iceberg with the help of a giant.

One Greenland story, unrelated to Kiviuq's, shows how women could survive in the absence of men. A mother and daughter had accidentally been left alone on an island. They made spiritual alliances and exercised shamanic power by calling food from a lake of their own creation. It is clear that although they survived, they were now set apart from human society. When a male relative turned up on the island to take the women home, the lake stopped producing (Sonne 1992, 170–1). The women had to give up seeking and receiving help from spirits in order to return to the community. This was part of the social contract. Siberian tales also show that help from the spirit world is reserved for serious emergencies. In ordinary times people should rely on their own work and their relationships in the community.

Although we later learn that Kiviuq had already married one or two Inuit wives before the storm, the daughter on the island is the first of Kiviuq's wives that we actually meet. The relationship is short, but it is the first time we see him growing fond of a woman. From here we go on to meet his two human wives and then the fox-wife and goose-wife. All of the animal wives show their animal natures at some point. The fox-wife retains her smell and the goose-wife her migratory instinct. The wolf daughter retains her physical strength.

It's easy to forget that the daughter is really part of the scheme of wives. The story focuses our attention on the mother, who creates one of the major challenges of Kiviuq's first journey, while the daughter inaugurates a series of female images that corresponds to the idea of Kiviuq leading multiple lives. While he stays in one body, the female appears in many, some of which are reincarnations of the same being and others that most likely are not. I find it fascinating that Kiviuq's competitions with female characters, such as the human grandmother and non-human Bee Woman, are on the level of magic. With males like the man we'll soon meet who lived with Kiviuq's wife while he was away, he engages in tests of physical strength. With males like the grizzly bear and the Fishmaker, he engages in a bit of trickery.

The first appearance of a female partner of Kiviuq's is a pivotal moment in the story and may explain why this part appears sometimes before and sometimes after the homecoming. It serves as both the end of the male initiatory journey and the beginning of the wife's development and Kiviuq's marriages.

Obstacles

Δ The mother suspected that Kiviuq was staying not because he was fond of her, but only to collect new clothing from her. She said, "If you leave me, you will have bad times ahead."

And so it was. He left and went to the mainland. The lower halves of two female bodies kept moving to wherever he tried to go. Finally he had sex with them and they disappeared. A boiling pot appeared. He jumped from rim to rim and the pot disappeared. He was on a point of land and wanted to walk on, carrying his kayak. He saw two grizzlies fighting and tried to go around them but finally had to go between. They disappeared after he passed. He went forward and came to two mountains clashing together. He turned his kayak sideways, put it on his head, and ran between the mountains, but they almost got him – the back of his *atigi* was caught

> but he escaped unharmed. The message is clear – if you face your fears head-on, they will disappear. You might lose something external but nothing essential.
>
> Kiviuq was tired. His troubles were slowly ending. He came to the games rope and did all his tricks, even when there was a snow knife in the middle. Many had died there. Blood and carcasses were all around, but now they too disappeared. **Δ**

The hamlet of Arviat has printed a leaflet showing some of the Inuit rope games. I've heard that these games develop upper-body strength and the agility essential to saving oneself from a flipped kayak. A rope is set up either between poles or hanging inside an igloo. Competitors engage in gymnastics while hanging in the air, which develops muscle strength. Here is an example of a game: "Lift body with arms and try to rotate body around the rope without touching stomach to rope. Competitor must not rest on rotation but movement must be continuous. The person doing the most rotations wins." Other variations include balancing on the rope with the knees or on one hand, jumping on the rope, doing handstands, taking off clothes, and rotating around a knife. While hanging, a person could do chin-ups, hang by the feet, balance, and swing.[5]

Netsilik storyteller Kuvdluitsoq and others told the wolf story after they told of Kiviuq's homecoming, whereas today's elders tell it before. In parts of Greenland, however, the mother and daughter story appears close to the beginning of the whole Kiviuq legend, with a different series of events motivating his journey away from home. He left after his wife died, they say. He had buried her under stones and was grieving, but his small son said to him, "Mama is outside now, with another man." Kiviuq looked and it was so. He was so angry that he killed both his wife and her lover. "Now perhaps you'll stay dead," he said, and then set off on a long sea journey. As Kiviuq swirled through a heavy storm, he heard a voice telling him that he was at the middle of the world and that a whirlpool he negotiated was the navel of the sea. He was plagued by sea lice eating his kayak, by clashing icebergs, by cannibal women who wanted to eat his body parts, by a cannibal baby, and by an eagle who tried to carry him off. The ghosts of his wife and her lover came back to clamber into his kayak, weighing it down. His wife said it was unkind of him to kill her, and he replied that she was already dead. "To kill a person who is already dead is the unkindest thing of all," she said.

There's one problem with walking away from interpersonal trouble. It means there is no immediate resolution – in this case the walker is really running away and not truly leaving painful emotions behind. Greenland Kiviuq left because of the pain of his wife's betrayal, and he met jealousy in a different form when the mother killed her daughter. After his terrible trials at sea, he met the human women who were living with a log of wood. He introduced himself saying, "I left home because I was jealous." It would seem that his journey was about this emotional issue. There is no abused orphan and the hero is not shown as compassionate – at least not at the story's opening.

I have heard a number of life stories around the North in which a person realizes he has done wrong in social terms and leaves the community for a period of time without being told by anyone to do so. Greenland Kiviuq may have gone into a self-imposed exile after murdering his wife and her lover. Some say Kiviuq comes home and wins his wife back from the young lover (now alive!), while another says he meets their ghosts and does not arrive home again. Clearly there are many ways this situation can be worked out.

The incident with the two women appears near the beginning in the minds of Henry Isluanik and Elizabeth Tunniq. They told the story of the wolf women immediately after the stories of the seal-child and the storm at sea, before Kiviuq's meeting with Bee Woman. Here too the wolf women story kicks off the whole journey, but from a different starting point. The rest of the elders told it at the crucial midpoint.[6] This episode connects Kiviuq's otherworldly adventures with his human family life and plays a vital role in his relationships with women.

Beads and Tiny Spiders

Δ In Henry and Elizabeth's versions, Kiviuq met Bee Woman right after his involvement with the mother and daughter, while everyone else went on from here to tell of the tiny spiders and the beads.

Samson Quinangnaq says that at this point Kiviuq got sleepy. He placed his paddle between two rocks to hold the kayak and slept. He woke up and saw snakes crawling over the kayak; he picked it up and ran. He rested again but awoke when he heard spiders crawling on the kayak. He moved on.

He came to some little spiders who were stringing beads or making beaded clothing.[7] Although they wanted him to stay, Kiviuq took the beads and clothing and left the spiders weeping on the shore as he paddled on towards home. ∆

This episode gives the hearer the feeling that a piece of recorded history has made its way back into mythic time, given that glass beads appeared in the Arctic only with the arrival of Europeans. We'll never know if this part of the legend was told before contact, when perhaps beads made of local materials were used, or if the episode intentionally refers to the foreign nature of the beads. Another mystery is why Kiviuq took the beads and left the spiders crying. Several non-Inuit listeners have suggested that their tears could have turned into shiny webs. They made a mental association between the spiders' skills in geometric design and the intricate motifs used in embroidering beads on clothing. Philip Paniaq says the beads' appearance in the story reminds him of the way spiders carry their eggs on their backs in bundles that look like beads. When I asked Aupilaarjuk about why Kiviuq might have stolen the beads, he responded very strongly, saying that Kiviuq didn't steal the beads. It's only stealing if you make sure the person doesn't see you do it. The spiders definitely saw him. Inuktitut has precise words for different kinds of taking.

We were mystified by this part of the story until a year later, when John returned north and spoke with several of the elders again. Now Henry Evaluardjuk told him about the *nigjuarjuit*. At a later date, most likely after Kiviuq's homecoming, these tiny spiders came wielding tiny knives and attacked Kiviuq's community, covering the water with their kayaks. They were likely friends of the larger spiders who had the beads. Kiviuq told his people that when you take something from non-humans, they can exact a heavy revenge. He had his companions make arrows, and with them they defeated the small beings.

Annie Peterloosie spoke about this incident: "The lesson is, don't mistreat anything, even insects. And don't burn them. If you are going to kill them, then squash them. If you are afraid of them, they will show up in greater numbers. This part about the spiders is something that should be known today. The legend has a valid use. But people don't tell Kiviuq's words any more." Being unkind gives power, it seems, to those small beings, who can then exact a powerful revenge on people.

Kiviuq brought the beads back to his human wives, and they all began to have trouble that could not be understood or resolved. As Danish ethnologist Birgitte Sonne pointed out to me, Inuit women were very attracted to glass beads in their shining beauty, but later found them difficult to keep. The beads were shown up as being non-functional, basically useless in a practical sense. Spiders come from heaven (as they do in Chukotka), and Sonne feels that their bringing beads could be a warning of things to come. Unpredictability makes its way into a story that is otherwise subject to solid rules. Certainly Europeans followed a code that was different from that of the Inuit and often incomprehensible to them. But when we add Henry Evaluardjuk's story of the spiders' revenge, the lesson takes on the same clarity as other parts of the story that had seemed mysterious on first hearing.

In the history of northern contact, useful and attractive trade goods came first: rifles, sewing machines, beads. Then, as outsiders searched for resources and vied for control of the territory and its sea routes, the door was open for disease, government control, cultural degradation, decline in health – loss of the old way of life. This didn't happen all at once, but gradually. One would not immediately foresee a problem on the basis of bits of coloured glass for decorating clothes. For Kiviuq personally, the shift entailed a certain loss of power, just as shamans in many lands found themselves powerless to deal with the deadly diseases brought by foreigners.

Beads as adornment seem to go back to dawn of the modern human race and are found among all peoples. Before contact, arctic beads were made of local materials. Northern people used soft stone, bone, ivory and other teeth, shell, and sometimes amber. Porcupine quills were also used in some areas.

Glass beads could have come to the central Arctic from two directions.

Most foreign trade came from Europe and North America through the whalers and traders, but some may have arrived from Alaska and Siberia. Many of the glass beads used around the Bering Strait had travelled all the way from Venice and Bohemia, as well as from China and Central Asia (Francis 1994, 284–8).[8] Beads in the eastern Arctic could easily have travelled just as far via Europe instead of Asia. I love to think of how these tiny objects could have changed hands many times, travelling from the glass-blowers of one of Europe's most sophisticated and international cities of the eighteenth and nineteenth centuries, to be worn by masters of the world's harshest climate. Neither had heard of the other, and the glass artists became mythical creatures to those who wore the beads.

Beads are the only tangible thing Kiviuq brought home from the worlds he visited on what may have been a visionary journey. I wonder if by bringing these physical objects, which may have been made or at least passed on by those evil beings he met, he introduced something that worked like bacteria in his human relationships at home. Generally, shamans cannot bring objects back from their journeys. Physical gifts should not cross those boundaries. Perhaps this is why epic storytellers (who in some ways resemble shamans) describe receiving gifts at the feast that ends the story they have told, but always emphasize that they had to leave the gifts behind when they came home.

Homecoming

Δ Now Kiviuq was truly tired. He wanted to get home and called upon his sandpiper spirits to help him. He had gained strength in his journey and now could call them, whereas before they appeared in the storm of their own volition. Rasmussen often refers to these delightful birds as "harmless snipes and redshanks." The word harmless stands out – so little in this story truly offers no danger. Kiviuq said, "I am really tired. Can you help me?"

"Go to sleep," the birds replied, "and we will tow your kayak." He gave up control, and they carried him along. Perhaps this means that Kiviuq was in a deep shamanic trance or that this was one of his deaths. The sandpipers woke him up from time to time, asking if he was seeing any familiar landmarks. At first he saw nothing, but then began to see features of the land that became more and more familiar. Artist Simon Tookoome told us how he had loved hearing this part in childhood. He had first seen it in a vision and then had created a lovely representation of sandpipers pushing the kayak.

At one stop Kiviuq met two young men who had come out to get meat from their cache.[9] Because they were humans, they told each other stories. Elders use the word *unipka*, the same word used to describe the whole legend. *Unipka* is also the root for the word "explain." The young men told of how their father was lost at sea long ago, and Kiviuq told of his own journey. One of the young men finally recognized Kiviuq from his teeth. He was their father and they were his two sons – just small children when he left home, now grown to manhood. Some say they took him home by dog team and others that he continued his journey by kayak. **Δ**

The appearance of the two sons acts as a forerunner of the welcome Kiviuq would receive on returning home. But there's something odd about them. They could be no more than a dramatic device showing the passage of time, like the kayak filling with urine or Kiviuq's moving the kayak through the cycle of tides. They show that he had been gone long enough for small children to grow into men. The passage of years ties in with Kiviuq's identification with seasons, which increases as the story continues, until he becomes almost solidified at the end, his body gaining and losing mobility from summer to winter. Or the sons could be real, the source of Kiviuq's descendants, who are mentioned on certain rare occasions in conversation. Simon Tookoome tells us that Kiviuq's descendants are white people.

There's no logical problem in Kiviuq having these sons if he was an adult when he was blown away at sea, but on the other hand a number of elders indicated that it was young people, even children, who pursued the seal-child. They say Kiviuq was a boy in a learner's kayak and thus not fully grown. If this was so, the wives who met him on his return could have been promised to him as children. They would not have been married to him when he left, so it would have been unlikely for them to have had his children. However, several of the elders said that

Kiviuq *was* the seal-child, and they too spoke of his wives meeting him on his return, although none of them told about the two sons. A bigger problem would be explaining how and when he had learned the shamanic knowledge that seems clearly to have been taught to him by others, unlike the knowledge he gained from experience on the journey. We are not looking for logic or the one correct storyline – each version has its own truth.

Characters in stories almost always have symbolic functions that go beyond their actions. In fact, they are sometimes little more than symbols. These sons, whether real or not, showed us that Kiviuq had been gone for years, and that now he was getting close to home.

Δ Coming ever closer, Kiviuq sang his personal song – a song full of the elation he felt. "*Aasiggai, aasiggai, aasi, aasi, aasiggai*! Here I am!" People on shore recognized his voice – Jacob Peterloosie says his wife sang the song back to him. His parents had been watching for his return. Even today we can see the indentations in the rocks formed by their long wait. Δ

In company with Henry Isluanik from Arviat, we visited the rock where Kiviuq's mother had stood. We rode out along the shore on all-terrain vehicles and came to a point of rock looking out over a cloudy and seemingly endless Hudson Bay. The mother's rock itself is simply marked with a stick. Henry pointed to the indentations, one bigger than the other, and to a calcified cross that had formed between them on the rock – a sign of its importance. Leo Ahmak says the mother's tears and mucus formed the calcification.

As we approached the rock, Henry said, "Although I had heard the story all my life, it was only when I saw this rock in 1999, on moving to Arviat, that it became real." It had a similar effect on me, as did seeing a dragon in the rocks in the Russian Far East and hearing that the couple who survived the great flood in Tuva had landed on a mountain visible from the storyteller's window. It was easy to imagine Kiviuq's mother standing year after year in that desolate place, never giving up hope that her son would return. People brought her food, Henry says, but she never left the spot.

The rock where Kiviuq's mother waited for him to come home, located south of Arviat. Elder Henry Isluanik explains the rock's significance to interpreter Percy Tutannuaq.

If we had been in Siberia, our arrival on a visit like this would certainly have been celebrated with offerings to the spirit of place, anything from a quiet personal act to an elaborate group ritual. It felt odd to me not to do this, and even odder that we were staging our arrival so as to catch it on video. The technology did not faze Henry, but I felt disoriented by our approach and privately made an offering of some snacks I had in my pockets. We then recorded interviews. When we had packed up and were ready to go, Henry produced a large thermos of tea and some fresh bannock from the back of his Honda. We sat on the rocks and warmed our hands and hearts together, and I realized that the old celebrations live on here too.

When we got to Taloyoak, we heard about the stone seat where Kiviuq's father had waited, although we didn't visit the place. They say the old man had been unable to walk for a long time, but when he heard Kiviuq's song, he got up and made the rounds of the tents, telling everyone that his son was back. Here was another hint of the Christian Bible, reminding me of the man who picked up his bed and walked. Although most told of the parents separately, Margaret Nakashook described them together. Kiviuq's mother and father used up the last of their energy in the joy of hearing their son's voice, Margaret says, and died just before he arrived onshore.[10]

In the 1970s elder Marcel Akadlaka of Labrador said that members of the community doubted at first that it was really Kiviuq they saw paddling towards them. They refrained from telling the parents until they were sure of his identity, fearing that the joy would kill them. This turned out to be the case: "Kiviok's parents died without seeing their son, but Kiviok saw his parents" (Blake 2001, 7). Dale Blake, editor of *Inuit Life Writings and Oral Traditions: Inuit Myths*, points out that Inuit stories often do not have happy endings and that hearing them prepares children for the disappointments of life. In a deeper sense, there may have been sadness about this homecoming, but the important thing was the fulfilment the parents felt on knowing their son had returned.

Δ Kiviuq's wives recognized the style of his paddling and the sound of his singing voice. One wife had taken another husband, and she was well dressed and healthy. The other wife had not taken another man, and she appeared in tatters, painfully thin, her cheeks still

> puffy from tears. Henry Evaluardjuk says Kiviuq killed the wife who had taken another husband. Most say the wife who had waited came down to the shore saying, "Kiviuq, my husband. I have waited so long for you. All this time my vagina has been closed, but now it is wide open!" **Δ**

The cheeks puffy with tears may be another storytelling convention, showing the depth of her sadness. Although earlier translations said that one wife was faithful and the other unfaithful, I appreciated the neutrality of Inuktitut words as translated to us. One wife took another husband and the other did not. There were good reasons to take a husband. Kiviuq was gone for many years and we have already seen how difficult it could be for a woman to live alone. This wife made one choice and the other one waited. But the easier choice led to retaliation.

Some say Kiviuq had only one wife. Two wives show that he was a powerful man and an able hunter. In story terms his having two allows us to see two different possibilities working out for a woman. Percy Tutannuaq and Albert Kimaliakyuk discuss the idea that one marriage had been arranged for him in childhood, while the other was an affair of the heart. Annie Peterloosie says there was one wife and that she had been living with an eider duck. Others say she wore eider duck clothing.

I wonder what the community was like when he returned. How different was it from the one he had left so long ago? The grandmother most likely would have died by now, but what about the seal-child? There is no mention of him. I can only imagine there would have been resentment on the part of the women who had lost their husbands and sons – perhaps grandmother and child were driven out of the community, although she may have succeeded in fooling the people into thinking she had had nothing to do with the storm. Now we hear about his wives and parents, who were not mentioned at the beginning. Perhaps their existence is simply assumed by Inuit elders and others like them, who see Kiviuq's circumstances on the basis of his current behaviour.

Even though Kiviuq's family was there, it doesn't feel like the same community. True, Inuit communities shift over time, with small groups joining and separating with the seasons, but it seems odd that there is no memory of the loss of men, even if the mourning for them would have been finished years ago, and no sense that it had become a community composed almost entirely of women, at least for some time. By the time Kiviuq got home, a lot of the young male children would have grown up and men would have been absorbed from other communities. Nonetheless a whole generation would be missing. Jacob Peterloosie was the only one to mention that all the hunters had been missing and that Kiviuq's wife was glad her husband was back at last. Although it would be interesting to know how things had changed, this is not information that propels the story and so it is not mentioned. Kiviuq sees his parents and his wives, and for our purposes that has to suffice.

Δ Kiviuq came up onshore and greeted everyone. He distributed beads to the women in recognition of their loss – not much comfort for having lost their men, although Kiviuq could not be blamed for that. Cornelius Nutaraq says he provided for all the widows on his return. Joanasie Macpa tells us that all the boys had grown up. When they pulled the kayak up, the bottom fell out, again showing just how long he had been gone. It appeared that Kiviuq had given beads to all the women except the wife who had waited patiently for him. This seemed cruel and upset her further, but then he said to her, "Go and look in the prow of my kayak." She looked and saw that he had saved a big sockful of the most beautiful beads for her alone. Alternatively, he ripped her tattered clothing from her and dressed her in the magnificent beaded clothing he had brought back from the tiny spiders. **Δ**

This gift of clothing is reminiscent of a scene in the film *Atanarjuat, the Fast Runner,* and so too is the exaggerated weeping. Even here the wife's torn clothing resonates both with the seal-child and with the daughter who lost her skin. Here the wife received new clothes from the non-human world, which could be a harbinger of trouble to come.

For Kiviuq, this homecoming is the fruition of the gift bestowed on him in childhood by his grandmother – that he would always get home no matter what the obstacles. His initiatory journey is complete.

Wolf Cousins

When my grandmother was released from the gulag she wanted to hurry home as fast as possible so she turned into a wolf. As she neared her village a hunter caught sight of the wolf and tried to shoot her, but his bullets were unable to touch her. She got home safely and told everyone about how she had turned into a wolf. The hunter backed her story.

– Musical instrument maker Marzhymal Ondar, Tuva, 1993

Tuvan Epics

The Tuvans are a Turkic-language people living in southern Siberia. They have a long and brilliant history as storytellers – a *toolchu* can tell epics that go on for several evenings. Before the Soviet era, people would gather from far and wide to listen to these storytellers at large community gatherings. The dramatic and multi-layered imagery of their tales connects cultures as far away as the Celtic and Inuit.

I first went to Tuva on the invitation of musicians I had worked with in Canada. On my first trip I met with storytellers and shamans, heard music, and got thoroughly acquainted with the holdings of the wonderful local museum and with the people who keep it alive. But the country was deep in economic crisis and at first things weren't easy. Many of the people I wished to meet lived far from town. Cars broke down and were difficult to repair, gas was expensive and in short supply, people were busy with their own problems. I spent a lot of time walking by the river and playing the bone game with the children of my hosts.[1] And then I discovered the research library – a pleasant second-storey room with a welcoming librarian. She brought me a number of books, including a dog-eared copy of the popular epic *Boktu-Kirish and Bora-Sheelei*. I had already read stories about women warriors from the area, but was amazed that this one had two parallel heroes – a brother and sister. At certain points they each seemed to absorb qualities and skills generally belonging to the opposite sex, becoming fully balanced heroes. I loved it.

In the absence of photocopiers, I took every spare moment to translate the story into my notebooks. It took weeks. Once I got it into my computer back home, the whole story was more than 25,000 words or fifty single-spaced pages. Short by epic standards, but much longer than any of the stories I heard told. I then kept my English translation – "Boktu-Kirish and Bora-Sheelei" – at home for ten years. It didn't seem to fit into any of my books, and it was too long for me to tell in an evening. At last the opportunity arose. In 2006 "Boktu-Kirish and Bora-Sheelei" became part of a community gathering halfway around the world from its source – Vancouver's sixth annual "Epic Weekend." I was joined by eight other storytellers to tell the story. It took us a whole day and evening. The story came to life – even I, who had painstakingly worked and reworked the translation, heard new insights in the telling. This was the first time the story had been told in English and outside its homeland, and because the epic telling tradition has fallen on hard times in Tuva as in other parts of the world, perhaps it was the first time it had been told at all for many years. I felt tremendous gratitude to the storytellers, who had worked so hard getting acquainted with a culture different from their own.

After many adventures, the sister, Bora-Sheelei, went to live in seclusion in the forest, where her brother would visit and bring her food. Two of the three wives she had won for him became jealous and decided to do away with her. They visited her and, like the mother in Kiviuq's story, offered to do the heroine's hair. When she was well relaxed, they stuck needles into her ears. She did not die, however, but fell into a death-like sleep. Her brother, thinking her dead, sent her body away on the back of a heavenly stag, who delivered her to an elderly herding couple. The old woman found the needles, removed them, and restored the girl to life.

This image comes down to us in European story as the long sleeps of Snow White and Sleeping Beauty. In these tales, the image has turned 360 degrees – the passive and beautiful European heroine is qualitatively different from the Asian warrior heroine who falls under a spell but eventually regains her power. The European image is also different from that of the strong but vulnerable Inuit daughter who dies at her mother's hands. Story images persist through time and space, but their meaning can shift significantly.

Tuvan and Inuit societies were relatively egalitarian right into the twentieth century. Their heroines were powerful compared with the women portrayed in European folk tales, who had become more passive over time. The European heroines reflected the life of the upper classes in many parts of the world – women were perceived as inactive and exercised power only very covertly. In contrast, Tuvans and Inuit (among others, of course) respected female wisdom highly and publicly. Women and men shared skills that could be used in time of need, even if in normal times there was a pretty strict division of labour between the sexes. Although Tuvan and other Siberian women did not routinely hunt with their husbands as Inuit did, they were well able to provide for their families while the men were away on hunting and trading trips that could last months. In 2005 I heard a young Udeghe man grieving the fact that the last of the strong female hunters in his community had died, thus depriving young girls of that important role model. His sense of loss was just as great as that expressed by people who say that the last of their great shamans had died.

When I first heard that the Inuit mother had stolen her daughter's skin, a tingle went down my spine – and not just from the horror of it. I thought of Bora-Sheelei going under a spell as the two women played with her hair. And I thought of several Siberian tales about identity theft in which a woman steals another's face, or sometimes just her clothing, in order to marry her bridegroom or steal a baby. Many of these stories don't involve putting needles in ears, but there is often some act of violence. Killing through the ear can exist with or without the subsequent theft of identity. The totality of story as held by a given culture is like a mosaic made up of interchangeable pieces. It is my belief that this body of knowledge holds information about cycles of change and the results of life choices. I had been fascinated for years by the Sakha story "The Horsetail Girl," which embodies the image of identity theft in detail.[2] It is the story that came immediately to mind when I heard of the wolf mother stealing her daughter's skin. What appears as a brief interlude in Kiviuq's life is central to the Sakha people's understanding of who they are.

Ceremony of welcome, Sakha Republic

The Horsetail Girl

A long time ago there lived a little old woman named Beiberiken. She had five cows, which she pastured out in a wide field behind her yurt.

One day the old woman went to look for her cows but for a long time could not find them. She worried, knowing that they were about to give birth. She asked crow and raven but they refused to help her. At last the eagle directed her to a small hill where the cows were resting with their new calves under a tree with deep roots and low branches. As the old woman prepared to take them home, she found a beautiful plant growing nearby, a five-jointed horsetail with leaves of many colours.

"I'll take this plant. I'll carry her home. She can become my child," said the old woman. Carefully she dug the horsetail up, without damaging so much as a tiny root or twig. She carried the plant home, laid it on a pillow, and covered it with a blanket.

Then she went to milk the cows. After she had finished milking the second cow, she heard the tinkling of little bells on her drum coming from inside the yurt, and then the thimble fell. The old woman jumped up, spilled the milk, ran into the yurt, and turned back the blanket. The horsetail was still lying on the pillow. Nothing but the plant, just as it had been before.

She was mystified and went back out and sat down to milk the cows. By the time she had finished the third cow, again the sound came – the tinkling of little bells and the needle falling down.

The old woman jumped up, spilled the milk, ran into the yurt, and turned back the blanket. Again the plant was lying there on the pillow just the same as before.

"What was that sound?" thought the old woman. "Surely it wasn't just ringing so that I would spill the milk!"

Again she went away to milk the cows. As she finished the fourth cow, she heard the sound – again little bells were ringing and the scissors fell. For the third time the old woman jumped up, spilled the milk, and ran into the yurt. And there on the blanket sat a beautiful little girl. Her face was like white marble, her eyes like chalcedony. She had lips like dark stone and her eyebrows were like two black sables that lay touching each other's paws in the middle of her forehead. Through her dress the old woman could see the girl's body, through her body the bones. The nerves spread this way and that, like mercury through the bones.

Old woman Beiberiken was very happy.

"At last I have a daughter!" she said. She went out and milked the last cow holding the little girl in her arms. She fed the child the last of the milk.

The two of them lived together, and together they looked after the cows. As the girl grew, her clothes grew with her.

Several years passed. One day the brave Harzhit-Bergen was hunting in those parts. He was the son of Kharakh-Toyon, the *toyon* with the eye of the Eagle. Normally he was a crack shot, but this day he caught sight of a squirrel and shot, but missed. He chased the squirrel from morning until sundown but he could not make a hit. Then the squirrel ran up a spruce tree, jumped from there to a birch, and finally to a larch tree right next to old woman Beiberiken's yurt. The brave hunter shot one more time but the light was failing. His arrow missed the squirrel and fell into the smoke-hole of the yurt.

"Hey, old woman!" called Harzhit-Bergen. "Bring out my arrow!"

There was no answer. And then he shouted still louder.

"Come out, old woman! I am Harzhit-Bergen, son of Kharakh-Toyon! I'm waiting for my arrow!"

Again, no answer. He flushed with anger. A wave of arrogance sprang from the back of the hunter's neck and he rushed right into the old woman's house.

When he got inside, he saw a beautiful girl, more lovely than any on earth. Her face was like white marble, her eyes like chalcedony, her lips like dark stone, and her eyebrows like two black sables that lay touching each other's paws.

Harzhit-Bergen stood stunned for a long time. When at last he came back to himself, he had fallen in love. He ran out of the yurt, jumped on his horse, and rode home.

"Father, Mother!" he cried when he got there. "I have seen the most beautiful girl, so lovely that her equal does not exist anywhere on earth. She lives in the yurt of little old woman Beiberiken! I must marry her!"

His father, the tribal leader Kharakh-Toyon, sent nine horsemen on nine red horses. The horsemen flew like the wind to the old woman and ran into her yurt. They were all stunned when they saw the beautiful girl. And when they came back to themselves, they quietly went out. Just one stayed behind, the eldest one.

"Old woman Beiberiken, our leader, the illustrious Kharakh-Toyon asks that you give this girl, your daughter, to marry his son."

"I am not against it," said the old woman, "but first ask the girl if she agrees."

The girl smiled. "I will marry him," she said.

"Then bring me the bridal payment," said the old woman. "When the Toyon has filled my whole field with horses and cows, then his son can come for the girl."

The messengers returned to the Toyon. They told him everything that had happened. The Toyon gave the order to fill the woman's field with horses and cows. His people drove them there.

On a fine day at the new moon Harzhit-Bergen came for his bride. He brought a dappled talking horse with a silver saddle and a harness decorated with silver. A silver whip was fastened to the saddle. He carefully led the girl out of the yurt by the silver whip and seated her on the dappled horse. She sang her farewell to her mother and they set off for his home.

But on the way he stopped.

"I have fox traps in this forest," he said. "I want to go and check them. You ride on alone. You'll come to a fork in the road. Beside the road leading east a black sable skin is hanging from a tree, and by the road to the west a brown bearskin with white at the throat. Take the road with the black sable skin."

He then disappeared into the forest. The girl was frightened. But there was nothing to be done, so she rode on alone. And when she came to the fork in the road, she forgot what her bridegroom had told her. She took the road where the bearskin was hanging.

She rode into a dark forest and soon came to an iron yurt. An *abaasi* woman, daughter of the eight-legged evil spirit Adzharai-Böga-Abaasi, lived there. When the girl rode up to the yurt, the *abaasi* woman rushed out to meet her. She wore iron clothing. She had one twisted leg, one twisted arm, and one terrible cloudy eye in the middle of her forehead. She had a long black tongue, which hung all the way to her belt. She could cut firewood with her nose.

She invited the girl into her house. Frightened, the girl went.

The *abaasi* woman offered her human meat to eat. Not wanting to refuse, the girl took the meat but did not eat it. Instead she put it down her sleeve when the evil woman was not looking. Now the *abaasi* woman asked if she could try on the girl's clothing and adornments. Afraid to refuse, the girl took off her clothes and jewellery. But now the monster tore the skin from the horsetail girl's face and attached it to her own face. She dressed in the girl's bridal finery. She threw the girl's body to the left side of the house, where there was a big hole in the floor. The girl felt as if she were stepping on a dry skin and then falling.

Then the *abaasi* woman jumped up on the dappled horse and rode to the palace of Kharakh-Toyon.

The bridegroom caught up with her right at the gate. He suspected nothing. All the Toyon's relatives, all his subjects, and all his servants came out to meet the bride. Harzhit-Bergen's nine brothers ran up to the golden hitching post from the right to take up the reins of the horses. His nine sisters came up to the golden hitching post from the left to tie the horses.

There was whispering in the court of the Toyon.

"When the bride speaks, precious red beads will come from her mouth. Where she walks, soft black sables will run in her footsteps."

The girls had prepared unbleached threads for these precious red beads, to collect them and string them. The boys had prepared bows and arrows for these soft black sables, in order to shoot them.

But for some reason the bride tied her horse to an old willow post at the back of the yard. Everyone who came to meet the bride felt uneasy. Sorrow fell upon them.

When the bride spoke, stinking green frogs fell from her mouth. It made the girls feel sick. In her tracks ran ugly red ermines. The boys put down their bows and frowned.

As custom ordered, the area from the hitching post to the door of the palace was strewn with green grass. As custom ordered, the bride was given the tops of three young larch trees.

She went into the house along the green grassy path and started the fire on the hearth with the three tops of young larches. Then the wedding feast began.

When they finished feasting, they returned to everyday living.

But all was not well for Harzhit-Bergen. A hunter who had previously never missed his shot, he now came home empty-handed. His wife's body was bumpy and uncomfortable. He asked her why, and she told him that from childhood old woman Beiberiken had dressed her in heavy jewellery and that was why she had bumps on her back and on her breast. She was also totally inept at sewing and cooking. Everything she cooked tasted bad and the things she sewed fell apart the first time he wore them. He was disappointed in his marriage.

One day not long after, old woman Beiberiken had a dream. She saw her daughter in a dark underground place. She went into the forest and came to the home of the *abaasi* woman. She went in, and from under the floor on the left side she heard a barely audible voice. She found her daughter and took her home. She healed the girl's body and soul and then asked her, "What happened, my dear?"

And the girl told her.

"My bridegroom Harzhit-Bergen was taking me home with him. Along the way he said, 'I'm going to check my fox traps. You ride on alone. Take the road where the black sable skin is hanging and don't go where the bearskin is.' I forgot what he said, and went the wrong way. I came to an iron yurt. The daughter of the eight-legged *abaasi* rushed out. She tore the skin from my face and put it on her own face. She dressed in my clothes and took on my appearance and went to the palace of Kharakh-Toyon. She became the wife of my bridegroom, the brave Harzhit-Bergen. Clearly I am not destined to die. I am destined to have children. But the monster's daughter broke my fate, she stole my bridegroom. How is he now? Most likely her spirit has been absorbed into his blood. Am I destined ever to see him again?"

"You will see your Harzhit-Bergen," said the old woman.

"And meanwhile, stay here with me."

At the same time, the talking dappled horse spoke to Kharakh-Toyon.

"The daughter of the eight-legged *abaasi* killed my mistress," he said. "She took her appearance and became your son's bride. She lives here at your palace. My mistress came back to life. She lives again with old woman Beiberiken. If your son does not marry the horsetail woman, I will complain to the White Khan on his seat of white stone, by the lake with silver waves and golden floating ice and blocks of silver and black ice. I will shatter your home and hearth and leave you no means of living.

"You must tie the evil daughter of the *abaasi* to the tail of a wild horse and let the horse go in the steppe. You must cleanse your son, the brave Harzhit-Bergen, from the spirit of the *abaasi*. You must wash him for thirty days in the current of a cold river, and then dry him for thirty days on the top of a tall pine tree, so that the winds of the north and the winds of the south may blow through him. After that he may go to old woman Beiberiken and convince his bride to take him back."

The old Toyon wept as he listened to the horse. And then he hurried to his son. When he ran into the palace, the daughter of the *abaasi* instantly understood everything. She frowned, her face darkened.

"Son," said the old man. "Tell me, where did you find your wife?"

"She is the daughter of the little old woman Beiberiken," answered Harzhit-Bergen.

"Which horse did you bring her on?"

"I brought her on the dappled talking horse," answered Harzhit-Bergen.

"And what do you know about her origins?"

"Beyond the third heaven the White Khan sits on the white stone seat. His younger brother gathered together all the migratory birds. Then he changed his seven daughters into cranes and they came to earth and danced in a circle. Their teacher selected the best of the daughters and told her that her mission was to come and live among the Sakha people, saying, 'You will live among them and bear children. You will marry Harzhit-Bergen, son of Khan Kharakh-Toyon.'

"She turned the girl into a horsetail plant. And old woman Beiberiken changed her into the woman I took for my bride."

His father explained what the talking horse had told him. When he heard his father's words, Harzhit-Bergen was enraged as he had never been enraged before. He dragged the evil one outside and tied her by the neck to the tail of a wild horse. The horse galloped off into the steppe. The horse turned her into food for the sun and moon. Her eyes turned into the stars that shine in the cold time, bringing hard frost and disease. Her body was torn to pieces and became the reptiles and worms which crawl on the earth to this very day.

The people washed Harzhit-Bergen in the cold rapids; they dried him at the top of a tall pine tree and brought him home barely alive.[3]

The brave hunter rested. He came back to himself and then hurried to the yurt of old woman Beiberiken. The old woman came to greet him, rejoicing as if the lost had been found, as if the dead had risen.

According to custom, she spread green grass from the hitching post to the yurt. She butchered her best cow and prepared a wedding feast.

But the girl came to Harzhit-Bergen and wept.

"Why have you come here to me? You let the daughter of the eight-legged *abaasi* tear off my delicate skin, spill my red blood. You let the grey dogs tear apart my white body. What are you looking for, coming here again? There are more girls in the world than perch, there are more women than hariusi-fish in all the rivers of Siberia. Among them you will find a wife. I will not go with you."

"I didn't give you to the daughter of the eight-legged *abaasi*," said Harzhit-Bergen. "I didn't tell you to take the wrong road in the forest."

Old woman Beiberiken sat down between the girl and the

hunter. She wiped the tears from both eyes on both sides.

"The lost is found, the dead is risen," she said. "You must take joy in your meeting. Embrace each other! Do not turn away from your fate."

"Mama, I will not disobey you," the girl said softly. "I will forget everything."

Harzhit-Bergen leapt up, he jumped for joy. He hugged her and kissed her. They laughed and talked and played all the best games until it was time to go.

Outside, the dappled talking horse stood ready in the silver saddle and the harness decorated with silver. The silver whip was fastened to the saddle. The bride dressed and adorned herself for the wedding and they set out on their way.

They rode for a long time. They knew the winter by the snow that fell, they knew the summer by the rain that poured down, they knew the autumn by the fog.

All the Toyon's relatives, all his subjects, and all his servants came out to meet the bride. Harzhit-Bergen's nine brothers ran to the hitching post from the right, to take the reins of their horses. His nine sisters came up from the left, to tie their horses.

There was whispering.

"When she speaks, precious red beads will come from her mouth. Where she walks, soft black sables will run in her tracks."

The brothers and sisters got ready to greet the bride. The sisters spun threads; they worked so hard that they rubbed the skin from their palms. The brothers made arrows; they worked so hard that the ripped the skin from their fingers.

The bride and bridegroom arrived. The young men took the reins, and the young women tied the horses to the golden hitching post. Harzhit-Bergen helped his bride down from her horse. When she spoke, precious red beads came from her mouth. The girls gathered them and strung them. When she walked around the yard, soft black sables ran in her tracks. The boys began to shoot them.

Green grass was strewn from the hitching post to the doors of the palace. As custom ordered, the bride was given three larch tops. She came into the house and started the fire in the hearth with the three larch tops.

And the wedding feast began.

And what a feast it was! The guests came from lands both near and far. Nine ancestral spirits came from the upper world and twelve ancestral spirits came from under the ground. Everyone came from the foreign tribes and from the nomad villages.

There were singers and dancers, acrobats and storytellers. Nine friendly sorcerers were there drinking *kumiss*.[4] Heroes competed in fighting and shooting.

The feast lasted seven days and then the guests rode off to their homes. The ancestral spirits rose to the upper world and the others sank into the ground. Harzhit-Bergen and the horsetail girl began living together. They were both happy and friendly.

And even today their descendants are living in our land.

Face Stealing

"The Horsetail Girl" is one of the most popular and vitally important stories in the long cycle of the Sakha people's physical and spiritual history. That fact provides a hint that face stealing or identity theft is something very deep and basic to human experience. The horsetail girl's story parallels the Sakha wedding ritual, which began at the bride's home. After a few days of celebration the bride put on a headpiece with a veil that completely covered her face, blinding her. Guided by her new husband, she rode away from her family. The couple arrived at a place between her parents' home and his. There she removed the veil. They stayed in this "no-man's-land" for a while and really got to know each other, just as the young people do at the end of the story. And then they continued on to his home, where the wedding concluded and the couple settled down to live.

Those who study initiation often feel that while the male engages in dramatic initiatory feats, the female receives her initiation in the course of marriage and childbirth, which can be represented in story as violence and dismemberment. In some stories from the Amur region an evil spirit steals the girl's tongue, an act that suggests that a new wife might not have been able to speak in the husband's home because a different dialect was spoken there. Or the girl might simply have had to remain silent in deference to her mother-in-law. In this story both Harzhit-Bergen and the horsetail girl experience initiation, she through death and rebirth and he through the rigorous cleansing he undergoes on the instruction of the talking horse.

Pursuing my fascination with the image of identity theft, I traced the horsetail girl story all across Asia and into Europe. The Tungus-language peoples, who live throughout eastern Siberia, have many variations on the story. In an Oroch tale, a foreigner with short hair named Pegeliktu pours tin in the heroine's ear to kill her.[5] Set apart by her hide clothing, Pegeliktu seeks to disguise herself by stealing girl's fish-skin coat, typical of peoples of the Amur River region. She deceives the husband, convincing him to move across the river. But the true wife's brothers find her body. She comes back to life and eventually returns to her husband. A son is born. The foreigner Pegeliktu, now relegated to the status of a servant, drowns the child and blames the wife – an epic theme the world over. In his rage the husband dismembers the true wife, cutting off an arm and a leg – her second dismemberment. A goat heals her and reunites her with her child, who has been raised in the water by friendly fish. In the end the child meets the father and tells the whole story, thus reuniting the family. Pegeliktu runs away into the forest. This story unites elements of dismemberment as initiation with the child reconciling the family.[6]

The Nanai tell a tale similar to "The Horsetail Girl" in which the fox who distracts the husband from the path actually is the evil spirit. The deception is unmasked by the girl's mother.

In North America the Gwich'in story of Shaaghan is similar to the mother and daughter story in the Kiviuq epic except that in the former the young woman has two husbands. The mother becomes jealous of her daughter's happiness and success, and steals the younger woman's skin after lulling her to sleep by picking lice from her hair. The two husbands are not deceived. Every day their young wife would jump over a stick when they arrived home. The older woman cannot jump as high as her daughter, and she knocks the stick over. The husbands kill the mother, but the story emphasizes that they are not able to bring the young wife back to life and are left grieving (Ruppert and Bernet 2001, 113–14).

The Yupik of Chukotka on the Bering Strait, linguistic and cultural relatives of the Inuit, tell the story of Kitsiniku. It goes to the unelaborated heart of the matter as surely as does Kiviuq's.

Kitsiniku[7]

This happened a long time ago. A man named Kitsiniku was living in the tundra with his wife and baby. They had seven reindeer.

Once there was a bad storm – a strong wind blew. They couldn't go anywhere. Kitsiniku had to kill one of his reindeer.

They ate.

They lived.

Now six reindeer were left. The storm did not abate and the food ran out. Kitsiniku killed a second reindeer. They ate it up. The storm did not abate and he was forced to kill a third reindeer. Now four were left.

The storm continued until there were only two reindeer left. Kitsiniku wanted to keep the pair so his herd would regenerate. But his son was crying. One by one he killed the last two reindeer.

Now the wind quieted down and the weather cleared up.

Kitsiniku and his wife decided to move to a place where there were many people, so that he could find work and they would have food. They took down the *yaranga* (tent) and tied it to their sledge. His wife and son sat on top of the *yaranga* and he harnessed himself to it.

On the way south the child began to cry.

"Wait for me here," said Kitsiniku. "I'll go look for water."

"Go, Kitsiniku," his wife replied.

When he was out of sight, a woman appeared out of nowhere. She came up to the sledge.

"Where have you come from?" asked Kitsiniku's wife.

"I come from far away," the woman replied. "Come here to me."

Kitsiniku's wife got down from the sledge, leaving the child, and approached the woman, who took her head in her hands and rubbed their faces together. As she rubbed, her face became exactly like that of Kitsiniku's wife.

"I'll look after the child," said the stranger. "You go look for water."

The mother trusted the stranger and went looking. As soon as she was out of sight, the woman got up on the sledge and took the baby in her arms.

Soon Kitsiniku came back. "I was unable to find water," he said.

"Hurry, let's go!" said the woman. He did not notice that it was not his wife, since her face was now so similar.

Kitsiniku harnessed himself up and they moved on.

His wife returned to the spot but no one was there.

"Kitsiniku!" she called. "Why did you leave me?"

Kitsiniku heard her voice. "Sh," he said. "I feel I'm hearing my wife's voice."

"Let's get away from this place quickly," said the other woman. "My shadow is walking there in the snow and crying out."

They moved on, and at last they came to a big settlement.

They went into a big *yaranga* – it was warm and clean. The people were wealthy reindeer herders. They greeted the strangers and invited them to eat and drink. Kitsiniku asked only for water for his son, but the hosts served food to them all.

After they had eaten, Kitsiniku happened to look at his wife's forehead. He froze. On her forehead she had a second mouth!

"Something happened – that is not my wife," he thought. Quietly he spoke to the daughter of the house. "Come outside with me. I have something to tell you." She went with him.

"Add more fuel to the fire," he said. "When it gets very big, tell that woman to sit closer to the fire and warm up."

And so the girl did as he asked. The woman moved right up to the fire and Kitsiniku pushed her in. At that moment the woman turned into a big black beetle. It often happens that an evil spirit turns into a black beetle, and that's just what happened this time. The beetle tried to fly up to the smoke hole, but its wings were scorched and it fell into the fire and burned to ashes.

Kitsiniku went looking for his wife in the tundra. He found her and brought her back. The people fed and warmed her.

That is when they began living here. Kitsiniku began to work for the reindeer herders, and soon they lived in their own *yaranga* and had their own food.

The next year Kitsiniku received a pair of reindeer for his work and in time his herd regenerated. They lived well.

As I looked at the similarities between this story and Kiviuq's, I thought again about the growth of the family concept and how over the course of time certain behaviours have become unacceptable. The killing of one's rival to get the man (or woman) of one's desires has certainly persisted up to our own time, but today it is viewed as a serious crime rather than as one of the dangers of everyday life. Another example can be seen in certain stories from the Amur region that hark back to the time when older sisters routinely married their younger brothers. In one, told by Udeghe elder Evdokia Kimonko, the sister tricks her brother into marrying her. When he finds out the truth, he kills her and deserts their two children. The girl is raised by a bear and the boy by a tiger. Each becomes the ancestor of a different clan. Although ancient stories like this one have sacred roots – this one is honoured as telling the ancestry of the Udeghe people – over the centuries they have come to carry a negative message about incest.

I have spent years telling "The Horsetail Girl," using it to come to terms with what it means to steal a face or to have one's identity usurped. The story strikes a chord for many women. What levels of anger and frustration motivate a person to want to be someone else? Beauty seems to be incredibly vulnerable to that kind of destructive power. How can the victim find her way back to wholeness? One important point is that it is never the man who makes her whole. The girl achieves that integrity herself, sometimes with the help of the old woman, before she and the man can truly come together. The situation is different with Kitsiniku's wife, who does not die. As soon as the imposter is out of the way she is able to return with the help of her husband. And, of course, in the North American versions, that transformation never takes place – the old woman *is* the usurper and the girl dies.

A major difference between the North American and the Asian versions of stories of identity theft arises in this question of whether the victim comes back to life or not. There is an interesting parallel in the prevalence, or lack, of soul retrieval in shamanic practice.

In North Asian shamanism, soul retrieval was the predominant method of healing. This was reflected in the many stories of a hero or heroine who set out to bring back a person who had been abducted, either within our own world or to another. The shaman's first task was to find out where the soul had gone and who had taken it. Mongolian shaman Tsenin-zaarin boo told me that another complication was knowing which part of the soul was missing, since that would make a difference to the process of retrieving it. Once the soul was located, shamans would use anything – from pleading, deal-making, and trickery to outright threats – to get it back. A typical story of soul retrieval is found in the Buriat-Mongol tale of their first shaman, Morgon Kara, who transformed himself into a wasp and stung the god Tengri, who was holding a man's soul in a bottle. Morgon Kara succeeded in returning the man's soul to his body but lost some of his power in the process.

Although Inuit shamans practised certain forms of soul retrieval, it seems to have made up a smaller part of their practice than it did among Siberian shamans. Inuit stories show the same pattern – there are fewer cases where a lost soul is found and returned. This may reflect the harsh reality of the arctic climate and the phenomenon Philip Paniaq refers to when he says there are no second chances. In the world of story as told by true nomads, it looks as if the girl dies permanently. Resurrection comes when the story is told by the more relatively settled people, including semi-nomadic herders. I'm not sure if this is universally true or what it might mean, but it's interesting to see that in spite of the fact that hunting peoples tend to believe that both people and animals reincarnate into new bodies, it is the people closer to an agricultural way of life who believe in human resurrection in the same body.

As the story travels westward, it gains stepmothers and stepsisters. The rival is now the same age, rather than older. In "Cinderella" the older woman splits into good and evil – the stepmother and the fairy godmother. In "Rapunzel" we see a reversal. It is the man who is dismembered, not the girl. But the Inuit version shows the simplest and deepest of all female jealousies – that of an older woman for a younger. The mother is afraid of being left behind, afraid of the shift that happens when the parent becomes dependent on the child, ultimately afraid of the death that stares her in the face. In more settled societies the mother's goal is to see herself cared for in old age by the daughter's husband, although probably the root fear is the same.

In Eurasian versions of the face-stealing story, the male and the younger female are reconciled in the end. Of course, this reconciliation is dependent on her coming back to life. The two competing women, whom we could see as two sides of the same woman, are never reconciled. The good and life-giving woman is never reconciled with the destroyer in stories of this sort. In human or even animal form, the goddesses who in ancient times ruled both creation and destruction have split in two. In Eurasian cultures the shadow has been inexorably split from the positive image. The two are now distinguished by their appearance – for example, Turkic cultures equate beauty with goodness almost without exception. "The Horsetail Girl" strongly emphasizes the contrast, describing in detail the heroine's beauty and the imposter's ugliness. There may also be two old women – one lovely and helpful and the other ugly and evil – or two siblings. If we think of the two female images as different facets of the same woman, perhaps they do become reconciled in "The Horsetail Girl": the girl becomes more assertive and careful as a result of her death and rebirth, while the young man learns to look beneath the surface.

ΔΔΔ

Kiviuq meets the tiny spiders and finally makes his way home. This part of the story fulfils a listener's desire for a happy ending. But the story is not over. Soon Kiviuq will leave his community again, this time in the company of his two wives.

The Penis in the Lake

Our tales are men's experiences, and the things one hears of are not always lovely things. But one cannot deck a tale to make it pleasant, if at the same time it shall be true. The tongue must be the echo of the event and cannot adapt itself to taste or caprice. To the words of the newly born none give much credence, but the experience of older generations contain truth. When I narrate legends it is not I who speak, it is the wisdom of our forefathers, speaking through me.

– Osargaq, early twentieth century (Rasmussen 1908)

Taima!

Δ Kiviuq felt a kind of emptiness in the community since his parents had died. Elders say this is why he took his two wives and set off caribou hunting, although it could also have been a normal seasonal activity. Ollie Ittinuar says they intended to camp through spring and summer. They set up their camp, and Kiviuq went hunting daily while his wives stayed at home.[1] There was no shortage of work – they cooked food, prepared hides, and made clothing, all labour-intensive activities. At first they worked well, just as he expected, but after a while things changed. He would come home and find them sleeping, their work undone. Samson Quinangnąq says they were cold and shivering in their sleep. Kiviuq asked them what was going on but got no sensible reply.

One day he stayed behind and watched to see what they were doing while he was gone. The two wives set out as if they were going to collect fuel for the fire, but instead they went to a nearby lake. They threw pebbles into the water and called, "Penis, come up!" A large penis rose above the water level, moving up and down. According to Samson Quinangnaq and Simon Tookoome, the women now sang using ancient words, "My vagina is open!" Δ

At this point most non-Inuit laugh heartily – both women and men. Even female Inuit elders show signs of amusement. As in the story of the cannibal Bee Woman, humour shows up in close association with the heaviest parts of the story, facilitating the healing of issues raised. But Inuit men get very serious.

Δ The wives took turns going into the water and having sex with the penis. When they were done, they collected a token amount of brushwood, returned home, and went to sleep.

Kiviuq was angry seeing his wives there. The next day he sent them on an errand far away from camp and went to the lake himself. Some say he went while the wives were still sleeping, and that he woke them later. He too threw pebbles and called the penis. When it came up, he waded out and cut it off at water level with his sharp snow knife.[2] The lake became entirely red. I asked if the lake is still red today, and Samson Quinangnaq told me that it is red and that it can be found south of Gjoa Haven, where there was once a trading post.

After cutting the penis off at water level, Kiviuq brought it home, cut it up, and boiled it. When his wives came back, he served it to them. One said, "What is this, so tough but so delicious?"

"It is your other husband, you two!" said Kiviuq. Δ

Female Shamans

More laughter from Inuit and non-Inuit listeners at this point. But here the mystery begins. Who is the owner of the penis in the lake? I asked a number of elders and got only the vaguest of replies. Most said they didn't know. Bernadette Uttaq said it was a *tuurngaq*, but didn't go further. Although the word can refer to a spirit independent of a shaman,

I began to wonder if it was really a helping spirit, the way the word is more often used.

Did the penis attract the women or did they attract it? At first I debated whether it was one of those things sent by Kiviuq's enemies to cause trouble. In that case the wives might have fallen under a spell. Something like this could happen in Siberian stories I've heard, but only if the women found it by chance. That seemed unlikely in this case, since we hear about the women actively calling it. And who can call *tuurngait*? Shamans, of course. This opens a whole train of thought about female shamans, their power, and their possible competition with the male. That Kiviuq's wife was a shaman in her own right now seems so obvious that it's hard to believe that it took me weeks to come to the realization. If a woman was calling a *tuurngaq*, she had to be an *angakkuq*. Later events bear this idea out, notably when one wife returns to life in an animal incarnation, as many shamans do between human lives. I think my slowness in seeing the point was the result of the intense focus on the male hero that prevailed both in ethnographic works and in our own questioning. The woman's power might have been clearly understood before contact but became less so as social change altered the way relations between men and women were portrayed. Ethnographers and missionaries, even down to very recent times, may have unconsciously superimposed their male-oriented focus.

In world epics the wife of a male hero is generally a woman of great power, if not a deity. The very courting of her is a challenge, and the coming together of the hero and the woman of power enriches their people from both sides, creating a powerful lineage. It makes sense that a man of Kiviuq's strength would have a very strong wife, equal to him in many ways. In terms of the telling, a story stays better in memory and has a stronger effect when we choose the interpretation that most empowers the characters and the listeners, and in this case that would include the powerful wife.

Women are known to have practised shamanism among the Inuit from early memory right up into missionary times. Some elders say they were equal to men in power, and a few, including the respected Mariano Aupilaarjuk, say they were even stronger (Saladin d'Anglure 2001, 21). Some Siberian peoples agree that female shamans were often at least as powerful as the male, but they were quieter and less showy, and thus got less attention.

Many cultures have stories that tell how shamanic power was first acquired. One recorded by Rasmussen described a man who went behind a curtain during a time of terrible need and journeyed from there to the mother of the sea beasts, just as shamans did right up until very recent times (Rasmussen 1929, 110).[3] Oddly this is the only story about the first appearance of shamanic power I have found among the Inuit. It shows that in a time of desperate need new powers and abilities can suddenly appear in an individual and the person simply does what must be done. Many stories about first shamans have been recorded in Siberia. They tend to have a mythic quality, unlike the Inuit stories, which seem almost to have happened in living memory.

It's interesting that the female image of a lake is completely balanced in Kiviuq's story by having a penis in it. An artwork by Victoria Mamnguqsualuk depicts many penises, which in the Baker Lake graphic tradition shows the passage of time – the fact that the penis was appearing here and there in the lake. The drawing is part of a collection of artistic vignettes from Kiviuq's life.[4] Encouraged by the abundance in the drawing, I wondered if the wives going to the lake was a kind of fertility ritual. And how would that relate to the animals that come out of one wife's body after her death? Although we'll return to consider the significance of the animals, I dropped the idea of fertility for two reasons. First, it simply didn't feel right. And second, the kinds of rituals that women actually did for fertility looked very different from this. Rasmussen, for example, tells us the Igloolik people would ask the moon spirit for help. He would shine in the woman's lap, lie with her, or take her to his own home until she became pregnant (1929, 75). Some say a shaman could bring back the soul of a child that had died and give it to an infertile woman. There was another reason the fertility interpretation didn't quite add up: if these were the same two wives Kiviuq had before going to sea, they might already have given birth to children – the two sons he met on his way home.

If not as a fertility ritual, then why were the women calling the penis? Clearly not for simple pleasure, since sex is never casual in the world of high myth. When it is mentioned at all, it is an important joining of forces and rarely goes without a subsequent pregnancy. Here there are no offspring unless you count the image of lemmings emerging from one wife's body. Just as Philip Paniaq's motto is "No second chances," mine is "Nothing happens in a traditional story without cause or result." The story's structural economy demands that everything be relevant. There has to be a good reason the women called the penis – it was not just a whim or an act of self-gratification, and it did not result in children.

I asked Annie Peterloosie who the penis was. She thought it over, looked a trifle disconcerted about not having a ready answer, and then said with a big grin, "At least it's edible!" We laughed heartily, my face turning red. And then it got worse! Annie and interpreter Philip Paniaq went on to discuss at length the kinds of animal penises that Inuit ate and how they were prepared. So much for the idea lurking in the back of my mind that the penis might have been a plant! What to me was the most horrible part of the tale turned into a riotous recipe swap. Later, when I read a full translation of Annie's telling, I realized she had said from the start that the penis belonged to the lake spirit. This had not been translated, and my question probably made no sense to her.

School at Pond Inlet. A polar bear was found here the day before we arrived. The bear had to be destroyed, since it had come too close to the community.

At some point both Kiviuq and his wife have sex with disembodied sexual organs. To Kiviuq, the lower halves of female bodies appear as obstacles. Sex with them most likely raises his life force in a difficult moment. The wife goes into a trance as a result of having sex with the penis in the lake. Is that what she needed?

In 1973 the elder Kupaaq told Bernard Saladin d'Anglure a similar story about an unnamed man similar to Kiviuq. According to Kupaaq, there was just one wife and the couple was childless – a cause of great distress. He pointed out that when an individual goes alone on a long journey, there is always the risk of attracting spirits. The hunter and his wife both put themselves in this position. The risk is even greater when one is suffering, as was the case for this man and wife, who had no children (2006, 171–2).

Listener Responses

In the words of Canadian storyteller Dan Yashinsky, "Some parts are hard to tell, some parts are hard to hear." Elders call this part of the story "embarrassing." As a non-Inuit woman, I find it a difficult part to tell. It's hard to reconcile Kiviuq's behaviour with that of a hero. Although Inuit elders tell this part in front of small children, it would be unlikely fare for school storytelling in other parts of Canada. Because I have been urged by Inuit colleagues to present the whole story without leaving anything out, I need to understand this episode as best I can and come to terms with my own emotional responses and those of others. I've thought about all this and discussed it with storytellers, anthropologists, and Inuit from various walks of life. Here I present no solutions – just several different ways of approaching the story, some of them contradictory, all in the search for understanding. I have come to see that the whole legend has much to do with the relations between male and female. The story reveals how their life paths diverge and how they intersect. Inuit elders would be much less likely than I am to speak of those paths separately.

Facing the possible distress of my listeners, I realized that telling the story to a non-Inuit audience required a different level of preparation than I was accustomed to. Humour following on a long serious section can go completely unnoticed without a signal from the teller that it's okay to laugh. A sudden shift from laughter to seriousness is even harder to deal with. Although non-Inuit listeners find the first part of this story hilarious, that soon changes as Kiviuq responds to his wives' behaviour. Too sudden a shift in the telling would shock listeners – it would be like dropping them off a cliff. At this point I may leave a space, take a breath, and shift to take a less chatty, more deliberate tone.

Polygamy and Jealousy

Some men in our company found the episode an affront to Kiviuq's manhood and were offended on his behalf. Inuit elders seem more saddened than angered. Without fail, female non-Inuit listeners think that Kiviuq must not have been able to satisfy the two women sexually and that is why they went elsewhere. This is a curious point about polygamy that is rarely discussed. Indeed, how could one man satisfy two lusty wives? Surely there must have been a lot of frustration and jealousy. After all, these were not Victorian wives, raised to believe that a man's sex drive was stronger than theirs. If they engaged in a ménage à trois, I have never heard it mentioned. One wife came down to shore calling out that her vagina had been closed for a long time and now she was eager for action. Would she have wanted to wait her turn?

Polygamy is a delicate situation for all those involved. Udeghe elder Valentina Kyalundzyuga recalls that when she was a child her father had two wives. She says they got along fine, with no jealousy. Many might agree with her child's-eye viewpoint, and indeed the logistics were often worked out according to a careful hierarchy. In Valentina's family, there was a huge age difference between the wives – the first wife had already given birth to several children when the second one came into the family as a child of five and subsequently grew up to be a wife and mother. But as seen through adult eyes, polygamy has observable problems. Educator and storyteller Johanna Kuyvenhoven describes the women in the African villages she lived in for several years. In their faces and words she sensed the constant tension of having to balance a three-sided relationship. It was difficult for the men as well. Keeping up with the sexual needs of several women drained their energy. One African man told Johanna that it could even be life-threatening if each of his three wives demanded all the time allotted to her. Enough conflict can arise from simply negotiating the details of living together, but with a sexual element added in, it could get really difficult. The vulnerability of all concerned is portrayed strikingly in the film *Atanarjuat*, in which the man and his two wives are shown to sleep close together in one small tent. It was more rare but not unheard of for an Inuit woman to have two husbands, a situation that leads to a different dynamic.

An explanation for Kiviuq's problems that focuses on the sexual dissatisfaction inherent in polygamy does not hold up well, since the story is the same when told about just one wife. I believe the sexual aspect must be part of the equation, but it doesn't explain everything. Elder Zippora Innuksuk points out that the wives were neglecting their work and that this was a serious offence. Survival in the North requires that all pull their weight. The women's contribution in preparing and preserving food, as well as in doing everything related to creating all-important arctic clothing, was a critical one. Kiviuq could not survive long without their work any more than they could without his. The important lesson here is that we must all contribute to the good of the whole, even when it is uncomfortable for us.

To me, visiting the penis in the lake was a curious offence for these women to have committed. The storytellers emphasize that at first everything had gone well and the wives had done their work normally. After all, it is very possible to conceal a love affair and keep up with one's work at the same time. We have no sense that the lake was very far away and that getting there would have taken much time. What changed? One day things were fine and the next they were not.

The answer may have to do with shamanic time. Calling a *tuurngaq* brings up the entire shamanic reality and everything that goes with it, including a very fluid sense of time. If one or even both of the wives were shamans, they would have entered this shamanic time while visiting the lake, represented by their sleeping deeply on returning. The sleep could at one and the same time represent their trance state and be a forerunner of death. We have no idea how much time passed, but it was time out of normal life – including their work.

In real life this story could represent a situation where someone dies unexpectedly. Perhaps the wives became ill and died and the rest happened in Kiviuq's vision. He went through various stages of grief, including denial and anger, and eventually buried them. This is similar to the way the seal-child may have lain sick in bed while the grandmother tried to heal him. Perhaps the child had died and the story represents the grandmother's vision. This part of Kiviuq's adventures also parallels, in an odd way, the story of the Greenland wife and her lover, mentioned in the "Wolf Women, Tiny Spiders, and Homecoming" chapter.

It was here that our crew came closest to serious disagreement about the story and even our line of questioning about it. As I noted earlier, the Inuit elders referred to this as the embarrassing part of the story, and I've been assured that there is no translation discrepancy about the word embarrassed. Inuit men seemed to be most embarrassed about the sexual part, whether because of the way sex was portrayed or because of the suggestion of Kiviuq's inadequacy. They lightened up as Kiviuq took his revenge, enjoying his cleverness. Inuit women were mainly neutral, although most responded to my amusement when the penis appeared in the lake. Younger Inuit men were not outraged but they still took this episode seriously. Non-Inuit listeners were most disturbed about the killing that was to come, its brutal and premeditated manner. Male listeners responded in much the same way as the female – if anything they seemed more disturbed by the murder. Although we reached different conclusions, John and I were highly involved emotionally – we both wanted to find a way to understand and even justify our hero's actions so that we could portray him in a positive light. If a villain had been engaging in the same acts, we would of course respond differently, whereas Inuit might not. They recognize that this wanting to explain and find a positive outcome is a cultural tendency of ours. They gently remind us that stories tell of both the good and the bad – they simply portray life as it is, without interpretation or justification. To outsiders the Inuit stories sometimes seem stark for this reason. There is no sugar-coating in the telling.

An important thing to remember is that sex outside marriage was not necessarily considered wrong in pre-Christian Inuit life. Keeping it secret was the problem. This was much like the distinction drawn between taking something with the owner's knowledge and stealing it in secret. I wonder if sex with a non-human wouldn't have been more disturbing to one's partner than sex with a human. It was considered highly dangerous and of course couldn't result in human children. On the other hand, Kiviuq himself had had at least one extramarital relationship unknown to his wife by this time, possibly also with a non-human if the daughter killed by her mother was really a wolf. Non-Inuit listeners often comment on the double standard involved in his jealousy.

Death and the Social Contract

Δ Kiviuq's anger did not abate after he had cooked the penis and fed it to his wives. He went out and collected maggots, keeping them in a caribou skin. Some say he got the wives to make him new mitts and that he used them for the collecting.

He cornered his first wife and asked her, "Which are you most afraid of, maggots or the knife?" She chose maggots, saying, "We can squash maggots. I am not afraid of them." He made her sit on the caribou skin. At first she tried to put her parka flap under herself, but he cut it off and held her there as the maggots entered her body through every opening. She spoke, describing which parts they were eating – intestines, womb, stomach, liver, lungs, and heart. At last she died.

Now the maggots came back out through every body opening in the form of small animals, including weasels and squirrels but mainly lemmings. Kiviuq was still so angry that he took a burning brand from the fire and burnt one lemming, who went away with a bent nose.

Kiviuq was not finished. He asked his second wife, "Which are you more afraid of, maggots or the knife?" She chose the knife, saying, "It will be quick." She knew there was no way to avoid her death. Bernadette Uttaq says the second choice was fire, a punishment with a sense of Christian hell about it. When he had pierced her with his knife, he buried both wives under stones and moved his camp. Δ

Only one of the wives seemed distressed when they learned that they were eating the penis. We're not sure which one. If it's her *tuurngaq*, that could explain either why she doesn't mind eating it or why she's upset, depending on your point of view. The wives are never differentiated in the telling, but I always think that the wife who was first to wade into the water, the one who was distressed by Kiviuq's cutting and cooking the penis, and the one who was murdered first and came back as the fox must have been the same, and that she must have been the one who had waited unpartnered while he was away on his long journey. If this was also the one he most loved, it would explain why his rage focused more on her. Percy Tutannuaq and Albert Kimaliakyuk point out that the other might have been an arranged marriage, perhaps with less passion in it. In story terms, two parallel characters allow two different possibilities to work out, showing listeners the results of each side of a choice. One had taken a new husband and lived well, the other had waited and lived poorly. Now, oddly enough, they are both in the same boat. We have already seen other pairs of women – the two irontails, who were mother and daughter, and then the women who lived with the log of wood. When one is older than the other, there are issues of power. In the case of the two wives, the question is about both power and love.

A number of elders were distressed about Kiviuq's flagrant injuring of an animal. This is one of the worst sins among Inuit hunters, who are well aware of how their entire existence depends on animals. To them, burning the lemming had more significance than killing his wife, which came as a shock to me.[5] But clearly Kiviuq had broken a vitally important law, which would have had serious consequences. It could have been the point where Kiviuq's fate was sealed in terms of his living in the community and having a successful marriage. A person who does not care for animals properly will live poorly at best. The situation seems to be remedied when Kiviuq pursues the fox to her den. Although the mechanism is not clear, he is forgiven. But it is still possible that he misused shamanic as well as physical power when he called his wife's helping spirit and when he killed by using maggots. That killing pursues him later in life.

With my outsider's focus on the human, I asked elder Henry Evaluardjuk, "Wasn't it wrong of Kiviuq to murder his wives?" and he replied sadly, "Of course it was wrong. Very wrong." Samson Quinangnaq also stated unequivocally that Kiviuq had done wrong. Philip Paniaq emphasizes that even when justified, murder was not tolerated and a murderer could expect to have to move away or to engage in a lengthy blood feud. Clearly, if someone was behaving insanely, any execution needed to be a group decision. Generally an individual should not take things into his or her own hands.[6]

In Rasmussen's work on the Netsilik, we read that Kiviuq was exiled to the south on account of a murder he committed among his own people (1931, 376). We wondered if this was a reference to the murder of his wife/wives, either in this story or in the one where he murdered his wife and her lover. The answer is not clear. It makes sense but feels wrong to me.

In a strange reversal of the maggots' usual association with death, the insects re-emerge as live lemmings. Although maggots usually eat bodies that are dead or dying, here they eat the wife's body while it is very much alive, acting as agents of her death. The whole process is a graphic example of the way a body decomposes and contributes to new life, and it is especially striking in a culture where the belief in reincarnation is so strong that death is nearly synonymous with birth. And so, as birth comes from death, it almost seems that these animals are the offspring of the wife and the lake spirit.

If the wives' shamanic sleep is actually death, the maggots make perfect sense, tying in with the stories of other characters who seem to have died more than once, including Kiviuq himself. There is probably a connection here with the words Kiviuq's Greenland wife spoke as her ghost climbed into his kayak. "To kill someone who is already dead is the unkindest thing of all." I wonder if killing a dead person has anything to do with the irrational anger we often feel towards a person who has died, leaving us alone.

These possible connections become even more interesting when we hear that one wife returns in the form of a fox who becomes Kiviuq's next wife. Although Inuit do not eat lemmings, foxes depend on them. The wife now appears to be recycling her body as food for her next incarnation. The lemmings will also help the wife several times in her fox incarnation, acting as though they are her helping spirits, just as the polar bear or snow bunting is Kiviuq's. This may partly explain how Kiviuq is forgiven for injuring the lemming – the forgiveness comes through the wife whose helping spirit is the lemming.

Birgitte Sonne points out that lemmings were often shamanic helping spirits and that they could burrow through a person's body, killing them. She relates this image to the way lemmings burrow through snow and earth. The emergence of the lemmings is an interesting reversal of the way the Fishmaker later makes fish, some say by passing wood chips through a hole in his body.

Women and Community

One Udeghe story, which we'll see in the next chapter, "Lake Cousins," tells of a hunter who went badly astray, died, and returned to life. Presumably he became a better hunter as a result of his transformation. Kiviuq's wife also comes back to life, in the form of a fox, and takes good care of the housework.

I began to feel that there is a female cycle in the epic that runs parallel to Kiviuq's male journey. The two wives seem to begin a cycle about his marriages that continues with fox and goose, each female character highlighting a different stage in a woman's life and character. In the fox-wife's story we'll see her forgiveness, her innate shyness and fidelity, and her relationships with other animals. With the goose-wife come children and a woman's need to stay true to her own nature. But what if we also work back from the story of the penis in the lake?

In the legend's opening, Kiviuq is both challenged and protected by female shamanic power, and develops in the process. The female characters are mother figures or teachers rather than wives. The grandmother, the wife of Tuutalik, Bee Woman, and others propel or protect the hero. Even the threat of death can be a form of mothering, as we see when Bee Woman or the big spiders bring Kiviuq back to life. A man grows up under the influence of elder women, who protect, teach, and challenge him. Only after this tutelage is he ready to form adult partnerships with women and grow into a provider and leader. So it is with Kiviuq. Later he is fully empowered, while the female figure dances between animal

Zippora Innuksuk and Kira Van Deusen, Igloolik

forms and human incarnations, learning about being human through contrast.

A girl also grows up under female influence. The daughter who was murdered by her mother was the first one Kiviuq seemed to be really fond of, but in her own terms she had no authority over her own life, remaining under control of her mother. Had she survived, she would have set out on the road to her own wisdom, becoming a mother and later an elder, ready to help younger people on their way. It's not an easy road.

We are still on the cusp of the story's midpoint. In one version that Rasmussen recorded in Greenland, the penis in the lake appears after Kiviuq's wife has taken another husband and he has killed them both (Ostermann 1939, 52–5). He meets the two women living with the log of wood after the storm at sea and finds out that they visit the penis in the lake. The key details distinguishing this story from the one we heard about Kiviuq's two wives is that the lake spirit gives those women eider ducks, contributing to their survival. They were living alone, whereas the two wives were living with their husband. While the log gave them food from the sea, the lake spirit gave those women food from a border area, since eider ducks live both on land and on water. Thus the food cycle was complete.

I've wondered before about the composition of the community after the hunters died at sea. While male-female balance would eventually have been regained, there must have been a period of time when women had to provide food in the absence of men. Kiviuq's adventures at sea recall this absence of men in his home community in that he meets so many females living alone. The situation at home would have been very much like that of the two women who live with the log of wood, except that there would have been more women and they would have been on the mainland, which would have made a big difference in their ability to get food, at least in summer.

While Kiviuq was away on his long journey, the wife who did not take another husband must have had to work harder to provide for herself and her children. At the same time, her refusal to believe he was dead must have been a help to him on a spiritual level while he was gone. Perhaps a number of widows were also providing for themselves after their men were lost at sea. Over time other men joined the community, some of the women remarried, and children grew up. But the wife who waited was still alone. If the single wife had developed the habit of getting food by calling on the spirit of the lake, she should have given the visits up when her husband returned. But it may not always have been easy to integrate a man back into the family after a long absence. Old habits are hard to break, even when the man is much loved and valued.

The two wives return to the lake together. I'm assuming that the wife who had lived alone while Kiviuq was away led the other wife, although I can't be certain. Now there are no eider ducks, only sex. Samson Quinangnaq says the sex leaves the women cold and shivering – sluggish instead of invigorated as they might have been. At some time in the past they may have received food from the lake's spirit, but they have already lost that ability when this story begins. In fact, this may be the exact moment that they realize they've lost it.

The wife has held on to a habit that is no longer serving her, and she has lost track of what her job is in this very different family arrangement. A willingness to adapt quickly must be one of those Inuit survival mechanisms. In many cultures there are rules about what is appropriate for men and women to do when they live together as opposed to when they are separated. These rules create situations mysterious to an outsider. In Tuva it's considered shameful to a man if a woman slaughters a sheep or does throat singing. No one can explain what is shameful about it, just that it is, and that is enough for them. It's only the outsiders who want to analyse further. At the same time, it is completely acceptable and even obligatory for a woman to slaughter animals when the man is away, and she may do throat singing any time she is alone and feels like it. Both Inuit and Tuvans have been discouraged from questioning their elders about such things.

It's also possible that the wives called the spirit for a completely different reason, one we know nothing about. Bernadette Uttaq says there were greater numbers of strange beings in those days, and scarier ones. I wonder if Kiviuq's hunting suffered while this was going on. In the story of the horsetail girl the man's hunting suffered while he was being deceived by the false bride, but we have not heard that things went wrong for Kiviuq.

Retribution

In holding on to behaviour that is no longer appropriate, the wife acts wrongly, and the punishment is swift. There are no second chances. Kiviuq does not talk to his wives sensibly or try to convince them to return to normal behaviour. He doesn't call in mediation from elders; nor does he walk away, leaving them alone again. Instead he is overcome with rage, almost as if possessed. His behaviour is so out of character that it seems some other power is channelling through him. If seen strictly from the wife's point of view, he becomes her retribution. As we'll see in the Udeghe story of the good/bad hunter in the "Lake Cousins" chapter, a person who makes a mistake so serious that it will over time endanger the wider community is in need of transformation. Both the Udeghe hunter and the Inuit wife are reborn wiser. Interestingly enough, that transformation comes the same way in both cultures – by having the body eaten by creepy small creatures.

Shamans in many cultures report being eaten by spirits during their initiation. The story seems very different if we look at it shamanically rather than from the human point of view. Instead of appearing cruel and almost insane, Kiviuq can be seen as taking on a task beyond his human calling and as assisting his wife's transformation, which is perhaps a further stage in her initiation. Both are powerful people when we meet them, and yet they go through trials that seem to be more involved with their own further development than with helping others – they undergo another stage of initiation. If the daughter we met in the last chapter does come back to life, we might look at her mother the same way, although in that case the daughter doesn't appear to have done anything wrong. Perhaps, the daughter being young, this was her first initiation. It's interesting that both of the people who "bring about another's transformation" are motivated by jealousy. Murder is still an obvious invasion of the other and brings its own burden.[7]

Shamanic researcher Gizelle Rhyon Berry pointed out to me that the elemental harshness of the environment Inuit live in encourages them to think of harsh solutions to their problems – such as the execution of those who create a danger to others, the banishment from the community of wrongdoers, or the voluntary death of elders in times of hunger. For that reason she believes that Inuit story life contains more violence than that of certain more southerly indigenous peoples who live in plant-oriented cultures and a more inviting climate. For them, violence is almost unknown in daily life and even in stories and shamanic journeys. This does not mean that Inuit are more violent than southern peoples in their ordinary lives – after all, strong social mores have evolved to prevent waste of life – but the harshness of their lives finds expression in story and dream. Gizelle told me she had discussed dreams with a number of Inuit when she lived in the North. Many of them had extremely violent dreams, but since their waking lives were peaceful, they were not disturbed by that violence. Between waking and dreaming, a balanced life was achieved. Perhaps the story works like that too.

Nanai shaman Mingo Geiker once said that those who make our lives most difficult are those who help us grow the most. As hard as that seems, it is true. Both Kiviuq and his favourite wife have dual roles, as human beings and as shamans. As a human woman, the wife indulges her need for sex and is cruelly punished for it. As a shaman, she has a parallel marriage with a spirit helper and undergoes transformation into her next life form, where she becomes helpful to the very man who killed her, healing his jealousy. Clearly, their destiny goes further along the same road. As a human man, Kiviuq makes a serious mistake by indulging his anger and hurting an animal, and suffers afterwards by losing his two animal wives. As a shaman, he helps another person through an initiation, as he has been helped by the grandmother and Bee Woman.

None of this makes it easier to tell the story of the penis in the lake to a non-Inuit audience, especially in the atmosphere of political correctness that permeates our public life. Inside or outside school, one would never want to condone male violence against women. Today's Inuit are also concerned with this problem.

Colleen Rusk of Kitikmeot Heritage Society speaks with amusement about her own reaction when she saw one of the stories chosen by the society and Nunavut Arctic College for inclusion in a publication.[8] "The Man with Two Wives" is the story of the penis in the lake but is told about an unnamed man. The women do not die at the end of this story but instead get the flu from being forced by their husband to sit on seaweed full of worms. Colleen was shocked, first by the man having two wives and then by the rest, concerned about responses from outside the area. Later she came to respect the compilers' choice, even if it did make her and other outsiders uncomfortable.

Canadian storyteller Nan Gregory speaks about this kind of discomfort in relation to telling long stories in a retreat situation: "The feeling of doing homage to a tradition is strong in our group epic tellings. Maybe this is because we're able to let the strangeness be, and don't feel the necessity of shaving off the sharp edges to make the story work for our audience. I think that kind of revision is the greatest disservice a teller can do to a culture, story, and audience."

Social Change

By the time Kiviuq's life was first written down in the late nineteenth century, Europeans had been in the Arctic for some time. They had brought trade, guns, religion, schooling, and disease. Social disruption was already beginning, as life began to centre more on the trading posts.

Between Rasmussen's time and our own there has been massive change in language, housing, education, religion, government intervention in community affairs – a whole way of life.

Elders who were raised on the land frequently refer to how noisy and distracting life has become, how it has lost its sense. Jacob Peterloosie describes himself as having two brains that are out of touch with each other. "There are things we'd like to think over but it all gets lost in the din. It's as if my brain is divided in two – one for the older generation and one for the new. What's back here can't seem to make friends with what's in front. They don't seem to get along any more. I want to use old ideas that can help today. Thoughts up front are drifting on the surface of our lives. As if we don't care how we live. Back here the rules are not to be treated that way." He adds that he doesn't even have time to think things over the way he would like because of the constant intrusion of telephone, television, and other aspects of modern life.[9]

People tell the episode of the penis in the lake much more frequently today than was recorded in the past. Eleven elders told it to us, and none of them mentioned gifts of food from the lake's spirit. This discrepancy cannot be accounted for by regional variation, as the early ethnographers recorded in all the regions we did and even more. Stories do reflect social change over time, even when they do not mention any of the outside influences. Although details such as the appearance of glass beads make their way into traditional stories, tellers rarely include the actual events that precipitated the change in ways that are obvious to an outsider. With the exception of family story and historical narrative, we hear nothing of the arrival of strangers and the conflicts that may have arisen. Nonetheless, the shifts make their way into the very fabric of the story.

In pre-contact society the injunction was to walk away from trouble. But it gets much harder to walk away in a settled society. In spite of the difficulties of nomadic life, there was much more space. Being free to walk out into the tundra, perhaps even with a different partner for a while, would be much different from being tied to a settled community, with a paid job and permanent house. Even shamans were powerless to deal with problems in the old way, since new problems had sources outside their ken – guns, diseases, drugs, and alcohol. There was no previous experience, no story that helped in dealing with this new world. For Kiviuq, the problem was amplified by the fact that he and his wives were away from the community. There was nobody to turn to for help, nobody to raise a sensible voice.

The defection of Kiviuq's wives is incomprehensible to him, happening as it did without reason or balance, and thus his rage is greater than it might have been otherwise. He reacts by striking out at those he loves – a familiar picture in today's Inuit communities, where domestic violence is increasingly a problem. I heard a sad story on our trip about a young woman who had walked out into the tundra and died, leaving children behind. The story that circulated publicly was that she became lost in a storm. Privately I heard that she deliberately walked away to escape a brutal husband. Walking out into the tundra today, as this girl did, feels like a tragic dead end, not the intelligent solution it so often was for Kiviuq. Yet the issue of abuse is relevant. Many will say this interpretation goes counter to the way Inuit would have understood the story fifty years back, and that is so. But the issue jumps out and hits a modern audience so graphically that it would be impossible to bring the story to the public today without addressing it. It could be a good jumping-off point for a discussion about what Kiviuq and his wives might have done differently and how a community, past or present, could deal with such situations. In public situations, the telling requires some preparation and the feelings aroused may need to be addressed through different forms of discussion. I came to see that the return of scatological humour in the following section does help lighten the energy. Although it does not provide resolution, it gives an outlet for emotion, allowing movement.

Sometimes meanings shift as the social setting of the listeners changes, even when the words stay the same. The Udeghe story of the good/bad hunter is a good example. With practically no change in words or nuance, a modern audience gets the idea that the parents were lazy and that they were stupid to kill their son, who was bringing back such an abundance of animals. But it would have been clear to listeners less than a hundred years ago that the son had to be stopped. Every day he had to go further and further from home because he had killed all the animals nearby. He was clearly taking more than he needed, and the hunting became much easier with a rifle than it had been with a bow and arrow. This was as great a sin for the Udeghe as for the Inuit. The change in interpretation shows how an ancient story has taken on the social history of contact with the outside world and all the resulting damage. The process is especially amazing to observe among the Inuit, since they are so exacting about passing things on exactly as they heard them. The truth of immediate experience shines through the telling of a tale that has been passed down through the ages. An old story becomes the vehicle for a new message. In order to retain the old message, sometimes the words need to change.

Storyteller Johanna Kuyvenhoven feels that stories change over time in part because of the way we perceive them while listening and telling. I had described to her my sense that the storytellers were "dipping into the well" when they provided fresh details and when they looked for motivations and links. What we find in "the well" today is different from what our grandparents found partly because the world we live in changes our imagery.

In her work with children, Johanna came to describe three circles of listening. The first is the outer circle in which we are aware of our surroundings, the teller, and other listeners. In the second circle the outside world falls away as we enter the story and we are alone with the teller. And in the innermost circle even the teller disappears and we are fully in the story. This is the experience that children, by their own testimony, crave most strongly (Kuyvenhoven 2009). I believe people down through the ages have craved it. This is the place that provides rest from the day-to-day world and healing on a spiritual and even physical level. In spite of the listeners' having fallen away in the second circle, we feel connected with others. From that sense of connectedness spring cultures and friendships.

The well is held not only in the teller's memory. It is also created by the presence of listeners – their memories, hopes, fears, and concerns. Johanna understands the well as being something a bit more deliberate than what is understood as "collective unconscious." In our experience, tellers and listeners come together in the state of being that makes us receptive to the well's information – outside our individual heads, inside the story. As one of the ten-year-olds Johanna interviewed said, "When our teacher tells a story, there are no words." An odd description of an art that uses words as its main tool – and it yet very aptly captures the feeling.

Both while telling and while listening, people often "see" details that have not been mentioned. Listeners sometimes "remember" words that the teller did not speak, and tellers "see" material that was not in their source. We've already seen that Annie Peterloosie's grandmother recognized this phenomenon and attributed regional change to the way it works.[10] I was once part of a storytellers' panel at a meeting of the American Folklore Society. Each of the panel members shared an occasion where our listeners were positive they had heard something in the story that in fact had not been told. Equally surprising are those times when we find that we've done it ourselves – looking back at the source, we see that a detail we told was simply not there. When I was preparing to tell the Tuvan epic "Woman of Steel," I saw in my mind an old man walking eagerly down a desert hill to join the heroine and her family, as well as the woman he had loved in his youth. But I couldn't place exactly where in the chain of events this happened. I went back to the original – and it wasn't there. I was shocked, having seen it so clearly in my mind's eye. I believe this is one way stories change over time – we enter and live in the story and sometimes we see something that wasn't mentioned by anyone else. And we retell what we see.

This was the section of Kiviuq's story that was most challenging to me, as listener, as storyteller, and even as writer. The best lesson I've learned as a teller is that I should not try to explain the story or even to subtly include an explanation in my telling by means of words and expression. Instead, when a story is difficult for me, I should first sit with it until I feel ready, and then tell it simply. It's also important to create a climate for discussion, so that the storytelling won't be just a performance, but will allow room for listeners to speak.

Δ Now Kiviuq was disconnected again. He moved on and set up camp in a new place, not too far away.[11] Δ

A new trend appears. Prior to his homecoming, Kiviuq travelled entirely by kayak, but now he embarks on a land journey. He is a master of both elements, although more successful at sea. His story lives in the dichotomy that controls Inuit life, especially their food.

Lake Cousins

In long stories there is less moralizing than in the short ones. They are more descriptive of the human condition. Lessons and messages become more complex and ambiguous. The "listener-storyteller" is not a judge as you may be in a short tale, but instead grows sympathetic to all.

– Linda Stender, Canadian storyteller, 2006

Udeghe storyteller Valentina Kyalundzyuga and I were working on a trilingual book of folk tales. We had selected, translated, and typed the stories and had them illustrated. Before going to press, I visited her in order to try out the preliminary version in the local school and to have Valentina check for typos in the Udeghe. It was my first trip to Gvasyugi village in winter. Crisp, sunny, beautiful, and very cold, even indoors. The teacher of the Udeghe language had her pupils acting out the phrases they learned, striding like valiant hunters across the classroom to keep their bodies warm as they spoke.

Valentina had been away and her house was cold. Generous as always, she had made sure that the best supplies of firewood had gone to those with the greatest need. By the time it had come to her own supply, the community truck had broken down out in the *taiga* and it would be impossible for it to bring in good dry wood before spring. What she got was hopelessly wet. We developed a routine – piling pieces of wet wood on top of her stove, where they lay spitting and crackling until we hoped they were dry enough, and then putting them inside the stove to burn. The second afternoon Valentina peered at the thermometer and announced proudly, "At last! We've achieved 15 de-

Schoolchildren in Gvasyugi village exercise to keep warm while learning the Udeghe language. The heating system in their school is severely inadequate, given the outside temperatures of -40°C and below.

grees!" Not bad, as it was minus 45 outside. Meanwhile we sat huddled in coats and boots, discussing the cultural quirks I needed to understand in order to get the English translation right. At night we slept under warm camel hair blankets.

The first question had been which stories to include – we were aiming for young readers. Valentina wanted to publish a certain story that disturbed me. In it a man beat his wife to the point that her body became severely deformed – into that of a frog. In Udeghe folklore, any inept housekeeper is jokingly referred to as a frog, and Valentina assured me

Valentina Kyalundzyuga drying firewood on her stovetop.
The outside temperature was -45°C.

that this story was meant to point out in an amusing way the necessity of doing a good job at cooking and sewing. True, the tone was light, but I worried that readers might take the story as licence for wife-beating. "Ridiculous," said Valentina. "Nobody would think such a thing. The story is a joke." She won – the frog story is in the book, although it would be unlikely to pass muster in a Canadian school.

This is the same kind of problem I have in telling the story of the penis in the lake. Although Inuit don't treat it as a joke, most of them aren't worried about the story encouraging a man to murder his wife. A few, though, are concerned about the violence and work to find solutions. But in the story's own culture, there is no perceived reason to treat the subject with kid gloves. Stories convey truth – not just comfortable truths but also unpalatable ones.

Kiviuq's is only one of many stories that we non-aboriginal storytellers may find difficult to tell to our own audiences. But there are advantages in their telling and hearing for those who are willing to dig in. Linda Stender points out that long stories offer greater possibilities than short ones, for they allow the difficult truths to be spoken aloud without negative judgment. Characters develop fully. Solutions can be found. Things just are as they are in such stories. Sometimes it is the only way the truth can be spoken at all. Some short tales, including Valentina's frog story, can speak the truth as well, although their characters are more black and white than those in longer stories. It seems to take a certain length to allow for deeper development.

Part of the problem lies in what we expect of a story. Most Westerners, consciously or unconsciously, want a happy ending – at least from a folk tale. We expect the good guy to be unfailingly good, or at least to improve over time. Ancient epic stories don't always work that way – no matter which continent they originate on. Their cultures tend to judge heroes not by what they did wrong but by what they did right, forgiving lapses. People are loyal to their heroes, accepting their human frailties. Contemporary Western cultures, on the other hand, may turn on a former hero if he makes a serious misstep. The epic approach shows more compassion for the hero, although this may be hard on those who must learn to forgive or overlook his mistakes, no matter how hurtful. People who survive together in harsh and severe climates understand the importance of each individual – there are no throw-away people.

Perhaps we are too influenced by television, a visual medium where values are conveyed without layering. In contrast, when we listen, we visualize, and this allows us to identify at some moments with the bad guy as well as the good. We come to realize that we may later be judged as we judge. Mainstream television programming doesn't give us that kind of room. But simplistic and moralistic thinking is much older than television. It has often been used in the service of a political agenda and may take its source in pain too deep to allow for the expression of compassion.

Another Udeghe tale, "The Good/Bad Hunter," has several points in common with the lake part of the Kiviuq legend – an important rule is broken and a person is killed by insects and snakes. It tells of a hunter who was so incredibly successful that his aging parents got exhausted carrying the take home. They decided to kill their son. Nowadays the parents appear foolish and cruel, but in the old days everyone would have understood that the boy was overhunting and had to be stopped.

The Good/Bad Hunter[1]

Old man Kanda and his wife had one son. The son would go hunting, and the parents carried the meat home. Old man Kanda wore the skin off his shoulders with the rubbing from the straps on the sled. He got tired of carrying meat day after day. The parents started to think about killing their son. They made a coffin, and when it was done, they placed it on their son's sleeping place. They lined the coffin with soft fur bedding. Now they went out and collected insects, worms, and snakes in a basket and kept it close at hand.

That night when their son came home, his parents said, "Lie down in this coffin, little son. When you are very tired, this will give you a good rest." The boy lay down in the coffin and fell asleep.

The parents shouted in the night to see if he would wake up, but he slept on. Then they filled the coffin with the crawling creatures they had collected and quickly closed the cover. They harnessed the dog to the coffin with a bast rope and pushed it in the water. The dog ran along the shore pulling the coffin downstream until the rope broke.

The coffin floated down the river until it came to the place where a girl named Emenda lived. If you knew Udeghe stories well, you'd realize that Emenda is the one who always does things wrong – and that's what happened this time. She came out on the shore with her bucket to get water and there she saw the coffin. "That's strange," she thought. "People usually bury their dead in the earth, but this one is floating on the water!" She wanted to drag the coffin in to shore but she heard scratching and grating from inside. Her fear overcame her curiosity and she let the coffin go. It floated further downstream.

The coffin floated on and came to the place where Belye lived. And if you had heard Udeghe stories before you'd know that she is the one who always does things right. She is an excellent seamstress, a fine artist and housekeeper, and always seems to know what to do. When she saw the coffin on the water she too thought it was odd. But although she too heard the scratching and knocking, her courage overcame her fear and she pulled it in to shore.

She opened the coffin and out crawled the insects and snakes. All that was left of Yegdyghe was one bone from his little finger.[2] She washed the bone, wrapped it in lynx fur, and placed it in a cradle with rattles made of lynx bones. She rocked it for seven days and seven nights without stopping, and sang the whole time.

Son of old man Kanda,
Seven days and seven nights I will sing you to sleep.
Rattling with lynx claws, tightly wrapped in lynx fur.
A strong man will grow up.
I sing you my lullaby!

On the seventh day Yegdyghe got out of the cradle and stood up. He went out hunting so that Belye would have food to eat.

And so they lived. One day Belye told him how he came to be in that place, how his own father and mother had closed him in the coffin with crawling creatures while he slept. She told him how he had floated down the river and how he had come back to life from his one finger bone. And about the girl Emenda who had not saved him.

Yegdyghe and Belye set off upstream. They came to the place where Emenda lived and she invited them in. "What news do you bring me?" she asked.

"I was floating in a coffin and you did not save me. Instead you pushed me back into the deep water," Yegdyghe told her.

Emenda was so upset that she had missed the opportunity to get a good husband that she took her belt and hung herself on a dry tree branch.

Yegdyghe and Belye continued on their way. At last his old dog came out to greet him – just skin and bones now. The dog told Yegdyghe, "Your parents do nothing but fight – each blaming the other for the death of their son."

Yegdyghe came to his parents' bark hut. He climbed up the wall and looked down through the smoke hole. They were boiling up an old hunter's boot to eat. He threw a piece of fat down into the pot. Old man Kanda saw fat on the surface of the water and said, "Look! Fat has cooked out of our son's hunting boot – the boot of a successful hunter!"

"I can't stand listening to you!" said the mother. "You put him in the coffin just so you wouldn't have to haul the meat home. It's your fault he died." And the two of them pulled each other's hair.

Yegdyghe and Belye did not go in. They continued up along the river until they came to a place where there was much fish and many animals. They built themselves a hut and lived there. And in time they had two children, a boy and a girl.

"The Good/Bad Hunter" belongs to a type of story called *ningma*. These stories have their basis in the storyteller's inner vision, as opposed to the *telungu*, whose basis lies in a historical life story. A *ningma* shares with several shamanic activities a linguistic root with the meaning "to see with the eyes closed." Generally, *ningma* is translated as magic tale and *telungu* as legend. Both may contain magic. There is more leeway in making changes to a *ningma* than to a *telungu*, according to shamans and native scholars. A visionary story contains a different kind of truth than the historical type – a deep internal truth that transcends time and place. As Annie Peterloosie pointed out in relation to Inuit storytelling, each storyteller may see something new, and thus the story detail shifts while its heart remains the same. Of course, in terms of social values, any story can be subject to shifting interpretations.

Female Shamans

Besides evidence of initiation through dismemberment, Kiviuq's story shows us how females went on to practise shamanism. We saw this first when the grandmother turned the child into a seal and called the storm, and then when odd beings like Bee Woman brought Kiviuq back to life and competed with him. And now Kiviuq's human wife calls her helping spirit.

There were certainly many powerful female shamans in Siberia as well. In fact, there are some who believe that women were the first shamans. A number of recorded stories tell how the first shamans came to be in Siberia. They feel more mythic than the Inuit story of the first shamans – more *ningma* than *telungu*. The Sakha people of central Siberia tell of a woman who conceived from a raven and gave birth to the first two shamans. The Buriat (relatives of the Mongolians) tell of a woman who received the gift of shamanism from an eagle and retained the powers herself instead of passing them to her children. Some Buriat say that the two children of a swan maiden became the first shamans.

The English word shaman comes from the Tungus-language word *sama* (shaman). Any similarity to "man" is purely coincidental. Linguistic evidence also supports the idea that women practised shamanism before men did, at least among the Turkic peoples. The word for female shaman, *udagan*, comes from the root word for fire and is found with many small variations over a large geographic and cultural area. The words for male shaman, on the other hand, vary greatly among those far-flung peoples, sharing no linguistic roots. Linguists believe that this shows that the words were adopted after the peoples had separated. Although female Siberian shamans were powerful, they were less showy than their male counterparts. For this reason, more females survived the Soviet persecution, living into the 1990s when I met them.

In the story of the good/bad hunter, the main shamanic figure is Belye. Using the most time-honoured shamanic skill, she sings Yegdyghe back to life from a single bone. The Tuvan warrior-heroine Kang Kys also sings to bring her father back to life from his bones. Bringing the dead to life seems to be an ability possessed only by female Siberian shamans – the male can heal the sick by bringing back lost souls, but once people are truly dead, it takes a female to resurrect them.

But for the most part shamanic skill crosses gender lines – in fact, that's part of the point of it. Male and female skills and activities are much less distinct and separate in shamanic practice than they are in the everyday life of nomadic peoples. In the course of their initiation, men and women learn to partake of each other's experience and wind up with a more complete range of understanding.[3] Lessons also cross lines. A Khakassian hunter learns that otherworld gifts should be used only in emergencies, as does the Inuit woman who calls food from the lake. When the Khakassian hunter was in desperate straits, a mountain spirit helped him home and gave him a wealth of valuable furs on the condition that he not share them with the brother who had accompanied him on the hunt but had gone home when things had gone badly.[4] Under normal rules, hunters would share the take, but in this case the mountain spirit told the man to break that rule. The final outcome was problematical – the man wound up rich but lonely (Kazachinova and Van Deusen 2003, 30–3).

The Udeghe hunter learns to obey the rules through his death and rebirth. Kiviuq's wife learns to partake in the work of human society through hers. The two are at different phases in life – Kiviuq's wife is already in her power, she has a spirit helper, and she has helped her husband home through her unflagging belief that he would return. The Udeghe hunter has learned practical skills but still lacks understanding about living harmoniously with nature. In this he gains help. It's possible he is undergoing a hunter's initiation rather than a shamanic one.

One other detail of the story of the penis in the lake reminds me of several stories told by the Siberian Udeghe and Nanai people of the Amur River region. Their territory has several lakes whose water appears red – and stories to go with them. Nanai storyteller Maria Kile tells of a red lake, saying the red colour resulted from the death of a crocodile that had eaten a girl (Van Deusen 2001, 217). The crocodile is a complete oddity in their climate, and thus it is surprising that the Nanai have a word for crocodile in their own language, a word not imported from Russian, Chinese, or any other language. This adds to information that leads some anthropologists to believe that ancestors of the Nanai may have lived further south in the past and brought the memory with them. The Udeghe story Kakta Ni (in the "Seal Cousins" chapter) tells of the red water that brought the hero's seal-wife back to life. When Kiviuq cut off the penis, the water turned red, and Samson Quinangnaq tells us it is red to this day – he can point to the location. Interestingly, all three of these are murder stories that involve otherworldly beings. Red is associated with blood, symbolizing life. Science tells us that the red colour in the Siberian water is caused by mineral deposits, but story always associates it with extraordinary events.

After all these extraordinary events, the Siberian characters continued living normally. Kiviuq moved his tent and went hunting.

The Fox-Wife

We sing to make the thoughts pleasant since a man is dangerous when angry.
– Tatilgak[1]

Taima!

Δ Kiviuq lived on his own for some time. He hunted and returned lonely to his tent. After a while though, he began to notice that someone had been there in his absence. He found cooked food waiting for him in the pot. The first day it was cold, the next day a bit warmer, and after a little time had passed, he arrived to find the food steaming hot. His mysterious helper must have just left.

Next day he pretended to go hunting and hid near the tent. After a while an arctic fox came sniffing. She went into the tent and a few minutes later a beautiful woman came out. She hung a fox skin over the tent ropes to dry and went back in to start cooking. Much attracted by her beautiful white hair, Kiviuq watched until she left.[2]

Next day he hid and kept watch. Each day he moved a little closer, careful to stay out of the wind.

At last he was close enough. He stepped forward and grabbed the fox skin, holding it tightly.

The woman came right out, demanding, "Give me back my skin!"

"I will give you back your skin only if you become my wife."

At first she was insistent but at last she gave in. The two began living together. Δ

At first I pictured Kiviuq hiding close to his tent, but I soon realized that a good hunter would have stayed far away from the animal's sensitive nose. Some people say he built a series of *inuksuit* to hide behind as he crept closer. Although it seems far-fetched to think the fox wouldn't have noticed abnormal activity when stone cairns were being built leading to the tent, this motif reflects the way Inuit used to hunt caribou. They built a double line of *inuksuit* in the shape of a funnel, luring migrating caribou into a river or lake where hunters waited in their kayaks, or into an area where they waited in blinds. Women and children would stand near the entrance of the funnel waving and yelling to chase the caribou into the trap. The people might howl like wolves. Sometimes the *inuksuit* were made to look like human beings to scare the caribou (Bennett and Rowley 2004, 65, 258). Here the use of *inuksuit* shows us Kiviuq's intelligence as a hunter; it also shows his patience – rewarded when at last he comes close enough to snatch the fox skin from the tent rope.

Several Inuit elders mentioned that Kiviuq saw the fox emerge from the grave of one of his wives, which suggests that the human woman had reincarnated as an animal. This lends strong support to the idea that she was a shaman in her own right, since *angakkuit* often take animal form between human incarnations. It is a sign of her power that the fox managed to get out of the grave even though she was covered with rocks. While I had assumed this was the first wife, Elisapee Karlik feels it was the second one.

Rasmussen recorded a story about one such cycle of incarnation from Netsilik storyteller Nakasuk of Ilivilermio.[3]

Arctic fox

The One Who Lets Himself Be Born Again

There once was one who let himself be born again in all forms, a shaman. Bear he was for a time. It was tiring, it is said; they walked so much, even in darkness they used to walk. Fjord seal he was for a time, they were always playing, it is said. The fjord seals amused themselves with sport, and out over the sea the waves came into movement after the fjord seals, it is said. They were very clever at shooting with the bow, they set something up in the snow as targets. They used to appear in human form then.

Wolf he was for a time and famished. They say one of the wolves gave him this hint: "You must grip the ground and in that way you must always follow us!" And then he could keep up with them, it was said, and he began to bring down caribou. Then he became a muskox. In among the muskoxen it was warm. Then he was a caribou. Just when they had gone sound asleep, the caribou used to jump up and start galloping. One became so terrified, it was so unpleasant.

They say that when the shaman came back to the people he related his experiences.

There is much one can learn from actually living inside an animal body. This breadth of experience contributes greatly to a shaman's power in human body. Nakasuk's tale, however, shows up the advantages of also being human.

Elder Joe Issaluk says that all animals can turn into humans. In his mind, the fox appeared to Kiviuq as a naked woman. He also recalls that people sometimes see lights in polar bear dens, which means the bears are in human form. Polar bears and other animals have the idea that humans are hard to beat, he says, and that is why they want to change form.

In realigning herself with Kiviuq, his former wife becomes a valuable partner. Beginning by cooking his food, she shows that she has learned an important lesson about living in relationship with humans. She has to hold up her end of the work. First she provides the warmth and nourishment of a good meal at the end of a long day's work. It's her decision to join the social contract.

When I first heard that the fox was a reincarnation of the wife, I was much surprised. Why would a woman be so willing to help the man who had murdered her? Wouldn't she have wanted him to learn a lesson? I've debated at length the question of whether Kiviuq actually did learn something, and it seems to me that for him the tragic result of the murders lies in the fact that both of his subsequent marriages fail, at least as told today. Sitting in our cozy hotel dining room in Igloolik chatting with Philip, I came to see that the fox-wife was able to forgive the murder because she knew beyond doubt that his act would come back on him. Her knowledge was so strong that she had no need to be the conscious agent of his comeuppance. This makes forgiveness easy for her. In light of her own transformation, she no longer looks like a victim and can rejoin him without rancour. A tough lesson but a good one.

But I came to wonder whether my using the word forgiveness might reflect only an outsider's view. Inuit do speak of the importance of letting things go, of not dwelling on them, but is that the same thing as forgiveness? We see that the wife didn't need to exact revenge, and we can learn from that. One thing is clear. If the wife had retaliated against Kiviuq, it would then have come back on her. She was better off to walk away, to let things go. Staying immersed in negative emotion has a bad effect on us.

The point here is that what may seem to be gaps in story logic are not deficiencies, even in story form. The information is filled in by listeners from their pool of common knowledge. This happens in any culture – it's just that most of us are not aware of all the information and assumptions that we hold in common and thus do not need to communicate to others. Confronting stories outside our own sphere can be confusing. But as storyteller Jan Andrews points out, it allows us to try things on: "With long stories we have the opportunity to take part in the sometimes baffling, incomprehensible differences of action and belief in different cultures. We can try these things out for ourselves and find out what they really mean."

I have learned something profound from this about forgiveness and acceptance. In a society where everyone is needed, there has to be a way to integrate even those who are most difficult to get along with. True, there may come a time when behaviours cannot be tolerated, but that limit must be stretched as far as humanly possible.

Mariano Aupilaarjuk emphasizes strongly that marriage with animals can be dangerous and can shorten a person's life. Rasmussen recorded that there was a real taboo against men having physical sexual intercourse with animals (1929, 98). But perhaps shamans and story heroes were an exception – they would be powerful enough to survive it. This was marriage on the spiritual plane rather than in the world of ordinary reality. Aupilaarjuk says, though, that people were not supposed to have sexual intercourse with spirits, and if they did, they needed to talk about it right away (Saladin d'Anglure 2001, 69).

Viewed in shamanic reality, the wife may have become Kiviuq's helping spirit, much like the polar bear and snow buntings we have already met.[4] The fox has several of the characteristics attributed to *tuurngait*. She is flighty and extremely shy. Spirits are often described in precisely those terms. Ollie Ittinuar told us that dead shamans often return as helping spirits to living shamans. Marriage with helping spirits is well known in many shamanic cultures, although it is quietly spoken about. One elderly Nanai shaman described herself to me as having a second family in the spirit world, whom she visited on her journeys, often just before returning home to this world.

Both Niviuvak Marqniq and Henry Isluanik put forward the idea that Kiviuq married animals because the human population was so small. There was a shortage of human women available. Theresa Kimaliadjuk cites Kiviuq's marriages with animals as proof of his strength. Could the danger stem from the fact that a human could only marry a shape-changing animal, not an ordinary one? Or is it true that any animal can change shape? A normal animal living temporarily in human form is called an *inuruuqqayuk*. This seems to be distinct from the *inurajait*, which are human-like beings who may also sometimes appear in animal form and can cause dangers of their own. Elders have not entirely clarified for outsiders the relations between people and various kinds of animal beings. This is an important focus for research in the near future, when there are still people alive who can explain such things.

If the fox-wife is a helping spirit, it could make a difference which one courted the other. We've seen that it is dangerous for a shaman to accept a *tuurngaq* who solicits him, and better to take one given by a mentor. Our sources don't mention the possibility that a shaman might court a particular spirit, but it would seem that if Kiviuq courts his wife again while she is in the form of a fox, the outlook would be better than if she courted him. In fact, they both work at it with clever determination. She's busy cooking and tidying up while he labours building *inuksuit*. The courtship seems at first glance to be mutual, so the result could be mixed, as it turned out to be. But since she started cooking before he crept up and grabbed her skin, it's fairly clear that she has taken the initiative, and thus there may be dangers involved.

Here we again have the motif of skin and its role in shape-shifting. The fox removes her own skin, though, instead of being skinned like the wolf daughter. The main way animals change shape in stories worldwide is to pull off their animal skin. The grizzly bear Kiviuq meets later does this, as do animals in many cultures. The image of the fox-wife hanging her fox skin out to dry has a double implication. If the skin was wet from rain or sweat, it would need care, just as a fur coat does, and her hanging it out to dry proves that she intends to use it again. And if an animal had been killed, its skin would have to be dried prior to treatment. A shy animal, sensitive about her odour, the fox may simply have wanted to remove the fox smell from the house so that Kiviuq would not notice it when he returned. However it was, as soon as the agreement was reached and the skin returned, Kiviuq and the fox became true partners, living and hunting together. Surely a natural predator made an ideal partner for a hunter. And perhaps he had gone through enough hard trials to now be ready to marry successfully in the animal world. Annie Peterloosie tells us that after this the fox took very good care of her skin.

Igloos and the Wolverine

The story has parallels in tales worldwide about men who marry in the animal world – parallels that include mysterious housekeepers and the withholding of a skin – but from here on Kiviuq's adventures depart on a purely Inuit path.

Δ As winter arrived, Kiviuq and his fox-wife moved to new hunting grounds. They stopped at a place where a wolverine was living and he helped Kiviuq build an igloo next to his own. Δ

Cooperation in igloo building and other such activities would be normal for the Inuit. Even when they met up with people they didn't know, it made sense for them to build adjoining igloos for the sake of warmth and companionship.

Snow makes excellent insulation. Inuit and their ancestors of the Thule and Dorset cultures long ago developed sophisticated architectural structures using snow as a building material. Although a temporary igloo could be built quickly on a hunting expedition, great care was taken in building one to last the winter. The blocks had to come from an exact consistency of snow, and they needed to be the right size and thickness. When the dwelling was well designed, the air circulated inside, keeping occupants comfortable, but if the construction was wrong, people would inevitably be cold. Windows and doors needed to be well placed in order to catch sun and to avoid drafts and drifting snow. It was important to provide a view of the ocean without opening the dwelling to the prevailing wind.

In a permanent camp an igloo could have several rooms. The main dwelling area needed to be higher than the entrance porch or corridor to prevent cold air from coming in. Other rooms could be added for meat storage, clothing storage, cooking, and even a toilet. Sometimes two families would build igloos that shared a wall while having separate entrances. I believe that this is what Kiviuq and the wolverine did. A whole camp might build a large common area for celebrations and for working on tools (Bennett and Rowley 2004, 232–7).[5]

Δ Some elders tell us that the neighbours were a wolverine couple, and others say they were a wolverine with his muskox or grizzly bear wife. In east Baffin, Cornelius Nutaraq and Naujarlak Tassugat say it was a raven. But our crew was most amused by the storytellers who told us the male wolverine was living alone. After a little while he began to envy Kiviuq his lovely wife.

"I wish I had a nice wife like that. I can just see her, with long hair, rosy cheeks, chewing coyly on the tip of her mitt," he thought to himself. Then he got an idea. "I'll shit out a wife for myself!"

And he succeeded!

The wolverine proposed to Kiviuq that they trade wives for the night.

Kiviuq knew his fox-wife wouldn't like the idea, since she was terribly shy. Add to this the fact that foxes mate for life. She was also self-conscious about her strong fox smell. He resisted as long as he could but the wolverine was persistent.

At last Kiviuq consented, but said, "My wife is very shy. Don't do anything to offend her. Whatever you do, don't mention her smell. Don't sniff around while she is urinating. And make sure you close the igloo up tightly."

The wolverine agreed.

They went their separate ways, each into the other's igloo. The wolverine remembered to close the igloo, rubbing chunks of snow into the cracks and letting it freeze, but he didn't pay close enough attention and left one small crack open. Ollie Ittinuar says the fox didn't realize it wasn't her husband under the covers until she heard his voice. Then she wanted to pee and she went shyly into the place at the end of the bed that people use for the purpose.

"Ugh," said the wolverine. "Where's that nasty smell coming from?"

"Maybe from me?" said the fox-wife. She was so embarrassed that she found her fox skin, quickly chewed it pliable, put it on through the mouth, and made her escape through the crack that the wolverine had left open. Off she ran. The wolverine went over to his own igloo and said to Kiviuq, "I wasn't able to lie with your wife."

"I told you not to offend her," Kiviuq replied, preparing to go in pursuit. But before he left he noticed a bad smell in the wolverine's igloo. The dream wife had reverted to her original state! **Δ**

The wolverine's naming the fox's animal nature made it impossible for her to stay. And while his shitting a dream wife is always good for a laugh, the meaning of this goes deeper. "In Inuit culture, excrement (*anaq*) is much more than body waste. It is a dynamic link in the chain of life from the animal world, through the human body, and back to the environment. It has a strong symbolic value … It should therefore be no surprise that animal excrement, beginning with dog dung, was used in shamanism" (Angilirq et al. 2002, 145).

Gizelle Rhyon Berry told me that "in many cultures, and not surprisingly in numerous contemporary westerners' shamanic initiatory dismemberment journeys, it is not unusual to be eaten by a power animal and shat or vomited out." This is true in Inuit culture, where the apprentice shaman would be devoured by Nanurluk, the spirit bear, and emerge as a shaman, part animal and part human.

Inuit listeners hold this deep knowledge and share a hearty laugh at the same time, whereas the deeper sense might go unnoticed by a non-Inuit listener, who comes away wondering why there is so much scatological humour in aboriginal stories.

Why does the wolverine make a wife for himself this way? Is he too facing a population shortage? It seems he only wants a wife in order to trade with Kiviuq – to use as a ploy to get the fox-lady. Members of the weasel family, wolverines are notorious food thieves, but this wolverine wouldn't get away with stealing the wife of a hunter like Kiviuq. He is pretty creative in coming up with this solution. It works well for him, and for us too, in terms of storytelling. When I tell the whole epic, listeners are distressed when Kiviuq murders his wives and their mood often remains heavy until this point is reached, where the obvious slapstick of the wolverine shitting a wife seems to give them permission to laugh again. This only became clear to me in the telling.

Wife swapping for various periods of time was fairly common among pre-contact Inuit. Sometimes a man whose wife was pregnant and unable to travel would trade with another man in order to have a partner who could go with him on a hunting trip. Sometimes it was just a matter of personal preference. But to believe that it was always done with complete agreement on all four sides is to romanticize Inuit life. Some of the women we talked with indicated that wife swapping might be an unpleasant necessity when a husband owed another man a favour. And this was the case with Kiviuq. After all, the wolverine had helped him build the igloo, and now he wanted to swap wives. Mary Ittunga spoke strongly about how the wife had been abducted and traded against her will, pointing out that people often had no choice but to do things they didn't like.

Tracking the Fox to Her Den

Δ Kiviuq tracked his fox-wife for a long distance as she ran from the wolverine. At one point he noticed that he was following both human and fox tracks. When he found her dung and urine marks on the snow, he ate them. Elders say this was his way of keeping in touch with her. Again, excrement carries important information along with the food being transformed on its journey through the body, linking animals, people, and the environment. It may have been as much help to Kiviuq as her tracks on the snow were. Some elders took a more romantic view, saying that he ate it so that others would not see her potentially embarrassing leavings.

Margaret Nakashook and Henry Evaluardjuk say that Kiviuq stopped everywhere, asking at igloos and kicking at mounds. At last he came to a place that some describe as a series of igloos and others as the entrance to an underground fox den. This is where the tracks ended. A lemming came out – some say a lemming with a smoking head. Jacob Peterloosie and Henry Evaluardjuk say it was a spider with a smoking head. Annie Peterloosie adds that he stopped at two dens – the first inhabited by a being with vertical eyes. At the second den a caterpillar with a smoking head invited him in.

The lemming is the first of a series of animals who offer themselves coquettishly to Kiviuq, saying, "Have me!" A strong rhythm develops in the storytelling as Kiviuq replies, "I won't have you because your nose is bleeding." He refuses offers from lemming, weasel, ground squirrel, arctic hare, wolverine, and wolf, telling each one what he finds wrong with them – too skinny, too fat, eyes too close together or too far apart, nose too short or too long. Besides these animals, Jimmie Qiqut mentions a seagull whose beak is too long, Gideon Qitsualik talks of a raven whose beak is too big, and Annie Peterloosie speaks of a spider who has vertical eyes. Samson Quinangnaq says that there was a fox but that Kiviuq realized it was not his wife. The animals return to the den and report to the fox-wife.

The lemming came back out and told him he had passed the test. "You can come in. But you have to come backwards. And keep your eyes closed."

Kiviuq obeyed, but in a move typical of most story heroes and heroines, he couldn't resist taking a peek. The opening squeezed him tightly, and if he hadn't closed his eyes again quickly, he would have been squashed. ∆

Annie Peterloosie attributes the smokiness of the caterpillar to the fact that some of them have furry heads. Philip wondered about a possible connection between the lemming who greeted Kiviuq at the second den and the one he helped up the sandbank earlier in his journey. It makes a nice balance – each has now helped the other. His idea was confirmed by Henry Evaluardjuk and others.

Henry tells us that when a lemming shows up in an unexpected place it is an important sign. This time it reminds Kiviuq that he did wrong by injuring the lemming, who was both the one he had helped up the cliff and the one he had burnt after it came from his wife's dead body. He should have confessed to this wrong as well as to the murder of his wives.

The rhythmic repetition in the proposals emphasizes the importance of what is happening and acts as an aid to memory for tellers and listeners. This part of the story seems to be an amusing test of the husband's fidelity, as the offers get more tempting. The first few aren't too hard to turn down, but he's very attracted by wolves, as we know already, and the wolverine is also pretty. Nonetheless he manages to resist temptation while confirming his ongoing relationship with the animals.

But what else might be going on here? As Kiviuq is known as an *angakkuq*, it occurred to me that the animals might be offering themselves as shamanic helping spirits. It struck me as odd that he would refuse them until I learned about how spirits that solicit are considered dangerous and should not be accepted. On both scores, human and shamanic, he makes the right choice. And there's something important in his naming a characteristic of each of the animals. It may give him power over them. This is similar to the way the wolverine drove the fox away by naming the nature of her smell. We'll see it again when Kiviuq's mother names the qualities of the goose, thus driving her away. Bee Woman or Irontail gained power over Kiviuq by saying "It's a person" while bringing him back to life, naming his nature. The wolverine might have gained a similar power over the fox by mentioning her smell, had he been stronger or smarter. Now Kiviuq is doing the same in an odd way by confirming something about the nature of each animal as grounds for refusing them.[6] Naming conveys power.

Philip Paniaq points out that entering the den backwards is physically safer than forwards, since the back is less vulnerable. It is good hunter's practice. Perhaps Kiviuq is learning it at this point – at the least it stands as a lesson to listeners. His entry to the fox den runs parallel to the way Tuutalik entered the breathing hole and his child went down through the wet spot in the house; each is an entry to another world. Gideon Qitsualik says that by closing his eyes Kiviuq called on his shamanic power and managed either to shrink his body or to make the opening bigger. Entering a womb-shaped dwelling backwards seems to me to be a reverse image of birth. If Kiviuq is indeed living many lives in succession, this could be one of the transition points.

Rasmussen recorded this description of a shaman finding the entrance to the lower world: "He almost glides as if falling through a tube so fitted to his body that he can check his progress by pressing against the sides, and need not actually fall down with a rush. This tube is kept open for him by all the souls of his namesakes, until he returns on his way back to earth."[7]

Δ Kiviuq arrived inside and saw that the lemming was living in a little space over the door. Herve Paniaq says it was a deformed lemming. Annie Peterloosie quotes the lemming with a bent nose as saying, "Is he the one? Let's stab him," although this didn't happen. A number of elders agreed that this was the lemming he had injured after killing his wife. Cornelius Nutaraq tells of a separate incident in which Kiviuq meets a lemming living over a door. The tiny animal looked down and said, "This is the one who injured me. Now by coming here he has healed me." It seems that his sin in relation to animals is now forgiven, perhaps because he searched the animal out. Margaret Nakashook, who did not tell the story of the penis in the lake, says that the lemming was one that Kiviuq had injured in childhood, which is why the relationship needed to be healed. All elders point out that injuring any animal is a great sin and needs to be confessed.

Now Kiviuq looked around some more. A couple of ground squirrels were making up their bed. He looked at them and without speaking aloud he thought, "They look exactly alike."

One of the squirrels spoke aloud, "He thinks we look exactly alike." So he had arrived in a place where small animals were capable of mind-reading!

He looked into the next room and saw his fox-wife combing her beautiful hair. She had wept a stalactite of tears and mucus that reached all the way to the ground. He tried to sit next to her but she moved swiftly away. After several tries he spat in front of her, and she stopped. The two were reunited. Δ

Bodily fluids all carry power. It's interesting to notice that Westerners might find the fox's tears poignant and the mucus disgusting. But in this context the mucus simply adds to the sense that she missed him tremendously. The measurement of quantity – a stalactite that reaches the ground – shows how very long she has wept.

Saliva carries not only personal power but shamanic power as well. In the stories of many cultures we see it used for its healing properties. In the Udeghe tale of the hunter who traces his seal-wife in the underwater world, he heals her wounds by rubbing his own saliva around them.[8] In another tale from the same people, a hero wounds his beloved in a contest and uses his own saliva to heal her; the saliva also seems to contribute to winning her over, affectionately softening her anger with him, as it

June Shappa portrays the fox-wife in the film *Kiviuq*.
Photo by John Houston for drumsong communications inc.

does in Kiviuq's story. Most of us can recall instinctively putting a cut finger into our mouths, and now science agrees that saliva has healing power.

Herve Paniaq says that instead of spitting, Kiviuq let out a great fart and all the animals scrambled for the door. This is yet another place where a funny interlude in the story holds deeper meaning. Like excrement, body gases hold power of the soul. "Farting and belching could either ward off bad spirits or cure sick people by ridding them of evil influences" (Angilirq et al. 2002, 145). The subject of farting (*niliqsiniq*) came up in Bernard Saladin d'Anglure's work in Igloolik in 1971–72. Elders Ijituuq, Ujarak, and Iqallijuq were discussing amulets (*aarnguat*) and agreed that in a case where a person had an amulet and was afraid of something, farting would have driven the fearful thing away, while the amulet would have provided protection (Saladin d'Anglure 2001, 144–5).

The Feast and Lampoons

Many say the animals called for a feast before dispersing.

Δ Each of the animals brought a different kind of food to the feast, generally what we might expect. Wolf and wolverine brought caribou meat, although wolverine's was stolen. The seagull brought arctic char. It's interesting that although the fox has learned to cook and provide food in this incarnation, only one elder mentions that she brought anything at all to the potluck. According to Samson Quinangnaq, it was oily meat. Raven was the only one to bring something that no one else wanted. They told him to go out in the porch and eat his frozen dog shit by himself, as it was disgusting to them.

At this point Jimmie Qiqut adds an episode in which a wolf steals Kiviuq's snow knife. Wolverine tells wolf that the others are uncomfortable with his taking the knife from a guest and tells him to give it back. The wolf returns the knife.

After supper the animals paired up for a session of singing lampoons at each other. Δ

Gideon Qitsualik says the feast was to celebrate the fact that Kiviuq was now one of the family. His family relationship with animals is one of his greatest powers as a shaman, and it has been carried on by *angakkuit* from that time forward. Inuit shamanism is strongly related to hunting, as it is in many indigenous cultures, and a deep understanding of animals is what makes a shaman a success – an understanding much like that within a family. As I considered the idea of this greater than the normal closeness, I began to wonder whether Kiviuq was determining the parameters of shamanic power, especially male shamanic power, at the same time as he was mapping the physical and spiritual geography of the known world. After all, many things are created in this story. Bee Woman formed the first ice on the sea, and the fog we'll encounter in the next chapter was the first fog. Perhaps certain social and spiritual matters have their start here as well. Clearly shamanism already existed – we've seen not only Kiviuq but several female shamans at work. But why should certain shamanic acts not be the first of their kind? Perhaps Kiviuq's story shows how Inuit hunters and shamans gradually gained their unique understanding of animals and thus also gained more powerful helping spirits.

Many things in this story are enjoyed for a laugh, but nothing stops at that level of meaning. I wonder if this picture of the raven shows anything beyond the fact that his eating habits make him an outcast in animal society. It certainly shows us the social structure of the animal world. Simon Tookoome adds that the raven turned black from eating excrement. But we've heard a lot about excrement and its symbolic value. Kiviuq himself has eaten the fox's droppings. This might be a bit far-fetched, but I wonder if the dog shit is an oblique reference to incomers. Inuit say white people are descended from dogs, the children of Nuliajuk. Their leavings could be particularly distasteful. This could be an example of coded language, often used by oppressed peoples. For example, American slaves used to talk about their masters and even make fun of them using secret words and expressions. I've heard that even to this day speakers of south German dialects engage in such secret conversations.

After supper the animals prepared for lampooning. Samson Quinangnaq calls it a drum dance. In a lampooning session, funny songs in which the animals made fun of one another served to defuse tensions among them. Some expressed their own frustrations with the difficulties of their lives. Lampooning was also an important way to solve interpersonal problems.[9] These songs are called *iviutiit*. If, for example, two people were in conflict, the whole community would gather. The two, generally from different communities, would get up and sing, expressing fully their critique of each other. Each would have prepared carefully beforehand. This was a good way to speak a truth that could otherwise not be spoken, and there was no hesitation about speaking to a person of different status. It was important that the duellers stick to the facts; anyone who went beyond them would be soon corrected by listeners. The singing would go on until all the frustrations were expressed. If a fight broke out, the listeners who had gathered would laugh heartily. My understanding is that in the end the offended parties often wound up laughing as well. This levity could sometimes be a pretence, since it was important to appear nonchalant, but it was often sincere. Children were encouraged to listen, as it was a good way for them to learn socially accepted norms. Singing duels allowed all the grievances to be aired, and they became less serious as a result. Sometimes the duelling parties would drum, and in such cases their wives would sing for them (Bennett and Rowley 2004, 100). Gideon Qitsualik says that the lampoons prevented people from getting into physical fights. He cites a hypothetical example where a man lampoons a woman for being unable to bear children and she responds by telling the assemblage that he is an inept hunter.

If the animals in the den are shamanic spirits, their lampooning implies a fairly good-natured form of competition with each other. Most pair up with those they compete with for food: wolf with wolverine, raven with gull. Fox and hare pair up, although they are not food competitors. Hare lives on plant foods and fox on small animals. Wolf and wolverine engage in the worst accusations, the birds make fun of each other's habits, and the fox bemoans her own fate. Among our forty storytellers, only Margaret Nakashook recalled the fox's song and no one could sing the hare's (I have added the latter here, drawing from Rasmussen's work, for the sake of completion). The melodic lines are simple, generally two notes in the relation of a falling fourth or fifth.[10]

Δ Beginning with Gideon Qitsualik's version, the lampooning went like this:

The wolverine sang to the wolf: "The wolf is cunning and boisterous. He tells stories that seem to be true. But when he ran up the brow of a cliff chasing a hare, I clearly remember watching him unsuccessful in his chase, *ajaajaa*. Everybody laugh at him!"

Wolf replied to wolverine: "The wolverine has a snout like a grizzly's. He's always around the meat cache, frustratingly irritating. He creates anger. He should be forced with howling to go to where people are. *Ajaajaa, ajaajaa.*"

Jimmie Qiqut continues:

The gull sang to the raven: "*Last spring as the river's mouth was opening, as I took my spear to catch fish, I could hear raven's call in the distance, now where oh where is this disgusting eater?*"

Raven replied: "*During the cold time you won't be here at all while I'm feasting on dog droppings and getting fat on garbage.*"

Margaret Nakashook continues:

Fox sang to hare: "*I am a predator looking for seal breathing holes. I smell them but can't find them. This is the hard part for me – and the same goes for the nest with eggs.*"

And finishing from Niaqúnuaq, recorded by Rasmussen (1931):

Hare sang to fox: "*Can you catch swimming caribou from a kayak?*"

"*Yes!*" says the fox. But of course it's ridiculous, and her snout grows longer! **Δ**

In the ethnographic works, the fullest versions of the lampoons come from the Netsilik group, as sung to Rasmussen by Niaqúnuaq and Kuvdluitsoq (Rasmussen 1931, 352–5, 372–3). Niaqúnuaq had the most complete versions, including songs of the wolf, wolverine, lemming, raven, gull, ptarmigan, long-tailed duck, hare, fly, worm, water beetle, and blowfly. Rasmussen himself could only guess at the meaning of the lemming's song, which involves snaring marmots, while the rest of the songs are similar to the ones we heard or continue in the same vein by making fun of the other's peculiarities. Today the fullest versions are still sung mainly by the Netsilik elders Jimmie Qiqut, Gideon Qitsualik, and Margaret Nakashook.

Although he had now become one of the family, Kiviuq did not take part in the lampooning. Given the important role played by lampooning in Inuit justice, I think the animals may have taught him this non-violent way to solve problems.

Inuit Music

Lampooning is just one form of Inuit music-making. Another is the drum dance. As a musician, I naturally gravitate to musical instruments and songs, and I was delighted to be invited to a drum dance in the community of Arviat on the west coast of Hudson Bay. Our unit manager, Tiffany Muckpah, walked us over to a modern building where the dance was already in progress. We entered, were warmly greeted, and sat down on the floor. A group of women sat along one side of the room, beautifully dressed in the beaded clothing Arviat is famous for. They were the singers. The drum was on the floor in front of them. I later learned that these hoop drums are called *qilauti*. The head is traditionally made from the skin of caribou, mountain sheep, or seal, although intestine or stomach lining of walrus or whale is also occasionally used. The skin is stretched over a wooden hoop with a cord made of sinew or rawhide, holding the head in place. The one external handle is made of bone or antler. The player can tune the drum by warming it. Nowadays drums often have synthetic heads.

Urged by his friends, a man came forward, picked up the drum, and faced the singers. They consulted among themselves and then began singing. Percy whispered to me that the song would have something to do either with the drum dancer or his family. I have read that the women would have composed the songs themselves (Angilirq 2002, 75). The dancer began drumming, beating on the frame, not the head, turning the drum from side to side as he danced and sang to his own beat and the steady rhythm of the women's song. I was soon mesmerized. One by one various men got up and danced – each one unique in his movements, drumming style, and singing, a moving expression of individual creativity. Much of the community had gathered, from eldest to youngest. Many were urged to get up. Even the police officer was there, greeting everyone in a friendly way but declining to dance.

I was burning to try it. "Do women ever do this?" I whispered to Percy.

"Yes, sometimes," he replied, curious about my eagerness. I've since learned that some men resent women taking part in drum dances, although Percy is not one of them. Mary Piercey, who lived in Arviat for a long time and participated in many drum dances, believes that the men's resentment comes from the fact that they have lost their role as providers owing to social change and so resent having one more thing taken away from them (Piercey 2005, 1–6).

Finally a couple of women did get up and drum, and I felt encouraged to jump up in one of the gaps. I took up the drum and faced the singers, who smiled at me. Their consultation about what song to sing took a little longer than usual, but then they started. I later learned that although most of the songs are personal, there are always some with no ownership that can be sung for visitors from afar. Right away I discovered that drumming was trickier than it looked. Who would have believed that it was possible to miss hitting the frame of the drum altogether? But I thoroughly enjoyed exploring the drum's sounds and the ways to move and sing in harmony and rhythm with them.

Long ago drum dancing was used for celebrations of birth, marriage, the changing seasons, a successful hunt, or a first kill, or to greet visitors or honour someone who had died. It may have emerged from shamanic ceremony. The songs contain the refrain *ajaajaa*, which has a spiritual significance. For religious reasons Inuit today are hesitant to speak about the meaning of *ajaajaa* songs, drum dances, and throat singing. *Ajaajaa* is always used in songs about journeying, in both shamanic and ordinary reality. Joe Issaluk tells us that story songs such as the one Kiviuq sings while following his goose-wife were not used in drum dances, although they too may use the *ajaajaa* refrain.

Inuit throat singers Trisha Marie Ogina and Jerilyn Kaniak perform at the school library in Cambridge Bay.

Although lampooning, *ajaajaa* singing, and drum dancing were forbidden by missionaries, singing played a big role in Inuit life of the past. When old friends, called *illuriik*, met, they would engage in song and dance contests as a way of enjoying their friendship (Bennett and Rowley 2004, 129). Songs in general are called *inngiruti*, and several forms exist. There are the songs of the newborn (*aqausiit*), which are often inherited from a namesake and remain part of the child's lifelong personal identity.[11] There are also songs of exploits (*pisiit*) that people compose after an exceptional performance or a painful test of their abilities. There are duelling songs (*iviusiit*) that are composed to ridicule one's opponent as the animals do in lampooning each other. There are magic songs, or spells (*irinaliut*), that summon spirits to act, as the grandmother did when sewing the seal-child's clothing. There are the songs that accompany the shaman's trances. The two brothers Peter Suqaksiork and Phillip Kigusiutnak told me that only namesakes could sing each other's personal songs. Translator and story collector Marie-Lucie Uviluq pointed out to me that many songs originated in life's most trying personal times and should not be sung by others, although they often are today. She says their meaning can be truly known only to the composer.

Women compose and perform a special kind of throat song, called *katajjait*. Two women (nowadays occasionally men) alternate in rapid succession as they make panting and puffing sounds with their throats (Angilirq et al. 2002, 75). Throat singing, or *katajjaq*, is one of the best-known and most unique aspects of Inuit culture. The style has also been referred to as a vocal game. Forbidden by the churches for decades because of its role in Inuit spiritual life, it has been enjoying a revival for a number of years now. Singers Pauline Pemik and Inukshuk Aksalnik spoke about throat singing at their performance of "Inuit Games," by Pat Carrabre, with the Winnipeg Symphony Orchestra. The piece incorporates Inuit singing with Western music to stunning effect. The singers described three uses of throat singing, as a form of prayer, as entertainment, and as competition. The competitive aspect determines the form, a kind of call and response. One singer states a musical phrase, and then the other imitates it. Each singer may add something that the other then incorporates into her own part. The song gets more complex as each singer adds and imitates, always keeping in perfect rhythm. At a certain point one singer will be unable to keep up or will run out of breath, and the whole thing breaks down in laughter. I've tried it myself, and my laughter came almost immediately, largely as a result of my being in such close proximity to another person and the intimate nature of the sounds produced.[12]

The music produced by accomplished throat singers includes both voiced and unvoiced sounds made on inhalation as well as exhalation. Good singers can keep going a long time, the result being something like circular breathing. Words and meaningless syllables can be used, but even the real words are used more for their sound value than their meaning.

Sometimes the sounds imitate animals and birds. Such imitations are an important skill for Inuit hunters and are also raised to the level of art among Siberian hunters.

The Party's Over

Δ The vast majority of elders end this section either when Kiviuq is reunited with his wife or after the feast and do not tell about the animals dispersing. They say they are not sure about how he lost her before meeting the Canada goose.[13]

Those who do go on to tell of the party breaking up say that the fox ran out the door. Kiviuq was stopped from following her by a scratching being that fell down from over the door. He had to go out a window, but by that time he had lost the fox, since it was now spring and there were no tracks to follow. The scratching being, who some say was an old woman, was the reincarnation of the second wife he murdered, now getting back at him by making it impossible for him to track the fox-wife. In the words of Henry Evaluardjuk, "If you do wrong, you'll have trouble." Even a small act, such as delaying him, can have far-reaching results. And so the murder has come back on him, at least in the minds of those few who tell this part.

Leo Nimialik says he travelled with the fox again, but Henry Isluanik says he lost her tracks and found the geese. Many don't recall what happened. Δ

Scratching beings are mentioned in another of the Inuit's most important stories – that of the brother and sister who became the moon and the sun. The sister was attacked by what Rasmussen calls "claw-trolls" and one scratched her seriously (Bennett and Rowley 2004, 161–6; Rasmussen 1931, 232). Interestingly enough, she too was instructed to enter an igloo backwards, but in her case she was being deceived.

When the Inuit fox story is told independently of Kiviuq's life, the unnamed hero always gets back together with the fox-wife. As I've noted, a few tellers think Kiviuq did too. It could also be that she is a helping spirit and thus, because she can be with him in spirit, she does not need to be with him in body.

My sense is that the idea of a reunion with his wives may have been lost in the post-contact shifts. This is the only part of the legend that does not connect to the next in anyone's telling, except for that of Henry Evaluardjuk, who says that Kiviuq lost track of the fox only to come upon the women bathing in the lake, which is where the goose-wife story begins. But most elders now take us to the story of the grizzly bear.

Fox Cousins

My mother's father was out hunting. One day he came back to his hunting tent and found a female tiger there. "I am a tiger woman," she said. "Lie down and sleep with me. Eat what is in the bowl." He lived with her for three years – she taught him much about setting traps. When he finally returned home she warned him not to wear boots made for him in his absence, saying that if he did she would take him away for good. He forgot her injunction and as soon as he put the boots on, he died. People found a mark on his body shaped like a tiger with the head and tail coming around his waist.

– Ulchi shaman Anga, 1995

The only living person I've ever met who speaks of marrying an animal was the Ulchi shaman Anga. She was much respected up and down the Amur River for her abilities to heal and to find people and animals that were lost. I visited her one rainy summer day after a long search for the bottle of vodka that's obligatory when visiting shamans. She put on a traditional robe to talk with us and sang into the back of her large single-headed drum. She told us many things, including how she had come to marry the tiger. "When I was young, I married a tiger. He came over the hills in the depths of winter to find me. He set up his home next to ours and washed himself in deep clear water until he was shining. When he came to me in my childhood, it was like sleeping with a warm fur coat. Later he scratched me and I became pregnant. My father recognized signs that I would be a shaman. The first time I gave birth to tiger babies I didn't want them, but the second time I kept them. Those babies have become my helpers – they fly me to other worlds."

Ulchi shaman Anga with her drum, Bulava village

The mountainous taiga of the Russian Far East is one of the few places on the planet where tigers still live. When Anga was young, the tigers kept to themselves, like the cougars of my British Columbia home. Although the animals might be nearby, they did not show themselves to people. To see one was fearsome and awe inspiring. Now it happens more often, although the meeting still inspires high emotion. Apart from Anga, the first person I met who had seen one was a woman named Svetlana. She walked seven kilometres to work every day along a deserted forest road, and one day she met a tiger halfway along the way. Although the animal didn't chase her, she ran the rest of the distance. The next year a tiger came even closer to people's homes. Valentina Kyalundzyuga's daughter looked out the kitchen window and saw a tiger prowling in her garden. Right in the village. A tree beside the much-used footbridge shows marks where he sharpened his claws. This change has happened since I first visited the area in 1993. At that time people who had lived in the area all their lives had never seen a tiger. Even most of the hunters hadn't seen them. Now sightings are much more frequent.

In spite of the fact that people see tigers more often, their numbers are in decline. Loss of habitat and poaching have reduced their numbers to the point where they are under the careful watch of scientists. Tiger parts are highly valued in neighbouring Asian countries, fetching money no local hunter could hope to get in any other way. Organized crime plays its role. People are stealing the tiger's skin, but no longer marrying the animal. And unlike Kiviuq, no one thinks of returning the skin, making a fair exchange. Although tigers are still alive in story, marriage with the animals is at a dead end in ordinary life. Change of lifestyle and ecological damage have broken that intimacy.

Experiences like those of Anga and her grandfather are reflected in numerous magic tales and legends of women who married tigers and started clans. As shamanic helping spirits, few beings can rival the tiger in power – he is the master of the taiga forest. Even I have a small carved figure of the tiger spirit guarding my home, a gift of the animal's human descendants.

Marriages with animals, birds, and even fish and snakes abound in stories from North America, Siberia, Asia, Europe, Africa, and likely all around the world. Both men and women enter such marriages, although generally it is only the human women who produce cross-species children who live full lives in human community. (We'll get back to this with the goose-wife and her children.) In my Siberian experience I have heard traditional stories of women marrying tigers, bears, whales, snakes, raccoon-dogs, crows, and even a hunting bag and a human skull. Most of the animals help the women produce powerful offspring, sometimes starting new clans. Men enter marriages with seals, foxes, tigers, swans, and fish. The land mammals produce powerful hunting alliances, while the birds and fish attract the man's romantic side through their beauty.

In Tuvan folk tales a man who visits the underwater world is offered a reward by its ruler. The man is advised to ask for nothing but the mangy puppy who sits at the ruler's feet. When he gets home, the puppy turns into a wise and beautiful woman, but trouble ensues when he burns the dog skin in the hopes this will ensure that she never leaves him (Van Deusen 1996, 35–44). Kiviuq abides by the rule about honouring his wife's origins, whereas the Tuvan proves the rule by breaking it.

With Anga's grandfather, the exchange that establishes his relationship with the tiger almost seems to take place in the dream world. Some boundary is always being passed. The high language used in the telling of Kiviuq's courtship of the fox reflects this otherworldly aspect. Practically every teller uses the same words to relate the conversation.

The story of the man who married a fox is often told independently both in the Inuit world and across the Bering Strait. Here is a version that was told to Chukchi writer Antonina Kymytval by her elder relative Entu in Snezhnoe village, Chukotka, in 1970.

The Chukchi Fox[1]

An orphan child was living with his aunt and uncle but they left him behind at one campsite. He tried to grab hold of the boat but his uncle hit him with an oar. As he was weeping from loneliness that evening, a fox showed up. "Why are you crying?" she asked.

He told her everything and she took him over to a small hill where there was an ancient earth hut. It would be warmer to spend the night there. She encouraged him. Next day he found an old bow string and strung it onto a bow stick. He made arrows and learned to shoot. He got partridges and sometimes eggs, and so he and the fox lived. When he grew up, the fox became his wife. Now he made a big bow and began to shoot wild reindeer.

Two children were born and the wife constructed a *yaranga* – an elaborate and highly efficient type of tent used by the Chukchi. Although she was now his wife, the fox retained some of her animal habits. Sometimes she affectionately called him a lump-head, which is the term animals use to refer to humans. He paid no attention to her animal ways. They lived well, and he enjoyed watching his children grow.

Time passed and the uncle who had left the boy said to his wife, "Let's go and look at our nephew's bones. They've probably gone white in the sun." They arrived and were surprised to see the thriving camp. The orphan and his fox-wife invited them in and offered them food. But the aunt and uncle offended the fox-wife by speaking about her claws, which they saw emerging from her boots. She left her family never to return. Chukchi storytellers always state a moral clearly at the end of a story, and Entu commented that people offended the fox even though she had done them much good.

The Chukchi story emphasizes different lessons from those of Kiviuq's fox-wife, although it has interesting connections with lessons we find in other parts of his life. Like the story of the seal-child, it emphasizes the wrong done to an orphan and the way he found help – a very common theme in both Inuit and Chukchi storytelling. The Chukchi hero lost his wife because someone else offended her, just as Kiviuq later lost his goose-wife.

In Chukotka, foxes are kept for their fur, which is mainly used to make winter hats.

Search for a Spouse

Having tentatively traced the wife from her human form to that of the fox, as some elders do, I wondered if we could trace her further – into the story of the Canada goose. That would give a lovely completeness to the cycle, although I didn't believe the connection would be as direct as it was when the fox appeared from the wife's grave. This connection would come in a different way. The goose-wife story clearly follows Kiviuq's cycle of searching for the ideal relationship with the female. For this reason we can expect the goose to show another aspect of the female, although she doesn't necessarily need to be another incarnation of the same being and it seems unlikely that she is.

We might look at Kiviuq's courtship of the fox-woman as part of the enduring theme of searching for a spouse, which takes on aspects of a heroic journey among nomadic peoples. Their nearest neighbours might be very far away and always on the move. The search is a major theme in stories from the Amur River peoples, as we saw in the tale "Yegdyghe and the Bones" ("Bee Cousins" chapter). It shows up in a more formal way in Turkic epics about a young person searching for a spouse. The usual social pattern was that the man travelled more, hunting and trading, and thus came into contact with other settlements where he might find a wife to take home. But sometimes circumstances dictated that a woman undertake the search. She might have been left alone or fallen on hard times. It would be suicide to sit around waiting for a man to show up – she had to take things into her own hands. Among the Udeghe of far-off times, it was accepted practice for an older sister to marry her younger brother. With the passage of time, custom changed. Later it was forbidden not only to marry a sibling, but even to marry inside one's own clan. The search became more difficult. It was the subject of many stories, especially as it parallels the way a shaman may journey to find spirit helpers or to return a lost soul.

Whole story forms, including that of the fox-wife, may have crossed the Bering Strait intact with the Inuit's ancestors, but other themes and details may have come from an ancient homeland on the Asian side only to be expressed in a different way over here. Still others seem to have been freshly minted on the North American side. The wife-swapping episode, the courtship of the animals, and the lampoons have their basis in Inuit life and have been added to the fox story as known in Asia.

The Grizzly Bear

When you grow up with stories it's hard to see you've learned from them, but when you go hunting it's apparent that stories help. You seem to just know what to do partly because of the stories. In old times stories were passed on. You picked the knowledge up without realizing it.

– Joe Issaluk, 2004

Taima!

One evening we were invited to a party by Aaju Peters, an Inuit friend of John Houston's from Greenland. She was studying law in Iqaluit, and there was a gathering at the home of one of her fellow students. We taxied uphill away from the centre of town and arrived at a home on a residential street where the houses overlook Frobisher Bay. We took along "country food" – *paqqutik*, or caribou marrow, mixed with *nirrukkaq*, the rumen from a caribou first stomach. John had been given this treat as well as some caribou meat in Chesterfield Inlet. We added a few items from the Co-op Store and joined the potluck.

After supper Aaju took out her guitar and sang. Then she asked me to tell a story. I chose a Chukchi tale about a man who wintered in a bear's den. The bear helped him survive and regain his courage.

Now Killaq Enuaraq, the young daughter of one of the guests spoke up – she was about eight years old.

"I know a story," she said.

In the darkened room we were re-enacting an age-old storytelling ritual. One story leads organically to another as a listener picks up on a striking detail offered by the previous teller. Sticking with the theme of the bear, the girl told the story of Kiviuq hiding in the meat cache. Her audience was delighted – she told it with gusto. John loved the evidence that the story is still alive, and I also enjoyed the way she made the link from my story to her own.

The elders tell about Kiviuq and the grizzly like this:

Δ Kiviuq was living in a community at this time. Jimmie Qiqut tells us it was a place called Upiniviq, located about thirty miles south of Gjoa Haven. Meat had been disappearing from the cache. The food supply was threatened. Aupilaarjuk says it was Kiviuq's own cache. No one was sure who was stealing the meat, but they suspected it was a bear. That being so, it took a lot of courage to volunteer to face the thief. Kiviuq said to his neighbours, "Hide me in the cache and I will find out who is stealing our food."

The people took Kiviuq out to the cache and removed some rocks. He got inside and they replaced the rocks on top of him. The hero lay there like a dead man. The cache resembled the grave he made for his wives – he had "buried them under rocks" – and he lay there longer than any ordinary human would have been able to. Judas Aqilgiaq told us he stayed there for a whole year waiting for the thief to show up. People came and went, taking meat from the cache and ignoring Kiviuq. Δ

As always with Kiviuq, there is more to the grizzly bear than meets the ear. Mariano Aupilaarjuk knew we would have little time together owing to flight schedules and he prepared carefully. After telling the part of the story from Tuutalik going into the seal hole to Kiviuq's return from his long journey, Aupilaarjuk stated that there are two parts of Kiviuq's life he most respects. One is the story of the grandmother and the storm at sea. He respects what it shows about Kiviuq's upbringing and the way he scrupulously follows the rules. The second place is the story of hiding in the meat cache, since it shows the shaman Kiviuq at his most powerful. Indeed, shamans worldwide share a common focus on protecting their communities, which is just what Kiviuq sets out to do in this story.

Aupilaarjuk is not the only one to speak of Kiviuq's legend in terms of respect. I'm fascinated by his point of view. In my experience, most peo-

Storyteller Judas Aqilgiaq with his wife, Mary. He portrayed the grizzly bear brilliantly.

ple speak of story in terms of enjoyment or emotional qualities, but Aupilaarjuk speaks of story as a living phenomenon with a shape and meaning worthy of respect. Contemporary storytellers in southern Canada have the same sense. Canadian storyteller Abegael Fisher-Lang says, "I believe that stories have a life of their own. To bring people together to share in the epic experience keeps them alive and vibrant and even imbues them with new meaning as well as a better understanding of the old."

Meat Caches and Graves

On their way home, northern hunters often cached meat that was not immediately needed. This meant they didn't have to carry it long distances only to have to move it again on their nomadic rounds. The place for the cache needed to be carefully chosen. Factors taken into account included the expected precipitation, temperature, predators, and length of time until recovery, as well as the nature of the product. Sometimes meat had to be dried or otherwise treated before caching. The hunters were careful to leave a marker that would stand above the level of the snow so that they could find the cache when they returned (Bennett and Rowley 2004, 247–9).

The meat cache might resemble a grave, but not all graves involved covering the body with stones. Sometimes the body was exposed on the ground, with a marker nearby. Special requests made before death were always honoured. One man asked those who passed his grave to tell jokes to make him laugh, adding that this would help hunters. Another requested not to be covered with rocks, so he could get out freely to help those in need (Bennett and Rowley 2004, 223–4).

If Kiviuq really spent a year in the cache, that long time would have completed a cycle and must at least have meant that his body went into hibernation the way bears themselves do. His being able to go dormant in this way is further evidence of his power.

Δ At last one day Kiviuq heard someone approaching on powerful paws. Rocks were tossed from the cache and Kiviuq found himself face to face with a big grizzly bear. The bear pulled him out, Kiviuq playing dead. The bear seemed a little disappointed that it was only a human but decided to take him home anyway.

But how to carry him? We might guess that this wouldn't be just any bear, but a shape-changing bear, and indeed he simply removed his skin as if it were a fur coat and laid it out on the ground. Underneath he was a man.[1] He pulled Kiviuq on the skin as if it were a travois. Δ

Bears

The bear is one of the animals most often described in the North as taking human form easily. Native people often point out that when a bear has been skinned, it looks very much like a human being. Besides this, the bear has great strength and intelligence. In my own neighbourhood we are acquainted with the bear's facility in opening "bear-proof" garbage cans and other containers. Although Inuit do not speak of human ancestry from animals, it is a common theme in other northern cultures. Korean, Northwest Coast, and Siberian storytellers tell us that bears have intimate relationships with humans. One Udeghe clan claims descent from a woman who married a bear.

Although the motif of fighting grizzlies is told all over the Arctic as one of the obstacles Kiviuq encounters, only people who live or grew up in areas where grizzly bears actually live – Kivalliq Region, the west coast of Hudson Bay, and the inland Back River area – tell the story of Kiviuq hiding in the meat cache. Today they never tell it about any other kind of bear. Outside grizzly territory, the story that was told to earlier ethnographers involved spirit beings and black bears.[2]

This bear and his whole family shift into human shape whenever it is convenient for them. For now though, the skin is useful as a type of sled.

Δ After a while the bear suspected that maybe Kiviuq wasn't really dead. He came sniffing around the man's nose and mouth. Kiviuq held his breath as long as possible and then had to breathe through his rear end. The bear suspected Kiviuq might be breathing through his rear end and sniffed around there – at which point Kiviuq breathed through his nose.

More or less convinced, the bear-man continued on his way, pulling Kiviuq. They passed a place where willow grew close on both sides. Kiviuq reached out and held on to the branches in order to make the bear-man work harder. Of course he let go when his captor looked around.

When they reached the bear-man's home, his children came running, asking what he had brought them. "I've brought a man. And after we've eaten, you can use his bones for your games." Δ

Kiviuq's breathing trick generally gets a roar of laughter from audiences, and at the same time it demonstrates the protective power of body gases that we heard about in the fox den. Grizzly bears are noted for their poor eyesight, which is compensated by keen senses of hearing and smell. Clearly Kiviuq was using shamanic power as well as quick thinking to trick the bear into thinking he was dead. Besides its amusement value, the story teaches listeners how to behave around grizzlies.

The bears may play a game with the bones of their prey that resembles the game that Inuit play with seal bones. The human game may have shamanic roots, as we've heard that the "dog" bone was also used in divination. If their game is similar, the bears must have some shamanic power as well. In referring to the bear's playing with the bones, Jimmie Qiqut used an ancient word whose meaning he himself doesn't understand, a word that may also have shamanic roots. Inuit often played games when a bear was killed, so it seems the grizzly was getting back at humans with this remark.

Δ The bear-man's wife, also in human form, carried Kiviuq's body into their igloo. She tried to cut him up, but he held his abdominal muscles so tight that she thought he was still frozen. She set him up beside the wall to thaw and set about sharpening her *ulu*. The bear-man was sleepy and lay down for a nap.

The bear children sniffed around Kiviuq, licking the mucus that came from his nose as he warmed up. It must have taken tremendous concentration for him not to react to this intimate contact. Meanwhile Kiviuq wanted to check and see if there was any kind of weapon in the igloo, so he opened his eyes slightly.

"*Ataata*, Papa, the dinner is opening its eyes!" called the children.

"Let him open his eyes. I thought he was holding the willow bushes on our way here, making me tired." Δ

We debated what the phrase "Let him open his eyes" meant. Some thought that the bear-man, half asleep, was just now coming to the full realization that Kiviuq had been alive the whole time. It made sense, but I wasn't quite satisfied. The verb form, used by virtually all elders, is something like the subjunctive in European languages, similar to the English expressions "Long live the king" and "May your every dream come true." This would indicate that the bear was calling or at least wishing Kiviuq back to life, likely to have another go at him. This reminds me of the irontail who used an incantation to call him back to life after he had seen her cut off her eyelids. (She used a different method – first the powerful naming of his nature and then a simple imperative, "Wake up!") Apparently animals and non-humans have a preference for freshly killed meat and want to bring the prey back to life before cooking it. If this is so, Kiviuq might have lain dead for a year in the meat cache and experienced the trip to the bear's home while still dead. But it must be a shamanic death, since he can still use his wits to fool the bear.

Δ Now Kiviuq opened his eyes fully and noticed an axe on the other side of the igloo. Jimmie Qiqut points out how odd it seemed that bears would have such a thing as an axe in their home, while Mariano Aupilaarjuk says that this is the moment he most respects, for it shows the shaman's power. Kiviuq struck the bear-man on the leg and left him howling with pain as he ran out the door. Once again, he did not kill the dangerous creature, just put him out of action.

The wife lit out after him, pausing in the porch just long enough to dress in her own bearskin. When I asked why she put on the bearskin, Gideon Qitsualik replied as if it were completely obvious – she was mad and would be able to run faster that way. Samson Quinangnaq says she managed to cut Kiviuq's parka as he ran from the igloo, just as Bee Woman did when he ran from her house.

As Kiviuq ran, the bear started to catch up. To slow her down, he created a mountain or an esker by running saliva around a small mound of earth with his ring finger. This hindered the bear for a while but she started gaining on him again. Kiviuq then created a river by running saliva along the bank of a small stream. Δ

Creation of Landforms

This image of creation is common to stories of many cultures. A landform grows from a smaller object with a similar shape. A hero, often a woman, throws objects out behind her as she runs. In the Udeghe story "Yegdyghe and the Bones" ("Bee Cousins" chapter), the hero throws objects his sister has given him, a comb that turns into a great forest and a sharpening stone that turns into steep rocky cliffs. In all cases, these creations turn into obstacles that slow the pursuer down. The objects contain personal power, as does Kiviuq's saliva. We'll see in the story of the goose-wife that Kiviuq's mother also uses personal objects as obstacles. Like her pot, lamp, and sharpening stones, the Udeghe sister's comb and stone are connected with her body and her work, and Kiviuq's saliva is one of the body fluids that has shamanic power.[3] Samson Quinangnaq explains that Kiviuq's ability to create landforms means he is either a shaman or another kind of talented man with helping spirits. I asked specifically about whether a good storyteller might be one of the kinds of people who have helping spirits and he said yes, although my impression is that it would be because of the person's talents in the practical world more than because of the storytelling. My question arose from the fact that Turkic storytellers often have helping spirits like those of a shaman.

Place Names

Elders Jimmie Qiqut, Gideon Qitsualik, Judas Aqilgiaq, and Samson Quinangnaq of Gjoa Haven and the Back River area could name the esker and the river and pinpoint them on the map, demonstrating that there is a very strong focus on this story in that area. The esker, or mountainous glacial moraine, is called Qimiqtaaq, which means "New Esker," with the implication that someone created it. One dialect includes the idea that inspired singing played a role in the creation. The esker is located at one end of Franklin Lake. The river, now called Kupta, runs from a small lake into Elliot Bay. These locations and the place where the bear's body came out of the water are all around Chantry Inlet, to the south of Gjoa Haven. Several of the elders had migrated from that area, which they would have become familiar with through their nomadic rounds. It is highly likely that the story reached its current form there, especially since no one, past or present, gave it specific locations in any other geographic region.

The story may also recall a time when the geography was changing radically. It is hard to believe that human memory can hold events in

Christianity comes to Chesterfield Inlet.

oral tradition over such long periods of time, but this has been shown convincingly to be so. The area known as Beringia, which once connected Asia and North America, has undergone huge climatic changes over thousands of years. Yukon storyteller Louise Profiet-Leblanc brings elders into the Beringia Centre in Whitehorse to tell stories that could well have had their source in that long-ago time and place. Yukon elders Edith Josie and Stanley Jonathon told the story of Tutatchukai, who made his way down the river killing off gigantic and dangerous animals, much like those described as living in Beringia when there were grasslands. A similar story was told to poet Tom Lowenstein in Point Hope, Alaska, by Iñupiaq elders. In it, the hero Qayaqturungnaqtuq defeated monsters and spirit beings while on a long series of journeys. He was the son of another wandering shaman, named Ukungniq (Lowenstein 1992, 54). Qayaqturungnaqtuq's story is told by Lela Kiana Oman as *The Epic of Qayaq: The Longest Story Ever Told by My People* (1995). Some draw parallels between these stories and the legend of Kiviuq.

Δ Kiviuq waited on the far side of the river as the grizzly approached. She came up to the riverbank and saw that she couldn't cross. She sniffed up and down the river and then called out, "How did you get over there?"

"Me?" said Kiviuq. "I just drank and ate and kissed and licked and fought the river, and then I crossed." And so the bear did just that. She drank and ate and kissed and licked and fought the river, and came across. When she got near the other side, she shook herself to get the water off her fur. Her big stomach burst, and because the water was so warm inside, it turned into mist and fog. And that was the very first fog that ever appeared on earth.

The bear fell back into the river and was washed to shore further downstream. Kiviuq followed on the bank. He skinned the bear on the riverbank and stretched the skin over a big boulder that you can still see today if you go to the place. Uriash Paqiqnak calls it Paniqsiivik, the drying place. Then Kiviuq walked off in the fog, unsure of what direction to take. Δ

The steam from the bear's stomach turned into the first fog that ever appeared on the earth.[4] The tantalizing and unanswerable question arises as to whether this story dates back to a time when there had not yet been a fog in the Arctic – or did the Inuit move from a place where there was no fog to one where it existed? It's also possible that this amusing explanation for an often bothersome and dangerous phenomenon helped people find the courage and patience to sit it out.

It seems that in Inuit culture creation did not happen all at once. Bee Woman has taught us about the creation of sea ice, and here we have the fog. Where was the real beginning? Asen Balikci quotes Netsilik people as saying that at first there was only darkness, no animals, no suffering or pleasure. They attribute the creation of people and animals to Nuliajuk, the girl who refused to marry. The animals and people then received joy and taboos, along with the ability to hunt and work. At this time there was no difference between animals and humans. The fox and the hare created cycles of darkness and light through resolving an argument. The power of words could transport people, as it still does today. There were no women until after the flood, when two male shamans gave birth to children, including girls (Balikci 1970, 209). This late creation of women is a good example of the cyclical nature of sacred story, where chronological time has no meaning.

Inuit creation sources are land-based. For them the earth has always been there, the first element. Many aboriginal peoples worldwide share the idea that creation did not emerge from a void. Rasmussen tells us that the polar people believed the earth fell from above. People were created from soil and children were found on the ground (1908, 99). The Igloolik people told him of a previous world that had collapsed. A flood ensued and then two men gave birth from the penis of one of them. That man turned into a woman and she gave birth with a song. Children and animals came from eggs buried in the earth with just their tops sticking out. Light and darkness came about through an argument between fox and raven, or fox and hare (Rasmussen 1929, 252–3, and 1931, 208; Bennett and Rowley 2004, 160–1).

The idea that one civilization was created after the fall of another is reflected in many cultures, and of course in the historic record as well. But it seems to me that there must have been earlier Inuit stories about the very first creation. It's odd that women would not have been involved in the first creation, since the ability to give birth is such an obvious and striking form of creation in human terms. The man who turned into a woman is reminiscent of Eve's creation from Adam's rib. Most stories that begin with male creation are known, or presumed, to have followed on earlier stories involving the female. Although I have not heard any earlier stories from the Inuit, it's easy to imagine that they existed at some time in the past.

Simon Tookoome says that Kiviuq made his tent out of the bearskin. He segues from this point to the fox story, adding that an ordinary fox would have been afraid of the bearskin and would not have entered the tent. The fact that our fox did enter proved that she was part human.

This story is alive in the present – more so than many other parts of Kiviuq's life, although other short sections, even the episodes about the penis in the lake and the mother who killed her daughter, have been published recently in Nunavut and elsewhere for use in schools and literacy programs. Generally, no more than one part of the legend appears in any one volume. It's easy to see why the bear story would be retold separately. It's a wonderful tale, full of the excitement of the chase, mystification and clever trickery, courage and creation. Its shape is clear – the story can be told or read aloud with full detail in ten minutes, the maximum length of an oral story in many modern contexts. The story also appears alone in many ethnographic works from the early twentieth century, indicating that parts of Kiviuq's story were also told independently in those days, sometimes about him and sometimes about an unnamed hero. Annie Peterloosie calls the grizzly story an "extra," something added on to Kiviuq's life story.

The story works easily with audiences of all ages. There are no issues of morality and political correctness to worry the non-Inuit storyteller, nothing like the issues that came up in the story of penis in the lake. And there are no complexities to trouble the listener, such as whether Kiviuq is the seal-child or the fox a reincarnation of the wife.

One possible reason for this story's popularity is the sense that it might have happened in real life. Unlikely but possible – a man could have been carried to a bear's den and then managed to escape, chased by the female after injuring the male. This has the same feel as stories of people who have been helped by wolves or other wild animals when stranded out on the land, including even the bear story that I told at Aaju Peter's party. On the shamanic level it is yet another journey and yet another death and rebirth.

Ijirait – Shape-Shifting Caribou

After Gideon Qitsualik told us Kiviuq's bear story, I was confused about when the bears were in human form and when they appeared as bears. Were they human only when at home or was there some other distinction? I asked him for clarification. He took us on an unexpected sidetrack into the world of the *ijirait* – caribou that turn into humans:

This happened not only long ago – it still happens now. I have spoken with someone who saw them. They are called *ijirait* [singular *ijiraq*] and they disappear as they turn human. It is very comfortable for them to change into humans but uncomfortable at the moment of becoming visible – the ground shakes. The people who meet them can't stay present and their clothes drop off. There is nothing you can do – they spin you around and ask you the direction to your home. If you know, they spin you again. If you don't, they let you go. You can't remember it afterwards – only years later it comes back to you.

They can see you when they are caribou, but when they catch sight of you, they turn into humans and disappear. People can't see them with the naked eye when they are in human form.

Gideon's acquaintance spent time with caribou, and when he looked at his own hands, they were hooves. Any animal can transform, says Qitsualik, but arctic hare and fox are particularly good at it. Those with helping spirits – shamans and others who see differently – can see the transformed animals.[5]

According to Igloolik people, *ijirait* are a type of *inurajait*, or human-like spirits, descended from Uinigumasuittuq (also known as Nuliajuk or Sedna) and the dog.[6] Most *inurajait* love humans and want to form lasting relationships with us. *Ijirait* have the ability to call storms in order to confuse their pursuers.

In an interview with Bernard Saladin d'Anglure, Aupilaarjuk once said, "I have seen an *ijiraq*. I once saw a *pangniq*, a bull caribou that looked really different. The antlers were very different, really bent down low. I saw this quite recently with my son. I didn't want to see this because I am a Christian, but this being was showing itself to us. I could see it through my binoculars. If it had been a real caribou it would have been thick, but it was very thin, even though it had the form of a caribou … It looked around while it was eating without lifting up its head. You could tell it was very scared. From what I had heard, I believed this to be an *ijiraq*. *Ijirait* can look like caribou. These *ijirait* that look like caribou were humans that turned into *ijirait* after they died. This is what I believe I saw."

In the same conversation another elder, Naturaaluk, agreed that *ijirait* may be deceased people's *tarniit* (souls) that remain on the land. Nowadays they are said to shop in stores (where stocks do not diminish as a result!) and use snowmobiles. They live in bushy parts of the tundra, called *miqqungaq* – places where there is a lot of willow, brush, and grass. These plants grow up after a camp is no longer in use. The *ijirait*'s houses are probably inside the earth.

Aupilaarjuk says that they can be *tuurngait* and can live in human communities and mingle with people. If people meet them, they should talk about it. Not everyone can see *ijirait*, but both shamans and non-shamans number among those who do. *Ijirait* are generally not frightening, not unless a person has done something wrong – then that person should be frightened.[7]

In one of his drawings, artist Zebedee Enoogoo illustrates people scaring *ijirait* away. As he explains it, "In ancient times when *ijirait* came, the Inuit would be afraid. So they would blow up their sealskin floats and toss them up in the air. When the *ijirait* saw them throwing the floats up in the air, they would become frightened and run away. They would think that the Inuit were very strong because they were tossing big boulders up in the air. The *ijirait* did not know about floats; they thought they were big boulders, so they would run away" (Bennett and Rowley 2004, 153).

It frequently happens in stories that a hero deliberately puts himself in a dangerous position only to be faced with the huge challenge of figuring out how to escape from it. I find that curious, but it seems to be part of solving the problem. Kiviuq manages to create landforms and he can be pretty sure that the bear won't be stealing from his neighbour's cache again. Clearly he has done his community a service. But he does not return home right away. Instead he walks away through the fog to his next adventure.

Now Gideon Qitsualik returned to the bear story and explained that before setting off after Kiviuq, the female donned her bearskin so that she could run faster. Clearly the sidetrack had been relevant to my question about whether the bears were human only when at home, enlightening us further on animals that can change shape.

Grizzly Cousins

My grandfather was an Udeghe shaman, and he competed with an Ulchi shaman who lived quite far away. One time his soul went out to battle with that Ulchi shaman. Each took the form of a bear. They fought to the death. When it was over, both shamans had died separately in their own homes, and two bears were found to have killed each other in the forest between.

– Udeghe cultural worker Nadezhda Kimonko, 2005

In Siberia, bears sometimes have associations with the lower world and its dangers but more often with the upper world and its gifts. The Nivkh and Ulchi peoples of the Amur River region and Sakhalin Island, as well as the Ainu of northern Japan, had a ceremony in which a bear was raised in a home as one of the family for a period of one to two years. Then the animal was sacrificed in a ritual rich in dance and music, sending its soul to the upper world to report on the people's behaviour. This kept relations between humans and bears in balance, clearing the channels through which an animal could take on new flesh (Campbell 1988, 147–51).

The bear ceremony was forbidden under communism. In fact, I've heard that in 1937 the authorities arrived in an Ulchi village and "arrested" the bear, taking him away on a steamship. The ceremony was not performed there again until 1992, but at that point people had changed. The human–bear relationship, which was formerly affectionate, meant far less to them in their current lives. In the words of elder Ymynda Ycha, "When I was young the bear had his own little separate house. There was a hole in the top and that was how we gave him food. Mama made it nice and warm – she put hay on top of his house. But now they kept the bear in a hut that was open. How that bear suffered. I couldn't even look."

The jawbone of a bear that killed a hunter is kept in a tree in Gvasyugi village. Other hunters killed the bear, then scattered his bones and hung the jawbone so that the bear would not return to harm other humans.

From that time forward the people have maintained certain parts of the ceremony, but without keeping or killing the bear.

On the other hand, there were also ceremonies to deal with breaches of the balance between humans and animals. Jansi Kimonko, the first Udeghe writer and a relative of the shaman described at the beginning of this chapter, describes a time when a bear had killed a man and the people in turn pursued and killed the bear. Ceremonial negotiations on the shamanic level indicated that the man had offended the animals by speaking badly of bears and shamans while he was out hunting. The ceremony ended with an agreement between people and bears not to kill each other any more (Van Deusen 2001, 152–5).

Many stories tell of women marrying bears, often giving birth to twins. Sometimes the children are bears, sometimes human, sometimes one of each. Twins and their mothers are considered sacred and receive special treatment. The story-song about Biatu tells of a time when things went badly wrong. In all similar stories I've heard told about bears, the children survive, so this story is more like that of the woman and the whale, where the cycle was interrupted.

I wonder if having both human and animal parentage facilitated shape-shifting, as in the case of Nadezhda's grandfather and perhaps the bear that took Kiviuq home. The name Biatu refers to a bear and is only used in story and song.

Biatu

A girl and her brother lived as man and wife. One day while he was away she called the bear to her. The brother was suspicious and set up a trap. He found out his sister had been seeing the bear, but when she realized he had spied on her, she left him.

After a while the brother went looking for his sister. Along the way he met two baby bears. "Uncle, uncle, smells like uncle," they said to him. He followed them and found his sister. She hid him, but when the bear came in, he smelled the presence of a human. The bear challenged the brother and in the end the man killed the bear. He tried to get his sister to come

> home with him but she refused. Leaving the children with him, she turned into a bear and left.
>
> When winter came, the man settled the two bear cubs down and left an embroidered robe with them, to show that they had human parentage. Nonetheless, when he came back in the spring, some hunters had killed the children.

Kiviuq's story tells more about the dangers of grizzly bears than about their protective powers or intimate relationships with people. Kiviuq deals with the bear by undergoing a voluntary experience of death and rebirth while buried in the meat cache. This shamanic death makes me think there's more to the story than just an encounter with a dangerous wild animal. It reminds me of the story of a Tuvan shaman's journey related by master storysinger Andrei Chuldum-ool. The great shaman Doilar-khaam had decided to compete with a female shaman who lived far away. To get there, he deliberately took ill for seven days and died. His body was taken to the grave just as Kiviuq's was to the meat cache. Doilar-khaam's body stayed in the grave while his spirit journeyed to the other shaman's home. The two engaged in a series of competitions involving shape-shifting and trickery. When he was ready to come back to life, he emerged from his own grave beating on his drum. A good trick, but it only worked while his drum remained unbroken. On a later journey his wife became angry with him and broke the drum head to prevent his getting back. At that point his body began decomposing (Van Deusen 2004, 27–31).

The image of throwing obstacles behind oneself while being pursued by a dangerous opponent appears in stories worldwide, including those from many parts of Siberia. The same effect is achieved when Kiviuq uses his saliva as he draws his finger beside a small landform, thereby turning it into a large one. Kiviuq's tricking the bear into drinking the river water and bursting wide open has parallels on Siberia's Kamchatka Peninsula, where the Kerek people tell of a monster, the iron *kala*. Some women tricked him into swallowing the sea. The monster burst open, turning into useful metal objects (Vatagin 1988, 310–13).

There are many real-life stories of people who are helped in desperate situations by animals, including bears. Here's one I heard in Chukotka in 1994 from a young dancer, Svetlana Chuklinova. It's the story I told at the party in Iqaluit.

Chukchi hunters

The Man Who Wintered in a Bear's Den[1]

They say this really happened, long, long ago. In one village there lived a man with his wife and children. They were very poor, and he worked as a herdsman for some rich reindeer breeders. The master was very strict, but in spite of that he paid the people something, and they managed to get by. They didn't die of hunger but at the same time they didn't live well.

The man reasoned to himself, "The more I work, the more the master will pay me." So he was rarely at home, always out with the herds. One day he went out to pasture the reindeer as usual. That day a terrible storm came up, with very strong winds. The reindeer ran off in all directions. No matter how he tried to chase them together, the wind beat him so hard that at last he fell to the ground, exhausted. He lost consciousness. When he came to, all the reindeer were gone.

"If I go back without the reindeer, the master will kill me," he thought. "And if I die in shame, my wife and children will die too. Better for me to go off into the tundra. Maybe I'll find the reindeer there. At least if I die in the tundra, people will take care of my family."

And off he went.

"Death awaits me," he thought.

Suddenly he was falling! Darkness – he couldn't see a thing. "I must have fallen into a hole," he thought.

He smelled her before he saw her. A bear! And what was worse, it was a female bear with a baby! Everyone knows that if a mother bear sees a human near her cub, she will rip him to pieces.

"Now she will kill me," he thought. He prepared to die – he lay down and closed his eyes. But then he thought, "Why should I die like this? I might as well accept it."

He sat calmly.

The mother bear was sleeping. She opened one eye and looked at him and went back to sleep.

"If I move," he thought, "she will attack." He sat without

moving for a long time. At last it got painful and cold.

He opened one eye. He moved one toe.

The bear opened one eye and closed it again.

Then he tried moving his foot.

Again she opened one eye and closed it.

"If she hasn't attacked yet, maybe I can move my foot a little more," he thought.

He moved and she opened her eyes and gave him a strange look. Was it the look of a friend or an enemy? She looked at him a long time, then turned her head away and went back to sleep.

"If she hasn't attacked," he thought, "it means I can move my arm."

And so it went. He stayed there in the den for a long time, moving only a very little.

He got very hungry. There was some meat in the den and it looked really good. But he was scared of the bear.

"If only I had something to eat!" he thought, looking at the meat.

The bear opened her eye. She looked at him and then at the meat. And then she took a piece in her paw and threw it to him!

He ate and felt new strength. Gradually he got braver and walked around on his side of the den, without getting close to the mother or cub.

He started to think, "I have to get out of here somehow." He had with him a *teviskhin*, a tool made of reindeer antler for beating snow out of fur clothing. If he could put it out over top of the hole, he would be able to pull himself out. But he couldn't reach high enough. The only way to do that would be to stand on the bear! What to do? He thought and thought.

Then the bear opened her eyes, got up, and moved right under the hole.

"If she hasn't hurt me, and has even given me a piece of meat, it means she is well disposed to me," he thought. "If I haven't died yet, it means death is not fated for me at this time. Whatever will happen, let it be!" He got up on the bear's back, got the *teviskhin* out across the top of the hole, grabbed hold and jumped out!

The bear looked up at him, wrapped herself around the baby and went back to sleep. He said, "Thank you, bear, that you didn't let me die and you saved me from starving."

He started home, thinking, "If I didn't die here, maybe I won't die back in the village either."

He went back to the village. People looked at him in amazement, as if he were a vision. "You were gone so long. Where have you been?"

"The bear saved me," he said, and told the whole story.

In several of our villages they worship the bear as a sacred animal. When people found out that the female bear had saved him, had even fed him, they all respected him. He started to live well.

When the spring holiday came, he killed several white reindeer and took them as a gift to the place where the bear lived.

They say of this story that good is repaid with good.

Kiviuq did good by ridding his community of a dangerous thief, and he was repaid with happiness – at least for a while.

The Goose-Wife

It's a mental inheritance – passed from mind to mind without paper.

– Annie Peterloosie, 2004

Taima!

Δ As Kiviuq walked through the fog, he heard laughter up ahead and it sounded like girls. He moved quietly and came to a lake. Several girls were splashing there, enjoying a swim.[1] Kiviuq stayed out of sight. The girls had left their feather clothing onshore. He crept close, and when they weren't looking, he grabbed all the clothes and held them.

The girls came out of the water and now they noticed him. One by one they approached. Each girl was a different kind of water bird, temporarily in human form. First the sandhill crane demanded her skin back. Since she was flat-chested and not very attractive, he returned her feathers right away.[2] The loon had a long beak and was eyeing the area of his kidneys. This made him uncomfortable, so he quickly returned her skin. Next came the northern brant. Some say he married her, but most agree it was the Canada goose, Nirlik (called Uviiqtuqijaaqjuq by some), who captured his heart. He was struck by her shapely beauty, and when she said, "Give me back my skin," he replied as he had to the fox. "I will give you back your skin only if you become my wife."

After a bit of argument the goose-woman agreed and they were married. Although she stayed in human form, he gave her feathers back. Δ

Bird Wives

Before we travelled north, John Houston had wondered what marriage with a bird was all about. I thought you could observe the birds to find out. It's their beauty, their ability to go where we cannot, to cross between worlds of air, land, and water, and to bring some of their wisdom into human embodiment by marriage with a human. My thinking came from hearing stories like the Sakha "Horsetail Girl," where the bride came to earth in the form of a crane and later enriched the people with her wisdom. She became a divine ancestor. Both in Siberia and North America, some aboriginal clans claim a bird ancestry, which shows how highly birds are valued.[3] For the Inuit, the bird's beauty and a basic love of animals and birds seem to be enough to explain the marriage.

Samson Quinangnaq emphasizes that he respects this story highly. Among Tungus and Turkic Siberian peoples, bird stories are also highly respected. A female duck plays a vital role as creator of the earth we live on. She dove to the bottom of the water and brought up mud to make a nest for her babies, and this is how the earth was formed. Some say she used the fluff from her own body instead of mud.[4] The Inuit may have taken the bird's divinity for granted in pre-Christian times, although today it is either forgotten or rarely mentioned.[5] That reverence may never have been distinguished from the respect and love due to all beings. It certainly recalls a time when people, birds, and animals could communicate more directly than they do today, and when they could change form more easily.

Courtship, followed by marriage, with swans and other birds, such as geese and doves, is one of the most enduring themes in world folklore, with versions recorded in many cultures across Asia, Europe, and North America. Usually the courtship involves withholding the feathers.[6] Some feel that the goose story shows the hunter's attraction to the beauty of the prey – which could explain some of what comes later. A Haida version recorded by Robert Bringhurst shares many features with Kiviuq's tale, although its major differences connect it more to the old world (1999, 32–44).

Within the Inuit world the story has long been told all across the Arctic, not only about the Canada goose but also about a northern brant and a duck. One of these tales appears in the next chapter, on Siberian cousins, in spite of the fact that it comes from Alaska. Since it was told right at the point of Asian connection, it has even more points in common with Asian and European versions than does the Canada goose version told in Nunavut, which is why I've put it there.

The ritualized telling of the birds' approach reminds me of the parade of animals that offered themselves to Kiviuq at the entrance to the fox den. But Kiviuq was courting the birds rather than rejecting them, as he had done with those animals. The feathers are like clothing, an external sign of the girl's identity. Exchanging one outfit for another indicates a new allegiance. But the feathers represent only her outward appearance, not her inner reality. In some stories the man does not steal the feathers, which could indicate a greater ease of transformation back and forth between animal and human. To me, the feather stealing simply confirms that the man is marrying one of the bird-people and that she is undergoing a major change.

Inuit elder Ollie Ittinuar feels that the goose story is more recent (or perhaps he meant more recently added) than the other parts of Kiviuq's legend. Others tell us it is not part of Kiviuq's life at all, nor is the fox story, although they tell them about other heroes without names. My own thoughts connect with theirs. If the goose and fox stories crossed the Bering Strait at some point, as they must have, then they were likely added on to the life story of a man who was born and lived in North America.

Inter-species Marital Problems

Δ After their marriage, Kiviuq and his wife lived happily and she gave birth to several children. Numbers vary. Samson Quinangnaq says she laid four eggs and that Kiviuq ate two of them.

The goose-wife lived with Kiviuq and his mother but didn't change her own eating habits. She continued to eat sand and a bit of grass, and taught the children to do the same. This upset Kiviuq's mother. She wanted the new bride to eat caribou and seal meat like everyone else, and complained that they were tracking sand into the tent, which damaged the caribou hides she was working on.

Some people say the wife refused to help with the women's work, since she didn't require their food or even their clothing. Others say she did pitch in and work just like a human woman. After all, one must help with the work in order to be part of the group. No matter which way it was, Ruby Eleeheetok tells us that Kiviuq supported his wife about the food, saying, "Sand is their natural food. Let her eat what she likes." He even collected grasses for her.

Fall came – the time of migration. The goose-mother heard her siblings, aunts, and uncles getting ready to fly south. As she thought of the harsh winter to come, she worried that the ground would be covered with snow and there would be no way for her to find food for her children. She loved them and realized that she would have to take them away from their father and fly south with the other geese. They collected feathers and she attached them between the children's fingers. She trained them carefully. When they were ready, they all flew around Kiviuq's mother, so she would notice their going. Then they circled around Kiviuq, who was out hunting. "I'll be back in the spring," his wife called. **Δ**

There's great variation among the elders on how many children were born to Kiviuq and his goose-wife. The magical use of numbers among the Inuit is not standardized into the threes, fours, and sevens familiar in other cultures. It seems shocking that Kiviuq would eat his own children and yet completely normal that he would eat eggs. Perhaps his wife is providing him not only with children but also with food, reminding us that stories of marriage between humans and birds play a role in resolving the dilemma of having to kill beings with souls in order to live. The hunter falls in love with the prey.

Listeners often question how Kiviuq's mother can reappear now, after her death at the end of the long journey at sea. I think her appearance could be related to the flexibility of time in story. The mother's presence reminds us that the goose story has long been told separately from the rest of Kiviuq's life story. And it's possible to tell the story in a different order. Samson Quinangnaq and others told us the goose story first. I also wonder if the death of Kiviuq's parents could have been a story convention. Their joy was so great that it used up the last of their energy. No joy could be greater than that complete fulfilment of a long-held desire. But perhaps they didn't actually die.

In the bird marriage story as told worldwide, the mother often plays an important role in the wife's leaving. She offends the younger woman by chiding her about her eating habits. In a version told by Kupaaq to Saladin d'Anglure, the husband also offends the wife by throwing fat at her when she refuses to help with the work (2006, 89). Some of the elders feel that the goose-wife left because the mother offended her, whereas others emphasize her strong instinct to migrate in the fall. Like the Inuit themselves, the goose is nomadic, but her seasonal round takes her beyond where her husband can follow.

Food Issues

Food is a strong determining factor. Inuit are very exacting about keeping food from the land separate from food from the sea, while depending on both for survival.[7] The mother was uncomfortable living with someone who not only ate no food from the sea, but also ate no animal products at all. Something in this discomfort seems stunningly contemporary, recalling the difficulties that come up between vegetarians and meat-eaters and the increasing number of diets that need to be honoured in contemporary society owing to cultural backgrounds and medical needs. The mother wasn't having any of that. Neither did my own mother, who held to the "Eat what's put in front of you" school of thought about food. Both came from a simpler time – a time when most people in a given region ate the same foods and when there weren't the foods available to cater to varying diets.

I've encountered a stringent ethic on my visits to Russia, where rural people still hold to old habits. To honour the hospitality of the host, a guest must eat and drink whatever is offered. It was no good protesting that you didn't drink alcohol, for example, and useless to apologize with reasons medical and social. Having just had lunch is no reason to refuse a large meal now. In my world such disclaimers are accepted, but I'm aware that a generation back they might not have been. It's natural for any cook to hope that guests will enjoy the food, and most conscientious guests do their best to eat, hungry or not. But I had a hard time shifting from my own understanding that the host should try to make the guest comfortable to one in which a guest must meet the host's demands in spite of how uncomfortable doing so may be. This latter approach could go back to a time when a guest was truly at the mercy of a host, depending on hospitality for survival. One of my Tuvan friends says, "When we have food, we eat it. Even if we are not hungry, even if it makes us sick." People who go hungry for long periods of time often feast hugely, eating quantities unthinkable to a person who eats more moderately but never goes hungry. This habit sticks even in times when starvation is a distant memory.

My heart goes out to the goose-wife, under pressure to change her eating habits. Whatever her reasons, Kiviuq's mother was upset, probably most of all by this evidence that her son had married outside the realm of human comprehensibility. This created a tension that inevitably contributed to the marriage breaking down.

The children seem to share their mother's nature more than their father's. Unlike children born of human mothers and animal fathers, they do not stay in human society. Inter-species children usually follow the mother. The goose-children can live as birds as well as people. Like their mother, they eat bird food even while in a human body. Both mother and children have something to learn. The mother, who seems to originate in the bird world, learns to work like an Inuk. Her children, more than half human, have to learn certain bird skills. Like the seal-child, they need to be trained into their animal nature. Tuutalanuaq had to learn to hold his breath under water, and the goose children had to be taught to fly. The mother chose to teach them at precisely the time when the skills were needed. The goose-children's human bodies differed from those of other children in one important way. Niviuvak Marqniq says they had little holes between their fingers where the mother could insert the feathers they had gathered along the shore to make wings. Placing the feathers is one of the gestures that almost all the elders used. The picture reminds me of the gloves that Iñupiaq and Yupik dancers wear, which have feathers attached to the finger ends that allow the dancers to "fly."

Detail can vary depending on the message one wishes to convey. Some people want us to learn about the necessity of taking part in the work of human society, others about the difficulties in marrying outside one's familiar realm and trying to adjust, or about the power of instinct. For some, it was the mother's jibes that sent the wife away. Cornelius Nutaraq says a male water bird wanted to swap wives for the goose-wife. But the most powerful motivation seems to be the migration instinct. The goose-wife heard her relatives getting ready for their fall flight south and longed to go with them. Torn between her bird family and her human husband, she found the genetic draw impossible to resist. It's easy to understand when we watch the Canada geese flying overhead in formation – an important marker in the year. Immersed in urban life on the west coast, where the seasons change only marginally, the geese remind me of the seasonal cycle. The sense of freedom in flight has always attracted people, and there is something about the formation that underlines the importance of that flight. And in practical terms, she needed to go where she would be able to find food for her children.

Here we have a different kind of woman from the ones we have met before. She is not affected by the opinions of others as the fox was. She is simply true to her nature, and Kiviuq respects that. Beyond this, she forces him to use shamanic power to follow her. Although he had used some shamanic power to follow the fox, he had also been able to track her physically, at least until the snow melted. When he traces the goose-wife, the shamanic song will be his primary transport.[8]

It's clear that one of Kiviuq's murdered human wives returned as the fox. I wondered if she returned yet again as the Canada goose, but this feels unlikely. There is nothing to link them, and in most versions the bear story intervenes, with a good year or more passing between. In the Inuit world, reincarnation generally happens quickly, almost immediately. And aside from that, we never heard that the fox had died – she simply seemed to move on. Nor is the goose-wife likely to be the other murdered human wife. The female evolution is happening in a different way now. It's not about the wife reincarnating to complete a destiny with her husband, and there isn't the kind of strong resonance we have seen between the daughter who was murdered and the human wife.

Owls

Kiviuq could have waited for his goose-wife to return in spring. Conventional wisdom would have told him it was insane to set off on foot following geese on migration.

Δ Moses Koihok says Kiviuna (as Kiviuq is called in parts of Kitikmeot Region) caught up with his goose family while they were resting along the way. His wife informed him they intended to fly further south and asked how he would follow. He turned into an owl, hovered over them while they were resting, but then got tired. He fell and sank into the water at an angle, since he didn't have webbed feet. He sank and drowned and that was the end. The geese went on their way and arrived at a place where they couldn't talk because it was too echoey.

Henry Isluanik tells of an owl who was not Kiviuq but who competed with an unnamed man for a snow goose woman. He kept her inside the tent. She tried to go out but forgot her bag of utensils. As she turned to go back, the owl grabbed her with his talons and held her.

The brothers knew the owl was holding her and asked the man, "What will you do when we travel?"

"I will follow."

They asked the owl. He too said he would follow.

And so they went. The snow goose was above them. The owl got tired and landed on her. His claws tore her feathers off. The brothers thought she would freeze. "Next time he comes, take a dive!" they called. Next time he came she dove and the owl sank.

Before this, the brothers had suggested to the owl that he wait until the next year, when the goose would return. But he was not one to listen. It seems now that the man had gone home when he learned that his wife was living with another.[9] Δ

The advice about waiting seems to apply to Kiviuq as well as the owl. He too was not one to listen. A break with what "everybody knows" is one of the markers telling us a hero is bent on transformational adventure. Many is the story that begins with this defiance. Kiviuq follows partly because he loves his wife and doesn't want to be without her, and partly because he is angry with his mother for driving her away. His big journey helps him to separate from his mother and to move across worlds. At the same time, he undergoes a new level of initiation by overcoming obstacles.

The goose and Kiviuq connect us to the elements and the seasons. She lives best in air and water, and less comfortably on earth. He lives best on land and fairly comfortably on the water, but he can take on the air element only in his shamanic state – his body has to follow along on the ground. He needs help to cross the huge bodies of water, since he is now travelling without his kayak. It is the stuff of high myth. A good number of similar heroes have been advised not to go on such dangerous journeys, but their passion overtakes them.

Obstacles

Δ To make the journey more difficult, Kiviuq's mother sent him off with a curse. Speaking in ancient Inuktitut, she said, "If you really leave me alone, may your goal be very far distant." Herve Paniaq tells us that the first three obstacles Kiviuq meets on the way are representations of the mother's belongings. The giant cooking pot is her pot, the giant *qulliq* is her lamp, the clashing rocks are her sharpening stones.[10] Δ

This is the last of several points where obstacles appear in the legend, and the one that appears most consistently in our forty tellings. But there are others. Some say everything that happens from the storm at sea to Kiviuq's homecoming represents a series of obstacles sent by the grandmother, who is bent on revenge. If not the grandmother, then Bee Woman might have sent obstacles, including the giant mussels and the fighting grizzly bears. And of course it is possible that Bee Woman was the grandmother's agent. Whether or not the grandmother's goal was to teach Kiviuq and strengthen him, the initiation he went through included dealing with serious obstacles.

Henry Isluanik says that the first place Kiviuq landed after the storm at sea was with the mother who murdered her daughter. She sent a series of obstacles when Kiviuq left her. In Greenland they say that Kiviuq set off after discovering his wife had a lover, and this journey too was fraught with problems, taking him to the middle of the earth and thence to follow his destiny.

Greenland Obstacles[11]

And then one day when he was out in his kayak, he rowed right out to the open sea. And when he turned round to look at the land, it was almost out of sight.

He rowed on again, and when he next looked round, he could no longer see the land. On his way he came to a place which was full of sea-lice. (When we see a piece of driftwood which is full of holes, then we know that the sea-lice made them.) He flung his bird arrow out at them, and they ate it up in a moment. And then, seeing that he risked losing his paddle if he tried to row through them, he took a piece of the skin that covered his seat, and cutting it into thongs, bound them about the paddles. In this way he rowed safely through the swarm, for sea-lice do not eat thongs.

And thus passing on his way, he came later to a place where the snouts of many spotted seal were to be seen sticking up above the water. And these he simply passed by.

And still passing on his way, he came to a place where the guts of bearded seal were to be seen, all bulging out as if they had been filled with water.

"Who can have filled them out thus," he thought, and rowed on.

But at the same time he heard a voice out of the air, which said, "This place is the Middle of the World!"

Then he rowed on and came to a place where the sea went bubbling round in a whirlpool.

"What can this be?" he thought.

"This is the Navel of the Sea," said the voice in the air.

In this story Kiviuq left home because he was jealous and it's uncertain who set the obstacles. But usually obstacles are sent by women as revenge for someone having left them or having hurting them or their relatives. With the exception of the seal-child's grandmother, these women are all in the wrong when they give him a hard time. Although on morally difficult territory, the grandmother is justified, if indeed she is taking revenge on Kiviuq at all. And we're not sure she is. Many elders say she spared him from her revenge and even helped him survive the obstacles rather than having set them.

As for the other women, the mother did a terrible wrong in killing her own daughter to get the man. In her disappointment when he rejected her, she hurled curses after Kiviuq as he left. The Greenland wife had a clandestine affair (and remember, it's keeping things secret that is the worst wrong, not extramarital sex itself). She also deserved a comeuppance, even though his killing her was too strong a reaction. And now Kiviuq's mother – Philip was the first to notice that she had acted wrongly by offending her son's wife, and now she was left alone, placing her own objects as obstacles in his way as only a mother can. On the other hand, Cornelius Nutaraq says the obstacles were set by shamans in Kiviuq's home community who wanted him to come back because his hunting skills were much missed.

Kiviuq's mother doesn't reckon on his shamanic power. He sings as he goes, and indeed this is the only way he can possibly overcome the obstacles and follow a wife who is flying through the air with a good head start while he toils along the ground on foot.

The Journey Song

We experience his journey to the south through his song. Although it may be difficult to determine where Kiviuq actually travelled, this kind of mapping is a time-honoured singing tradition. Travelling songs named the places the singer had visited and often served as an aid to navigation in the future (Bennett and Rowley 2004, 113–14). Six elders sang the journey song for us, and their melodies were very similar, although they lived far apart, in all three regions of Nunavut. A number of elders did not sing but spoke the content of the song. All agreed the song obstacles were metaphors for the physical obstacles Kiviuq overcame. Samson Quinangnaq had listened to it on a radio broadcast from northern Quebec. He said Kiviuq's journey song is the longest he's heard.

Theresa Kimaliadjuk told me that for her the singing is more real than the telling. We are all aware of the evocative way music expresses feelings without words, reminding us of times and places nearly forgotten. When I asked a group of high school students what music had added to my storytelling, one replied with a sense of wonder, "Music takes away the words." Other students have told me it makes the flow of internal pictures happen more easily. That reminded me of the Australian aborigines' belief that dream life is real and waking life an illusion. They map their territory and travel through it by singing song lines, similar to Inuit journey songs. When I actually tried Inuit throat singing and drum dancing, my experience felt much more real than anything I had read or heard about either practice. It gave me an intuitive feel for what it would be like to experience that music in a ceremonial setting when the song comes forward as one's primary reality. The eagerness with which the elders consider the story's geographical mapping may be partly ignited by a memory of the ancient use of song in navigation.

The song's power may no longer be acknowledged publicly, but it clearly still influences people. One of our elders stopped singing because he got a tingling in his back, signalling the presence of spirits. I don't know specifically why this made him stop, but Siberian people say it's dangerous to call spirits simply as a demonstration, when you don't really need them.

The Inuktitut term *silaup putunga*, which appears in the song, is difficult to translate simply. The best our interpreters came up with was "a hole in the environment."

This is the song Kiviuq sang, as rendered by Henry Evaluardjuk:

I'm walking past the mountains to the land of the birds, where winter never comes,
through a hole in the environment, ajaajaa.
Crossing the seal-oil lamp by jumping on chunks of fat.

I'm walking past the mountains to the land of the birds, where winter never comes,
through a hole in the environment, ajaajaa.
Crossing a pot of boiling meat by stepping on the chunks.

I'm walking past the mountains to the land of the birds, where winter never comes,
through a hole in the environment, ajaajaa.
Rocks are clashing together and I must go between them.

I'm walking past mountains to the land of the birds, where winter never comes,
through a hole in the environment, ajaajaa.
Two grizzly bears are fighting – I must go between them.

I'm walking past mountains to the land of the birds, where winter never comes,
through a hole in the environment, ajaajaa.
I see the lower half of a female body. I must have sex with it to get by.

I'm walking past mountains to the land of the birds, where winter never comes,
through a hole in the environment, ajaajaa.
At last I come to a warm place, with trees, a place where the water doesn't freeze.

Gizelle Rhyon-Berry says obstacles such as clashing rocks and fighting grizzlies test courage and help the traveller enter different levels of reality and power. Most of the objects belonged to Kiviuq's mother, but what about the grizzlies and lower half of the female body? My best answer is that those things never appeared in the telling of a person who said the obstacles were sent by the mother. Beyond that, why does sex appear as an obstacle here, as it does in other lists of obstacles? Perhaps it's a way of raising Kiviuq's life force through sexual energy so that he'll have enough strength to achieve his goals.

The syllables *ajaajaa* that are used in the shamanic song frequently accompany travel songs and are also used in drum dancing. These syllables mark the song's rhythm even when there is no drum. In many cultures, shamans sing their journeys, usually accompanied by drumming. The drum acts as a riding animal, providing the rhythm, while the melody and words report where the shaman has been and what he or she has encountered.[12] The songs could be very long. It seems to me that today's elders quote only short sections of shamanic song because of the spiritual dangers and their reluctance to bring the old ways into the glare of community critique.

The song follows Kiviuq's journey. *Silaup putunga*, the hole in the environment, represents a type of shamanic travel that shortens distances by folding the earth or creating a kind of tunnel. Elders say that using the folds is very dangerous, as it could shorten one's life. Use of the folds remains a last resort, usually to help someone in a dire emergency (Aupilaarjuk et al. 2002, 35–6). Anthropologist Edith Turner describes a similar phenomenon among the Alaskan Iñupiat in which a "tube in the weather" opens up, allowing people to get home safely during a storm (1996, 162). Rasmussen describes how ice can be crumpled for the same purposes (1931, 521).

I heard about a similar kind of travel in Chukotka. A shaman who had been passed by while hitchhiking on a lonely road somehow managed to arrive at a distant destination before those who had travelled by truck – in spite of the fact that there had been no other vehicle on the road and the truck had made no stops.

Henry Evaluardjuk told us that the pot symbolizes salt water. When we asked which body of salt water, he said it could be the Foxe Basin or Hudson Bay, but that it's hard to say because everyone tells it as "here." Henry has travelled a lot in his life, which has given him a broad perspective. He decided to tell us just one of the three versions he knows. Major stories are usually told with local centring, and this one is no exception. One of the interesting aspects of story among nomadic peoples is the way they map the known areas, which can be very large. As Kiviuq moved further from home in the storm, the land became completely unfamiliar and was peopled by unusual creatures. Henry says that this can't be a normal land because of all the creatures in it. To me, it includes elements of spiritual as well as physical reality, although likely most traditional Inuit would not make this distinction between the physical and the spiritual, since they view both as parts of one larger truth.[13]

One story listener in Ontario was struck by how different the sense of "home" among nomads must be from that familiar in settled societies. "It's not a hero's castle," he said. "Anything you construct doesn't matter. It's just the land." After hearing his insight, I began to notice how many Siberian stories say things like, "He returned to his native river." The hero could feel at home at any point on the river, just as Inuit can feel at home at any point in the large area they cover in their seasonal rounds. But truly feeling at home comes with getting back to one's people.

Henry said Kiviuq was blown by a north wind, which led Philip Paniaq to think he must have started on the south side of an island and moved southwards. Thus Foxe Basin and Hudson Bay would make sense. It was only later that I realized that since Kiviuq set off on foot, this would necessitate journeying shamanically rather than physically. He crossed the bodies of water in large steps.

The only concrete location mentioned for the goose-wife story – and that from hearsay – is Pikiulik Island, off Chesterfield Inlet on the west side of Hudson Bay.[14] Since the story likely migrated east from Asia, this must be a case where a location was attributed to a story, rather than the other way around.

Evaluardjuk feels that details vary from region to region because dialects have evolved over time, breaking off from one another, and certain words take on different meanings in different regions. A precise word may be retained as a story moves through time and space. Then the meaning of the word shifts as dialects diverge. Eventually people no longer remember that the word had a different meaning and the story develops according to the new meaning of the old word.

As we flew from one community to another, I watched the ever-changing landscapes from the plane. There were times when I looked out and saw big chunks of ice swirling in the sea, bounded by land and sea ice on several sides. The view reminded me of the chunks of fat in the *qulliq* or the chunks of meat in the pot that Kiviuq describes in his song. How could shamans describe what land and seascapes looked like as seen from above? Participants in ceremonies emphasize that the shamans saw them in soul flight. Inuit shamanic languages use the ordinary word for lice to describe caribou, which could indicate that the shamans saw the animals from far away, perhaps from above. I've heard that Siberian shamans described seeing the planet Pluto before it had been "discovered" by scientists. In their sketches, they show the constellations from various perspectives, as if not seen from the earth but from another angle. Although Kiviuq is generally not described as the kind of shaman who can fly, he partakes of this knowledge as well.

The Fishmaker and the Hole in the Environment

Δ At the end of the song, Kiviuq arrived at a place where he could see a big lake or river in the distance. Tired from the journey he'd taken so far, he decided to approach the water the next day when his energy would be stronger. He lay down and went to sleep.[15]

The next morning Kiviuq got up and continued down to the shore of the lake. It was so vast that he could barely see the opposite side. As he approached, he noticed a very large man working with an axe. There was something odd about the man, even apart from his enormous size. Kiviuq could see daylight all the way from his anus to his mouth – a tunnel through his body. Guessing that the man might be sensitive about this, Kiviuq crept around and approached him from the side.

He was right to be cautious. The man raised his axe and spoke threateningly: "Which way did you come from?"

"I came from your side."

At first the man did not believe him, but Kiviuq treated the Fishmaker carefully and respectfully. After a few more assurances he calmed down.

This man was Iqaliraq, the Fishmaker.[16] He was working on a large piece of driftwood. He put the chips into the water, where they became fish. From the hardwood he made arctic char and from the softwood he made lake trout. Niviuvak Marqniq told us, "When fish meat is sliced, the grain of the meat is similar to the grain of wood."

Theresa Kimaliadjuk, Madeleine Ivalu, Annie Peterloosie, and several others told us that the Fishmaker rubbed the wood chips on his penis before putting them in the water, which explains why fish are slimy. Moses Koihok adds that this was the first creation of those kinds of fish. Judas Aqilgiaq says that the Fishmaker put the fish through the open passageway in his body. Δ

The passageway seems to be related to *silaup putunga*, the hole in the environment we met in the shamanic song. The Fishmaker personifies that connection, which may explain how he helps Kiviuq cross the water, shortening the distance using shamanic means. Henry Evaluardjuk thinks of the hole in the environment as a barrier, but he's not sure if the river or lake where the Fishmaker stood forms part of it.

Tuutalik's entry through the breathing hole, Tuutalanuaq's descent through the wet spot in the house, Kiviuq's descent into the fox den, and now the hole in the environment all remind me of how Siberian shamans enter other worlds using the smoke-hole or the hearth. The ceremony of accompanying the dead to the next world often includes entry through a hole in the earth. If the same kinds of portals exist for Inuit shamans, this may be another of Kiviuq's deaths. I have wondered before whether Tuutalik may have died in the water before being killed by the hunter, and whether the seal-child may have been dead before the grandmother summoned the storm. Kiviuq's wife may have died either before or after her visit to the penis in the lake. In a similar way, Kiviuq could already be dead here. The story may be showing us how very porous the line is between being alive in body and being in the realm between incarnations. Naujarlak Tassugat reasons that Kiviuq can no longer die, since he already died before meeting Bee Woman. (In his understanding, Kiviuq died over the winter after pulling his kayak up onshore.) Does this mean that once a shaman has died and been reborn in the same lifetime, he cannot die again with finality?

Δ Now Kiviuq asked if the Fishmaker had seen his family of geese. "They crossed this lake," the Fishmaker replied, "and now they are somewhere on the other side."

"I truly wish I could get over there and find them," said Kiviuq.

"I will help you," said Iqaliraq. He called out into the lake. That which Kiviuq had taken for an island turned out to be a giant fish who helped him cross the big lake. Annie Peterloosie says that the Fishmaker made Kiviuq a wooden kayak to cross in and that Kiviuq listened to the ground before setting out.

"Get on, and sit behind the second to the last fin," said the Fishmaker. "He will take you across. When you see the shallows on the other side, the fish will move very quickly and shake with excitement. That's when you must jump off. When you get up on shore put your ear down to the ground and listen carefully – then you'll find out where your family is." Niviuvak Marqniq says Kiviuq was told to listen to his palm.

Samson Quinangnaq tells us the crossing was very long. "You can do whatever you want at any time," said the Fishmaker. "If you need to sleep, then sleep. If you need to piss or shit, go ahead. It's no problem." **Δ**

The crossing can't help but remind listeners familiar with Greek myth of Charon ferrying travellers across the river Styx, the boundary to the land of the dead. The image of crossing water is common in many cultures, including those of many Siberian peoples. The Amur region, which is laced with rivers like much of Nunavut, produces many stories in which people cross water symbolically – the water representing either the boundary between death and life or an important point on the life path. The characters may be crossing from life to death or vice versa.[17] Whether or not the bird's territory is in the realm of the dead, it is clear that Kiviuq survives the crossing, as elders insist that he is still alive today.

Who is this Fishmaker, whose very body reflects a portal to another world and who helps Kiviuq cross the water? According to Daniel Merkur, a specialist in religious studies, this character appears in stories across the Arctic, from southern Alaska to west Greenland. The Fishmaker's story is often connected to a story of a man pursuing a bird wife, but it also appears independently.[18] There is a similar character in the Haida story recorded by Bringhurst. Ethnologist Inge Kleivan feels that Kiviuq is similar to the North Alaskan hero Qajartuarungnertoq, who also had a long series of adventures. These included meeting the Fishmaker, although Qajartuarungnertoq did not marry a bird.[19]

Merkur believes that the Fishmaker is associated with Tapteq or Moon-Man, one of the major Inuit deities. He tells us that Moon-Man spat on sticks and made animals from them and that the land of the birds is his realm. Inuit elders have told Bernard Saladin d'Anglure that animals live on the moon and that Moon-Man is a hunter, keeper of all the animals. He is associated with water and many of his helpers are people who drowned, so it would make sense to me that he might appear beside a large body of water just after Kiviuq has shamanically crossed two other bodies of water. Tapteq is also known to have a kind heart and to help those in need. A well-known story tells of how he helped a woman who had been abused by her husband (Saladin d'Anglure 2001, 166–9).

Merkur goes on to say that Kiviuq's meeting with the Fishmaker is part of his initiation and results in his having a helping spirit, but he doesn't offer an opinion as to whether the spirit is the Fishmaker himself or the large fish that helps Kiviuq across the water.[20] To my way of thinking, the Fishmaker and the fish help Kiviuq only once and neither is referred to by a word indicating a helping spirit. I see the Fishmaker more as the guardian of the boundary between north and south, the lands of humans and of birds. It's entirely possible that the giant fish is the Fishmaker's helping spirit. Kiviuq gains his goodwill by being sensitive to his embarrassment, but this is not a relationship that continues – witness the fact that Kiviuq does not return home by the same route and never calls on the Fishmaker again.

Reunion and the Story's Ending

Δ Kiviuq got on behind the fish's fin and rode across the huge lake. He jumped off as instructed and put his ear to the ground. He could hear the sounds of geese, and he followed their laughter. As he came near their camp, his two children recognized him. "*Anaana, ataata* is here!" they called, running back to their mother.

"He can't be here," the goose-mother said. "We left him far away, beyond the second step." She meant they had left him beyond two large bodies of water, the ones represented by the *qulliq* and the pot of boiling meat in the song.

But now he arrived and she saw that it was truly her husband.

> In the meantime she had taken another husband, also a goose, or an eider duck. He said, "Kiviuq is not one to be afraid of." Nonetheless he came out of the house and jumped into the lake. But then he rushed back in because he had forgotten his bag, which turned out to be his stomach. Some say instead of a bag he had left a bait box, and Herve Paniaq says he opened a wooden box, took out feathers, and distributed them among the geese, who flew away. **Δ**

It is almost always the children who carry the news of their father's arrival to the mother. They recognize him immediately, while the mother does not. It's interesting that it's also his grown children who are the first to recognize Kiviuq at the end of the first journey. This motif shows up frequently in Siberian stories as well. Children are closer to the otherworld and not as much bothered by physical logic. The mother's words "It can't be your father, we left him too far away" do not convince them.

"We left him beyond the second step, *adluq*," she says. There was much debate among the elders and interpreters about what this step referred to. At last they reached a general agreement that the two steps refer to the two bodies of water Kiviuq crossed during his shamanic journey. They are represented by the pot and the lamp in the song, but do not include the large body of water the Fishmaker helped him over. The goose-wife knew he would have to use shamanic means to find her and perhaps was not sure he would be able to do it.

The goose-husband's words, "Kiviuq is not one to be afraid of," are reported so faithfully by so many people that they must be important. But they remain mysterious. It is true that people use the whole skin of birds as bags, which clarifies how his bag could be his stomach. We don't understand why the goose-husband feels Kiviuq is not to be feared and yet runs away, but it usually gets a laugh. The wife's taking another husband is interesting in light of the fact that Canada geese normally mate for life. Here the goose-wife has behaved more like Kiviuq's second human wife than like a true goose.[21]

In swan maiden stories worldwide, the two return to the man's home. I wonder if this could have something to do with marriage customs, since in many traditional cultures, including the Inuit, the woman went

Bernadette Uttaq demonstrates starting a fire.

to the man's home after marriage. This is what we would expect to happen, but this woman adheres to a different marriage system just as surely as she eats different food.[22]

Δ At this point the elders part company. Some say Kiviuq and his wife were reunited, others that she was unable to return to her human body. Some say she came out to greet him but she had forgotten a small amulet and the words to the song that she had to sing in order to transform back into a human. And now it was too late. She stayed in the form of a goose, and when the time came, she flew north again with her children.

Kiviuq is now stuck in the warm southern lands. Naujarlak Tassugat thinks he is probably in Scotland, having gone there on the ships. Others speculate that he is in Britain or in southern Canada. When John asked Niviuvak Marqniq whether Kiviuq is still alive, she replied, "He must be. If he were not, I would have heard about it." Δ

This is very different from Kiviuq's first journey, the one that began with the storm at sea and ended in a successful return home. Even after the fox-wife story he seems to return to his community. The journey following the goose-wife story is the only time he is unable to get home. It's as if his gift of returning has been broken – or that he's a different person now than the one he'd been when he had received that gift.

In the earliest recorded Inuit versions, the goose-wife has married another by the time Kiviuq arrives and she pretends to be dead to avoid going back with him. He sees her with her new partner and kills her. He buries her and she then comes back to life. This is strongly reminiscent of the beginning of the entire Kiviuq legend as told in parts of Greenland, perhaps indicating that for Greenlanders the goose-wife came first. According to other versions of the story, Kiviuq kills his goose-wife and perhaps even eats her body. Once she is fully committed back into her bird incarnation, the goose-woman becomes prey to the hunter rather than a beloved wife, so that killing her and eating the eggs is completely normal.

In my view, the shamanic reality holds the key to many of these differences. For cultures where shamanism was practised or was well remembered within the period when the story was recorded, the kind of travel that one would have to undertake in order to follow and bring back a bird-wife was considered physically possible. This ability, which is so akin to soul retrieval, was lost when shamanic journeying and the hunter's intimacy with animals were decimated by religious and political forces. Likewise, the word that has the ability to transport people (it is mentioned in the Inuit creation story) is now only known by the most powerful shamans. I have heard that Siberian shamans were powerless in certain situations after contact with Europeans. There were diseases they could not cure, and they were not very successful in dealing with the basic encroachment of the Western world. Perhaps Kiviuq's failure to return is something like that.

Could it be that after crossing from Asia it became that much more difficult to go back? Is it possible that this shift in story represents the trauma of that crossing? Or was it traumatic? What to us looks like a huge crossing could have been part of an ongoing journey, without the traveller having any awareness of moving from one continent to another. The idea sends a shiver down my spine. We'll never know, but the shift in today's story is abrupt. On the North American side the hero returns home only in the duck-wife story (in the next chapter), told at the closest point with Asia, and in the West Coast Haida story, in which a raven flies him back. As people moved across the continent to the eastern Arctic and Greenland, there would always have been some home that they never would see again and a time when a seasonal round turned into a permanent move. This could happen for many reasons – war, climate change, or the promise of better hunting up ahead. Although such conditions applied on the Asian side as well, after the crossing, different messages were attached to the story, having less to do with romance. In the case where the hunter eats the goose in the end, it seems almost as if he has awakened from a dream. He may have gone hungry so long that he began to see visions, and at last succeeded in killing the goose. He now ate but he was still far from home, and without his wife. It's also possible that the "hunter's version" is a more ancient one and that the change occurred on the Asian side, although that seems less likely to me, given the extremely wide area in which the story is told with the return home.

It is a real challenge to find a way to end the story as we heard it. Full of doubt about Kiviuq's return, saddened by his losing his wife and living far from relatives and friends, we are left wondering. Again, the Western expectation is that a story finds a clear conclusion, usually a positive one.

As told during the time of Rasmussen, the story offered a hope that Kiviuq would return to the North someday to help his people. Many world cultures have stories of a hero who will return. Today no one seems to expect to see Kiviuq again, but will this change in the years to come? It is our fond hope that he will return to life in the hearts and minds of his descendants as Inuit culture continues to develop and change in the twenty-first century.

Δ Samson Quinangnaq says that in the 1940s some of Kiviuq's descendants went to visit him and saw that his face had turned to stone. His spirit is alive on earth, says Madeleine Ivalu, but he has more and more difficulty moving. His body is calcified and his joints stiff. He moves around a bit in the warm days of summer but is almost motionless in the cold days of winter. He is shy about coming out where people can see him, since his face is covered with lichens. Ollie Ittinuar says he is alive, always changing from one animal to another. When asked if he would ever return north, Niviuvak Marqniq says he would not. Why? "It's too cold for him here!"

Samson Quinangnaq says that when Kiviuq dies there will be no more air to breathe and life on earth will end. But for now, he is still alive and has much to teach us about how to live a good life on this earth. **Δ**

Goose Cousins

"Kilae, Kilae! How will you come across? No ordinary person can do it. When a hail of rocks falls, when the salt sea burns, how will you come across?"

"I will cross over to you. I'll put seven pots on my head and the rocks will bounce off. I'll wear ice boots through the burning salty sea."

– Udeghe song/story

Approaching the end of Kiviuq's story, I wonder what it means in terms of today's Inuit culture. Stories and other aspects of culture, particularly shamanism, have played a big role in the post Soviet revival of culture in Russia. Although indigenous peoples there are in a different position from those in Canada, both are considering the implications of bringing ancient culture back into the public eye in a way that lives and breathes and, most of all, that supports contemporary people as strongly as it did their ancestors.

One of the people who is strongly involved in this process in Tuva is Dr Mongush Kenin-Lopsan. Himself a poet, he has dedicated his long working life to preserving Tuvan culture in the face of terrible odds – including Soviet oppression and even the opposition of his own family. He assiduously collected shamanic poetry and fortunately has lived long enough to see it published and read since the fall of communism. He also collected shamanic equipment, storing it in the attic of the museum, where it lived uncomfortably until it was safe to bring it out. Night watchmen reported strange sounds and energies from the storerooms and some refused the job. But the costumes, drums, and spirit figures finally saw the light of day again and have served as models to those involved in reviving shamanic practices. In the post-Soviet period Kenin-Lopsan was instrumental in setting up shaman clinics in the cities, adapting ancient healing and divination to a now predominantly urban population. He has forged links with healers and cultural activists beyond his borders.

Sergei Duger was one of the shamans who gave his things to Kenin-Lopsan. This happened on the collective Tere-khöl, located on the southern boundary of Tuva. On 17 May 1970 in the village of Kungurtug, Sergei Duger met with Dr Kenin-Lopsan of the Tuvan Museum and offered him his complete set of ritual equipment: drum, drumstick, headgear, *küzüngü* (mirror), ritual costume, footgear, and bear-spirit figure. In parting he said, "My time has passed, sons. I am sixty-nine years old. I have held my shamanic equipment in secret for thirty-four years. Soon I will see the sun set on my last day. I want my things to be held eternally in a clean and bright place in my native land. Yes, I voluntarily leave my equipment to my descendants, who are fated never again to see the likes of me, a living shaman. I was born on the banks of the river Karga and maybe I will die here. Just allow me to put on my shaman's clothing one last time and to carry out a ceremony in the depths of the night. And then let my shaman's things go away from me into a different world, the people's museum" (Kenin-Lopsan 1999, 109–10).

Duger has a lot to say to us. Not too many years would pass before his descendants would begin practising publicly, something only a shaman could have foreseen in 1970. Some shamans and Buddhist lamas hid their belongings, entrusting their location to a grandchild; after the fall of communism, these family members brought them forward.[1] In giving his belongings to the museum, Duger took a more public step than those who kept the objects in secret places, where so many things were lost. Although he may have felt that shamanism had died, he still wanted to carry out one last live ceremony – who knows what his wishes were as he did so? How can we confidently pass our heritage to descendants who will live so very differently from the way we have? One thing he knew for sure – the ancient tradition was taking a new form. He had done his part.

What does this have to do with a man who remained living in the south after losing his wife? Perhaps Kiviuq too is alive but knows his story will have a new meaning in the future. Younger people today are picking up the ball, adapting their ancestors' solutions to their own problems. Inuit youth work with their elders to decide what to keep and what to

Contemporary Tuvan shaman and his wife, outside the city of Kyzyl in 2002

leave behind. Siberians have had both success and failure – their children today have a greater sense of their roots than did the last generations growing up under Soviet power. Tradition informs intelligent approaches to serious ecological problems. At the same time, shamanism has been commercialized, and competition is just as damaging as ever.

We are coming to the end of our parallel journey through Siberian stories – some with their sources close to the Bering Strait and others more distant both in geography and connectedness. Similarities with the goose-wife are rich, not only in Siberia but around the world.

As I began reading the numerous North American versions of the story of the man who married a water bird, I came across the story of the duck-wife, recorded by Diamond Jenness from an Eskimo storyteller named Fred of Nome, Alaska. Something about this story felt familiar to me. I immediately felt at home with it and learned to tell it quickly, with no stumbling. I think this is because it is like so many other Siberian stories I tell, in form, detail, and feel.

As you'll see, the man who married the duck-woman has much in common with Kiviuq and a few major differences.

The Duck-Wife[2]

Long ago, near Tapqaq (Cape Prince of Wales), there lived a man, his wife, and one son, a youth. The woman constantly urged her son to go and find a wife for himself, but the youth refused, saying that he did not want a wife.

"Nay," said his mother, "I am growing old, and shall soon be unable to dress the game that you kill. You had better find a young wife who can help me." However, the youth refused; later, he said he might look for a wife, but for the present he was quite content without one.

Then one day he went off in his kayak to look for ducks and other game. All day he paddled up the river, but he saw nothing. When night came, he made a rough shelter for himself among the willows that fringed the bank, and lay down. But he felt a little nervous and did not sleep very well, so before daylight he rose, ate a little seal meat that he had with him, and set out again up the river.

All that morning he paddled along without seeing any signs of game. Dense willows lined the riverbank on one side, but on the other there were short stretches of beach. In the afternoon the youth turned his kayak towards the more open bank and went ashore to examine the country ahead, for it was all strange to him. He took the kayak out of the water, turned it on its side, and propped it against a stake, intending to return after a while.

He pondered a moment as to which way to go, then started off inland.

Evening was drawing near when suddenly he noticed a number of girls playing hide and seek (*imutaq*); strangely enough, they wore no clothes. He crept near to watch them. "I never saw girls like this before," he said to himself, and crept closer and closer until he had a good view of them. There was one he particularly admired; she was more beautiful than the rest; but how was he to seize her and carry her off?

"Here is a fine place for you to hide," he thought. "Come over this way."

Even as he thought thus, she began to run towards him. He concealed himself cautiously behind a bush, and when the girl approached, sprang out and seized her. "Let me go," she said. "Let me go."

"No," he answered, "You are my wife now."

"Let me go. I'm cold."

"No, no. I'll give you a skin shirt and you won't be cold any more."

"I don't want it," she said. "I never saw one like that before. I don't want it."

However, he took her away to the place where his kayak was lying. "I'm hungry," the youth said, and she answered, "So am I."

"Well, I'll give you some seal meat."

"I don't know that kind of food," she said. "I don't want any."

"Why, it's good food. It's what I eat all the time at home." Nevertheless she hardly touched it. By this time it was dark, so they slept there that night. The next morning he put his wife inside the kayak and started off home. All that day they travelled, and at sunset they slept on the bank again; the following day they reached his home.

Meanwhile his mother had been anxiously watching for his return, but when several days passed and still he did not appear, she lost hope and began to weep. "Alas! I shall never see him again," she mourned. Still she kept going outside to look and at last saw him paddling down the river in his kayak. Presently she caught sight of the girl in the bottom of the canoe. "Why he's bringing a wife back with him. Well done, my son, well done."

At last the kayak put in to the beach and the old woman went down to greet them. "You have found a wife at last," she said. "Yes," he replied, "I found one." "Well, I expect she's hungry," his mother said. "There is some seal meat and caribou meat in the house. Let her come in and eat." So the young man turned to his wife and said, "Go inside and have something to eat."

"No" she said, "I don't want that kind of food." And she ate but little of it. But when all was quiet and the rest had gone to bed, she gathered a lot of grass and ate that, and so appeased her hunger.

The days passed quietly. The young man went out hunting while his wife stayed at home and made his mittens and boots and whatever other clothes he needed. In time she bore him a son and later a daughter, but still she continued to eat grass as before.

One day the old woman said to her, "What kind of girl are you that you are always eating grass? Are you a duck?" Then the girl was very angry. She went inside, weeping, dressed her two children, and went out again with them.

Her husband was away hunting on the ice. When he came home in the evening he looked round for his wife, but could not see her anywhere. "Father, mother," he said, "Where is my wife?"

"I don't know," the old woman answered. "This afternoon she came inside, dressed the two children, and went out again. Perhaps she has run away."

The youth was vexed with his mother and said, "What did you say to make her run away? I shan't stay with you any longer."

The old woman began to weep bitterly, but all in vain. In the morning the young man went to look for his wife. He found her tracks and followed them day after day. One evening he came to a rude shelter. "Ah," he thought, "this is where my wife slept last night. I'll sleep here too, and in the morning I'll overtake her."

So he rose early the next morning and hurried forward, hoping to catch up with her very soon. But when night came there was still no sign of her. Another evening, just when darkness was drawing on, he discovered the ashes of his wife's fire, and they were still warm. He lay down beside them, but slept very little for thinking of how he should overtake her on the morrow.

Again he rose early and pressed forward, but suddenly, looking at her tracks, he exclaimed, "Why, one of her feet is webbed like a duck's! Perhaps I shall never find her now." Nor indeed did he catch up with her that day. Still he continued to follow her tracks day after day. Once he found the remains of a fire she had kindled, and this time the ashes were very hot, but still there was no sign of the girl herself.

The next evening, though, he saw a house in the distance and hurried towards it, thinking to find his wife there. As he drew near, a man called out from within, "Someone has reached me," meaning "Hello."

"U, u," the youth replied. "Where is my wife?"

"How should I know?" the man answered. "I know nothing of your wife."

"Oh yes, you do," the young man said. "Tell me where she is and I'll make you a present."

"What will you give me?" he asked.

"I'll give you an axe."

"All right," the man said, "I'll tell you. Your wife was here last night, but she went away again this morning. She's a long way off now."

"Never mind," the youth said. "I'll find her."

"Well, stay here tonight and in the morning I'll show you which way she went." So the youth slept with him that night.

In the morning the man said, "This is the way she went, but she is a long way off now and you are tired. You had better give up the pursuit."

"No, I'm never tired," the young man said. "I'll soon catch up with her." And he gave the man his axe and went on.

Day after day he travelled along until he came to another house. A man inside called out, and the youth answered.

"U, u, where is my wife?"

"I don't know anything about your wife. What are you talking about?"

"Yes, you know all right. I'll make you a present if you tell me."

"What will you give me?"

"I'll give you a pair of sealskin trousers."

"Well, your wife was here last night but she went away again this morning. She had two children with her, a boy and a girl."

"Yes, that was she. Tomorrow I'll overtake her."

All the next day he hurried along and in the evening he came to a third house. This time he offered a skin coat.

Yes, his wife had been there yesterday but had gone on that morning. He slept at the house that night. Early the following morning the man said, "This is the way that your wife went. Very soon you will come to a big lake. But you are worn out. Perhaps you will die on the trail. Better give up the chase."

"No, no, I'm not tired. I'll overtake her soon," and away he went.

Presently he came to a great lake. "Alas!" he said, "How am I to cross. I have no skin boots, no kayak, no axe. I shall never catch her now. I may as well lie down and die." So he lay on the edge of the lake and fell asleep.

He was awakened by something tugging at his leg, and looking down he saw a red fox. He sat up. The fox pulled back its hood, changed into a man, and said, "Where have you come from?"

"Oh, I have come from a long way off in pursuit of my wife. Now I have reached this lake and cannot get across. I shall never find her now."

But the fox said, "You see that big mountain on the other side. You must climb that. There will be dead Eskimos lying all about the path, but you must take no notice of them. You must keep on and on and on, however tired you are. If you stop even once you will surely die and never see your wife again. Never mind the dead bodies, keep on going until you reach the top.

Then when you get there, you will see down below a large village containing many people. One house will be bigger than the rest. That is where your wife lives. Around it there will be plenty of reindeer, and inside is where your wife lives. Around it there will be plenty of reindeer, and inside abundance of everything that you can wish. Your boy you will find as tall as yourself, and your little girl has grown too. Now sit on my back and close your eyes. Don't look, but just hold on tight."

So the young man climbed on to the fox's back, closed his eyes, and the fox started off. Presently it stopped – the lake was far behind them and they were at the foot of the mountain. Here the young man alighted, and the fox said, "We are both glad," meaning "Goodbye."

"Goodbye," said the youth. "Some day I'll requite you with a piece of caribou meat or something."

"Very well," said the fox. "Only remember, don't stop until you get to the top, however tired you may be."

So the young man set out to climb the mountain. All day he walked, never turning to right or left, never heeding the dead bodies with which his path was strewn. No darkness came to obscure the way now, but his legs began to ache long before the top was in sight. Still he struggled on. Once he stumbled and almost fell, so terrible was the aching in his limbs, but looking up he saw the summit just a little way beyond, and with one last effort he managed to gain it. Slowly he recovered and looked around him.

There below was the village, as the fox had told him, and there was the big house with the reindeer near by. Hurriedly he descended and approached the houses. But now two men came directly towards him from the big house. "What does this mean?" he said to himself. "What do they want?" He searched about, found a stout willow stick and hid behind a bush. The men came close up and were passing by when he sprang out and smote them one after the other on the back of the neck and slew them. Quickly he dug a hole in the ground and buried them, then hurried on to the big house.

In the passage he stopped to brush the snow off his clothes and boots. Suddenly the door opened and a boy came out, said something, and quickly went back inside again, calling out, "Mother, Father is here." But the young woman within laughed at him. The boy went outside again and the young man said to him, "Boy, give me some water, I'm thirsty. Tell your mother to bring it out."

So the boy went inside and told his mother that his father wanted her to take him out some water. Still she did not believe, but said, "What are you talking about, my son? Your father is a long way from here. Your father's mother was a bad woman, so we left them," and she refused to go out.

Then her husband went inside himself and found another man sitting on the sleeping platform. "What are you doing here?" the young man said. "She is my wife, not yours." The other man was afraid and said never a word, but presently took his mittens and coat and departed.

Then the young man turned to his wife and said, "How the boy has grown, and the girl too."

But his wife answered, "You are not my husband. He is far, far away and can never come here."

"Oh, but I have come. I am he. You know the river beside the house. I followed you up the river and walked day after day, never stopping until I reached here."

"No Eskimos ever come here," she rejoined. "This is my country, the ducks' country. I think you must be some other man, not my husband."

"Do you remember the big mountain on the side of the lake? I climbed right up that mountain, never stopping once. My legs ached, my body ached, often I nearly stopped, often nearly dropped down, but I was afraid I should die if I did and should never reach the top, so I kept on and on, and at last I reached it."

Now at last his wife believed him. Her old mother said to her, "Perhaps your husband is hungry and would like something to eat." So his wife went outside and brought in some food – berries and a few small fish, for, being ducks, they had no seal or caribou meat. Her husband was not used to this kind of food and ate but little, but when his wife's mother asked him if he had finished he said, "Yes, I have eaten plenty."

Then they settled down to talk and his wife's father said to him, "You know, in your country there is an abundance of everything: plenty of caribou, plenty of seals, plenty of white fish, plenty of white ducks, plenty of willows, plenty of wind. Sometimes it is very hot, sometimes very cold. Everything is in abundance."

The young man said, "Yes, that is so." And the old man continued, "Well, how long do you expect to stay here?"

"I don't know," answered the young man. The old man went on talking and said, "Sometimes strange people come here to attack us, so we have to keep watch."

The young man settled down with his wife and her people. One day a villager went outside and, looking around as usual, saw a dark cloud like smoke coming down from the mountain. He watched it come nearer and nearer until at last he could distinguish what it was – a host of duck Eskimos. The villagers turned out to oppose them, and a great battle ensued. The young man – the only real man amongst them all – looked round for a weapon with which to help his wife's people. He found a stick and laid about him mightily, slaying the enemy by hundreds. All day he pursued them ruthlessly, and ceased at night only because he was tired out. Some of the slain he took home with him, and he said to his old mother-in-law, "Cook some of these ducks for me. I've been hungry for ever so long."

But the old woman said, "No, no, we don't eat that kind of meat. I don't want to cook them."

"Well, but I like them," he rejoined.

"Well then, I'll cook them outside away from the house," said the old woman. So she cooked them outside, and the young man went outside and ate them.

"They were fine," he said when he came in again. "I had an excellent meal from them and am not hungry any more."

He stayed in that place for some time longer, and his wife bore him another son. Then he said, "I shall return to my home again. My wife and her baby, they shall come with me, but the boy and the girl shall stay here."

His parents-in-law asked, "When will you be coming back again?"

"I don't know," he said. "Perhaps we shall never come back at all. It is a very long way." So he departed with his wife and baby.

Several points in the duck-wife tale, told about an unnamed hero, set it apart from Kiviuq's story. Urged by his mother, the young man sets out specifically to find a wife. This is a common theme in Siberian folklore, but it's not what Kiviuq was consciously doing when he met the goose-wife. The man who married the duck does not steal the feathers – instead he grabs the girl herself and dresses her in his own clothing, which seems to tie her to his world, at least temporarily. Later he gives away his own belongings while searching for his wife, who had left because his mother offended her. The men who receive these gifts may well be reminders of the spirit masters of place, so important in Siberian and Inuit culture.

The man meets a helpful fox instead of Kiviuq's Fishmaker, and after crossing the water he has difficulty climbing the mountain where many have perished. At last he arrives at the land of the duck-people and engages in a great battle on their behalf. Most important is the hero's return home with his wife, leaving the children behind in the duck country. In Europe and Asia not all bird-marriage tales include the quest to find the runaway wife, but in those that do the husband and wife always return home. Looking back, I was surprised to realize that the return never appears in any of the Inuit versions recorded in the past, either as part of Kiviuq's tale or separately, although in some versions he does get his wife back and stays with her in the land of the birds. However, in others he kills the goose and eats her body.

Journey to the Land of the Dead

When Kiviuq journeyed to the south, overcoming obstacles, and when he seemed even to pass through the mysterious hole in the environment, I was reminded of the Udeghe land of the dead. People usually say that this land is far away from their known territory, accessible through a distant mountain. The seasons are reversed from what they are in the land of the living, as the Inuit land of the birds is perpetually warmer than Kiviuq's land. The souls of the dead arrive there guided by shamans. Udeghe storyteller Valentina Kyalundzyuga participated in the ceremony several times as a child, before the days when Soviet power all but eradicated open shamanic work, sending the more elaborate ceremonies underground. Her memories are vivid: "A female shaman accompanied my father's soul to the next world, *Buni*. She described descending through a hole in the earth. People were holding her by a strong rope around her waist. They went through darkness until it got light. The seasons there were the opposite of what they are here. Then a man came out to greet my father – it may have been his own father or someone else from his clan. People present at the ceremony asked questions to determine exactly who it was. Once she was sure he was in the right place, the shaman left my father there and she came back. Her assistants were pulling on the rope so she wouldn't get stuck there in the land of the dead."[3] This is a clear example of the kind of reversals we've seen so often in Kiviuq's story, but the fact that Kiviuq meets his wife's family instead of his own ancestors sets it apart from the Udeghe journey to the land of the dead.

Seagulls

One of my favourite Udeghe stories resonates strongly with Kiviuq's crossing the water to find his bird bride. It tells of a man who hears seven seagulls calling to him from across the sea. This story is sung as often as it is told, and singing itself crosses worlds. Around the world, crossing water is an image for reaching the land of the dead, and in this case it connects bird marriages with that realm once again.

Long ago the Udeghe lived close to the sea, south of Kamchatka Peninsula, which has live volcanoes. At some point their heroes must have been caught in an eruption and found themselves having to contend with a burning sea and falling rocks. On the return journey, Yegdyghe seems to be flying like the birds.

Kilae[4]

Yegdyghe lived on the bank of a river. He lived and hunted. One day he thought, "I'll go and find myself a bride." He made a boat and set off down the river. After a while the water opened out into the sea.

He got out on the shore and thought, "How will I get across? You can't cross that water in a little boat like mine." Then from the other side he heard seven girls singing, inviting him across.

"Kilae, Kilae! How will you come across? No ordinary person can do it. When a hail of rocks falls, when the salt sea burns, how will you come across?"

"I will cross over to you. I'll put seven pots on my head and the rocks will bounce off. I'll wear ice boots through the burning salty sea."

And so he crossed. The rocks rumbled – *guangutata, guangutata* – and bounced off his head. The boots melted and sputtered – *chaulili, chaulili.* He leapt onto the shore and ran to the place where the seven girls lived. A servant woman was looking out.

There were seven beds inside the house and outside seven *jiagda* – places with poles used for praying to the ancestors.

"Who lives here?" he asked.

The servant woman replied, "I live alone."

"If that is so, why do you have seven beds?"

"I use one for sleeping, one for sewing, one for feeding my dogs ..." and she counted them all off.

"Why are there seven spirit figures?"

"Those I don't need. You can break them."

He started to break them. And then the seagulls came flying and sang to him, "Why are you breaking our spirit figures? You are destroying our souls!"

"She told me to. She said nobody needed them. But don't be angry. You invited me and I came. I want to take you back as my wives."

"We won't go until you put the spirit figures back together. They are the spirits of our ancestors."

And so he put them back together. The girls got ready for the journey and they set off. They flew a long time and the oldest one started to cry out.

"I am dying. I am going to the place of my ancestors."

"Don't die!" called Yegdyghe. "Keep flying!" But at last she fell into the sea and Yegdyghe's tears fell like lead.

One by one they fell into the sea until only the youngest was left. Already he could see his own shore. "Don't die!" he called to her.

He took her and threw her the last distance to shore. The bird fell on the sand. He rushed to start a fire and burned the sacred Labrador tea plant.

The girl came to life.

They returned to his native river and they lived there together – Yegdyghe and the beautiful girl from the other side of the sea.

This story is similar to Kiviuq's because of its romantic theme of marriage with a bird. It does not have the elements of stealing feathers or the bride leaving her husband, but listeners sense the birds' beauty and the young man's determination to get to where they live and bring at least one of them home with him. The telling of the journey and its obstacles in song also connects the two stories strongly.

In Siberian folklore, women as well as men marry in the animal world, but they never employ the ruse of stealing the skin. But there are a number of cases where the woman, while her husband is either sleeping or away, finds the skin in the place he had concealed it. She destroys it in order to try to keep him, but this often leads to her losing her beloved for good. In Tuvan tales it leads to trouble but not loss, and for the Udeghe it simply resolves the problem of whether this shape-changer will stay in human form or not.

Kiviuq's inability to bring his wife back resonates with a north Asian story in which a man helped the Snake King defeat an enemy and took a small puppy as a reward. The puppy turned out to be the king's daughter. She married the hero and had three children. After some time, she decided to go home to visit her parents. She fell asleep in ordinary reality and forbade her husband to wake her under any circumstances. He was too impatient to wait out the time period she specified, and lost all (Kazachinova and Van Deusen 2003, 42–8).

At the end of Kiviuq's story he is living in the south, turning to stone and becoming more immobile with every passing year. Will he ever come back to the North? We did not hear about it on our journey. But in the South Siberian republic of Khakassia a great warrior named Tadar Khan is said to have gone off into the mountains to sleep after being defeated by the Mongols. His story has come to be connected with the post-Soviet cultural revival.

Khakassian musical instrument maker Petr Topoev told me of his own experience with a sleeping warrior: "Once I had made a new drum. My brother played it and said it would be a warrior's drum. I went up a mountain to consecrate it. I came to a place where I could see five peaks and there I began to play. Beside one of the peaks I saw a huge warrior sleeping and another one trying to wake him. I stopped playing and they disappeared, and when I began to play again, they reappeared. I was frightened and ran away."

Will the time come for Kiviuq's return? If so, it seems clear that the arts will continue to be his means of expression, despite changes in language and genre. Films, visual art, and the age-old art of oral storytelling continue to carry the hero on his journey.

Conclusion

Story Architecture

Having now spent a long time immersed in this story, I see a complex architecture emerging that is not obvious at first glance. Of course, the legend has a structure involving the various episodes presented in the chapters in this book – and these can be rearranged in several ways. The episodes are more like interlocking building blocks than like the links of a chain with a beginning and an end. Some people begin with the seal, others with the goose, fox, grizzly bear, or penis in the lake. The episodes with Bee Woman, the *inuksuit*, the lemming and seal bone, and the mother and daughter can be told in different orders. These arrangements allow for differing explanations and lessons. Herve Panaiq says that the story moves from the goose to the fox, since Kiviuq was a bachelor when he met his goose-wife and a previously married man when he met the fox. Cornelius Nutaraq says that the story of the penis in the lake leads directly to the goose-wife, and only after all of that does he tell the story of the seal-child. Each of these arrangements opens pathways to understanding.

The architecture I'm speaking of is different from this plot-centred structure but goes hand in hand with it. It involves recurrences of theme and imagery, parallels and opposites, humorous and serious sections, the intersection of the male story with the female, the use of ancient language and music, the interaction of shamanic and ordinary reality, the dichotomy of sea and land, mapping in physical reality and in the spiri-

Elder Samson Quinangnaq with John Houston. Photo by Alethea Arnaquq-Baril for drumsong communications inc.

tual world, and the passage of time as well as variations caused simply by dialect change as the story moves through time and space.

The storytellers dip into a multi-dimensional structure to find the information they need at a given moment. No one knows the whole, and all acknowledge that the parts unknown to them do exist. When we asked questions, the Inuit elders dipped deeper into the well. Some said that although they couldn't answer a particular question, most likely someone else would. A listener at one of my own performances asked if I felt that the storytellers sometimes made something up, and the answer is that I truly don't believe they do. Not in the sense of indulging a whimsy, and not in the sense of just saying anything to get an irksome questioner off their backs. True, they were coming up with new information, but it came from inside the story world and sometimes from shared experience. Because they were still in the story world when the question came to them, they could simply look. Answers may differ, since we do not all visualize the same way, but even contradictory details contribute to the whole.

Elders speak of the way the story was told to them – not all at once but in pieces tailored to the particular evening. "The story has no end," says Herve Paniaq. "I'm not aware that the story has either a beginning or an end," says Celestin Erkidjuk. Like the cycles of life where death leads to rebirth, the story goes on.

Ancient Words and Music

Certain phrases are spoken in the same way by many tellers, often in the ancient language. Some involve singing – either a full song or a chant. Let's see what we can learn from listing the incantational phrases and singing used by today's elders. See if you can identify where they come from in the story – reading them aloud works powerfully.

I am an Inuk. Don't spear me.

I want to be reborn through you.

Grandmother sings while stretching the sealskin.

Will you be afraid if I put you down through this wet spot in the house?
I will not be afraid.

Grandmother sings while putting seal-child down through the floor.

Silaga nauk, ungaa! Where's my weather?

I can't hold on any longer. Let me go. You go ahead.

Nuna tauvva, iqqaq tauvva. There's the land, there's the bottom under shallow water.

Get up! You need to move your kayak.

If you don't want to turn out like me, get out of here fast!

I put 'em up. You get 'em down!

Nanurluk, come and get your woman!

Don't go! I won't harm you!

This is the way I would have sliced/speared you.

tee hee, tee hee

Come and help me clean the dirt from my eye.
Come and help me climb this cliff.

This house has never dripped but now it's dripping.

Oh, it's a person! *Inunguna!*

Kubluruq is lying.

Let me pick the lice from your head.

I think you are going to leave me.
I won't leave you because I'm fond of you.

May you meet many obstacles on your way.

Aasiggai, aasiggai, aasi aasi aasiggai! Kiviuq's homecoming song.

My vagina has been closed, unused for so long, but now it is wide open!

Penis, come up! My vagina is open!

What are you more afraid of, maggots or the knife?

Give me back my skin!
I will give you back your skin only if you become my wife.

Take me!
I won't have you. You're too ...

Let him open his eyes! (He was holding the willows ...)

May this grow a mountain/esker/river.

If you really leave me, may your goal be very far distant.

The whole journey song.

Which way did you come from?
I've come from your side.

We left him beyond the second step.

Sure enough, these are the words and sounds that propel the action. Many of them are expressed as imperatives or use a grammatical form that expresses strong desire. In the mouth of a powerful being, such words, songs, and incantations actually call things into reality. They move a person through time and space. They provide a skeleton for the action. They mark death and rebirth, passages from physical to spiritual reality. I have a sense that the story could somehow be portrayed using only these words just as successfully as it could be portrayed in wordless pictures. The power of incantation and song is proven even when it fails in the story. The goose-wife forgets the song that would allow her to turn back into a human, and thus she and her husband cannot be truly reunited.

We've seen that actions in spiritual reality may have different meanings than actions in the world of human relationships. Sometimes they are almost completely opposite. This may be one reason so many elders are reluctant to engage in interpretation. The nastier things get, from cannibalistic bees to a mother murdering her daughter, the more powerful Kiviuq's initiation becomes. He will be stronger in the future as a result of dealing with these obstacles. The wife survives long periods of loneliness and then is murdered, being eaten from the inside by maggots. She is stronger, if more elusive, as a result. The goose-wife loses her skin temporarily and lives with a carping mother-in-law, but she gains children who partake of human as well as bird nature. Those who commit the most reprehensible acts may actually facilitate such transformations, although it is a skill easily abused. Inflicting such a transformation on another is wrong for the doer even if it has a positive result for the victim. This is clearly recognized by Inuit. I've heard that one shaman might send spirits out to curse another. It is better for the one receiving the curse to deflect the enemy's spirits back than to use his own spirits to counteract the spell. Using his own spirits would set up a powerful negative energy that could bounce back on him, while deflecting the enemy's spirits is an act of protection.

Death and Rebirth

We read before embarking on the trip that Kiviuq had died and been reborn many times, always coming back at the age where he left off. Where could those places be? Nobody answered this question, since today's elders mainly believe he lived one long life. I see a few possible places, suggested largely by the points where incantational language is used to bring him back. He may also be entering and leaving shamanic trance at each of these points, a transition shamans call dying and being reborn.

The cycle begins even before Kiviuq enters the story, with other characters dying and returning. Tuutalik may have died as he went down into the breathing hole, before he was pulled up in the form of a seal. Perhaps his son Tuutalannuaq died as the grandmother put him down through the wet spot in the floor of the house, before coming back as the baby seal that led the hunters out to sea. Tuutalik reincarnates as his own child, and Tuutalannuaq seems to have been called back to shore by the grandmother, having either survived the storm or come back to life.

Kiviuq may have died during the storm at sea or just as he pulled his kayak up onto shore. The mysterious voice called him back to life by telling him to move his kayak. Alternatively, he may have died of horror when he saw Bee Woman or the irontail woman eating her own eyelids. He fell off the house and lay dead through the winter before she called him back to life by speaking powerful words about his nature as a human being – *inunguna!* To avoid being killed again, he called on his spirit-helpers, the snow buntings or the polar bear. With their help he made his escape. Was he now dead or alive? It seems possible he was dead from that point until he got home, or even more likely that he was now alive, paddling and paddling, encountering obstacles such as the fighting grizzlies and the giant mussels. Naujarlak Tassugat says that because he died when he arrived on the shore, he could not die again later on and thus must still be alive today. Whether we can equate these events with acts of soul retrieval may depend on the motivations involved. Soul retrieval benefits the patient, whereas some of these events are designed to benefit the one doing the calling.

Kiviuq lived with the mother and daughter, whether they were wolves or human, and after that episode he seems to have turned a corner and was then really on the way home to human reality. Did he die again as he lay sleeping in his kayak, being pulled by the sandpipers, only to be brought back to life again by meeting his own two grown sons? We don't know, but it seems possible that his parents and the wife who waited had been holding an energy that kept him returning to the land of the living, right up until he pulled his kayak back onto shore. Having accomplished what they set out to do, the parents were able to die.

Did Kiviuq die again as he went into the fox den? Maybe he did, and somehow he brought himself back as he fought his way through the chaos at the end of the feast and lampoon session. Surely he lay dead in the meat cache. I think he came back to life while standing frozen in the bear's igloo, experimentally opening his eyes. The bear said, "Let him open his eyes!" That was all Kiviuq needed, and now he was all action again.

Kiviuq was certainly in another realm while negotiating the many obstacles on his journey to the south in pursuit of his goose-wife. The Fishmaker arranged to have him ferried across the water, but was that a trip from death back to life or from life to death? Trying to figure out which direction each transformation was taking is probably a task only an overactive rational mind would take on. More to the point is the easy permeability of the membrane and the fact that every death is a birth. People live in a continuum of life and death, including areas in between. "I think he led one life," says Henry Evaluardjuk. "If the story is true, the kind of life they led in Kiviuq's time is so different from ours that we cannot relate to how they lived their lives."

Parallels, Opposites, and Dichotomies

One architectural aspect that struck me repeatedly was the number of things that are parallel or opposite. There are strong parallels between Kiviuq and the seal-boy and between the fox-wife and the goose-wife. At least four times someone goes down into a hole or tunnel – Tuutalik into the breathing hole, the seal-child through the wet spot in the floor through the earth to the sea, Kiviuq into the fox den through a small opening, and later Kiviuq through the "hole in the environment" to the land of the birds. Kiviuq and his wives have parallel disembodied sex, he with the lower halves of women's bodies that appear as obstacles and they with the penis in the lake. Both Kiviuq and one of his wives have the flaps of their parkas cut, Kiviuq's by the giant mussels or Bee Woman's door and the wife's by Kiviuq himself in the episode with the maggots. There is a certain parallel between the women who lived without men that Kiviuq meets on his travels and the women who were presumably left for some time without men in his home community after the storm. Kiviuq meets a parade of animals who offer themselves to him, and he also meets a parade of water birds from which he chooses his goose-wife.

A number of things are reversed from the normal. A woman tries to penetrate a man with her iron tail; Kiviuq enters the fox den backwards, in a reversed image of the birth canal; the sod house appears at the wrong time of year; and maggots caused a death, rather than coming after. Elders pointed out that when the seal-child bobbed up in the water, he was all white, which was wrong for the time of year. One elder thought it odd that bears would have an axe in their igloo.

The story architecture includes the intersecting lives of male and female. Kiviuq travels while his human wives and certain strange beings stay put on their own territory. The animal wives journey and he follows them. The perceptions the males and females have of each other vary; at times they look attractive to one another and at other times life-threatening. Sexual imagery abounds in the contrast of *ulu* and spear, in fish being created when wood chips are rubbed on a male penis and then thrown into a lake – an image recalling the waters of the womb. Kiviuq searches for a wife, while the female moves towards greater autonomy.

Another ever-present image is the dichotomy of sea and land. Kiviuq's first journey is all about the sea – his paddling from one place to another, the transformational power of the water and its threat. Bee Woman stands with one foot on land and one in the water, reminding us of her powers and their limits. After the hero's return to wives and parents, the story takes place on land. Kiviuq seems to beach his kayak, never to take it out again. Even his pursuit of the goose-wife moves over the land. She refuses to eat food from the sea, identifying her story even more strongly with the land.

Mapping in Time and Space

Part of the architecture of our quest involved attempts to map the story in Nunavut's geography. We saw the places the hero started from and where his mother stood outside of Arviat, but there was much debate as to where the storm took him. Was it east across Hudson Bay to Quebec? Or was it to the north? We heard about his father waiting on a rock outside Gjoa Haven, and people from the Back River area could map the grizzly bear story precisely. We debated where the two bodies of water might be that are represented by the lamp and the cooking pot in the shamanic journey song. Foxe Basin and Hudson Bay? It's still difficult to map the story entirely or to know where the historical Kiviuq lived, although there's a strong sense that it was among the Netsilik, simply because the story is so strong there (this in spite of the strong Arviat connections). Of course, we don't know what further mapping would emerge were we to record the story as told in the western Arctic or in Greenland. For now it seems possible that the first part of the story takes place on an east-west axis, while the goose-wife journey moves from north to south.

The passage of time is another part of the architecture. How many seasons passed? Kiviuq was lost at sea long enough to fill his kayak with urine, he slept through a cycle of tides, he was gone long enough for his sons to grow up, he was in the fox den from winter to spring – and more.

It seems to have gone like this.

The seal hunt took place in winter, and the following summer came the ball game and the storm at sea. All winter Kiviuq slept on shore, and in spring he left Bee Woman. All summer he travelled. We don't know how many years the remaining adventures took but he arrived home in the summer to find his sons grown up.[1]

Still in summer, or perhaps fall, come the episodes about the penis in lake and Kiviuq's meeting the fox. In winter he travelled with the fox, built the igloo with the wolverine, and followed the fox to her den. In spring he lost the fox – although these seasons could all have been in different years.

Kiviuq lay in the meat cache for an unknown period that could have been a whole year. He escaped the grizzly bears. In summer he met the goose. Several seasons passed. Children were born and grew. In fall the goose flew away on migration and Kiviuq journeyed south. Although we can trace a good twenty seasonal rounds, we don't really know how long it all took. On another level, Kiviuq outlived all those whom he started out with, and seems to have lived from the time of creation to the present day. Some say that heroes who live such long lives do so because they have very large tasks to achieve, as does our hero. And thus hearing his story is a very large experience, encompassing many levels. One can hear it again and again with different insights.

This brings us to an architecture that is revealed when it is spoken with listeners – that of emotional levels. When I first told the whole story at once, the audience got very serious when Kiviuq murdered his wives, and stayed serious through the beginning of the fox-wife story, which has a much lighter feel if told without the preceding murders. The energy stayed serious up to the place where the wolverine shat himself a wife. This was taken as a clear signal that it was appropriate to leave heaviness behind and return to humour. Other transitions seem to require space – either a break in the telling or a musical interlude. Silence also serves well to allow listeners to digest and continue.

Stories form in various ways. Some are taken from history, others from vision. In the words of storyteller Dan Yashinsky, "Stories follow heroes." Some migrate through time and space, adding and dropping details as they go. Certain epics, or quasi-epics, have been formed like conglomerate rock – by adding episodes to a "frame story." A good example of this is *The Tales of the Arabian Nights*, which is based on the story of Sheherazade and the Sultan but goes much further afield between set-up and resolution. The Chinese tales of the Monkey King (*Journey to the West*) are another example. The tales are based on the travels of a seventh-century Buddhist monk but incorporate many fantastic and magical stories from earlier times. It's possible that many world epics have been formed in this way; the main story focuses on the life of a historical hero but other stories are added, some of them more ancient. Kiviuq's tale might have worked the same way, since his name only appears in what are now Canada and Greenland, while some of the added parts exist in the old world as well.

One last piece of architecture is the imperative that certain things must be accomplished. Kiviuq cannot go on until he has performed acts of kindness to the seal bone and the lemming. He must experience tragedy before being able to return home. His wife must undergo transformation in order to function in human society.

The Inuit Hero

While I was thinking about what the hero might be learning in the story, interpreter Philip Paniaq kept pointing out that there are no second chances in the Arctic. We may learn from the mistakes of others in story and in life, but once we make a mistake ourselves, there is no opportunity to try again. This idea about "no second chances" of course doesn't mean the Inuit don't learn from their own experience, but it underlines the fact that in an unforgiving climate one must stay alert and calm, and do one's best to "get it right" the first time. It is important to follow the rules (*maligait*) established through the learning of people in the past. The precision of life skill that goes into that way of life is a large part of Inuit heroism. Like any good hunter, Kiviuq is highly observant and learns from his partnerships with animals – the wolves, the fox, and the Canada goose. In a story recorded by Alfred Kroeber, he also learned to cut up narwhal from a woman he pursued (1899, 177).

What are the elements of Inuit heroism? Are arctic heroes different from those of other cultures? We see kindness to orphans, correct treatment of animals, courage, perseverance, control of emotion, getting things right the first time, walking away from trouble, clever dodges, creativity, hunting skill, willingness to give and receive help, and strict adherence to the rules of Inuit life. Most of these elements show up as the morals of the various parts of the story, and indeed the overriding moral can actually shape the story. It's no coincidence that today the story of the seal-child usually comes first, given that most elders consider the need to be kind to orphans the most important moral of the whole story. But in nineteenth-century Greenland the hero paddled away from home through a storm, surviving many obstacles after murdering his wife and her lover. He arrived at the home of the wolf women and announced, "I left home because I was jealous." It's just a guess but I wouldn't be surprised to learn that the need to deal with sexual jealousy was identified as the most important lesson to be learned in that time and place. On the other hand, across the water in Chukotka the moral drawn from the fox-wife story involved the fact that the fox had been helpful and the people failed to recognize it. Other value differences across the Bering Strait include whether or not Kiviuq's mother offends the goose-wife and his returning feathers and skins to his animal wives.

I believe many stories have their source in some gut-wrenching individual human experience and then are elaborated and generalized for a wide audience. On the other hand, certain parts of stories can also fall away. The basic skeleton suits many elaborations. Take the fact that the Inuit hero gives the animal and bird skins back immediately after marriage, something that heroes in other cultures do not do. Part of the moral involves respect for the animal, a respect that has become less emphasized over time in Asian versions. Perhaps a sacred story about bringing gifts from the upper world (for example, "The Horsetail Girl") suits a larger society and doesn't have much to say to a small family group, whereas a story about respecting your wife's true nature is very useful indeed. In fact Kiviuq runs amok when he fails in this regard. By the time the story had been analysed by folklorists in Europe, the goose-wife's marriage with a human man is covered under the motif involving "disenchantment," as if she were a human who had been stuck in the form a bird until the husband rescues her. In the Inuit world it seems to be just the opposite. She is basically a bird, living temporarily in human form.

Kiviuq is an epic hero whose function is different from that of a folk tale hero.[2] The latter, often portrayed as foolish at the beginning, learns from his mistakes or comes out well because of his very simplicity. This story form has been much taken up in novels and in Hollywood movies, where you can be sure that the worse a character appears at the beginning, the greater the possibility for transformation by the time we leave the theatre. In fact, we are so trained to this kind of story that we come to expect it and have a hard time relating to a different format. The fact that even the greatest heroes fall victim to traps laid by enemies as well as to their own emotions perhaps shows us how powerful such things are and how our heroes are only human. Storyteller Hazel Lennox says, "We can see that the 'good' person may do something that is not admirable and likewise the 'baddie' can show compassion or kindness. I feel the characters in long stories become more alive and real. I think about them as I do about actual people I know." Johanna Kuyvenhoven adds, "Not only do I get to know the characters as more than caricatures or symbols. I extend myself while sharing or being part of the adventure – I try out different dilemmas, ways of being and relating. I also get to feel intensely such things as the field of battle, jealousy, and magic places."

On the other hand, epic heroes often don't appear to learn much in the story – they already know. It is the listener's learning that is important. Inuit elders emphasize that Kiviuq was a good man and a good hunter who lay things out for people so we could see how to live good lives. This seems incompatible with his being the kind of hero who makes mistakes and learns from them, in spite of the fact that it's clear he does make mistakes that *we* can learn from. The hero (and in some cultures also the heroine) is set up as a pillar of goodness around whom the action swirls.

Epic heroes may even appear static as characters, unfailingly good, intelligent, kind, beautiful – less interesting psychologically than the villains but essential to the culture. They are of interest because of the situations they deal with, rather than because of their character. We should never forget, however, that Inuit storytellers like to encourage listeners to think for themselves. Elisapee Karlik says, "Some parts we want to follow and others we don't." It's up to us to know the difference.

Central Asian and other heroes are known as healers. Recalling them by telling their stories can be a healing process for listeners and even readers. I have a feeling that this is one reason we must see them whole, with their mistakes. Their stories include the whole gamut of human experience. We can't be healed without entering that flow.

Kiviuq strongly resembles the heroes of the Finnish Kalevala, who make serious mistakes while remaining staunchly and unswervingly heroic. It's interesting that the Finnish hero Väinamöinen fails in love and in the end leaves the world after the advent of Christianity. The Tibetan hero Gesar makes the mistake of falling asleep, leaving his people to be overrun by enemies. When his wife at last manages to wake him up, he puts things right only to leave the world and return to the heavens from which he came. Some say Gesar will return to help his people. Kiviuq too lives and learns.

Knowledge and Belief

Mariano Aupilaarjuk speaks about the difference between knowledge and belief. For him, knowledge includes the things that have been passed down directly from his elders. Belief is one step removed, based on his own thoughts and experiences in relation to his knowledge. Like him, other elders reported to us faithfully what they had learned about Kiviuq from their ancestors, and they made it very clear when they crossed the boundary into what they themselves believe about the legend and even when they made the occasional speculation or brought up an unresolved question.

Whenever my writing departs from precise quotations from the elders, I have taken you to a place that in my thought system precedes belief – exploration. Coming to understand a culture different from the one we were brought up in involves a lengthy process of setting ideas out to be looked at, turning them to show different angles. The same thought will look very different depending on whether it is seen from a traditional Inuit perspective or from a cyber-age global perspective. Trial-and-error testing may work in the realm of ideas, but it does not work while hunting on the sea ice. Inuit did not have the luxury to try such things out, nor the need. The wisdom of the ages stood behind them.

My ideas about Kiviuq are not cast in stone, but they do represent where I've arrived at from listening and also from retelling the story for audiences outside the Inuit world. Listeners try to grasp some familiar elements in the story, which for them is even more unfamiliar than it initially was for me. Their explorations can result in a new understanding and occasionally in a misunderstanding. But I'd like to emphasize that this is a process that has taken place down through the ages as people move to new circumstances and stories are shared over vast distances in time and space. When there are many versions of a story, no one version is more correct than another – all are equally valid.

When we asked what could be learned from the story, elders spoke about correct treatment of orphans and animals, hunting skills, and the importance of walking away from trouble – all of these showing aspects of the Inuit hero. At a deeper level, it becomes clear that the story includes a code of conduct that would not be complete if it covered only the human world. In order to work in the traditional Inuit environment, this code must cover the spirit world and the natural world as well. Individual points of the code are shown in the story when things go as they should, and most clearly when things go wrong.

When I retold and performed the story in English, my understanding was enriched through audience responses – where people laughed, where they were confused or distressed, and what they spoke about afterwards. In moving from listening to storytelling, certain things became clear only as I spoke them aloud. That process, together with this writing, has shown me things that go beyond this story and into the value of all long traditional stories. I've come to believe that the long form of the epic is important not so much because it allows us to absorb a large quantity of information as because it allows tellers and listeners to spend extended periods of time in the trance-like state that constitutes the story world.

Chesterfield Inlet

While there, we learn not only about spiritual and physical history, but also about ourselves.

I'm not the only one who has engaged in this process. While John Houston and I both do our best to stay true to the original, John presents in his film his own sense of the storyline and the details that most struck him. The differences in our approaches have something to do with our medium of presentation and even more to do with the fact that each and every listener down through the ages has experienced the story in his or her own way. We have different audiences, John's films being widely played in Nunavut and my storytelling so far being geared mainly to non-Inuit. We have faced common problems. For example, both of us worked hard to figure out how to introduce the hero at the beginning. As we heard the story, Kiviuq did not appear for quite a long time, and this is confusing to viewers and listeners. John chose to portray the hero as he appears at the end of the story, with rocks growing on his face, and have him flash back to earlier periods of his life. I began with a song about Kiviuq.

My listeners come from diverse cultural backgrounds. Their cultural assumptions influence the decisions they make about the characters and their motivations, and almost force them to find an arc that fits their own idea of story form. Even Inuit have widely divergent perspectives. As far as forgiveness goes, Philip Paniaq spoke about redemption, a possibility that came into Inuit thought with the adoption of Christianity, as opposed to the "no second chances" idea that is behind so many older rules and ideas. The makers of the film *Atanarjuat*, facing similar decisions, created a very powerful ending for their story. The hero states, "The killing must stop." The troublemakers are forgiven but banished from the community, whereas in earlier versions of the story the hero killed them, in line with rules of traditional justice.

The reincarnation of Kiviuq's wife as the fox is satisfying as a connection between sections of the story, and it ultimately works in the same way as Atanarjuat's strong statement. At first I wondered how she could have found it in her heart to come back so quickly and serve the man who had murdered her, even flirting with him. To someone like me who comes from a society where male violence against women is a huge issue, it felt wrong, even shocking. Not only in a moral or sociological sense – it also felt wrong in terms of the balance of the story. When a man murders his life partner (an act that Inuit call a wrong just as people from other cultures do), there has to be some lesson, some payback, in order for the story to feel right, at least to a contemporary non-Inuit audience. I needed the details – the wife's rebirth, the lemming's critique, and the presence of the scratching being – in order to understand the wife's behaviour and find a way to tell the story in my own social context. At least specifics like this open doorways to discussion. Many Inuit appear not to need the details, perhaps because the moral can be understood without elaboration. Or perhaps they take a different view. They have a very stark and true sense that things are as they are – and there's not much we can do about it. This is in contrast to the somewhat romantic tendency in contemporary Western art and society to show things turning out well, especially in art geared for children. Almost without thinking about it, we may "pretty things up" or even leave them out in order to satisfy that powerful need for the happy ending. But this practice wouldn't be true to Inuit tradition, even though today some Inuit might adopt it.

Siberian Connections

I was first invited on this venture because of my connection with the world of Siberian story. Following the threads took me not only back across the Bering Strait but also into world oral literature, whose connections are ancient, and to the Christian Bible, a connection that for the Inuit is very powerful and recent indeed. This has allowed me to speculate about the story's possible migration.

Clearly the fox-wife and the goose-wife have parallels not only across the Bering Strait but nearly worldwide. Did they cross with the Inuit ten thousand years ago, catch up with them later over the trade routes, or spring up independently? It's not a question I can answer, nor have folklorists of the past (Kleivan 1962, 32). More interesting to me are the smaller connections – a motif here, an image there. It seems to me that over such a long time period these are the elements that are more likely to stick than any but the most basic story forms, those that go to the root of human experience.

I was most struck by the connections the Kiviuq legend had with Siberian Udeghe story and world view. This may be because I am more deeply involved with Udeghe culture than with many others. On the first day I noticed how Inuit elder Bernadette Patterk spoke using similar intonations to those of Udeghe elder Dusia Kimonko. A few days later Henry Isluanik called out like the Udeghe elder Eofu Kimonko. My many memories of the Udeghe village of Gvasyugi resonated with the gentle warmth and hospitality of the Inuit.

As days went by, I felt the Udeghe connection more strongly but wondered if I was making it up. The two peoples are far removed from each other linguistically and geographically, too far distant in time and space for there to be any real relationship, but the connections kept on appearing. The Udeghe are people of the taiga forest, the Inuit of the arctic tundra. But both were nomadic hunters whose lives remained relatively untouched by outsiders until much later than those of some of their neighbours. This means that many of the ancient and rather mysterious parts of their culture are still available in story. I think of how an Udeghe heroine was mutilated by her husband because the "other woman" had accused her of killing their child. The imposter wanted to get the man for herself. There's a tantalizing similarity to the story of the wolf mother. But in the Siberian story, the true wife is brought back to wholeness by the child, who had been thrown into the sea to be raised by fish, while in the Inuit story, the woman is mutilated by her own mother but doesn't recover. I wonder if she ever had another story of her own, one that has somehow been lost. Here the lack of a return is just as disturbing as Kiviuq's failure to return home from the south. And as the thread continues, the woman returned to wholeness by her child reminds me of the way Kiviuq's children were the first to recognize him after a long absence.

I was also fascinated by several connections with the Udeghe story "Yegdyghe and the Bones." The hero's sister bestowed gifts on her brother just as Kiviuq's grandmother did on him. The sister advised her brother to listen carefully in much the way the Fishmaker advised Kiviuq. Dangerous cannibals reminiscent of Bee Woman masqueraded as friendly in-laws, and the whole story is about the man's search for a wife, which also is the theme of the latter part of Kiviuq's tale. Attempts to stab Yegdyghe were foiled by the heroine's cleverness, while Kiviuq himself outsmarted the irontail women. Attempts to poison Yegdyghe backfired on the cannibal daughter. The poisoned food offered to Kiviuq backfired on the giver. The young Udeghe couple escaped the cannibals by throwing out objects that turned into a forest and a rock cliff. Kiviuq escaped the grizzly by creating a mountain and a river. This is certainly a lot of common detail for one story, even if the events are arranged differently.

In other Udeghe stories the hero is helpful to those in need along the way. Of course, this is a common theme in stories around the world. The hole in the environment is similar to the tunnel Udeghe and other Siberian shamans use to escort the souls of the dead to the next world. The seasons are reversed in that next world, which reminded me of the Inuit land of the birds, a place where winter feels as warm as the northern summer. Udeghe storytellers sing conversations across worlds of body and spirit, bringing to mind the way the ancient Inuit language is preserved in the most propulsive moments in the story. In both, we see instances of shamanic knowingness along with common world images, such as crossing water to arrive at the land of the dead. An Udeghe man's marriage with a seal has the same level of devotion as Kiviuq's with his animal wives. There are knife fights and tug-of-war in Udeghe stories similar to the threats Kiviuq and Bee Woman hurled at each other. Red water plays a role in both story cultures. An Udeghe song-story tells of a hero who crosses a burning sea, rocks falling around his head, to bring back a seagull girl to be his wife. Kiviuq meets similar obstacles while searching for his goose-wife. A hunter who takes more than he needs undergoes death and rebirth to learn the necessity of obeying the laws. Kiviuq's wives die and are reborn to learn about the work involved in the social contract. Customs that make social life go smoothly and ensure survival are learned, not natural. Hunters must decide to stop when they have enough. Women and men are capable of doing each other's work but must learn to abide by the rules that keep the gender skills separated except in emergencies.

Ulchi people, neighbours of the Udeghe, tell of shamans who keep children's souls in a place of safety – much in the way the seal-child's grandmother transforms him to protect him from the hunters. In a different part of Siberia, Turkic epics follow the form of Kiviuq's story, with an initiatory first half and further adventures in the second. These adventures often involve bringing someone back who had been abducted or had died. Killing a person by sticking something in the ear is a common theme in the Turkic world, although the victim always comes back to life. Again, no return in the Inuit world. No second chances. This lack of return reflects a change in focus in shamanic work. The continuing practice of soul retrieval would have led to more stories with the pattern of return.

I was also interested in the differences between Nunavut and Siberia in terms of contemporary life, politics, and social concerns. The people have a lot in common in terms of the process of colonization and schooling. Nowadays the Inuit are much better off in material terms, with solid houses, impressive stores and public buildings, Internet connection, and marketing opportunities for their artwork. Their language is much changed by contact with English, in terms of both vocabulary and syntax, but it is more widely spoken than any Siberian language, with the possible exception of Tuvan. Many Siberian people live in small villages with no running water, few vehicles, only part-time electricity, and the nearest phone a two-hour drive away. On the other hand, for many decades a great number of Siberian people have received higher education, which has led to Siberia having a bank of professional workers and a rich cultural understanding of the outside world based on literature, comparative religion, and myth. Until very recently Canadian schooling seems to have given the Inuit little more than Sunday school imagery and television as sources of information about the outside world. Very few Inuit graduate from high school, although many of those who do go on to further training.

In terms of culture and spirituality, there were times when Nunavut felt like the Siberia I had first visited fifteen years earlier. Not only a new and deceptive political freedom but also the subsequent social breakdown and considerable outside interest in shamanism have contributed to old Siberian ways coming back to light since 1990. In Nunavut, I felt traditional spirituality and law bubbling up, but people are still reticent about trying things the old way. In both countries there has been a backlash. In Siberia, laws benefiting native language and culture have been repealed and giant Russian Orthodox churches have been erected on native territory. In Canada, we hear of the destruction of ancient petroglyphs by fundamentalist Christians in Nunavik.

In spite of humanistic rhetoric in both countries, communism enslaves the body but Christianity threatens the soul – a much greater danger. Communism was easier to throw off in cultural terms, although corrupt policies returned quickly. Most Inuit, on the other hand, don't want to throw Christianity and Canadian culture off; they only want to find a balance. In the words of Philip Paniaq, "We live a fragmented life. Before we took care of our own food, cleanliness, and water. Today others do those things, and all in different departments. We have lost order and self-esteem. We should be involved in all of our story."

In Siberia, people began to talk openly about shamans right from the early 1990s. True, some were hesitant to speak of having them in the family. But it was commonplace to talk about them and to draw conclusions about the spiritual underpinning of stories. As time passed, shamanism became a regular industry, called "shamanic tourism" by skeptics. Nunavut is largely silent and uncomfortable about shamanism, for better and for worse. At this point, most Inuit experience neither its benefits through healing nor its misuse through commercialization. I've heard that there are still some shamans, but this information has come to me only second and third hand, as it did in Siberia fifteen years ago. But there is a lot of interest in spiritual and cultural matters, a sense of their coming back to life.

It seems that visual art is the only place where things have stayed out in the open all along. Somehow it is permissible in art to express things that are not spoken of otherwise. Some young people who have received the age-old gift are using it with tremendous talent. Vancouver art collector Lorne Balshine says that missionaries had told artists that it would be all right to portray the animal and spirit beings of earlier times as long as the artists believed in Jesus. John Houston adds that the artworks are mute. The church recognized that the power of the spoken word was greater than that of a work of visual art.

I wonder if the priests also understood that native art would be a sorely needed economic success story, that the portrayal of ancient spiritual imagery, more than portrayal of everyday life, would appeal to an art market fascinated by the exotic. For whatever reasons, the artists have been the ones to record an array of information unavailable anywhere else. And so it turns out that those who encouraged the growth of Inuit art also helped create a spiritual outlet permissible under the church, whether or not they saw it that way.

Change over Time

When I looked at how Kiviuq's story had changed since Rasmussen's time, I was amazed. Although I heard a number of previously unpublished stories in Russia, the ones that had been recorded a century ago were often fuller and less "cleaned up" than what we read and hear today. Just the opposite was true with this Inuit story. Nothing that had been previously recorded was removed as a result of a moralistic church education. Nothing changed, and the story was much richer in detail, as if a lot had been held in memory that had not been recorded a century ago. The only pieces that we had read but did not hear were those that came from Greenland and Alaska.

Today's storytellers connected sections that had not been connected before: the fox was reborn from the wife's grave; Kiviuq found the goose by walking through the fog formed by the explosion of the bear's stomach; the lemming over the door in the fox den is at least tentatively identified as the one he helped up the sandbank and/or the one he wounded when it emerged from his dying wife's body. A year after our collecting, Annie Peterloosie, who had heard the sections separately from her grandmother in childhood, remarked on how she had now learned that all the pieces *could* be connected.

New to us was the prevalence of the story of the penis in the lake. It had appeared only once in the past – at least as told about Kiviuq's human wives. The hole in the environment was a new concept to us, and we were pleased to hear about the game played with seal bones and about how a gift bestowed at birth stays with a person all his life. There were anecdotes about poisoned food and tiny knives, and about an owl who tried to abduct the goose-wife. The Fishmaker appears in more lively detail in the elders tellings, as does the wolverine who created a wife in order to swap with Kiviuq for his fox-wife.

Are there more Christian elements in the story nowadays? The father who had not been able to walk and who got up when his son returned home reminds some elders of Lazarus, and the fact that the *tuutaliit* came back to life after three days seems biblical to me. Kiviuq's pointing with his finger to break open the sea ice reminds one Vancouver listener of Moses parting the Red Sea. Killing by fire reminds me of Christian hell, and the mother standing on her rock is like Jesus's mother Mary. None of these were recorded by Rasmussen.

One more very major difference between older versions of the story and those we heard is that nowhere in our travels did we meet an elder who told us that Kiviuq had ever returned to the North or that he was expected to come back in the future. Most agree that he is still alive, but they are uncertain about where he is. They say that when he dies, there will be no more air to breathe and life on earth will end. But until then he lives on in story.

ΔΔΔ

Comments from Nunavut Elders

As our journey comes to an end, I'd like to give you a taste of what the elders themselves had to say about the story of Kiviuq, about what we can learn from it, about the story's importance in Inuit life, and about the power of words. More of the elders' words have appeared throughout the text.

In Rankin Inlet

ELISAPEE KARLIK: What will we learn from Kiviuq's story? We learn about hunting on land and sea, how and where to do it. There are parts of his life you want to follow and parts you don't. Kiviuq goes through good times and bad times just like we do today.

BERNADETTE PATTERK: I learned the story by listening many times to my grandfather. If we listen carefully, we'll pick up what we need, but many will not learn.

NAALUNGIAQ MAKKIGAQ: Smart people learn quickly!

In Arviat

HENRY ISLUANIK: The rock where Kiviuq's mother stood is meaningful to me. I really believe the story happened because of seeing the rock.

If you are observant, you can learn how to live your life from the people in the story and their actions.

PETER SUQAKSIORK AND PHILLIP KIGUSIUTNAK: Today life is tangled and without direction. Life stories like Kiviuq's can help us direct our own lives. People who made the songs used to include whatever episodes from their lives they wanted, often about their struggles. They might include names of places where they got a wolf, things like that. Elders used to spend a lot of time with children to keep them out of trouble and to help them learn.

In Baker Lake

SAMSON QUINANGNAQ: I can say for sure that the Inuit had no writers. Instead we had storytellers for passing on the word. Everything is repeated so that people will remember it. Inuit had no written language, only the storytellers to guide their lives.

Here's a true story. When I was young, I had a dream that touched me greatly. We cannot see God, but in the dream I could picture the face and body of God. God appeared in the dream and said, "If you pass on what you know, you will be healed." I had gone to sleep with a sore throat and unable to eat, and woke up healed. This is when I was young. Now I have lived to 2004 and am still passing stories on as God asked me to.

SIMON TOOKOOME: You can learn from some of the stories. They help you survive as an Inuk. Our ancestors had hard times to survive. They worked hard. You learn how to live in the north, about hunting and things like that. Kiviuq may have turned to earth, and thus could be alive in the vegetation. To me as an artist, Kiviuq is difficult to visualize, since he is neither human nor god.

In Chesterfield Inlet

LEO NIMIALIK: I believe in this story, which has been passed down for many generations, from long before the time of Christ. I believe some parts and not others. There are some who know but keep quiet about it.

JOE ISSALUK: In old times stories were passed on. You pick them up without realizing. Just part of life. Today it's getting harder to pass stories to children. Some parents can't connect with their children or grandchildren because of language. If I could speak English, then I could pass them on.

THERESA KIMALIADJUK: There's lots to use out of this story. Our parents tell us things that are good to hear and make sure the kids don't hear the bad things. Kids would even be sent away while those conversations were going on. Kids heard all of the Kiviuq story because we encounter good and bad in life and the story contains it all. Which other stories should be recorded and re-enlivened? All of them!

In Iqaluit

HENRY EVALUARDJUK: I think that certain stories would be useful today – the ones that show how patience is necessary for survival. Today people go out on snowmobiles and are not careful; they don't stop when they should. I have found five different people dead because of this carelessness. Being patient and observant leads to survival. There are examples in Kiviuq's story of why we must not do wrong to any animal big or small.

In Igloolik

MADELEINE IVALU: Inuit were good storytellers because it wasn't written down. Even now my brother-in-law [Herve Paniaq] tells stories to his nephews while hunting. Stories are good for teaching language. Some of this story language is not used today, expressions like "the other step – *adluq*" and words used for calling the bear. Even I don't know the meaning of some of these words, although I use them. I'd like to see the story in a book. So would Herve Paniaq.

RACHEL UJARASUK: The strongest value shown is that of kindness and love, being good to those who are less fortunate than we are. We should help them, eat with them, laugh with them.

ZIPPORA INNUKSUK: I would like to see a book that would teach lessons like kindness to animals.

In Pond Inlet

JACOB PETERLOOSIE: The story proves that you'll have a long life if you are not cruel to anyone or anything. If you serve only yourself, your life will be short. That's the only meaning I see. We must strive not to be unkind. I was taught that lesson in childhood. If someone does you wrong, step away. If it's repeated a lot you can stop the person once.

I haven't heard this story since I was six. Why? Because they pass on things you'll remember at that formative time. Afterwards we have so many impressions that we may forget these things but they resurface later. But today it's as if even little kids are treated as adults – they are not given stories. Children don't know what to be afraid of, like the dangers of water and blizzards.

CORNELIUS NUTARAQ: Variations in the story come about because of dialect change. Stories have different purposes, but they all preserve words from the past which are lost otherwise. It's very important to teach correct Inuktitut. Not only the old language but ordinary everyday language should be correct. We can judge the locations in the story from landscape and dialect. With Christianity, storytelling stopped. The missionaries said you must give up storytelling, drum dancing, chanting, singing, and taboos. Now we realize that not all of traditional practice was bad. Some can be used for good. In Kivalliq they are using *ajaajaa* more because they understand it can be used for celebration and to help others. Stories come about because we need the information. Some things that are necessary today were thrown away, including the stories. As Samson Quinangnaq says, Kiviuq may have been a prophet in the Inuit understanding of the word – one who sees consequences. But I see that not only may Kiviuq be a prophet but Samson Quinangnaq is also a prophet.

ANNIE PETERLOOSIE: An important lesson is noticing who needs help even when others don't. Another thing is that Kiviuq just left all those beings, he didn't kill them. The message is just to step away from trouble.

Is it like a Bible story? Yes, I think so, just changed in time and space. Good shamans with helping spirits were prophets. We learn right and wrong from this story, as from the Bible. All stories guide us to do right by others and thus live a long life. It's very strong that people my age are remembering oral stories – I find the Kiviuq story easy to tell. It's a mental inheritance, passed from mind to mind without paper. I heard it at six and remember it now.

Missionaries tried to wipe out these kinds of stories. They scared people with hellfire. Only with things like Inuit Tapiriit Kanatami [ITK] are they resurfacing. [ITK, formerly Inuit Tapirisat, was concerned with politics and culture. The organization played a big role in the formation of Nunavut.] I'm thankful to my grandmother, who told in spite of that repression. The stories teach skills for survival on the land, about tools, making fire, and things like that.

JOANASIE MACPA: Don't think bad thoughts, much less speak badly of animals. Animals were the only thing that fed us.

In Gjoa Haven

GIDEON QITSUALIK: These are just stories. I doubt the truth of Kiviuq. People may have forgotten the written language and then they just had storytelling. There are some things you can learn but I haven't heard that was the purpose of it.

In Taloyoak

MARY ITTUNGA: Lessons? There is fiction and then there are legends that are real and historical. This story is separate from the legends about real life. In the practice of telling stories people learn often by analogy. For example, the fox-wife was driven to the point of leaving – she was worn down. This happens to people in life. I could tell lots of stories but the children don't understand the language.

BERNADETTE UTTAQ: Kiviuq is the same kind of being and the same age range as the biblical prophets. Kiviuq and other important story characters are in our lives today. Kiviuq was a good person, and like him we can be great. Their acts set a value, a way of living, of seeing consequences. Life has already been set out by Kiviuq for people and animals. I'm using analogy to simplify what will always be. It is set out but not written. It is very powerful.

In Cambridge Bay

FRANK ANALOK: There are good lessons for students in these stories about how life is enduring even when there are only a few women around, and about how hard life was and continues to be. The stories show a way of life that should not be lost. They can be used to carry that way of life on.

MOSES KOIHOK: Stories are very good for language learning and preservation, as well as for understanding the Inuit way of life. They were passed on down through many generations, and through them the awareness of life continues. They are important for passing on that way of life. Some are about the hardships our ancestors endured. Stories help children and youth to think about life, and they can help them with today's difficulties, including alcohol and drugs.

MARGARET NAKASHOOK: I am starting to regret not having recalled the story more regularly over the years. Why didn't I? Life has become more distracting. There used to be greater concentration because there were fewer people around. My parents lived with nobody nearby and so they used storytelling to keep us children from being bored. Stories help us to think about life and are also good for settling children down.

Glossary

Note: Pronunciation guides for Inuktitut and for the Siberian languages appear on pages 358 and 360 respectively.

Inuktitut

aarnguat: amulets
adluq: a step, as when Kiviuq crosses large bodies of water while pursuing his goose-wife
Airaqtuuq: the place where Kiviuq may have been born, near Arviat
ajaajaa: syllables used in songs about journeys and other spiritual matters
amauti: woman's parka with a back pouch for carrying an infant or toddler
anaana: mother
anaq: excrement
angakkuq (pl. angakkuit): shaman
anirniq: breath
ataata: father
atigi: parka, usually made of caribou skin
atiq: name or name-soul
ijiraq (pl. ijirait): caribou that appear in human form

ikajuqti (pl. ikajuqtit): helper or helping spirit
ilimmaqturniq: shaman's journey through the air
ilisiiq: hex
ilisiiqsiniq: act of putting a hex on someone
inngiruti: songs
Inuk (pl. Inuit): person, human being
inuksuk (dual inuksuut; pl. inuksuit): stone cairn used for various purposes, including showing directions and controlling a run of caribou
Inunguna: It's a person.
inurajait: human-like spirits
inuruuqqayuk: animal living temporarily in human form
irinaliuti (pl. irinaliutit): incantation
iviutik (pl. iviutiit): duelling song
kamik: boot; **kamiik**: pair of boots
katajjait: throat song
katajjaq: throat singing
kilangmiutak: collared lemming
maligait: things that have to be followed
miqqungaq: bushy parts of the tundra where there is a lot of willow, brush, and grass
nalauttaiji: prophet, one who understands consequences or foretells the future
nigjuarjuk (pl. nigjuarjuit): small, red-brown earth spider of barren lands. They are about one-fifth the size of ordinary spiders. May also appear as dangerous small beings, possibly *tuurngait*, who wield tiny knives.
nirrukkaq: rumen from a caribou first stomach
nunalait: evil spirits
Nuna tauvva, iqqaq tauvva: There's the land, there's the bottom under shallow water.
pana: snow knife
paniqsiivik: drying place
paqqutik: aged caribou marrow
pittailinik: forbidden behaviour
qaumaniq: shaman's aura or the ability to see clairvoyantly

Qikiqtaarjuk: place near Arviat where Kiviuq's mother's footprints can be seen
qilauti: hoop drum
Qimiqtaaq: New Esker or mountain
qulliq: seal-oil lamp, used for light, heat, drying, and cooking
sauraq: Dunlin sandpiper
sila: refers to many concepts connected with the sky, both physical and spiritual
Silaga nauk? Where's my weather? This was a call for the weather of the day one was born.
Silaup Inua: sky and weather spirit
taarniq: darkness
taima: now
Takulaarivuguk: We'll see each other again, after at least one sleep (two people talking to each other); **Takulaarivugut** (talking to more than two people)
tarniq: soul
Tikiraarjuk: place near Arviat where Kiviuq's mother waited for his return
tirigusuusiit: things that should be avoided, traditional laws
Tuniit (sing. Tunijjat): Thule people
tupilait: evil spirits
tuurngaq (pl. tuurngait): shamanic helping spirit
Tuutalannuaq: little Tuutalik
tuutalik (pl. tuutaliit): In Kiviuq's story, the word refers to a being that is half human, half seal. In everyday Inuktitut, it refers to a being that is half human, half fish.
ulu: crescent-shaped knife used by women
unipka: story or legend
unipkaqti: storyteller

Siberian Languages

abaasi (Sakha): evil spirit of the lower world
belye (Udeghe): a young woman who is beautiful, wise, and talented.

biatu (Udeghe): bear, a term used only in story and song
bua (Udeghe): word with many meanings relating to weather and place
jiagda (Udeghe): places with poles used for praying to ancestors
kakta ni (Udeghe): half person
kala (Koryak) or **kele (Chukchi)**: general word for an evil spirit
karang-körnür (Tuvan): clairvoyant person
kerker (Chukchi): woman's one-piece garment made of reindeer skin
khengginku bua (Udeghe): place for making offerings or prayers
khengki (Udeghe): a worshipful rendering of respect
küzüngü (Tuvan): shaman's mirror
ningma (Tungus-language family): magic tale, a story whose source is the vision of a storyteller
Öskiis-eeren (Tuvan): amulet representing an orphan
sagdi mama (Udeghe): oldest woman of all, literally "big woman"
sama (Tungus-language family): shaman
shoor (Tuvan): flute
telungu (Tungus-language family): legend; story whose basis is historical fact
teviskhin (Chukchi): reindeer antler tool used to beat snow out of clothing
toolchu (Tuvan): epic singer
toyon (Sakha): ruler
udagan (Turkic): female shaman
yaranga (Chukchi): dwelling; well-designed tent with interior subdivisions
yegdyghe (Udeghe): brave young man who is an excellent hunter

Inuktitut Pronunciation Guide (courtesy of Eva Aariak)

i is usually pronounced like **ee** in the English word d**ee**p. | **kisu**
Before **Q** and **R**, however, it sounds like **e** in the word b**e**t. | **tupiq**

u is usually pronounced like **oo** in the English word b**oo**t. | **iglu**
Before **Q** and **R**, it sounds like **o** in the word sn**o**re. | **uqsuq**

a is usually pronounced like **a** in the English word mama | **nuna**
Before **Q** and **R**, it sounds like **a** in the word fall. | **nuttaaq**

Long vowels, **ii**, **uu**, and **aa,** are pronounced as above, except that the sound is drawn out so that it is twice as long: **nakurmiik, pualuuk, ataata**

The following letters in Inuktitut are pronounced the same way in English:

p is pronounced as in **p**olicy. | **piqsiq**
t is pronounced as in **t**erms of reference. | **tuktu**
k is pronounced as in **k**ey. | **kamiik**
g is pronounced as in **g**overnment. | **kigut**
m is pronounced as in **m**onetary. | **matu**
n is pronounced as in **n**on-compliance. | **nipi**
s is pronounced as in **s**ystem. | **siku**
l is pronounced as in **l**egislative. | **igalaaq**
v is pronounced as in **v**erification. | **savik**
ng is pronounced as in English. | **kinguk**

The following letters are pronounced differently than in English:

j is like the English **y** in **y**am. | **qajaq**

r is a sound that is not made in English but is similar to the way **r** is pronounced in French or the way **j** is in Spanish. It sounds like a slight gargle at the back of the throat. | **tariuq**

q is another sound produced at the back of the throat. To begin, close your throat with the very back of your tongue, as if you were about to pronounce a **g**. Release air as if you were pronouncing a **k**. | **Iqaluit**

ł Put your tongue in the same position as you would to pronounce an **l**. Without using your vocal cords, breathe out, as if you were pronouncing an **sh.** | **akłak**

ll In the Qikiqtani (Baffin) dialects, this sounds like **d + l.** | **ullumi**
In the Kivalliq and Kitikmeot, this is pronounced like **b + l.**
Many speakers of Western dialects, write double **l** as **bl.** | **ublumi**

jj sounds like a **d + j.** | **sijjaq**

All other double consonants are drawn out, so that the sound is twice as long. | **naammattuq**

Siberian Pronunciation Guide

a as the **a** in father
i as the **ee** in deep
o is between the **o** in toy and the **aw** in awful.
u as the **oo** in cool
gh is similar to a French **r.**
kk as the **ch** in Loch Lomond

Double vowels are pronounced twice as long as single vowels.

Folklore Motifs

The motif list presented below was compiled by Michael Ballantyne and Murray Shoolbraid of the British Columbia Folklore Society and published by the society as part of their Pacific Folklore Studies (Van Deusen 2005).

Although comparing motifs across cultures leads to rich insights, the process also entails risks. The same image or action may be interpreted very differently in different times and places, depending in part on different religious and spiritual systems as well as different ways of life. A good example is the story of Kiviuq and his goose-wife. In the Inuit story she is understood to be a bird living temporarily in human form, whereas in European tales her transformation from bird to human is understood as "disenchantment."

Ballantyne and Shoolbraid write:

Motifs are the elements of a story that can be alphabetized and numbered according to category. The classification system for motifs, created by Stith Thompson, enables the researcher to cross-reference elements from tale to tale and from one culture to another. Some relatively new conventions in motif numbering have been incorporated here. For example, the sign § (a section mark) is now used at the end of a motif number to denote a newly suggested addition to Thompson's Index. This has replaced the asterisk in that position, which is now applied, elsewhere, in a different motif context (El-Shamy 1995). Also, the use of commas (rather than full stops) in all motif numbers likewise follows the lead of Hasan M. El-Shamy, one of the few people actively working with new numbers at the present time. Motif numbers are the first part of a sentence that is made complete by the description that follows the number.

This telling of the story of Kiviuq includes a number of motifs that appear elsewhere in the world but whose first occurrence in recorded arctic folk literature is here. The motif F1041.1.5, Death from excessive joy, is a good example of this. The most unexpected new motif is A945§, Origin of ice. An Origin of snow motif [A1135.2] already exists, but it has to do with weather rather than with a (semi-)permanent, physical earth feature. The fox-wife story, Mysterious housekeeper [N831.1], found throughout the world, will be familiar to folklorists, and the goose-wife is a variant of the swan-maidens [D361.1, B652.1, and H1385.3]. Many other motifs have parallels in Siberian folklore. It is worth noting that a number of previously unidentified motifs may be the product of acculturation, even though they occur in this ancient epic.

A0, Creator.
A1134, Origin of fog.
A1135.3§, Origin of ice.
A2100, Creation of fish.
A2100.1§, Fish created from wood chips hewn by creator.
B16.6.4, Devastating spider.
B17.2.5§, Hostile shellfish.
B29.10§, Man-seal.
B80.1§, Seal-man.
B80.1.0.1§, Seal-shaman.
B80.1.0.1.1§, Seal-shaman killed.
B80.2, Monster half man, half fish.
B81, Mermaid.
B82, Merman.
B211.2.4, Speaking wolf.
B211.2.6, Speaking hare.
B211.2.11§, Other speaking rodentia.
B211.2.11.1§, Speaking lemming.
B211.2.11.1§, Speaking ground squirrel.

B211.2.12§, Speaking mustelidae.
B211.2.12.1§, Speaking wolverine.
B211.2.12.2§, Speaking weasel.
B211.8§, Speaking shellfish.
B390.1§, Grateful lemming helps hero.
B457§, Helpful birds – columbiformes [was charidriformes].
B458§, Helpful birds – charadriiformes (cf. B457ff.)
B458.1§, Helpful sandpiper.
B470, Helpful fish.
B551.1, Fish carries man across water.
B649.11§, Helpful sandpipers.
B651, The fox-woman.
B651.1, Marriage to fox in human form.
B873.5§, Giant caterpillar.
C35, Tabu: offending animal wife.
C441, Origin tabu.
D127.1.1§, Transformation: man to seal.
D231, Transformation: man to stone.
D313.3, Transformation: bear to person.
D361.1, The swan-maidens.
D415, Transformation: insect to another animal.
D441.10, Transformation: chips of wood to animal.
D441.10.1§, Transformation: carved image to animal (cf. D441.10).
D483.2§, Stream transformed to river by spittle.
D489.3§, Mound transformed to mountain by spittle.
D522, Transformation through magic word (charm).
D523, Transformation through song.
D531, Transformation by putting on skin, feathers, etc.
D659.10.1§, Transformation to lure hunters out to sea.
D672, Obstacle flight.
D683.2, Transformation by magician (witch or sorceress).
D721, Disenchantment by removing skin.
D721.2, Disenchantment by hiding skin (covering).
D743, Disenchantment by sexual intercourse.
D996.0.2.1, Magic power of left hand for evil.
D998, Magic private parts.
D1001, Magic spittle.

D1013, Magic bone of animal.
D1274, Magic fetish.
D1274.2§, Amulet (cf. D1392.1; F403.2.2.7§).
D1275, Magic song.
D1344.3, Amulet renders invulnerable.
D1392.1, Amulet saves one from death.
D1442.7.1§, Magic of fart controls animal wife.
D1553, Symplegades.
D1610.5, Speaking head.
D1178§, Magic skewer. (cf. D1439.1.§)
D1439§, Magic object attacks people.
D1439.1§, Magic (caribou leg bone) skewer pokes up through floor.
D1610.5, Speaking head.
D1610.18.1§, Speaking inuksuk.
D1776, Magic results from spitting.
D1799.6, Magic results from performing good deeds.
D1799.10§, Magic results from jumping.
D1799.11§, Magic results from passing between.
D1962.2, Magic sleep by lousing.
D2011, Years thought to be days.
D2011.4§, Supernatural passage of time.
D2069.1.2§, Spear pointed at person knocks them down.
D2095, Magic disappearance.
D2131, Magic underground journey.
D2141, Storm produced by magic.
D2141.0.7, Storm raised by incantation.
D2141.0.11.2§, Magic storm raised by seal.
D2144.5.1, Ice produced by magic.
D2144.5.2.1§, Ice split by magic.
D2168, Magic used against poison.
E73, Resuscitation by incantation.
E586.2.1§, Dead returns third day after death.
E607.2.2, Rebirth by crawling into woman's womb.
F56, Sky-window.
F403.2.2.1, Familiar spirit in animal form.
F403.2.2.7§, Familiar spirit in bird form, or skin (sandpiper).
F525.7§, Person with only lower half of body.

F529.9§, Person hollow from anus to mouth.
F691.1§, Person with ability to breath through anus.
F811.25§, Log husband.
F811.25.1§, Log husband provides for human wives.
F851, Extraordinary food.
F851.1§, Excrement as food.
F1041.1.5, Death from excessive joy.
G11.18, Cannibal tribe.
G61, Relative's flesh eaten unwittingly.
G211.2.2, Witch in form of wolf.
G211.5.2.1§, Bee Woman (cf. G510.5).
G510.5, Ogress with knife tail defeated by hunter.
H96.1§, Seals recognize power of guillemot amulet.
J1761.1.3§, Fish thought to be island.
K1613, Poisoner poisoned with his own poison.
K1941, Disguised flayer.
M205.2, Curse as punishment for broken promise (cf. Q556).
N831.1, Mysterious housekeeper.
Q2. Kind and unkind.
Q263.2§, "Pinocchio" – liar's nose grows long.
Q556, Curse as punishment.
Q552.14, Storm raised as punishment.
S110, Murder.
S115.1, Murder by stabbing in ear.
S160.1, Self-mutilation (cf. 166.7§).
S165, Mutilation: putting out eyes.
S166.7§, Mutilation: eyelids cut off.
S176, Mutilation: sex organs cut off.
S176.1, Mutilation: emasculation.
S176.2§, Sex organs as trophy.
S467§, Tormented child or children.
S467.1§, Boy tormented by villagers.
S351.1, Abandoned child cared for by grandmother.
T141.2, Wives exchanged.
T257, Jealous husband.
Z71.1, Formulistic number: three.

Notes

Introduction

1 Metaphorically speaking. I did not visit all of the same places Rasmussen had. Many of today's communities did not exist in his time.
2 John Houston's 2007 film *Kiviuq*.
3 The term Siberia is not official. Although people in Russia generally associate it with specific areas, I am using "Siberia" in its broad general sense.
4 Ethical guidelines for university and medical research have been developed. See Van den Hoonard 2002 and Lischke and McNab 2005.
5 Permission was both oral and written. Each elder signed a release, written in Inuktitut and in English, for every aspect of filming and recording, and also for my storytelling performance and writing.
6 The website is www.unipka.ca. The word *unipka* means story.
7 Contact there was continuous up until the mid-twentieth century, when the border between Russia and the United States was closed. The border reopened in the 1990s, and Siberian Yupik re-established family relationships with relatives on the other side.
8 The Nanai are one of the indigenous peoples of the Russian Far East.
9 Results of this questionnaire were published in Van Deusen 2006.
10 Some of these appear in this book as alternate spellings used by other writers.

11 This unwillingness to explain is common in indigenous families in many parts of the world. I suspect it may also reflect a different time period in mainstream North American culture, since it reminds me of my own Dutch-American grandfather.

Kiviuq's Life Story

1 See the Glossary for hints on pronunciation of Inuktitut words.
2 *Inuksuut* is the dual form of inuksuk, whose plural form is *inuksuit*. In the works of Rasmussen, the word is translated as a stone cairn. Among many uses, they were used as beacons for travellers and also to control the movement of wild caribou.

Journey to Nunavut, 2004

1 A Canadian territory is an administrative unit similar to a province in Canada or a state in the United States. Although the territories receive their mandate differently from the provinces, their residents are Canadian citizens with full voting rights.
2 In this regard Kiviuq is not alone among heroes of world epics. Many others mistreat the women closest to them. A good example is the Indian Rama, who, after a long search and battle to rescue his beloved wife from a demon, subjects her to more than one severe trial. He does it because there are rumours among his people that his wife has been unfaithful. In his position as king, he cannot allow such rumours to go untested, as that would cause a drop in his people's morale. The king must put the people's welfare before his own happiness (and even before his wife's life). Some say Kiviuq murdered his wives for similar reasons. They had neglected their work, and such neglect would eventually harm the whole community. The correctness of both these heroes' acts is hotly debated among their own people.
3 Even though many elders live long lives, the life expectancy in younger generations is low, owing to teen suicide and other health issues.
4 Today, even communities with only a few hundred inhabitants are equipped with large Co-op and Northern Stores, which sell a very similar assortment of groceries, clothing, hardware, and home supplies.

The Co-ops are Inuit run, while the Northern Stores are descended from the Hudson's Bay Company.

5 Of course Boas, Bogoras, and others of the same period are equally well known in other geographic and cultural areas.

6 When interpreting is consecutive, one speaker delivers a few sentences, then the interpreter translates them. The second party may reply, in which case the interpreter translates back to the first speaker. Simultaneous interpreting generally uses technology. The interpreter sits in a booth and listens to a speaker, translating almost simultaneously. Listeners hear the interpreter through headphones.

Our interpreters occasionally stopped to clarify points with the elders. John and I took notes while listening and asked questions at breaks. Later, the English-language tapes were completely transcribed, and selected parts of the Inuktitut were re-translated from the tapes. Some of the videos are now available for viewing on www.InuitQ.ca and we hope that all of them will become part of an electronic archive.

7 Quinangnaq played a major role in Houston's film on Kiviuq, telling much of the story. He passed away two months after the filming, but now his voice brings the story into many Nunavut homes and into the lives of young people as he had wished.

8 In the 1920s native languages in Siberia were still in use, and folklore was collected and used in schools. It was not until later that policies became more repressive.

9 See pages 349–54 for more of the elders comments on storytelling.

Seal, Tuutalik, Storm at Sea

1 Rasmussen 1931, 365.

2 Tassugat was recorded in Clyde River by Jolene Arreak.

3 Other kinds of seals are hunted from kayaks, from the floe edge, and by approaching on foot as they bask in the sun (Bennett and Rowley 2004, 50–62).

4 *People of the Seal: Eskimo Summer*, National Film Board of Canada.

5 Balikci writes that seal, caribou, and bear have especially strong souls. If homage is not paid to them through observance of rules and rituals, the animal souls could turn into monsters (1970, 200).

6 *Tuutalik* is singular – plural is *tuutaliit*. It generally refers to a mer-person, half human, half fish, but here the being is half human, half seal.

7 Kivioq, *totalet*, and *totalik* are alternate spellings for Kiviuq, *tuutaliit*, and *tuutalik* respectively. This story was told by Nakasuk to Rasmussen (1931, 247). There is also a bilingual version on page 389 of Rasmussen 1931. On page 523 Tuutalik is described as half man, half seal. Of all the versions we read, only the Netsilik tell of the seal-man going down through a breathing hole.

8 See the story of the woman and the whale in the "Seal Cousins" chapter and the information about the bear ceremony in the "Grizzly Cousins" chapter.

9 See "The Fox-Wife" chapter. A similar concept is the hole in the environment discussed in "The Goose-Wife" chapter. The elders who said that Tuutalik went down into the seal hole were Mariano Aupilaarjuk, Peter Katorkra, Annie Peterloosie, and Leo Nimialik. Rasmussen recorded a related story in which one man, while seal hunting, killed another man in order to get his wife (1929, 103–4).

10 Leo Nimialik says that Tuutalik already had a son, who was living with the grandmother.

11 Told to Rasmussen by Markus Igdlukasik, published in Ostermann 1939 (24–6).

12 John Houston's film *Nuliajuk: Mother of the Sea Beasts* presents this story as a theatrical performance, using the words of Inuit elders.

13 Elisapee Karlik, Ollie Ittinuar, Bernadette Patterk, and Niviuvak Marqniq. Ollie Ittinuar adds that Kiviuq wore a sealskin hood.

14 Most parents are aware of the way children demand to hear stories repeated. It turns out that repeated exposure to a story's imagery helps the brain develop. In the words of educator and author Joseph Chilton Pearce, "The repeated exposure to stories and the subsequent triggering of mental images stimulates appropriate neural development in the brain. It is the reason that children will insist on hearing the same story again and again – the hearing of a story causes neural pathways to form and strengthen within the brain" (1992, 154).

15 Certain non-shamans endowed with the gift could do it as well (Aupilaarjuk et al. 2002, 93). Also, although most Inuit shamans were

mentored by elder shamans, some received the gift spontaneously and many of those were orphans (Bennett and Rowley 2004, 178).

16 *Tirigusuusiit* are things that should be avoided; *maligait*, things that have to be followed; and *piqujait*, things that have to be done. These concepts are basic to traditional Inuit law. Often, these terms are translated generically as taboo (Aupilaarjuk et al. 2000, 13).

17 The possibility of keeping the soul in a place of safety outside the body in times of danger is shown in stories of many cultures, from Europe to Canadian First Nations; the hero must find the place where his opponent has hidden his soul in order to defeat him.

18 In ethnographic versions only one unnamed storyteller recorded by Boas (1888, 638) mentions the child's return, saying he got home with dry feet.

19 Krill are shrimp-like crustaceans that serve as food for whales, seals, etc.

20 Baba Yaga often appears as a witch in Russian folklore.

21 See the Conclusion for a complete list of these moments.

22 For Annie Peterloosie, it seems that the voice belonged to Bee Woman, whereas other tellers did not identify whose voice it was, and thus we don't know whether Bee Woman was helping Kiviuq at that point or not. Cornelius Nutaraq says the warning voice could have been the sandpiper. He adds that not only shamans can call for help – "Everyone can call something."

Seal Cousins

1 Told to the author by Valentina Kyalundzyuga, Gvasyugi village, 1993. Images of the sea also appear in her story of Kilae and the seagull girls (see the "Goose Cousins" chapter).

2 This is portrayed in Akira Kurosawa's historical film *Dersu Uzala*.

3 Van Deusen 1999, 111–12. Another story that illustrates this theme is that of the boy who marries a fox (see the "Fox Cousins" chapter).

4 This is discussed in more detail in the "Wolf Women, Tiny Spiders, and Homcoming" chapter.

5 Translated from Yupik to Russian by the respected cultural activist Ludmila Ainana and from Russian to English by Kira Van Deusen.

Bee Woman and Other Adventures

1 Although Inuit are some of Canada's first peoples, they are not included in the term First Nations. They come from very different migrations, and their subsequent history, including that of contact with European culture, is very different. Inuit are those formerly included in the term Eskimo (still used by some groups in Alaska), while First Nations, known in the United States as Native Americans, include those formerly called Indians as well as the Métis.

2 For further information, see Laugrand, Oosten, and Trudel 2000.

3 Theresa Kimaliadjuk tells us that because of his power Kiviuq attracted the opposition of malevolent spirits but he had strong protectors to help him fend them off. Evil spirits are called *nunalait* or *tupilait*. They take the form of fabulous beasts, mountain spirits, and ghosts of the hostile dead (Rasmussen 1929, 144).

4 *Taarniq* is defined as darkness. Note that this is different from *tarniq*, the soul.

5 This information is from the website Hinterlands Who's Who: www.hww.ca/hww2asp?id=91.

6 In Millman 2004 (199–201), the women are not identified as irontails, although in Rink 1875 (159–60), they are.

7 The *tuutaliit* story was told mainly on Baffin Island.

8 In the 1920s Netsilik teller Kuvdluitsoq used the following order: seal-child son of Tuutalik; storm at sea; Bee Woman (with eyelids); caterpillars try to steal kayak (bee's helping spirits); giant mussel (also bee's helping spirit; Kiviuq was warned by a voice); spiders and beads; snipes (birds similar to the sandpipers) and homecoming; wolf women; fox-wife; goose-wife and Fishmaker; meat cache and grizzly; and living in the white man's land. In Greenland the story usually began with Kiviuq leaving home by kayak after murdering his unfaithful wife, and arriving first at the home of the mother and daughter.

Bee Cousins

1 "Kakta Ni," in the "Seal Cousins" chapter.

2 She reminds me of the female grizzly bear who later chases Kiviuq.

3 Told to the author by Udeghe storyteller Valentina Kyalundzyuga, Gvasyugi village, 1993. Published in Van Deusen 2001 (11–16).

Wolf Women, Tiny Spiders, and Homecoming

1 Although the log of wood was never mentioned by those who told of wolves, Niviuvak Marqniq said that the wolf-women were working on a piece of driftwood the size of a snow knife. In the past some said that it was a wooden pillar in the house that the women used, and that when Kiviuq discovered what the women were doing, he cut the knots off the pillar (Ostermann 1939, 53).

2 Some say it was a peg or one of the lice that broke the eardrum. Some criminals use this method today, since it leaves no obvious marks on the body.

3 We'll learn more about this when Kiviuq marries the fox.

4 See Ingerman 1991.

5 The pamphlet cites *Inuit Games* (1989), illustrated by Susan Shirley.

6 Samson Quinangnaq told it before the homecoming, but he told the story of the fox-wife before the storm at sea, and of the goose-wife after the homecoming.

7 Elisapee Karlik, Ollie Ittinuar, and Felix Kopak say that caterpillars were making the beads.

8 Francis's article offers a fascinating account of the sources, trade routes, and uses of beads, especially in Chukotka and Alaska.

9 This part was told only in Baffin Island.

10 Rasmussen recorded the parents standing together on the shore among the Caribou (1930a) and Netsilik (1931), although there is no discernible regional pattern in the tellings we heard.

Wolf Cousins

1 The game is described in the "Bee Cousins" chapter.

2 The Sakha people were earlier known as the Yakut. The story is also published under the title "Beiberiken of the Five Cows." It can be found in English in Yolen 1986 (72–9) and in two very different versions in the original Sakha and Russian in Ergis 1964 (156–77). What

follows is my own retelling from the two Russian versions.

3 Alternatively, word went around that old woman Beiberiken had a new daughter. Harzhit-Bergen convinced his unwilling wife to go for a visit. When they arrived there, the horsetail girl told the whole story. Harzhit-Bergen punished the evil wife, apologized to his true bride, and was reunited with her.

4 An alcoholic drink made from fermented mare's milk.

5 Published in Russian in Vatagin 1988 (282–7). Translation by K. Van Deusen.

6 This story has parallels with the European tale of "The Handless Maiden." The image of the child drowning and later returning to reunite the family appears in "Boktu-Kirish and Bora-Sheelei."

7 Published in Russian in Vatagin 1988 (346–8). Translation by K. Van Deusen.

The Penis in the Lake

1 Henry Evaluardjuk and Annie Peterloosie say he had only one wife. Ollie Ittinuar says Kiviuq had two wives on several occasions, including this one. Clearly there's more to the story than what we heard!

2 The snow knife, called *pana*, is used for cutting blocks for igloo building or other purposes.

3 This ceremony is artfully portrayed in Houston's film *Nuliajuk, Mother of the Sea Beasts.*

4 *Qiviuq Episode with the Spirit of the Lake,* 1983, collection of the Winnipeg Art Gallery.

5 Bernard Saladin d'Anglure believes that the lemming is the wife, returned on a lower level (2006, 176).

6 Sheila Grant describes this process in modern times in her enlightening book *Arctic Justice*.

7 One more possibility is that it could be the result of a contract between the two, made in another lifetime or reality.

8 *Inukkaknailak and Other Stories,* bilingual edition.

9 Peterloosie shared these thoughts in John Houston's film *Diet of Souls.*

10 In the "Seal, Tuutalik, Storm at Sea" chapter.

11 Cornelius Nutaraq goes from here to the goose-wife. In ethnographic sources, Boas is the only one to have the lake episode immediately precede the one about the fox-wife, while Ostermann includes the eider ducks in his telling of the episode.

Lake Cousins

1 Told by Udeghe elder Kyandu Kimonko to Valentina Kyalundzyuga and translated by K. Van Deusen.
2 The little finger bone is also the one from which a shaman reincarnates in the Nanai story "The Passar Shaman" (Van Deusen 2001, 111–12).
3 A good example is the parallel sister and brother heroes in the Tuvan epic "Boktu-Kirish and Bora-Sheelei," mentioned in the "Wolf Cousins" chapter.
4 The Khakassian people live in south Siberia near the border with Mongolia.

The Fox-Wife

1 Rasmussen 1932, 113.
2 Cornelius Nutaraq and Herve Paniaq say he met the fox on his way home from the goose-wife episode, Annie Peterloosie that he went from the fox to the goose. Eli Kimaliardjuk says Kiviuq married two foxes and later divorced one of them.
3 Rasmussen 1931, 382. Another reincarnation story is in the "Seal, Tuutalik, Storm at Sea" chapter – Maqo. This one is taken from an interlinear translation and is slightly edited for clarity by the present author.
4 For a full description of shamanic helping spirits, see the "Bee Woman and Other Adventures" chapter.
5 Elders in communities such as Arviat conduct learning projects with children that include building a traditional igloo and other related activities.
6 Another possibility is that this parade of animals reflects the fact that

Kiviuq *did* marry a number of times in the animal world. We already know about the wolf, and some elders refer in a general way to his marriages with other animals whose stories no one tells today.

Rasmussen recorded a story in which a man received a similar series of proposals from insects (1908, 326).

7 This sounds similar to what Aupilaarjuk says about how a shaman gets to the underwater world. See the "Wolf Women, Tiny Spiders, and Homecoming" chapter.

8 The story is in the "Seal Cousins" chapter.

9 A similar form of lampooning exists in Africa.

10 We are familiar with the musical interval of a fourth as the opening two notes of "Here Comes the Bride." The fifth begins "Twinkle Twinkle Little Star."

11 The namesake in this case is the person a child has been identified as reincarnating from. They both carry the same name. People with the same name always share a special relationship on the soul level, whether or not they have this reincarnational relationship.

12 Throat singing is becoming popular with composers. Witness the recent works by Derek Charke performed by the Kronos Quartet with singer Tanya Tagaq, known as the Jimmie Hendrix of throat singing, as well as a collaboration between the Kronos Quartet, Osvaldo Golijov, and Jeremy Flower in which string instruments imitate the sounds made by throat singers.

13 Two said he lost her, three that they stayed together, and the rest did not specify. In the ethnographic versions, as recorded by Diamond Jenness, Kiviuq gets his wife back (unspecified where they live). He goes home, presumably alone, in Rasmussen's *Eskimo Folk-Tales* (1921). He leaves her in one of Rasmussen's 1908 stories and she leaves him after the wife swap in another. He loses her in Ostermann 1939. They go home together in Rasmussen 1931. The fox puts Maqo to sleep by delousing him and he wakes up in another season and begins a big cycle of reincarnation. As recorded by Turner, the fox leaves and has been indisposed to visit a man ever since.

Fox Cousins

1 From Takakava 1970. Translation K. Van Deusen.

The Grizzly Bear

1 Artist Victoria Mamnguqsualuk Kayuryuk shows a bear instead of a human pulling Kiviuq on the bearskin in *Qiviuq Episode with the Spirit of the Lake*, collection of the Winnipeg Art Gallery.
2 Franz Boas (1888) recorded one version in Baffin Island but it was about a big man named Nareya instead of a bear. In Rasmussen's work on the Copper Eskimo (1932) and in the work of Diamond Jenness (1924), the story speaks of a hill spirit. Rasmussen's collection of Eskimo stories (1921) includes one about a mountain spirit. His works on the Netsilik (1931) and Copper Eskimos (1932) both have a story about a black bear. All the non-bear versions say the being was a grave robber.
3 Tuvan shaman Ai-churek Oyun teaches her students how to imbue objects with power in a mindful way, so that the objects can be called on for help later on. This, she says, is the principle of the shaman's spirit figures.
4 Not everyone agrees that it was the first fog. Simon Tookoome says, "If God wanted it to be the first fog, it would be so."
5 According to Ernest Burch, "Theoretically any empirical animal can have a non-empirical counterpart. These creatures are all regarded as highly dangerous" (Saladin d'Anglure 2001, 51).
6 There are many versions of this story, some of which are told in Bennett and Rowley 2004 (171–3). John Houston has made an insightful film about her entitled *Nuliajuk, Mother of the Sea Beasts*.
7 Saladin d'Anglure 2001 (52–63). For more stories about *ijirait*, see Bennett and Rowley 2004 (152–5).

Grizzly Cousins

1 Told to the author by Chukchi storyteller Svetlana Chuklinova in the town of Providenia in 1994, in Van Deusen 1999 (79–81).

The Goose-Wife

1 An interesting point here is that Inuit women did not swim (Kleivan 1962, 43). This is the first hint that the girls are not entirely human.
2 Judas Aqilgiaq says the sandhill crane eyed his gall bladder. Moses

Koihok says Kiviuq had two bird wives, a goose and a blackbird.

3 The horsetail girl's story (in the "Wolf Cousins" chapter) departs from that of the goose-wife in that it is her human skin that is stolen – this time by an evil spirit, not a prospective husband. The purposes in stealing the skin are different – the man uses the skin as a ruse to get her to stay earth-bound, whereas the evil spirit (or mother in the case of the wolf-girl) uses it as a transformational disguise so that she can take the girl's place.

4 This story is told by some North American peoples as well. In a Kutchin story, crow sends animals to the bottom of the water. Shoshone and others tell it in conjunction with a flood story.

5 The loon plays a healing role in stories such as "Aningaat" where the loon restores a boy's sight.

6 Folklorists classify the Swan Maidens as Tale types 400, 425. Motifs D721.2; D361.1.

7 As recorded by Boas (1901), the goose-wife says, "My food is not from the sea," and she refuses to help with the blubber, reinforcing the distinction of foods from land and sea as well as her own identity. In the Haida version there was a famine after the hero's marriage to the goose-woman. Her relatives provided food – pine needles and clover roots. Someone in the village spoke disparagingly of this food and the girl was offended and decided to leave.

8 Herve Paniaq notes that Kiviuq was a bachelor when he married the goose and a previously married man when he married the fox, which points to an opposite evolution.

9 Jacob Peterloosie tells a story in which a snowy owl tries to stay with a goose and sinks little by little into the water.

10 Saladin d'Anglure believes that the obstacles were set by the goose-wife and that the objects belonged to her (2006, 192).

11 From Ostermann 1939 (52–3).

12 Turkic shamans have many other kinds of songs as well, including those that describe their spiritual heritage, invoke their helping spirits, and are sung at various stages of ritual. Shamans also use songs in competition with other shamans. Some songs are dedicated to heavenly bodies, animals, fire, and hunting.

13 Some Inuit do look at these stories as parables with their strong and

simple morals, as apart from a more complex literal reality. This emphasis on the teaching aspect of storytelling may be the result of a Christian influence.

14 The name means "there are nests here in season."

15 In the Haida story as published in Robert Bringhurst (1999), an old man gives the hero the things he uses to help others along the way. At this point the hero enters the sky and meets two fishmakers there.

16 Sometimes called by other names, such as Eqalijaq, "salmon maker" in the Netsilik dialect.

17 The most striking Siberian parallel is the tale of the Nišan shamaness, a Manchurian shaman under Chinese law who had help crossing a river to the land of the dead when she went on an elaborate journey to retrieve a soul (Nowak and Durrant 1977).

18 According to Merkur, the Fishmaker appears with a man pursuing a bird-wife among the Chukchi, Koniag, Polar, and Netsilik peoples and in Baffin Island and west and east Greenland. He appears independently among the Kodiak, Kotzebue, Barrow, Copper, Caribou, and Igloolik peoples, and in Labrador and west Greenland (1991). Ethnologist Inge Kleivan believes the story may have travelled in either direction across the Bering Strait, since it appears frequently in North America and once on the Chukchi Peninsula (Kleivan 1962, 32). Presumably, the westward movement would have been part of a back-and-forth movement, originating in the west.

19 Qajartuarungnertoq seems to be a variant spelling of Qayaqturungnaqtuq discussed by Tom Lowenstein (1992).

20 Saladin d'Anglure also says that the Fishmaker can be a shamanic helping spirit. He cites the fact that the name Iqallijuq (variant of Iqaliraq) was given to a woman to help her survive (2006, 195).

21 In the version told by Kupaaq to Saladin d'Anglure, the goose-wife already had a goose husband before she met the human husband, and it is to him that she returned on migration. When the man arrives in the south, she is pregnant (2006, 196).

22 Ethnographic versions vary. Kiviuq kills the goose-wife in Boas 1888 and 1907. He kills her, she comes back to life, and he kills her again in Kroeber 1899. He kills her and her relatives and has a feast in Rasmussen 1908. She leaves and he does not follow in Jenness 1924.

He stays with her in the land of birds and she doesn't fly away in Rasmussen 1929. He gets the goose back and it's uncertain where they live in Rasmussen 1931. He loses her in Rink 1877. Among our storytellers, no one said he killed her or that they returned north together. Four said they stayed together and four that he lost her. Others either did not say what happened or did not tell this part of the story at all. As for related non-Inuit stories, the Haida tell us that the man wanted to return home and was transported there alone by a raven.

Goose Cousins

1 Tibetan Buddhism was widespread in Tuva for several hundred years, having come there from Mongolia. Since the fall of communism, it has enjoyed a revival.
2 "The Duck Wife," in Jenness 1924 (49A–52A). Edited slightly for style by the present author. Courtesy of the Canadian Museum of Civilization.
3 This is a different episode from the one Valentina described earlier (in the "Wolf Women, Tiny Spiders, and Homecoming" chapter) about the relative who wanted to take her along on his final journey.
4 Told by Valentina Kyalundzyuga in 1993 (Van Deusen 2001, 18–20).

Conclusion

1 Although it seems longer, Henry Isluanik told us that the whole adventure took one year.
2 Bruno Bettelheim distinguishes myth from folk tale. Myth is pessimistic, he says, and ends in tragedy, while the folk tale is optimistic and has a happy ending. He grants that this does not hold universally (1975, 37). Following this line of thought, certain epics are more mythic in their endings and types of heroism, while others tie up all the ends and wind up with peace and prosperity in the land.

Bibliography

References and Suggestions for Further Reading

Ainana, Ludmila. 1983. *Chelovek i velikan* [The man and the giant]. Magadan: Magadan Book Publishers

Allen, Paula Gunn. 1989. *Spider Woman's Granddaughters*. New York: Fawcett-Columbine

Angilirq, Paul Apak, Norman Cohn, and Bernard Saladin d'Anglure. 2002. *Atanarjuat, the Fast Runner*. Igloolik and Ottawa: Coach House Books and Isuma Publishing

Aupilaarjuk, Mariano, Peter Suvaksiuq, Felix Pisuq, Pujuat Tapaqti, Levi Iluittuq, Luke Nuliajuq, Ollie Ittinuaq, and Jose Angutinngurniq. 2002. *Inuit Qaujimajatuqangit: Shamanism and Reintegrating Wrongdoers into the Community*. Iqaluit: Nunavut Arctic College

Aupilaarjuk, Tulimaaq, Joamie, Imaruittuq, and Nutaraaluk. 2000. *Perspectives on Traditional Law*. Vol. 2 of *Interviewing Inuit Elders*. Iqaluit: Nunavut Arctic College

Balikci, Asen. 1970. *The Netsilik Eskimo*. Garden City, NY: Natural History Press for the American Museum of Natural History

Bennett, John, and Susan Rowley, eds. 2004. *Uqalurait: An Oral History of Nunavut*. Montreal and Kingston: McGill-Queen's University Press

Bettelheim, Bruno. 1975. *The Uses of Enchantment: The Meaning and Importance of Fairy Tales*. New York: Knopf

Blake, Dale, ed. 2001. *Inuit Life Writings and Oral Traditions: Inuit Myths*. St John's, NL: Educational Resource Development Co-operative

Boas, Franz. 1888. "The Central Eskimo." In *Sixth Annual Report of the Bureau of American Ethnology, 1884–85*. Washington, DC: Government Printing Office

– 1907. "Second Report on the Eskimo of Baffin Land and Hudson's Bay: From Notes Collected by Captain George Comer, Captain James S. Mutch, and Rev. E.J. Peck." *Bulletin of the American Museum of Natural History* 15, pt 2

Briggs, Jean L. 1970. *Never in Anger: Portrait of an Eskimo Family*. Cambridge, MA: Harvard University Press

Bringhurst, Robert. *A Story Sharp as a Knife*. Vancouver and Toronto: Douglas & McIntyre

Burton, Richard. *Arabian Nights*. On www.sacred-texts.com

Campbell, Joseph. 1973. *The Hero with a Thousand Faces*. Princeton, NJ: Princeton University Press

– 1988. *Mythologies of the Great Hunt*. New York: Harper and Row

Chaussonnet, Valerie. 1988. "Needles and Animals: Women's Magic." In *Crossroads of Continents*, edited by William W. Fitzhugh and Aron Crowell, 209–26. Washington, DC: Smithsonian Institution Press

Cruikshank, Julie. 1998. *The Social Life of Stories: Narrative and Knowledge in the Yukon Territory*. Vancouver: University of British Columbia Press

El-Shamy, Hasan M. 1995. *Folk Traditions of the Arab World: A Guide to Motif Classification*. Bloomington: Indiana University Press

Ergis, G.U. 1964. *Yakutskie skazki v dvukh tomakh* [Yakut tales in two volumes]. Vol. 1. Yakutsk: Academy of Sciences

Evanishan, Danny. 2000. *Carrots to Coins*. Summerland, BC: Ethnic Enterprises

Francis, Peter. 1994. "Beads at the Crossroads of Continents." In *Anthropology of the North Pacific Rim*, edited by William W. Fitzhugh and Valerie Chaussonnet, 281–305. Washington, DC: Smithsonian Institution Press

Fredericks, Linda. 1997. "Why Children Need Stories: Storytelling and Resiliency." *Resiliency in Action*, Summer, 26–9

Grant, Sheila. 2005. *Arctic Justice*. Montreal and Kingston: McGill-Queen's University Press

Hartland, Edwin Sidney. 1891. *The Science of Fairy Tales*. On www.sacred-texts.com

Hofman, Charles. 1974. *Drum Dance*. Toronto: Gage Publishing

Houston, James. 1973. *Kiviok's Magical Journey*. Don Mills, ON: Longman Canada

Ingerman, Sandra. 1991. *Soul Retrieval: Mending the Fragmented Self*. San Francisco: HarperSanFrancisco

Inuit Games [no author listed]. 1989. Illustrated by Susan Shirley. Rankin Inlet, NT: Department of Education, Regional Resource Centre

Inukkaknailak and Other Stories [no editor or year]. Cambridge Bay, NU: Kitikmeot Heritage Society and Nunavut Arctic College

Jenness, Diamond. 1924. "Southern Party, 1913–1916." In *Eskimo Folk-Lore: Myths and Traditions from Northern Alaska, the Mackenzie Delta and Coronation Gulf*, 49A–52A. Vol. 13, pt A, of *Report of the Canadian Arctic Expedition 1913–1918*. Ottawa: F.A. Ackland

Kazachinova, Galina, and Kira Van Deusen. 2003. *Mountain Spirits*. Vancouver: Udagan Books

Kenin-Lopsan, Mongush. 1999. *Tuvinskie shamany* [Tuvan shamans]. Moscow: Transpersonal Institute

Kleivan, Inge. 1962. "Swan Maiden Myth among the Eskimo." *Acta Arctica* 13:1–45

Kroeber, Alfred L. 1899. "'Tales of the Smith Sound Eskimo." *Journal of American Folk-Lore* 12 (46): 166–82

Kuyvenhoven, Johanna. 2009. *In the Presence of Each Other*. Toronto: University of Toronto Press

Kyalundzyuga, Valentina, and Mikhail Simonov. 1998. *An Udeghe Language Dictionary*. Steszew, Poland: International Institute of Ethnolinguistic and Oriental Studies

Laugrand, F., J. Oosten, and F. Trudel. 2000. *Representing Tuurngait*. Iqaluit: Nunavut Arctic College

Leary, Barbara Fass. 1994. *In Search of the Swan Maiden*. New York: New York University Press

Lischke, Ute, and David T. McNab, eds. 2005. *Walking a Tightrope: Aboriginal People and Their Representations*. Aboriginal Studies series. Waterloo, ON: Wilfrid Laurier University Press

Lowenstein, Tom. 1992. "Ukungniq: A Wandering Shaman." *Shaman's Drum*, Summer

Matthews, John. 2002. *Taliesin: The Last Celtic Shaman*. Rochester, VT: Inner Traditions

Melzack, Ronald. 1977. *Why the Man in the Moon Is Happy and Other Eskimo Creation Stories.* Toronto: McClelland and Stewart

Merkur, Daniel. 1991. *Powers Which We Do Not Know: The Gods and Spirits of the Inuit.* Moscow, ID: University of Idaho Press

– 1992. *Becoming Half Hidden: Shamanism and Initiation among the Inuit.* London: Taylor and Francis

Metayer, Maurice. 1972. *Tales from the Igloo.* Edmonton: Hurtig

Millman, Lawrence. 2004. *A Kayak Full of Ghosts: Eskimo Tales.* Northampton, MA: Interlink Books

Narby, Jeremy. 1999. *The Cosmic Serpent:* DNA *and the Origins of Knowledge.* New York: Jeremy P. Tarcher

Norman, Howard. 1990. *Northern Tales.* New York: Pantheon

Nowak, M., and S. Durrant. 1977. *The Tale of the Nišan Shamaness.* Seattle: University of Washington Press

Nyssen, Liesbet. 2005. "Traditional and Modern Khakas Conceptions of Sound and Music." *Oideion: Performing Arts Online*, no. 4

Oakes, Jill. 1987. *Inuit Annuraangit. Our Clothes: A Travelling Exhibition of Inuit Clothing.* Winnipeg: Thumb Prints Designs and Arts Studio

Oman, Lela Kiana. 1995. *The Epic of Qayaq: The Longest Story Ever Told by My People.* Ottawa: Carleton University Press

Oosten, Jarich, and Frédéric Laugrand, eds. 1999. *Introduction.* Vol. 1 of *Interviewing Inuit Elders.* Iqaluit: Nunavut Arctic College

Oosten, Jarich, Frédéric Laugrand, and Wim Rasing, eds. 2000. *Perspectives on Traditional Law.* Vol. 2 of *Interviewing Inuit elders.* Iqaluit: Nunavut Arctic College

Ostermann, H., ed. 1939. "Knud Rasmussen's Posthumous Notes on East Greenland Legends and Myths." *Meddelelser om Grönland* (Copenhagen) 109 (3): [3]–180

Pearce, Joseph Chilton. 1992. *Evolution's End: Claiming the Potential of Our Inheritance.* New York: HarperCollins

Piercey, Mary. 2005. "Gender Relations in Inuit Drum Dances." *Canadian Folk Music* 39 (3)

Qitsualik, Rachel Attituq. 2001. "The Unspeakable Tradition," pts 1–2. *Nunatsiaq News*, June

Rasmussen, Knud. 1908. *The People of the Polar North.* Edited by G. Herring. London: Kegan-Paul, Trench, Truebner and Co.

– 1921. *Eskimo Folk-Tales*. Translated and edited by W. Worster. London: Kegan-Paul, Trench, Truebner and Co.
– 1929. *Intellectual Culture of the Iglulik Eskimos*. Vol. 7 (1) of *Report of the Fifth Thule Expedition, 1921–1924*. Copenhagen: Gyldendalske Boghandel, Nordisk Forlag
– 1930a. *Observations on the Intellectual Culture of the Caribou Eskimos*. Vol. 7 (2–3) of *Report of the Fifth Thule Expedition 1921–1924*. Copenhagen: Gyldendalske Boghandel, Nordisk Forlag
– 1930b. *Iglulik and Caribou Eskimo Texts*. Vol. 7 (3) of *Report of the Fifth Thule Expedition, 1921–1924*. Copenhagen: Gyldendalske Boghandel, Nordisk Forlag
– 1931. *The Netsilik Eskimo: Social Life and Spiritual Culture*. Vol. 8, pts 1–2, of *Report of the Fifth Thule Expedition, 1921–1924*. Copenhagen: Gyldendalske Boghandel, Nordisk Forlag
–1932. *Intellectual Culture of the Copper Eskimos*. Translated by W.E. Calvert. Vol. 9 of *Report of the Fifth Thule Expedition, 1921–1924*. Copenhagen: Gyldendalske Boghandel, Nordisk Forlag
Rink, Henry. 1875. *Tales and Traditions of the Eskimo*. Reprinted 1975. Edinburgh: W. Blackwood. New York: AMS Press
– 1877. *Danish Greenland: Its People and Its Products*. Edited by Robert Brown. London: Henry S. King
Rousselot, Jean-Loup. 1994. "Watercraft in the North Pacific." In *Anthropology of the North Pacific Rim*, edited by William Fitzhugh and Valerie Chaussonnet, 243–58. Washington, DC: Smithsonian Institution Press
Ruppert, James, and John W. Bernet. 2001. *Our Voices: Native Stories of Alaska and the Yukon*. Lincoln: University of Nebraska Press
Saladin d'Anglure, Bernard, ed. 2001. *Cosmology and Shamanism*. Vol. 4 of *Interviewing Inuit Elders*. Iqaluit: Nunavut Arctic College
– 2006. *Être et renaître Inuit: Homme, femme ou chamane*. Montreal: Gallimard
Silko, Leslie Marmon. 1986. *Storyteller*. New York: Henry Holt and Company
Sonne, Birgitte. 1992. "Mythology of the Eskimos." In *The Feminist Companion to Mythology*, edited by Carolyne Larrington. London: Pandora Press
Sturtevant, William C., ed. 1984. *Arctic*. Edited by David Damas. Vol. 5 of

Handbook of North American Indians. Washington, DC: Smithsonian Institution

Takakava, Margarita, ed. 1970. *Kto samii silnii na zemlye?* [Who is the strongest on earth?]. Magadan: Magadan Book Publishers

Turner, Edith. 1996. *The Hands Feel It: Healing and Spirit Presence among a Northern Alaskan People*. DeKalb: Northern Illinois University Press

Turner, Lucien. 1894. "Ethnography of the Ungava District, Hudson Bay Territory." In *Eleventh Annual Report of the Bureau of American Ethnology for the Years 1889–1890*. Washington, DC: Government Printing Press

Van den Hoonard, Will C. 2002. *Walking the Tightrope: Ethical Issues for Qualitative Researchers*. Toronto: University of Toronto Press

Van Deusen, Kira. 1996. *Shyaan Am! Tuvan Folk Tales*. Bellingham, WA: Udagan Books

– 1999. *Raven and the Rock: Storytelling in Chukotka*. Seattle and Edmonton: University of Washington Press and Canadian Circumpolar Institute

– 2000. *Woman of Steel*. Vancouver: Udagan Books

– 2001. *The Flying Tiger: Women Shamans and Storytellers of the Amur*. Montreal and Kingston: McGill-Queen's University Press

– 2004. *Singing Story, Healing Drum: Shamans and Storytellers of Turkic Siberia*. Montreal and Kingston: McGill-Queen's University Press; Seattle: University of Washington Press

– 2005. *Kiviuq*. Pacific Folklore Studies No. 1. Central Saanich: British Columbia Folklore Society

– 2006. "The Spoken Quilt." *Appleseed Quarterly* 16 (1): 10–13

Vatagin, M.1988. *Skazki Narodov Rossii* [Tales of the peoples of Russia]. Minsk: Yunatstva

Walker, Barbara G. 1996. *The Woman's Encyclopedia of Myths and Secrets*. Edison, NJ: Castle Books

Walker; Barbara K. 1990. *The Art of the Turkish Tale*. Vols 1–2. Lubbock, TX: Texas Tech University Press

Yolen, Jane. 1986. *Favorite Folktales from Around the World*. New York: Pantheon Books

Websites

Acadia University. The Inuit Qaujimajatuqangit Adventure website: www.InuitQ.ca

D.L. Ashliman's Folktexts, a library of folktales, folklore, fairy tales, and mythology: www.pitt.edu/~dash/folktexts.html

drumsong communications website: www.drumsong.net

Hubert Wenger Eskimo Database at University of Alaska Library: www.wengereskimodb.uaf.edu

Joseph Jacobs website: www.pitt.edu/~dash/swan.html#jacobs

Kiviuq Trilingual website: www.unipka.ca

Sacred Texts website: www.sacred-texts.com

Films

Balikci, Asen. 1971. *People of the Seal: Eskimo Summer.* National Film Board of Canada

Houston, John, and Peter d'Entremont. 1999. *Songs in Stone.* Triad Films

– 2001. *Nuliajuk, Mother of the Sea Beasts.* Triad Films

– 2004. *Diet of Souls.* Triad Films

– 2006. *Kiviuq.* Triad Films and drumsong communications inc.

Kunuk, Zacharias, and Paul Apak Angilirq. *Atanarjuat, the Fast Runner.* Isuma Productions

Index